Foreword

National Security Agency whistleblower Edward Snowden justified the fears of the world that the United States, for years, had as its ultimate goal an omniscient surveillance capability that would render the concept of individual privacy obsolete. In releasing classified "code word" documents, Snowden proved what many other NSA whistleblowers had previously contended -- that NSA was engaged in a project to sweep up every telephone call, e-mail, and other electronic communication made every minute of every hour of every day all around the globe. Even the hallowed Fourth Amendment protections against unreasonable search and seizure enshrined in the Bill of Rights of the U.S. Constitution would prove no obstacle for NSA.

This book contains the collected works by the author that were mostly published by the website, WayneMadsenReport.com, since 2005. Many are based on inside information relayed by former and then-current NSA personnel, who, in the months after 9/11, grew increasingly alarmed by NSA's increasing tendency to scrap internal regulations and federal statutes designed to protect the privacy of "U.S. persons" from unauthorized NSA surveillance.

In many ways, the following pages represent the personal stories and observations of numerous NSA and other intelligence agency, as well as law enforcement, personnel who relayed to the author details of NSA abuses.

The reports are in chronological order. Hopefully, the reader will understand how the goal posts were constantly being moved at NSA and now the agency amassed greater and greater power to the point that the unthinkable occurred. NSA, which was once said to stand for "Never Say Anything," was seeing an outpouring of whistleblowers. Many were comfortable in approaching this editor because of my own experience working at NSA. I and they realized the risks they were taking and every conceivable measure was taken to protect their identities.

Front page headlines in mid-2013 introduced the world to Edward Snowden and his revelations about NSA. However, earlier individuals who were subjected to NSA abuse were mere footnotes in past news cycles: Ken Ford, Jr.; Russell Tice, Thomas Drake, and others. In many respects, Snowden's revelations brought past NSA abuses up to date, with new cover names that either represented new surveillance systems or were introduced to replace systems that were compromised due to past leaks.

The term that caught the attention of the public was a meta-data collection system called PRISM. According to an NSA briefing slide, PRISM connected directly to the servers of such web service providers as Google, Yahoo, AOL, Apple, YouTube, Facebook, Skype, and a number of others. PRISM also fed intercepted Internet communications to NSA databases like NUCLEON and PINWALE, as well as to FBI data interception units. Another system known as BOUNDLESSINFORMANT collected meta-data from global Internet connections.

Snowden rolled out for public consumption the NSA cover names for several signals intelligence systems and subsystems involved in metadata collection. NSA officials were traditionally content in their belief that the names and missions of such systems, both mission-critical systems and those that represented a massive waste of taxpayers' dollars for the benefit of greedy contractors, would never appear in the public domain. However, they reeled as the media carried stories about such meta-data collection systems like PRISM, PRINTAURA, OAKSTAR, FALLOUT, TRAFFICTHIEF, and BLARNEY. However, if the taxpaying public realized how many systems and subsystems NSA operated, many obsolete and others contractor boondoggles rife with non-performance issues, it would be horrified. This book uniquely presents literally hundreds of such systems known largely by only their odd cover names.

NSA has been caught eavesdropping on the public so many times, it has become a fool's errand to attempt to rein in the agency. The NSA surveillance abuses of the 1960s and 70s are legendary and, though noble, the statutory restrictions placed on NSA as a result of post-Watergate hearings by such congressional leaders as Senator Frank Church (D-ID) and Representatives Otis Pike and Bella Abzug, both Democrats from New York, were eventually superseded as a result of the 9/11 attack. The words of Senator Church had been largely forgotten in the aftermath of 9/11 and during NSA's unprecedented power grab. Church said, "Congress has a 'particular obligation to examine the NSA, in light of its tremendous potential for abuse. ... The danger lies in the ability of NSA to turn its awesome technology against domestic communications.'"

NSA began flexing its muscles into cyberspace in the 1990s. As this editor wrote in a report for the Electronic Privacy Information Center (EPIC) in 1998:

In response to the PCCIP's report, on May 22, 1998, President Clinton signed two Presidential Decision Directives - PDD 62 (Combating Terrorism) and PDD 63 (Critical Infrastructure Protection) - designed to defend the nation's critical infrastructures from various threats, including "cyber attacks" by computer hackers and terrorists. The White House summary of

National Security Agency Surveillance:

Reflections and Revelations

2001-2013

Wayne Madsen

National Security Agency Surveillance: Reflections and Revelations, 2001-2013

Copyright 2013 by Wayne Madsen

All rights reserved

ISBN: 978-1491211014
ISBN-10: 1491211016

Table of Contents

Foreword	5
2001	10
2002	11
2005	12
2006	80
2007	103
2008	127
2009	155
2010	168
2011	189
2012	200
2013	206
Appendix	256
Index	282

these two PDDs is contained in Appendix A. PDD 63 carried out most of the recommendations contained in the Report of the President's Commission. These include the establishment of several new boards and agencies, some with Internet surveillance authority. One of the new offices is the National Coordinator for Security, Infrastructure Protection, and Counter-terrorism within the National Security Council. This office is headed by Richard Clarke, a person who has spent a number of years in intelligence-related functions. Clarke reports to the President through the Assistant to the President for National Security Affairs.

PDD-63 also authorized the creation of a National Infrastructure Assurance Council (consisting of private sector and state and local government representatives), a National Plan Coordination (NPC) staff, the Critical Infrastructure Assurance Office (CIAO) (headed by Jeffrey Hunker), the Critical Infrastructure Coordination Group (CICG), and the National Infrastructure Protection Center (NIPC) under the FBI. Of most alarm is the fact that the NIPC may be assisted in its Internet surveillance activities by the Department of Defense and the U.S. Intelligence Community. The NIPC is headed by Associate Deputy Attorney General Michael Vatis.

In addition, PDD-63 encourages private industry to establish an Information Sharing and Analysis Center (ISAC). However, the Federal government is authorized to facilitate the start-up of the ISAC. Many observers believe that the NSA's Information Warfare Technical Center in Fort Meade, Maryland, has the right embryonic structure for the proposed ISAC. Such a facility, located within the structure of one of the world's most intrusive intelligence agencies, would constitute a grave threat to the privacy of not only law-abiding American citizens but citizens of other countries as well.

The EPIC report also discussed the NSA's expansion of domestic powers during the Reagan administration:

On September 17, 1984, NSA prevailed upon President Reagan to sign National Security Decision Directive 145 (NSDD-145). The directive authorized NSA to develop means to protect "unclassified sensitive" information. For the first time in its thirty-two year history, the NSA was assigned responsibilities outside its traditional foreign eavesdropping and military and diplomatic communications security roles. The agency was granted new powers to curb the use of public cryptography and to develop standards and techniques for automated systems security. In addition, NSDD-145 permitted NSA to control the dissemination of government, government-derived, and even non-government information that might adversely affect the national security. Some argued that such a broad definition included all information. NSA quickly began to exercise its new-found authority.

The directive also stated that NSA was to act as the government's focal point for information security and as such was to:

. . . review and approve all standards, techniques, systems and equipment for telecommunications and automated equipment security.

NSA also launched a program to take over the civilian use of cryptography during the 1990s. This expansion by NSA into the commercial sector was also highlighted in the EPIC report:

By early 1993, NSA was, once more, clearly in the driver's seat in protecting computerized information in the civil government sector. It, along with its allies in the Justice Department and FBI, sold the incoming Clinton administration on the technology of escrowed encryption. Most notable was the "Clipper Chip", a backdoor in digitized telephone scrambling programs that permitted law enforcement and intelligence agencies to listen in. The national firestorm that erupted forced many traditional NSA hidden agendas into public view, a situation which NSA found increasingly uncomfortable.

NSA's escrowed encryption proposals, the FBI's "Digital Telephony" proposals to give it virtual real-time access to the nation's digital telecommunications network, and the Clinton administration's continuation of arcane "munitions" export controls on acceptable strength cryptography, continued into the critical infrastructure protection debate. Within the business community, there is an underlying suspicion of government intentions, particularly in the computer and telecommunications industries. The privacy and civil liberties communities are inherently suspicious of administration intentions after witnessing a panoply of intrusive and anti-privacy measures being introduced in proposed legislation or by administrative fiat.

In the years prior to 9/11, NSA was regaining some of the unrestricted surveillance authority it enjoyed under the Lyndon Johnson and Richard Nixon administrations. During the administration of Bill Clinton, NSA produced three memos dealing with the application of the main internal NSA communications collection regulation, known as United States Signals Intelligence Directive 18 (USSID 18) against then-First Lady Hillary Clinton, former President Jimmy Carter, and 1996 presidential and other candidates for federal office.

A formerly CONFIDENTIAL July 8, 1993 NSA memo titled "USSID 18: Reporting Guidance on References to the First Lady" states: "Mrs. Clinton may be identified in reports only by title (currently, Chairperson of the President's Task Force on National Health Care Reform) without prior approval when that title is necessary to understand or assess foreign intelligence and when the information discussed relates to her official duties." One can only guess at the foreign intelligence aspect to NSA's interest in Mrs. Clinton's health care reform activities. The memo also states that no reports on Mrs. Clinton's private life could be published without evidence of criminal wrongdoing and then only after a "review by senior NSA management and the Office of the General Counsel."

A December 15, 1994 NSA memo deals with communications intercepts of former President Carter. The memo, titled "USSID 18: Reporting Guidance on Former President Carter's Involvement in the Bosnian Peace Process," states "former U.S. President Jimmy Carter has been invited to travel to Bosnia and Herzegovina by Bosnian Serb President Radovan Karadzic to participate in efforts to end the war there. "

The memo stipulates that intercepts of Carter's phone calls may only identify him as a "U.S. person" but also stipulates that "if Former President Carter eventually becomes an official envoy of the U.S. Government in this activity, could he then be identified as a "former U.S. President."

A June 6, 1996 formerly CONFIDENTIAL NSA memo, titled USSID 18: The 1996 U.S. Elections," states "We anticipate that as the 1996 election campaigns go on, there may be instances when references to political parties and candidates will be necessary to understand foreign intelligence or assess its importance. In such cases, unless you have prior approval for specific identification in accordance with the provisions of USSID 18, refer to the U.S. identity in generic form only: a U.S. political party, a U.S. presidential candidate, a U.S. Senate candidate, etc. "

After 9/11 and the enactment of the U.S. Patriot Act, even these questionable restrictions on NSA's authority to conduct surveillance of U.S. politicians, were tossed out. Today, with meta-data collection, it is a certainty that the NSA collects personal information on each and every member of the Congress and the executive and judicial branches. There was little surprise, therefore, that a bill introduced by Republican Representative Justin Amash and Democratic Representative John Conyers, both of Michigan, to repeal the meta-data authority of NSA contained in the Patriot Act, was defeated in a close 205-317 vote by the House of Representatives on July 24, 2013. NSA director Keith Alexander held closed-door classified sessions with key congressional members of both parties. Not surprisingly, the Republican and Democratic leadership, along with the White House, joined forces to ensure the defeat of the Amash-Conyers bill. The power of NSA to store sensitive and personal details on the lives of members of the Congress makes the intrusive personal files once possessed by FBI director J. Edgar Hoover appear relatively innocent by comparison.

A few days after the House vote, James Clapper, the Director of National Intelligence, admitted that NSA had some "compliance" problems with governing surveillance law but stressed that they were inadvertent. Nothing NSA does is ever "inadvertent" but coldly calculated to bypass or ignore the law and internal NSA regulations.

After reading the following pages, the reader will feel as if he or she just left a higher-than-top secret briefing on the NSA. However, unlike those who do attend those types of meetings, you are not under any restrictions on what you can discuss openly with others. The hope is that you the reader will sound the klaxons around the nation about the dangerous and unconstitutional powers now massed under the National Security Agency and its companion military activity, the U.S. Cyber Command. Complacency is not an option.

2001

Special Forces concentrating on "low-density" languages

U.S. Special Operations Forces are increasingly brushing up on what are termed "low-density" languages as they become involved in an increasing number of the world's trouble spots, including those where insurgents, narco-groups and organized crime syndicates are gaining increased power. African languages - Hausa, Fulani, Yoruba, Ibo and Twi -- are of particular importance to U.S. Special Forces, especially those in Nigeria and other parts of West Africa where U.S. military and private military contractors are increasingly active in Joint/Combined Exchange Training (JCET) projects. Central Asian languages such as Turkmen are also important because U.S. Special Ops personnel are providing training to the Turkmenistan state border service.

Special Operations Command personnel were also instrumental in setting up the Colombian Army's Counterdrug Battalion. It is at the center of the Plan Colombia program - a $1.3 billion initiative to beef up Colombia's counter-narcotics and counter-insurgency capabilities. Other Special Ops personnel were involved in a number of joint training programs with Latin American and Caribbean security forces. These have been code-named CABANAS, TRADEWINDS, ELLIPSE ECHO, BLUE ADVANCE, UNIFIED ENDEAVOR, and FUERTAS DEFENSAS.

Special Operations Forces are gaining a significant Signals Intelligence (SIGINT) capability. Through systems like Privateer provide maritime-based Special Forces with access to NSA SIGINT product and radio direction finding data with the support of Naval Security Group (NSG) personnel. A similar airborne-based system, code-named Silent Shield and operated by Air Intelligence Agency (AIA), provide Special Ops personnel with airborne communications intercepts and direction finding capabilities. A Special Forces SIGINT portable Manpack allows a single soldier to directly transmit communications intercept and direction finding intelligence to theater forces and NSA Headquarters in Fort Meade.

2002

<u>January 31, 2002 -- J'Accuse: Bush's Death Squads</u>

Abdullah Syafii

On January 22, 2002, Indonesian army troops assassinated the military commander of the Free Aceh Movement, Abdullah Syafii. The Free Aceh Movement demands independence for Aceh, a region in northwest Sumatra, and is a member of the non-violent Unrepresented Nations and Peoples Organization (UNPO), an international organization headquartered in the Netherlands. It has also been at loggerheads with ExxonMobil, which has extensive drilling and refining operations in the territory.

Aceh's Governor Abdullah Puteh, who is claimed by local activists to be on the payroll of ExxonMobil, had written a letter to Syafii inviting him to attend peace talks with the government. Syafii's lieutenants claim that the letter contained a small microchip that permitted Indonesian KOPASSUS troops to track him down and ambush him. The operation has all the earmarks of the CIA, which can rely on National Security Agency (NSA) satellites to track such microchip transponders.

2005

<u>May 10, 2005—General Michael Hayden, the man George W. Bush selected to be the deputy to new National Intelligence Director John Negroponte, has presided over the systematic dismantling and demoralization of America's premier technical intelligence collecting outfit— the National Security Agency (NSA).</u>

According to NSA insiders, Hayden's seven-year tenure at the agency, the longest for any NSA director, has witnessed the cashiering of experienced analysts, linguists, and field personnel and the crippling of America's ability to protect itself.

In the 1960s TV sitcom *Hogan's Heroes*, a motley crew of Allied prisoners of war at a German POW camp outwardly demonstrated to their captors that they were incompetent fools. In reality, this was a ruse. The prisoners established within Stalag 13 a behind-the-lines sabotage and espionage network, coming and going as they pleased through underground tunnels.

A sitcom about NSA could be called "Hayden's Heroes." The twist, however, is that Hayden, through a clever and unprecedented public relations campaign aimed at the major media and Congress, and a subservient staff of sycophants and apple polishers, has convinced the public that NSA is an ace intelligence agency successfully grappling with new communications technologies to maintain America's ability to have a keen "ear" on global intelligence indications and warnings. NSA professionals report a much different story. They point to an agency wracked by poor morale, questionable outsourcing contracts, and ineffective and corrupt management. After a number of interviews with NSA personnel, it is apparent that the agency even has its own Sergeant Schultz, the relatively unconcerned Deputy Director Bill Black, who was hauled out of retirement by Hayden and who, like the character in Hogan's Heroes, "Knows nothing! Nothing!" and "Sees Nothing! Nothing!"

For example, at a time when Negroponte and Hayden are charged with coordinating the activities of some 15 intelligence agencies within the U.S. government, Hayden ordered the transfer of NSA's Counter Terrorism branch ("CT"), operated as part of NSA's massive Signals Intelligence Directorate (SID), to the Georgia Regional Signals Intelligence Center at Fort Gordon, Georgia.

NSA is also farming out critical functions to other facilities around the country. For example, 350 electronic intelligence (ELINT) jobs have been transferred to the Buckley Air Force Base in Aurora, Colorado. However, most of the ELINT personnel have remained in Maryland resulting in a lack of experienced personnel in Colorado.

The Buckley ELINT facility, which operates in a super-secret facility known as the Aerospace Data Facility, does not even recognize NSA security badges and operates as an entity outside the control of the intelligence community and subservient to the Pentagon. The move of ELINT and other functions has disrupted various next generation collection programs with code names and titles like BEARTRAP, BEIKAO, BIRDHOUSE 1 & 2, BOOMVANG, CANYONDUST, CAPE LOOKOUT, CARIBOU, CENTERCOIL, CHARTVEIN, CHILLFLAME, DECKPIN, EAGLE REACH, E-SIGINT LOOK and FEEL, HOKUSAI, (CARS) IRISH DEN, GALAXYDUST, HARPSTRING, HIGHPOWER, HOKUSAI, JACAMAR, JETAVATOR, JOBMASTER, KEEPTOWER, KINSFOLK, MARINER II, MONOCLE, NEEDLEICE, PADDLEBOAT, PAPAYA, PLATOONWOLF, PATENTHAMMER, POWERPLANT, QUADRUNNER, RADIANT SPRUCE II, READOUT/IANA, REVERSE EAGLE REACH, ROADBED, ROMAN ALLIANCE, RSOC Development Program, SEADIVER, SENIOR SPUR/ETP, SHADOWBOXER, SHARKBITE, SHARPSHOOTER, SHILOH, SIDEKICK, Specific Emitter Identification (SEI), STARCICLE, STARQUAKE, STARSWORD, STOUTHEARTED, STRAIGHTSHOT, SUNBEAVER, and SUPERCODING.

In addition, 1,500 NSA jobs were transferred by Hayden to the Medina Regional SIGINT Operations Center (RSOC) at Lackland Air Force Base in San Antonio, Texas. NSA insiders report that Hayden's decision to move nearly 2,000 jobs from NSA's headquarters at Fort Meade, Maryland, was in revenge for Maryland Democratic Senator Barbara Mikulski complaining about the loss of government jobs at Fort Meade resulting from two controversial NSA outsourcing contracts—GROUNDBREAKER and TRAILBLAZER.

While critical NSA operational functions are being lost by Fort Meade to facilities in other states, Hayden has permitted his associate director for Security and Counterintelligence, Kemp Ensor III, to build up a security force whose sole mission is to unduly harass and intimidate NSA employees, some with over 15 to 25 years working for the agency in a variety of super-sensitive positions that would amaze the most ardent Tom Clancy fan. For example, in order that they can navigate the rugged wilderness of suburban Maryland, Ensor has purchased for his Praetorian force a fleet of menacing black Humvees outfitted with state-of-the-art electronics, including DVD players. Ensor relies on a network of East German Stasi-like snitches and security officers embedded throughout the agency—in SID, IAD (Information Assurance Directorate), the Logistics Directorate, and other agencies, including the Special Collection Service (SCS) or "F6," located in an office building complex between Beltsville and Laurel, Maryland.

Working hand-in-glove with Ensor is NSA's chief psychologist, Dr. John Schmidt. After a "problem" employee is identified and sent to Ensor's interrogators to be softened up, he or she is then sent to Schmidt who proceeds to identify the individual's mental problems to justify yanking their security clearance. NSA employees who have had the displeasure of being hauled to security on trumped up charges report a scene right out of *The Matrix* interrogation scene with Neo and Agent Smith. The accused is taken into a conference room with a table and a few chairs. An Agent Smith-type security officer produces a thick file bound by a rubber band and smacks it down on the table. During the initial interview, the security officer will periodically hold up a sheaf of paper close to his face, not allowing the subject to see what is written on the paper. However, employees who have never had a prior security incident and are hauled in for the intimidation "procedure," reason that the file is a stage prop and contains a meaningless ream of paper.

NSA insiders report that the NSA security division, still known by its old moniker "M5," maintains a database of problem employees. Of course, true to form for any Gestapo- or Stasi-like outfit, M5 does not include members of its own ranks in the database.

Spying on Unfriendly Journalists

The inquisition side of NSA is the one that Hayden and his advisers do not want the public to see. In fact, NSA maintains a database that tracks unofficial and negative articles written about the agency. Code named "FIRSTFRUITS," the database is operated by the Denial and Deception (D&D) unit within SID. High priority is given to articles written as a result of possible leaks from cleared personnel.

According to those familiar with FIRSTFRUITS, Bill Gertz of *The Washington Times* features prominently in the database. Before Hayden's reign and during the Clinton administration, Gertz was often leaked classified documents by anti-Clinton intelligence officials in an attempt to demonstrate that collusion between the administration and China was hurting U.S. national security. NSA, perhaps legitimately, was concerned that China could actually benefit from such disclosures.

In order that the database did not violate United States Signals Intelligence Directive (USSID) 18, which specifies that the names of "U.S. persons" are to be deleted through a process known as minimization, the names of subject journalists were blanked out. However, in a violation of USSID 18, certain high level users could unlock the database field through a super-user status and view the "phantom names" of the journalists in question. Some of the "source" information in FIRSTFRUITS was classified—an indication that some of the articles in database were not obtained through open source means. In fact, NSA insiders report that the communications monitoring tasking system known as ECHELON is being used more frequently for purely political eavesdropping having nothing to do with national security or counter terrorism.

In addition, outside agencies and a "second party," Great Britain's Government Communications Headquarters (GCHQ), are permitted to access the journalist database. FIRSTFRUITS was originally developed by the CIA but given to NSA to operate with CIA funding. The database soon grew to capacity, was converted from a Lotus Notes to an Oracle system, and NSA took over complete ownership of the system from the CIA.

Tens of thousands of articles are found in FIRSTFRUITS and part of the upkeep of the system has been outsourced to outside contractors such as Booz Allen, which periodically hosts inter-agency Foreign Denial and Deception meetings within its Sensitive Compartmented Information Facility or "SCIF" in Tyson's Corner, Virginia. Currently, in addition to NSA and GCHQ, the National Geospatial-Intelligence Agency (NGA), the Defense Intelligence Agency (DIA), and National Reconnaissance Office (NRO) routinely access the database, which is in essence a classified and more powerful version of the commercial NEXIS news search database.

In addition to Gertz, other journalists who feature prominently in the database include Seymour Hersh of *The New Yorker;* author and journalist James Bamford, James Risen of *The New York Times,* Vernon Loeb of *The Washington Post,* John C. K. Daly of UPI, and this journalist.

NSA abhors negative publicity. Anytime the agency is the subject of unwanted media attention, Hayden sends out an email known as an "All Agency." The memo reiterates NSA's long standing "neither confirm nor deny" policy regarding certain news reports:

NSA personnel must refrain from either confirming or denying any information concerning the agency or its activities which may appear in the public media. If you are asked about the activities of NSA, the best response is "no comment." You should the notify Q43 {Public Affairs] of the attempted inquiry. For the most part, public references to NSA are based upon educated guesses. The agency does not normally make a practice of issuing public statements about its activities.

The Calipari Slaying and the Cell Phone Diversion

One example of how poor management at NSA has affected the ability of U.S. intelligence to protect American and Allied personnel in combat zones is the slaying in Baghdad by U.S. troops of the number two man in the Italian military intelligence service—SISMI—Major General Nicola Calipari.

Accompanying freed Italian journalist hostage Giuliana Sgrena by car to Baghdad Airport after her liberation from Iraqi captors, Calipari was shot to death by troops of the 69th Infantry Regiment of the New York National Guard while talking to his superiors on his cell phone. The report issued by the United States that cleared the American troops of any responsibility for the killing of Calipari and wounding of Sgrena states that "Route Irish [the main access road to the airport] [is] a lucrative target area for insurgents to employ improvised explosive devices (IEDs) of varying types and to achieve effects in terms of casualties." A Secret/NOFORN [Not for Release to Foreign Nationals] sentence in the report states, "The use of radios or cell phones should be limited to essential communications and/or entirely prohibited as their transmissions may detonate any IEDs present."

Calipari's cell phone signal was likely picked up by tactical signals intelligence units in the area and may have been the reason the U.S. side opened fire on the Italian vehicle. However, according to NSA insiders, cell phones are not used to detonate either Remote Control IEDs (RCIEDs) or Vehicle Borne IEDs (VBEIDs). In fact, insurgents use cheap, Asian-made long-range cordless phones bought in the street markets of Baghdad to detonate IEDs. By using cordless phones bought from carpets strewn on streets in Baghdad, the insurgents know there is no way to identify the purchaser or track the use of the phones. The three cordless phones of choice for the insurgents are Senao and Voyager, which are made in Taiwan, and Anytone and Soontone, both made in China. Therefore, Calipari's cell phone frequency was a non-threat signal.

The U.S. report on the shooting death also refers in another Secret/NOFORN sentence to the use by the American Tactical Operations Center (TOC) of Voice Over IP (VOIP) phones and FM radio as the two primary means of communications. NSA insiders scoff at the reference to VOIP—claiming that such phones are not routinely used because of their inherent unreliability. Even the Secret/NOFORN sentence alludes to problems in VOIP communications between the 69th Infantry unit and a field artillery unit: "The 1—76 FA [Field Artillery] Battle Captain was using only VOIP to communicate with 1—69 IN, but experienced problems with VOIP, therefore losing its only communication link with 1—69 IN."

According to NSA officers, the failure of the agency to upgrade or change its ELINT parameter data, contained in two databases known as the Emitter Parameter List (EPL) and KILTING, has led to a number of friendly fire incidents in Iraq, including the killing of Calipari, an attack on a Kurdish convoy in the north of Iraq, and the shooting down of a British RAF Tornado jet fighter near the Kuwaiti border. Hayden's response has been to move SIGINT and ELINT functions to Texas and Colorado, respectively.

President Goofy's Talk with Putin about "Magic Mountain"

NSA's overriding interest in a Soviet-era underground mountain complex apparently caught the interest of George W. Bush. In a closed zone near the city of Mezhgorye in the Russian Republic of Bashkortostan, north of the Kazakhstan border, is a huge underground facility embedded deep within Yamantau Mountain in the Urals Range. Yamantau is Bashkir for "Evil Mountain." What amazes NSA is the absence of noticeable telecommunications support facilities for the complex, believed to be an alternate "doomsday" command center for the Russian government and military in the event of a nuclear, biological, or chemical attack. Costing over $7 billion, the complex is supported by 60,000 workers who live in the nearby towns of Beloretsk and Tirlyanskiy.

The Yamantau Mountain Complex covers an area of some 400 square miles. Construction of the mammoth facility began during the 1970s and the Leonid Brezhnev administration. To maintain operational security and prevent future leaks, the Soviets hired workers from different parts of the USSR to perform individual tasks.

The neoconservatives in the Bush administration and Congress, particularly Vice President Dick Cheney, Defense Secretary Donald Rumsfeld, UN ambassador nominee John Bolton, and Representatives Curt Weldon (R-PA) and Roscoe Bartlett (R-MD), have been pressuring the NSA and other intelligence agencies to come up with the goods on Yamantau. Wasting precious resources that could be used to combat terrorism, the intelligence agencies have been ordered to make Yamantau a top priority. The secrecy of the complex's telecommunications methods has resulted in NSA coming up empty-handed.

For reasons of communications security, NSA routinely listens in on the communications of executive branch officials, including, at times, the president and the vice president. In a conversation between Bush and Russian President Vladimir Putin, NSA operators overheard Bush asking in a rather inane manner, "You have a Yamantau, too?" Bush added, "It's like our 'Rock'?"

The "Rock" is a reference to the Joint Alternate Communications Center, or "Site R," bored into Raven Rock Mountain just across the Maryland border in Pennsylvania, near the town of Waynesboro. It is an underground alternate national command center constructed during the Cold War and the famous "secret undisclosed location" where Vice President Cheney is often transported during states of alert. Unlike Yamantau, Raven Rock is surrounded by a number of tell tale signs that it is a military-critical facility—satellite parabolic dishes, microwave towers, and various antennas sprout from the side of the mountain.

Apparently, Bush got nothing about Yamantau in his phone conversation with Putin, who is a former KGB officer.

Anyone "Butt" Him

Another prime NSA target is the Moscow-based Russian arms trafficker and human rights pariah Viktor Bout. Bout, pronounced "butt," has a long record of flying arms and various terrorist and mercenary ne'er-do-wells from one killing zone to another.

Bout, who has mysterious air cargo companies based in places as far afield as Burkina Faso, Sharjah, Ajman, and Ras al Khaima in the United Arab Emirates, Miami, Dallas, Swaziland, Democratic Republic of Congo, Gibraltar, Equatorial Guinea, Rwanda, Uganda, Pakistan, Kazakhstan, Central African Republic, Belgium, Gambia, Bulgaria, Cyprus, and, under contract to U.S. forces, Iraq, has long been sought by the international community for being involved in busting United Nations arms sanctions in places like Angola, Sierra Leone, Liberia, Congo, and Afghanistan.

Bout's clients have included Liberian dictator Charles Taylor, al Qaeda leader Osama Bin Laden, the Philippine Muslim extremist Abu Sayyaf Group, the Taliban government of Afghanistan, the Afghan Northern Alliance, Sierra Leone's brutal Revolutionary United Front guerrillas (who chopped off the hands and legs of children and other innocent civilians), and Zaire's dictator Mobutu Sese Seko.

During the last year of the Clinton administration, Viktor Bout was a number one SIGINT target for NSA. However, after Condoleezza Rice took over as National Security Adviser under Bush, she issued a change in orders on Bout. "Look and listen but don't touch" was the new policy. Ever since, Bout has flouted INTERPOL and Belgian and French arrest warrants.

Although the U.S. Treasury Department imposed sanctions on Bout's companies on April 26, 2005, and froze his corporate assets, one of Bout's airlines, Irbis, continued to operate from a U.S.-controlled airbase in northern Iraq.

Other Bout companies, which use a fleet of aging Soviet-era military cargo planes, are contracted to a network of seedy multinational private military contractors operating in Iraq. Bout's global enterprises closely intersect with the diamond, white slave trade, arms, and other illicit activities of Israel's Russian Mafia, made up of some 80 Russian and Ukrainian Jewish billionaires and millionaires who have escaped to Israel to avoid prosecution in and extradition to Russia and other countries. Considering the close association between leading neoconservatives like Vice President Cheney's Chief of Staff I. Lewis "Scooter" Libby to fugitive Marc Rich, who is linked to the crime syndicates in Israel, a reason for Rice's diktat, "Look and listen but don't touch," with regard to Bout, becomes abundantly clear.

Suicide is Painless and Common

The U.S. intelligence community has suffered a spate of mysterious and surprising suicides since the onset of the Iraq war. State Department Bureau of Intelligence and Research Iraq analyst John J. Kokal, former CIA officer Dr. Gus Weiss, and Washington's politically and diplomatically connected lobbyist Edward von Kloberg, who once counted Saddam Hussein among his clients, all jumped from the tops of buildings or out of window between November 2003 and May 2005. In addition, CIA officer Ben Miller was told to jump out of an open window at the National Security Council by Iran-contra felon Elliot Abrams, who is now an assistant national security advisor. In 2001, prior to the September 11 attacks, the DIA suffered a suicide in its Asia Area of Responsibility (AOR) unit.

NSA has apparently been no exception to the suicide epidemic. Before his departure from NSA to serve as Negroponte's deputy, Hayden sent a letter to all NSA employees in which he urged everyone to recognize "stress factors" at work. The letter also described the grief of losing a member of the NSA family from stress. NSA employees took the letter as an indication that there had been a recent suicide among the NSA ranks but no mention was made of the individual's identity. In fact, NSA insiders confirmed that an experienced NSA employee did commit suicide but the identity of the person remains a secret. In another mysterious case, a U.S. Air Force officer working clandestine SIGINT operations for NSA turned up missing with only a suicide note found.

NSAers are uniform in the way they describe Hayden and his team's tenure. The NSA is much worse now than it was seven years ago. Critical functions are being dispersed to incompetent contractors and distant military bases. Morale has plummeted to an all-time low. Retired NSA veterans are hopping mad about what has become of their agency. What the neoconservatives and their ilk are doing to America's intelligence, military, economic, and foreign policy infrastructures is nothing more than treasonous. And in what will amount to the greatest demonstration of the law of unintended consequences, the damage done to NSA by Hayden and his neoconservative superiors will result in more and greater intelligence disclosures that will shine a bright light on the behind-the-scenes machinations of the Bush administration and may, hopefully, drive a final nail in the coffin of neoconservative politics.

May 27, 2005 -- SPY AGENCY DISRUPTION REACHES FORT MEADE: America's "Ear" on Terrorism War Wracked by Poor Morale, Management Failures

Up to now, little has been reported on how the Bush administration's disastrous intelligence policies have affected the super-secret National Security Agency (NSA). According to NSA insiders, the chief U.S. signals intelligence (SIGINT) collection agency has been wracked by much of the same internal feuding, senior management failures, and external political pressure that have plagued other U.S. intelligence agencies, including the CIA, FBI, Defense Intelligence Agency, National Geo-spatial Intelligence Agency, and National Reconnaissance Office.

NSA insiders lay blame for the problems at NSA's Fort Meade, Maryland headquarters squarely on the shoulders of agency Director Air Force General Michael V. Hayden and his small coterie of close advisers, a few of whom have no substantive intelligence background. Hayden has been NSA Director since March 1999, the longest tour for any NSA Director. Not only did the White House extend Hayden's NSA tour, but also nominated him to be the first Deputy Director of National Intelligence, where he will serve under John Negroponte.

Hayden's reign at NSA has been marked by the emaciation of the career civilian corps through forced retirements and resignations, outsourcing of government positions to contractors, intimidation, forced psychiatric and psychological examinations for "problem" employees, increased work loads for shift personnel with no personnel augmentation, unreasonable personal searches by security personnel, and withholding salary increases for career personnel. A number of NSA employees are suffering from stress and fatigue and that is adversely affecting their job performance.

One of the most pervasive operational problems at NSA stems from the fact that when newly trained civilian and military linguists, analysts, and other operational personnel arrive at NSA for duty and are integrated into various operational work centers, they are soon quickly transferred to Iraq. This puts an inordinate workload on the career civilian NSA personnel.

In other cases, critical experienced employees have been forced out of NSA because of policy differences, especially those related to the war against Iraq. One linguist who was fluent in 14 languages, including Arabic, Russian, Japanese, Hindi, Chinese, Modern Greek, and Spanish was forced into retirement over policy differences with NSA senior management. NSA concocted trumped up charges against the linguist. Another analyst, who worked closely with the CIA's satellite imagery division on Iraq and other hot spots, was repeatedly harassed by NSA's Stasi-like security personnel. In other cases, experienced NSA employees who don't fit the mold have been charged with infractions as ludicrous as stalking, gun running, and personality disorders.

A senior NSA Intelligence Analyst and Action Officer ran afoul of NSA merely for doing his job for reporting a possible hostile intelligence agent while working in a previous sensitive all source intelligence Defense Intelligence Agency (DIA) job in early 2001. A U.S. Air Force veteran and experienced NSA hand in Afghanistan, Iraq, and post-911 operations, the intelligence officer believed a DIA colleague may have been a hostile intelligence agent. After the officer reported the individual to DIA's counter-intelligence office and after he transferred to NSA, he found himself subject to psychiatric tests ordered by the draconian NSA Security directorate. He was fired from his operational job, had his security clearance lifted, and sent to the agency's motor pool where he drove staff cars and cleaned buses as a "red badge" (uncleared) employee. A DIA source later informed the officer that there was "reason to be concerned" about the possible hostile intelligence agent he reported. However, the officer ultimately faced the permanent loss of his security clearance and dismissal from NSA.

When Hayden first began his civilian shake up at NSA in 2000, career professionals described it as an "internal coup." For many longtime NSA employees, the writing was on the wall and it was not a pleasant message. However, to the outsider, Hayden has represented a "kinder and gentler" NSA Director.

During the filming of the movie thriller about NSA, "Enemy of the State," Hayden invited lead star Will Smith to tour the National Security Operations Center (NSOC). Members of the film crew were allowed to buy NSA curios and souvenirs from the agency's gift shop. In addition, Hayden has thrown NSA's doors open to 60 Minutes, Nightline, and other news media. However, to NSA career employees, Hayden's iron fist tactics have earned him the nickname "Hitler Hayden."

Hayden also seems more concerned about public relations than NSA's mission. NSA insiders cite the presence of two female analysts in the Denial and Deception (called "D and D" in NSA parlance) branch of the NSOC who do nothing but scan the media for any stories about NSA, positive and negative. Their jobs are duplicated in Hayden's General Counsel's office. The NSA public relations mechanism went into red alert status in January 2000 when the agency suffered a massive computer failure.

Career NSA personnel claim that their most senior member, Deputy Director of NSA William B. Black, Jr., shows little interest in their plight. One long-time NSAer said Black often nods off at Hayden's staff meetings. In 2000, Black, a retired NSA employee with 38 years of service, was rehired by Hayden from Science Applications International Corporation (SAIC) to be his deputy. Hayden's selection of Black from outside the agency was considered a slap in the faces of those line NSA officers who would have been normally considered next in line for promotion to the much-coveted post. That slight began to severely affect agency morale a little over a year before the September 11, 2001 terrorist attacks on New York and Washington.

After 9/11 and subsequent revelations that NSA had intercepted two Arabic language phone calls on September 10, 2001 ("Tomorrow is zero hour" and "The match is about to begin") that indicated an imminent attack by Al Qaeda but failed to translate and analyze them in a timely manner to be effective, Hayden was looking for scapegoats. According to NSA insiders, he found one in Maureen A. Baginski, the Director of NSA's Signals Intelligence (SIGINT) Directorate. According to the NSA insiders, Baginski, a 27-year NSA veteran and Russian and Spanish linguist, was set up for a fall by Hayden and his team. In 2003, Baginski was named Executive Assistant Director of the FBI for Intelligence. According to NSA sources, it was Baginski who carried out Hayden's directives that farmed out many Fort Meade functions to other facilities. Another Hayden project, GROUNDBREAKER, the outsourcing of NSA functions to contractors, has also been used by Hayden's advisers to assign blame for the 911 failures at NSA. According to NSA insiders, GROUNDBREAKER has been a failure.

GROUNDBREAKER resulted in a $2 billion outsourcing contract being awarded in 2001 by NSA to the Eagle Alliance, a consortium led by Computer Sciences Corporation (CSC) and comprised of Northrop Grumman, General Dynamics, Keane Federal Systems, CACI, TRW, Verizon and other contractors. NSA government personnel report that the contractors, mostly former NSA personnel, have done nothing to streamline NSA operations and administration, the primary purpose of the contract. For example, the Eagle Alliance rents back non mission critical computers and phones at NSA back to the agency. However, according to NSA personnel, a number of mission critical computers have been included in the Eagle contract. Computers handling electronic intelligence (ELINT) and communications intelligence (COMINT) databases are leased by Eagle. Currently, technical support for the Dell computers is handled by a secured line to Eagle personnel. However, NSA insiders report there are future plans to provide technical support via non secured lines and that the technical support may very well be provided by off shore centers in India. The nickname for the Eagle Alliance inside NSA is the "Evil Alliance."

Another one of Hayden's projects that has been criticized by the NSA rank-and-file is TRAILBLAZER, the program to modernize NSA's SIGINT systems. For example, operators in U.S. electronic warfare aircraft rely on NSA to provide accurate electronic intelligence (ELINT) data in order to program their radar warning receivers and jamming pods. However, NSA data, provided from two databases known as EPL (Emitter Parameter List) and "Kilting." 70 percent of NSA's ELINT data is 30 years old. NSA management has forced field operators to use raw ELINT intercept data, culled from a database called WRANGLER, to program their ELINT systems. NSA operations and software engineers believe this function should be handled by NSA and not the "warfighters." Updated ELINT data is handled by ELINT Technical Reports or "ELTs." In 2003, the year the Iraq war started, there were 938 ELTs submitted on new emitter data. However, there were only 200 updates made to the ELINT databases.

The failure to update the ELINT databases may have had disastrous consequences in Iraq. For example, EPL and Kilting do not contain data on air traffic control radars and microwave communications links. Because current ELINT systems cannot differentiate between commercial signals and hostile target tracking emitters, U.S. forces in Iraq have launched attacks on non-threat targets in the belief they were hostile. NSA sources report that many of the cases of fratricide in Iraq has been due to faulty or old ELINT data. For example, the failure by NSA to update ELINT data and provide emitter parameter data to warfighting units led to the accidental shoot down by a Patriot missile of a British Royal Air Force Tornado fighter in March 2003 near the Iraqi-Kuwaiti border at the outset of the Iraq campaign. Two British crew members were killed. The ELINT data used by the Patriot misidentified the Tornado as an enemy missile and the U.S. Army blamed the British crew for the mistake, claiming they failed to switch on its Identification Friend or Foe (IFF) equipment. NSA insiders claim that allegation was false. They claim that "blue signals" (friendly) are not adequately included in the emitter data sent to field units by NSA and that claims by the Pentagon that the Tornado was shot down due to pilot error were false.

In other incidents, the radar warning receivers (RWRs) on U.S. F-16s flying over Iraq have either evaded or fired AMRAAM (Advanced Medium-Range, Air-to-Air) missiles on microwave communications towers because the microwave signals were identified as threat emitters from hostile aircraft. U.S. jammers are also adversely affected by the failure to update ELINT data.

In fact, many of NSA's developmental ELINT systems, with cover names like BEIKAO, BOOMVANG, CANYONDUST, CAPE LOOKOUT, CHARTVEIN, EAGLE REACH, GALAXYDUST, HARPSTRING, HOKUSAI, IRISH DEN, JETAVATOR, MONOCLE, NEEDLEICE, PLATOONWOLF, QUADRUNNER, RADIANT SPRUCE II, ROMAN ALLIANCE, SEADIVER, SHADOWBOXER, SHARKBITE, SHILOH, STARQUAKE, STOUTHEARTED ,and SUNBEAVER are not found in the master NSA ELINT project database, which also has a cover name: BRASSCOIN.

Many of NSA's other SIGINT systems are in the same conundrum. Rather than simplify and modernize NSA's SIGINT development and deployment, TRAILBLAZER has done nothing to modernize or cut acquisition costs. In a suspicious move by NSA, the TRAILBLAZER contract was sole-sourced to SAIC, the firm from which Hayden hired his deputy director. As with GROUNDBREAKER, TRAILBLAZER's contractors consist of a team led by a prime contractor. TRAILBLAZER's team overlaps with GROUNDBREAKER -- companies like CSC and Northrop Grumman are also found on the TRAILBLAZER team. Booz Allen Hamilton and Boeing are also on the SAIC team. According to NSA officers, one SAIC official left the firm to work for Hayden at NSA during the time the TRAILBLAZER bidding process was underway. The individual then returned to SAIC as a senior vice president, according to NSA sources. NSA employees, upset about the control that SAIC now has over the agency, refer to NSA as "NSAIC."

At his Senate Select Intelligence Committee nomination hearing for Deputy Director of National Intelligence, Hayden confirmed that TRAILBLAZER was over budget and behind schedule. He told the committee that TRAILBLAZER's "cost was greater than anticipated in the tune, I would say, in hundreds of millions." Hayden confirmed the report of the joint congressional committee that probed the 911 intelligence failures that TRAILBLAZER was several years behind schedule. NSA sources claim that TRAILBLAZER is at least five years behind schedule and $600 million over budget.

However, the career NSA operational personnel may be getting squeezed not so much for policy and management differences but because of what they know about the lies of the Bush administration. In addition to the obvious lies about Iraqi WMDs, many personnel are well aware that what occurred on the morning of 9/11 was not exactly what was reported by the White House. For example, President Bush spoke of the heroic actions of the passengers and crew aboard United Flight 93 over rural Pennsylvania on the morning of 9/11. However, NSA personnel on duty at the NSOC that morning have a very different perspective. Before Flight 93 crashed in Pennsylvania, NSA operations personnel clearly heard on the intercom system monitoring military and civilian communications that the "fighters are engaged" with the doomed United aircraft. NSOC personnel were then quickly dismissed from the tactical area of the NSOC where the intercom system was located leaving only a few senior personnel in place. NSA personnel are well aware that Secretary of Defense Donald Rumsfeld did not "misspeak" when, addressing U.S. troops in Baghdad during Christmas last year, said, "the people who attacked the United States in New York, shot down the plane over Pennsylvania." They believe the White House concocted the "passengers-bring-down-plane" story for propaganda value.

Morale at NSA has plummeted from repeated cover-ups of serious breaches of security by senior officials. While rank-and-file employees are subjected to abusive psychological and psychiatric evaluations for disagreeing with summary intelligence reports provided to outside users or "consumers" and even for more mundane matters, others are given a pass. Ironically, one of the psychiatrists used by NSA to evaluate problem or disgruntled employees was recently found by police to be growing marijuana at his home in Crofton, Maryland.

In another case, after suggestive photos of a female Air Force Captain, who was an aide to Hayden, were found on a pornographic web site under the title Captain amErika, NSA security did nothing to discipline or seriously investigate the officer in question. The web site was apparently set up by the Air Force officer's ex-husband. After NSA took legal action, the original web site was taken down. The NSA contended it was concerned about the web site because it contained the names of NSA field stations, including the Bad Aibling intercept station in Germany.

However, a group of non-commissioned officers who object to the double standards for conduct imposed on enlisted personnel and officers have re-created much of the original Captain amErika web site at www.captainamerika.us. The web administrator is based in South Bend, Indiana. The site continues to refer to Bad Aibling and the NSA communications intercept system known as "Echelon," contains the original pornographic material, and makes severe allegations about General Hayden's personal conduct. The web site claims the officer known as Captain amErika has been promoted to Major and is on the fast track for early promotion to Lieutenant Colonel.

There have been other sexual related scandals at NSA that resulted in little or no action being taken against the offenders. In 1999, a senior NSA officer, on assignment overseas, was arrested by police in his hotel room while filming a sex video with a child. The officer was forced to retire but became an NSA contractor in Florida making two to three times his NSA salary. In a more recent incident, an NSA SIGINT operator who was monitoring a targeted person's Internet activity involving access to child pornography web sites, lifted the NSA security filters to look at the pornography for himself, a violation of NSA operational procedures.

The 600-page report of the Presidential Commission on WMD intelligence failures in Iraq, co-chaired by Republican Judge Laurence Silberman and former Democratic Senator Charles Robb, concluded that there was no evidence that the Bush administration pressured U.S. intelligence agencies to "cook" or "cherry pick" the intelligence needed to justify the war against Iraq. Rather than focus on the pressure exerted on agencies by Vice President Dick Cheney, Defense Secretary Rumsfeld, and other neo-conservative officials in the National Security Council, Pentagon, and State Department, the report blamed the intelligence agencies for providing "worthless or misleading" information on Iraqi weapons of mass destruction to senior Bush policymakers. Silberman, a key player in the Iran-Contra cover-up scandal while a judge on the U.S. Court of Appeals for the District of Columbia, told Bush at the White House briefing in which the final report was submitted, "We did not see any evidence of false intelligence being injected by any policymaker into the intelligence community."

What is happening at NSA is also occurring at the CIA and other agencies. A senior CIA official is suing the CIA for being fired last August for refusing to falsify CIA reports on Iraqi WMDs in order to justify the White House's pre-emptive attack. As with the senior Arabic and Russian linguist at NSA, the CIA officer was falsely investigated for personal improprieties in retaliation for his refusal to cook intelligence for the White House. In the case of the CIA officer, the CIA's investigation was predicated on alleged financial and sexual misconduct.

The WMD Intelligence Commission's report failed to look at the underlying causes of U.S. intelligence failures: mismanagement and corruption at senior levels. That incompetence and malfeasance continues at the NSA, CIA, and other intelligence agencies. George Tenet, someone who was as damaging to CIA morale as Hayden has been for NSA's, resigned as CIA Director and then was given a medal by President Bush. His successor, Porter Goss, has carried out a top-down purge directed by the neo-conservatives in the administration. Hayden, who has allowed morale at NSA to sink to an all-time low, has been promoted to the Directorate of National Intelligence as deputy. By its failure to assign blame to the very top officials of the U.S. intelligence community and its continued harassment of career intelligence professionals, the Bush administration continues to send the message that it is okay to lie, cheat, and engage in inappropriate behavior. To challenge the administration, however, will result in firings, early retirements, harassment, and investigations based on sham charges.

NSA is also farming out critical functions to other facilities around the country. For example, 350 ELINT jobs have been transferred to the Buckley Air Force Base in Aurora, Colorado. However, most of the ELINT personnel have remained in Maryland resulting in a lack of experienced personnel in Colorado. The Buckley ELINT facility does not even recognize NSA security badges and operates as an entity outside the control of the intelligence community and subservient to the Pentagon. In addition, 1500 NSA jobs were transferred by Hayden to the Medina Regional SIGINT Operations Center (RSOC) at Lackland Air Force Base in San Antonio, Texas. NSA insiders report that Hayden's decision to move nearly 2000 jobs from Maryland was in revenge for Maryland Democratic Senator Barbara Mikulski complaining about the loss of government jobs at Fort Meade resulting from Groundbreaker and TRAILBLAZER.

It is anticipated that additional NSA jobs will be lost to a new Regional SIGINT Operations Center being built in Hawaii. The facility, consisting of three buildings and which resembles an eye from the air, will replace the current Kunia Regional SIGINT Operations Center, which is embedded in a mountain on Oahu. NSA sources report that the model for the building cost some $2 million.

According to NSA insiders, Hayden is taking many of his closest advisers with him to the Directorate of National Intelligence. They include his long-time public affairs officer, Judi Emmel.

June 1, 2005 -- NSA and selling the nation's prized secrets to contractors

On August 1, 2001, just five and a half weeks before the 911 attacks, NSA awarded Computer Sciences Corporation (CSC) a more than $2 billion, ten-year contract known as

GROUNDBREAKER. The contract was never popular with NSA's career professionals. Although GROUNDBREAKER was limited to outsourcing NSA's administrative support functions such as telephones, data networks, distributed computing, and enterprise architecture design, the contract soon expanded into the operational areas -- a sphere that had always been carefully restricted to contractors. NSA was once worried about buying commercial-off-the-shelf computer components such as semiconductors because they might contain foreign bugs. NSA manufactured its own computer chips at its own semiconductor factory at Fort Meade. Currently, NSA personnel are concerned that outsourcing mania at Fort Meade will soon involve foreign help desk technical maintenance provided from off-shore locations like India.

CSC had originally gained access to NSA through a "buy in" project called BREAKTHROUGH, a mere $20 million contract awarded in 1998 that permitted CSC to operate and maintain NSA computer systems. When General Michael V. Hayden took over as NSA Director in 1999, the floodgates for outside contractors were opened and a resulting deluge saw most of NSA's support personnel being converted to contractors working for GROUNDBREAKER's Eagle Alliance (nicknamed the "Evil Alliance" by NSA government personnel), a consortium led by CSC. NSA personnel rosters of support personnel, considered protected information, were turned over to Eagle, which then made offers of employment to the affected NSA workers. The Eagle Alliance consists of CSC, Northrop Grumman, General Dynamics, CACI, Omen, Inc., Keane Federal Systems, ACS Defense, BTG, Compaq, Fiber Plus, Superior Communications, TRW (Raytheon), Verizon, and Windemere.

In October 2002, Hayden, who has now been promoted by Bush to be Deputy Director of National Intelligence under John Negroponte, opened NSA up further to contractors. A Digital Network Enterprise (DNE) team led by SAIC won a $280 million, 26 month contract called TRAILBLAZER to develop a demonstration test bed for a new signals intelligence processing and analysis system. SAIC's team members included Booz Allen Hamilton, Boeing, Northrop Grumman, and Eagle Alliance team leader CSC. TRAILBLAZER, according to Hayden's own testimony before the Senate Select Committee on Intelligence, is now behind schedule and over budget to the tune of over $600 million.

But that is not the only consequence of these two mega-contracts for NSA's ability to monitor global communications for the next 911, which could be a terrorist nuclear strike on the United States.

NSA insiders report that both contract teams have melded into one and that NSA's operations are being adversely impacted. From simple tasks like phones being fixed to computers being updated with new software, the Eagle Alliance has been a disaster. The Eagle Alliance and DNE team members are rife with former NSA top officials who are reaping handsome bonuses from the contracts -- and that has many NSA career employees crying conflict of interest and contract fraud.

CACI, called "Colonels and Captains, Inc." by critics who cite the revolving door from the Pentagon to its corporate office suites, counts former NSA Deputy Director Barbara McNamara as a member of its board of directors. CACI alumni include Thomas McDermott, a former NSA Deputy Director for Information Systems Security. Former NSA Director Adm. Mike McConnell is a Senior Vice President of Booz Allen. Former NSA Director General Ken Minihan is President of the Security Affairs Support Association (SASA), an intelligence business development association that includes Boeing, Booz Allen, CACI, CSC, the Eagle Alliance, General Dynamics, Northrop Grumman, Raytheon, SAIC, and Windemere, all GROUNDBREAKER and TRAILBLAZER contractors, among its membership. SASA's board of directors (surprise, surprise) includes CACI's Barbara McNamara. One of SASA's distinguished advisers is none other than General Hayden.

Although contractors are required to have the same high level security clearances as government personnel at NSA, there are close connections between some NSA contractors and countries with hostile intelligence services. For example, CACI's president and CEO visited Israel in early 2004 and received the Albert Einstein Technology Award at ceremony in Jerusalem attended by Likud Party Defense Minister Shaul Mofaz. The special ceremony honoring CACI's president was sponsored by the Aish HaTorah Yeshiva Fund. The ultra-Orthodox United Torah Judaism Party's Jerusalem Mayor, Uri Lupolianski, was also in attendance. According to Lebanon's Daily Star, CACI's president also met with notorious racist Israeli retired General Effie Eitam who advocates expelling Palestinians from their lands. The U.S. delegation also included a number of homeland security officials, politicians, and businessmen. CACI has also received research grants from U.S.-Israeli bi-national foundations. A few months after the award ceremony for CACI's president, the Taguba Report cited two CACI employees as being involved in the prison torture at Abu Ghraib prison in Iraq. The U.S. military commander for the Iraqi prisons, General Janis Karpinski, reported that she witnessed Israeli interrogators working alongside those from CACI and another contractor, Titan.

When the Taguba Report was leaked, the office of Deputy Defense Secretary for Policy Douglas Feith issued an order to Pentagon employees not to download the report from the Internet. Feith is a well-known hard line supporter of Israel's Likud Party and, according to U.S. government insiders, his name has come up in FBI wiretaps of individuals involved in the proliferation of nuclear weapons material to Israel via Turkish (including Turkish Jewish) intermediaries. These wiretaps are the subject of a Federal probe of who compromised a sensitive CIA counter-proliferation global operation that used a carve out company called Brewster Jennings & Associates to penetrate nuclear weapons smuggling networks with tentacles extending from Secaucus, New Jersey to South Africa and Pakistan and Turkey to Israel.

According to the Jewish Telegraph Agency, some six months before the Abu Ghraib torture scandal was first uncovered, one of Feith's assistants, Larry Franklin, met with two officials of the American Israel Public Affairs Committee (AIPAC) at the Tivoli Restaurant in Arlington, Virginia. According to FBI surveillance tapes, Franklin relayed top secret information to Steve Rosen, AIPAC's then policy director, and Keith Weissman, a senior Iran analyst with AIPAC.

Franklin has been indicted for passing classified information to AIPAC. In addition, three Israeli citizens have been identified as possible participants in the spy scandal. They are Naor Gilon, the political officer at the Israeli embassy in Washington; Uzi Arad, an analyst with the Institute for Policy and Strategy in Herzliya (the northern Tel Aviv suburb where the headquarters of Mossad is located); and Eran Lerman, a former Mossad official who is now with the American Jewish Committee.

What has some NSA officials worried is that with pro-Israeli neocons now engrained within the CIA, Defense Intelligence Agency (DIA), State Department, and National Security Council, NSA is ripe for penetration by Israeli intelligence. NSA has a troubled past with Israel. In 1967, Israeli warplanes launched a premeditated attack on the NSA surveillance ship, the USS Liberty, killing and wounding a number of U.S. sailors and NSA civilian personnel. Convicted Israeli spy Jonathan Pollard compromised a number of NSA sensitive sources and methods when he provided a garage full of classified documents to Israel. But NSA is also aware of an incident where Israelis used a contractor, RCA, to gain access to yet additional NSA sources and methods. In the 1980s, against the wishes of NSA, the Reagan administration forced NSA to permit RCA, one of its major contractors, to develop a tethered aerostat (balloon) signals intelligence and direction finding system for the Israeli Defense Force. According to NSA officials, the Israeli-NSA joint project, codenamed DINDI, was established at a separate facility in Mount Laurel, New Jersey and apart from the main NSA developmental center at RCA's facility in Camden, New Jersey. Although NSA and RCA set up a strict firewall between the contractor's national intelligence contract work and the separate DINDI contract, Israeli engineers, who were working for Mossad, soon broke down the security firewall with the assistance of a few American Jewish engineers assigned to the DINDI project. The security breach resulted in a number of national intelligence developmental systems being compromised to the Israelis, including those code named PIEREX, MAROON ARCHER, and MAROON SHIELD. DINDI was quickly cancelled but due to the sensitivity surrounding the American Jewish engineers, the Reagan Justice Department avoided bringing espionage charges. There were some forced retirements and transfers, but little more. But for NSA, the duplicity of the Israelis added to the enmity between Fort Meade and Israeli intelligence.

With outside contractors now permeating NSA and a major Israeli espionage operation being discovered inside the Pentagon, once again there is a fear within NSA that foreign intelligence services such as the Mossad could make another attempt to penetrate America's virtual "Fort Knox" of intelligence treasures and secrets.

Thanks to some very patriotic and loyal Americans inside NSA, this author is now in possession of an internal NSA contract document from November 2002 that shows how GROUNDBREAKER and TRAILBLAZER have allowed the Eagle Alliance and other contractors to gain access to and even virtual control over some of the most sensitive systems within the U.S. intelligence community. One suspect in this unchecked outsourcing is the person Hayden hired from the outside to act as Special Adviser to his Executive Leadership Team, Beverly Wright, who had been the Chief Financial Officer for Legg Mason Wood Walker in Baltimore. Before that, Wright had been the Chief Financial Officer for Alex Brown, the investment firm at which

George W. Bush's grandfather, Prescott Bush, once served as a board member. As one senior NSA official sarcastically put it, "She's highly qualified to work in intelligence!"

According to the document, the future of some 10,000 Windows NT and UNIX workstations and servers that handle some of NSA's most sensitive signals intelligence (SIGINT) (the Signals Intelligence Directorate workstation upgrade is code named BEANSTALK) and electronics intelligence (ELINT) applications, including databases that contain communications intercepts, are now firmly in the grasp of the Eagle Alliance. Operational workstations are being migrated to a less-than-reliable Windows/Intel or "WINTEL" environment. The document boldly calls for the Eagle Alliance to establish a SIGINT Service Applications Office (SASO) to "provide and maintain Information Technology services, tools, and capabilities for all [emphasis added] SIGINT mission applications at the NSA." This is a far cry from the non-operational administrative support functions originally specified in the GROUNDBREAKER contract.

The document also calls for NSA to provide extremely sensitive information on SIGINT users to the contractors: "Identification of target sets of users in order to successfully coordinate with the Eagle Alliance modernization program." The Eagle Alliance is involved in a number of systems that impact on other members of the U.S. intelligence community, foreign SIGINT partners, and national command authorities. These systems include INTELINK, Common Remoted Systems, National SIGINT Requirements Process, Overhead Tasking Distribution, RSOC (Regional SIGINT Operations Center) Monitoring Tool, RSOC Modeling Tool, Speech Activity Detection, Network Analysis Tools, Network Reconstruction Tools, Advanced Speech Processing Services, Automatic Message Handling System, CRITIC Alert, Cross Agency Multimedia Database Querying, Message Format Converter, Central Strategic Processing and Reporting, Collection Knowledge Base, Language Knowledge Base and Capabilities, K2000 Advanced ELINT Signals, Speech Content Services, Speech Information Extraction, Dominant Facsimile Processing System and DEFSMAC Support, Data Delivery (TINMAN), High Frequency Direction Finding (HFDF) Database, Satellite database, Protocol Analysis Terminal, Global Numbering Database, Intercept Tasking Databases, DEFSMAC Space Systems Utilities, Message Server, Extended Tether Program, Language Knowledge Services, Trend Analysis in Data Streams, Signal Related Database, SANDKEY Support (SIGINT Analysis and Reporting), and the SIGINT interception database ANCHORY and the ELINT database WRANGLER. In fact, the document states that the contractors' plans foresee the inclusion of NSA's intelligence community partners (foreign and domestic) in the contractors' revamping of NSA's operational systems.

The servers include those that support mission-critical National Time Sensitive Systems (NTSS). These National Time Sensitive System servers have been assigned various cover terms:

CANUCKS
DOLLAR
EASTCAKE
HEALYCUFF
MUDDYSWELT
NEEDYWHAT

RIMTITLE
RISKDIME
ROWLOAD
SEAWATER
CURACAO
HALF
HEALYMINK
LEARNGILT
LINEFURL
MOBLOOSE
SPELLBEAK
THOSEHOT.

A number of SIGINT applications are also impacted by the outsourcing mania. They are also assigned cover terms:

ADVERSARY
ADVERSARY GOLD
CHECKMATE
FANBELT
FANBELT II
FIREBLAZE
GALE-LITE (the primary owner of which is DIA)
GALLEYMAN
GALLEYPROOF
JAGUAR
KAFFS
MAGNIFORM
MAINCHANCE
OILSTOCK
PATHSETTER
PINSETTER
SIGDASYS FILE II, III, and KL
TEXTA
SPOT

In fact, the document indicates that literally hundreds of NSA intelligence applications are now subject to the whims of outside contractors. These systems include

ABEYANCE, ACROPOLIS, ADROIT, ADVANTAGE, AGILITY, AIRLINE, AIRMAIL, ALERT, ALCHEMIST, ANTARES, APPLEWOOD II, ARCHIVER, ARCVIEW GIS, ARROWGATE, ARROWWOOD, ARTFUL, ASPEN, ASSOCIATION, ATOMICRAFT, ATTRACTION, AUTOPILOT, AUTOSTAR, AXIOMATIC

BABBLEQUEST, BACKSAW, BANYAN, BARAD, BASERUNNER, BEAMER, BEIKAO, BELLVIEW, BIRDSNEST, BISON, BLACKBIRD, BLACKBOOK, BLACKFIN, BLACKHAWK, BLACKNIGHT/SHIPMASTER, BLACKMAGIC, BLACKONYX, BLACKOPAL, BLACKSEA, BLACKSHACK, BLACKSHIRT, BLACKSMYTH, BLACKSNAKE, BLACKSPIDER, BLACKSTAR, BLACKSTORM, BLACKSTRIKE, BLACKWATCH PULL, BLOODHUNTER, BLACKSWORD, BLOSSOM, BLUEBERRY, BLUESKY, BLUESTREAM, BOTTOM, BOTTOMLINE, BOWHUNT, BRAILLEWRITER, BRICKLOCK, BRIGHTENER, BROADWAY, BRIO INSIGHT, BUCKFEVER, BUILDINGCODE, BULK, BUMPER

CADENCE, CAINOTOPHOBIA, CALLIOPE, CALVIN, CANDID, CANDELIGHTER, CANDLESTICK, CAPRICORN, CARNIVAL, CARRAGEEN, CARTOGRAPHER, CAT, CATCOVE, CELLBLOCK, CELTIC II, CELTIC CROSS, CENTERBOARD, CENTERCOIL, CENTERPOINT, CENTRALIST, CERCIS, CHAGRIN, CHAMELEON, CHAMITE, CHAPELVIEW, CHARIOT, CHARMANDER, CHARTS, CHATEAU, CHECKMATE, CHECKWEAVE, CHERRYLAMBIC, CHEWSTICK, CHICKENOFF, CHILLFLAME, CHIMERA, CHIPBOARD, CHUJING, CIVORG, CHUCKLE, CLEANSLATE, CLIPS, CLOSEREEF I, CLOUDBURST, CLOUDCOVER, CLOUDCOVER II, CLUBMAN, COASTLINE, COASTLINE COMPASSPOINT, CLIENT, CODEFINDER, COMMONVIEW, CONCERTO, CONDENSOR, CONESTOGA, CONFRONT, CONTRIVER, CONUNDRUM, CONVEYANCE, COPPERHEAD, CORESPACE, CORTEZ, COUNTERSINK, COUNTERSPY, CRAZYTRAIN, CRISSCROSS, CRUISESHIP, CRYSTALLIZE, CYBERENGINE, CYGNUS

DAFIF, DANCEHALL, DARKSHROUD, DATATANK, DAYPUL, DAZZLER, DEATHRAY, DECOMA, DELTAWING, DEPTHGAUGE, DESERTFOX, DESOTO, DESPERADO, DIALOG, DIAMONDCHIP, DIFFRACTION, DISPLAYLINE, DITCHDIGGER, DITTO/UNDITTO, DIVINATION, DOITREE, DOLLARFISH, DOUBLEVISION, DRAGONMAKER, DUALIST

EAGERNESS, EAGLESTONE, EASYRIDER, ECTOPLASM, ELATION, ELECTRIFY, ELTON, ELEVATOR, EMPERORFISH, ENCAPSULATE, ENGRAFT, ETCHINGNEEDLE, EXPATRIATE, EXPERTPLAYER, EXTENDER, EXTRACTOR, EUREKA, EYELET

FAIRHILL, FAIRVIEW, FALCONRY, FALLOWHAUNT, FANATIC, FANCINESS, FASCIA II, FATFREE, FENESTRA, FIESTA, FINECOMB, FIREBOLT, FINETUNE, FIREBRAND II, FIRELAKE, FIRERUNG, FIRETOWER, FIRSTVIEW, FISHERMAN, FISHINGBOAT, FISHWAY, FLAGHOIST (OCS), FLASHFORWARD, FLEXAGON, FLEXMUX, FLEXSTART, FLIP, FLOTSAM, FOLKART, FORESITE, FORTITUDE, FOURSCORE, FOXFUR, FPGA GSM ATTACK, FIRSTPOINT, FARMHOUSE, FLODAR, FLOVIEW, FOSSIK, FROZENTUNDRA, FREESTONE, FRENZY/GRANULE, FUSEDPULL

GALAXYDUST, GARDENVIEW, GATCHWORK, GATOR, GAUNTLET, GAYFEATHER, GAZELLE, GEMTRAIL, GENED, GHOSTVIEW, GHOSTWIRE, GIGASCOPE, GIGASCOPE B, GISTER, GIVE, GLIDEPLANE, GOLDVEIN, GOLDPOINT, GNATCATCHER-GRADUS, GOKART, GOLDENEYE, GOLDENFLAX, GOLDENPERCH, GOLDMINE, GOMBROON, GOTHAM, GRADIENT, GRANDMASTER, GRAPEANGLE, GRAPEVINE, GRAPHWORK, GREATHALL, GREENHOUSE, GREMLIN, GUARDDOG, GUIDETOWER

HACKER, HABANERO, HAMBURGER, HAMMER, HARPSTRING, HARVESTER, HARVESTTIME, HEARTLAND II, HEARTLAND III, HEDGEHOG, HELMET II, HELMET III, HERONPOND, HIGHPOWER, HIGHTIDE, HILLBILLY BRIDE, HIPPIE, HOBBIN, HOKUSAI, HOMBRE, HOMEBASE, HOODEDVIPER, HOODQUERY, HOPPER, HOST, HORIZON, HOTSPOT, HOTZONE, HOUSELEEK/SPAREROOF, HYPERLITE, HYPERWIDE

ICARUS, ICICLE, IMAGERY, INFOCOMPASS, INCOMING , INNOVATOR, INQUISITOR, INROAD, INSPIRATION, INTEGRA, INTERIM, INTERNIST, INTERSTATE, INTRAHELP, IOWA, ISLANDER, IVORY ROSE, IVORY SNOW

JABSUM, JACAMAR, JADEFALCON, JARGON, JARKMAN, JASPERRED, JAZZ, JEALOUSFLASH, JEWELHEIST, JOVIAL, JOBBER, JOSY, JUMBLEDPET, JUPITER

KAHALA, KAINITE, KEBBIE, KEELSON, KEEPTOWER, KEYCARD, KEYMASTER, KEYS, KEYSTONE WEB, KINGCRAFT, KINGLESS, KINSFOLK, KLASHES, KLOPPER, KNOSSOS, KRYPTONITE

LADYSHIP, LAKESIDE, LAKEVIEW, LAMPSHADE, LAMPWICK, LARGO, LASERDOME, LASERSHIP, LASTEFFORT, LATENTHEART, LATENTHEAT, LEGAL REPTILE, LETHALPAN, LIBERTY WALK, LIGHTNING, LIGHTSWITCH, LINKAGE, LIONFEED, LIONHEART, LIONROAR, LIONWATCH, LOAD, LOCKSTOCK, LOGBOOK, LONGROOT, LUMINARY

MACEMAN, MACHISMO, MADONNA, MAESTRO, MAGENTA II, MAGIC BELT, MAGICSKY, MAGISTRAND, MAGYK, MAKAH, MAINWAY, MARINER II, MARKETSQUARE, MARLIN, MARSUPIAL, MARTES, MASTERCLASS, MASTERSHIP, MASTERSHIP II, MASTING, MATCHLITE, MAUI, MAVERICK, MECA, MEDIASTORM, MEDIATOR, MEDIEVAL, MEGAMOUSE, MEGASCOPE, MEGASTAR, MERSHIP (CARILLON), MESSIAH, MICOM, MIGHTYMAIL, MILLANG, MONITOR, MONOCLE, MOONDANCE, MOONFOX, MOORHAWK, MORETOWN, MOSTWANTED, MOVIETONE III, MUSICHALL, MUSTANG, MYTHOLOGY

NABOBS, NATIONHOOD, NAUTILUS, NDAKLEDIT, NEMESIS, NERVETRUNK, NETGRAPH,   NEWSBREAK, NEWSHOUND, NEXUS, NIGHTFALL 16, NIGHTFALL 32, NIGHTWATCH, NOBLEQUEST, NOBLESPIRIT, NOBLEVISION, NSOC SHIFTER, NUCLEON, NUMERIC

OAKSMITH, OBLIGATOR, OCEANARIUM, OCEANFRONT, OCTAGON, OCTAVE, OFFSHOOT, OLYMPIAD, ONEROOF, ONEROOF-WORD 2000 TRANSCRIPTION, OPALSCORE, OPENSEARCH, OPERA, ORCHID, ORIANA, OUTERBANKS, OUTFLASH, OUTREACH

PADDOCK, PACESETTER, PALINDROME, PAPERHANGER II, PARTHENON, PARTHENON II, PASSBACK, PASTURE, PATCHING, PATHFINDER, PATRIARCH, PAYMASTER, PAYTON, PEDDLER, PEARLWARE, PERFECTO, PERSEUS, PERSEVERE, PICKET, PINWALE, PIEREX, PILEHAMMER, PINNACLE, PINSTRIPE, PITONS, PIXIEDUST, PIZARRO, PLATINUM PLUS, PLATINUMRING, PLUMMER, PLUS, PLUTO, POLARFRONT, POLYSTYRENE, POPPYBASE, POPTOP, PORCELAIN, PORTCULLIS, POSTCARD, POWDERKEG, POWERPLANT, PRAIRIE DOG, PRANKSTER,

PREDATOR, PRELUDE, PROSCAN, PROSPERITY, PRIZEWINNER, PROPELLER, PROTOVIEW, PUFFERFISH, PYTHON II

QUARTERBACK, QUASAR, QUEST, QUICKER, QUICKSILVER

RAGBOLT, RAGTIME, RAINGAUGE, RAINMAN, RAKERTOOTH, RAMJET, RAP, RAPPEL, RAUCOVER, REACTANT, RECEPTOR, RECOGNITION, RED ARMY, RED BACK, RED BELLY, RED DAWN, RED DEMON, RED ROOSTER, RED ROVER, REDALERT, REDCAP, REDCENT, REDCOATS, REDMENACE, REDSEA, REDSTORM, REDZONE, RELAYER, RENEGADE, RENOIR, RIGEL LIBRARY, RIKER, RIMA, ROADBED, ROADTURN, ROCKDOVE, ROOFTOP, ROOTBEER, ROSEVINE, RUTLEY

SAGACITY, SANDSAILOR, SASPLOT, SATINWOOD, SATURN, SAYA, SCANNER, SEALION, SEAPLUM, SCISSORS, SCREENWORK, SEABEACH II, SEARCHLIGHT, SELLERS, SEMITONE, SENIOR GLASS, SENTINEL, SHADOWBOXER, SHADOWCHASER, SHANTY, SHARK, SHARKBITE, SHARKKNIFE, SHARPSHOOTER, SHILLET, SHILOH, SHIPMASTER, SHORTSWING, SIDEMIRROR, SIGHTREADY, SIGNATURE, SILKRUG, SILVERFISH, SILVERHOOK, SILVERLINER, SILVERVINE, SINGLEPOINT, SINGLESHOT, SITA, SKEPTIC, SKILLFUL, SKYBOARD, SKYCAST, SKYGAZER, SKYLINE, SKYLOFT, SKYWRITER, SLAMDANCE, SLATEWRITER, SLIDESHOW, SMOKEPIT, SNAKEBOOT, SNAKECHARMER, SNAKEDANCE II, SNAKERANCH II, SNORKEL, SNOWMAN, SOAPOPERA, SOAPSHELL, SOFTBOUND, SOFTRING, SORCERY, SPANISH MOSS, SPARKVOYAGE, SPEARHEAD, SPECOL, SPECTAR, SPIROGRAPH, SPLINTER, SPLITTER, SPORADIC, SPOTBEAM, SPRINGRAY, SPUDLITE, STAIRWAY, STAR SAPPHIRE, STARCICLE, STARGLORY, STARLOG, STARQUAKE, STARSWORD, STATIONMASTER, STEAKHOUSE, STELLAH, STONEGATE, STORMCHASER, STORMPEAK, STOWAWAY, STRONGHOLD, SUBSHELL, SUNDIAL, SUPERCODING, SURREY, SWEETDREAM, SWEETTALK, SWEEPINGCHANGE, SWITCHPOINT

TABLELAMP, TALION, TANGOR, TAROTCARD, TARP, TARSIS, TART, TAXIDRIVER, TEAS, TECBIRD, TEL, TELE, TELESTO, TELLTALE, TELLURITE, TEMAR, TERMINAL VELOCITY, THINKCHEW, THINTHREAD, THUNDERWEB, TIDYTIPS III, TIEBREAKER, TIGER, TIMELINE, TIMEPIECE, TIMETRAVELER, TINKERTOY, TINSEL, TIPPIE, TOPSHELF, TOPSPIN II, TOPVIEW, TRACECHAIN, TRAILBLAZER, TRBUSTER, TREASURE, TREASURE TROVE, TRED, TRIFECTA, TRINFO, TRINIAN, TROLLEYTRACK, TROLLEYMASTER, TRUNK MOBILE, TRYSTER, TSUNAMI, TWILIGHT, TWOBIT

UMORPH, UNLIMITED

VIEWEXCHANGE, VEILED DATABASE, VEILED FORTHCOMING, VENTURER II, VICTORY DAEMON, VINTAGE HARVEST, VIOLATION, VISIONARY, VISIONQUEST, VOICECAST, VOICESAIL, VOIP SEED

WARGODDESS, WARSTOCK, WATCHOUT, WAXFLOWER, WAYLAND, WEALTHYCLUSTER, WEBSPINNER, WEBSPINNER -- ACCESS TO DBS, WESTRICK, WHARFMAN II, WHITE SEA, WHIRLPOOL, WHITE SHARK, WHITE SWORD, WHITESAIL, WHITEWASH, WILDFIRE, WINDSHIELD, WINTERFEED, WIREDART, WIREWEED, WORLDWIDE, WIZARDRY, WOLFPACK, WRAPUP

XVTUBA

YELLOWSTONE, YETLING

ZENTOOLS, ZIGZAG, and ZIRCON

June 4, 2005 – NSA in Management Uproar

With revelations that NSA permitted UN ambassador nominee John Bolton access to sensitive NSA intercepts of the communications of senior Bush administration and other elected U.S. officials, including New Mexico Governor Bill Richardson, the NSA is in a management furor. Many NSA officers are upset that the agency has been drawn into a political fight involving Bolton and view the current NSA leadership as too willing to allow heretofore carefully restricted intercepts to be used by neo-conservatives in the Bush administration to further their agenda.

Inside sources claim that current FBI Executive Assistant Director Maureen ("Mo") Baginski, fired by Hayden and his hand-picked deputy Bill Black (the current Acting Director) for the intelligence "failures" leading to 9/11, will soon replace Black as Deputy Director of NSA.

Baginski is a career NSA SIGINTer and linguist and is seen as more sympathetic

to the NSA rank and file than either Hayden or Black who have presided over the outsourcing of key operational and administrative responsibilities at NSA to a horde of outside contractors who have damaged the readiness and capabilities of America's largest intelligence agency, according to a number of NSA sources.

If Baginski does take over as Deputy Director, one NSA component that can expect a shake up is the Security and Counter-Intelligence Directorate.

NSA Security has been on a vendetta against any employees who show the least non-conformance towards the new order at the Fort Meade, Maryland agency.

NSA Security is now requiring employees to fill out a detailed financial statement that many long-time career people feel is an unwarranted invasion of personal privacy. For example, the form requires NSA employees to state how much they spend a month on such items and services as gas, water, cable/dish TV, cellular phone service, home owners' dues, union dues, lodge dues, social organization dues, church donations, newspapers, magazines, books, dry cleaning, laundry, school lunches, work lunches, new clothes, babysitting, children's clothes, pet care, auto payment, gasoline, day care, lawn care, groceries, and hair care.

As a result of the browbeating of NSA personnel by Security and the Director's office, morale is at an all- time low and is adversely affecting America's ability to defend itself from terrorism and foreign intelligence espionage.

NSA Security has purged a number of senior level NSA managers who were suspected of making contact with members of Congress. The Security directorate has threatened any NSA employee who cooperates with external investigations of the agency, including those conducted by the Defense Department Inspector General or the Congress.

June 5, 2005 -- As the AIPAC/Pentagon Israeli espionage scandal grows, more news about the non-reported Israeli penetration of the NSA and U.S. Navy in the 1980s has been revealed by NSA insiders.

Veterans of the RCA-NSA-Israeli joint SIGINT program code named DINDI report that Israeli engineer spies used the carve-out contract with NSA, through RCA, to gain access to NSA and U.S. Navy secrets. In an RCA facility in Mount Laurel, NJ, the Israeli engineers had their own secured lab, and for three years that DINDI ran, they were walking out with their briefcases loaded with equipment, including scopes. When RCA engineers finally gained access to their lab, they found the prints laid out for the Trident missile system. RCA had an ongoing contract top develop the Trident communications suite at the time of the security leak. The Israeli engineers on DINDI claimed they were from the Israeli Air Force but months later, an RCA engineer was in New York and he ran into the same Israelis, but they were wearing Israeli Navy uniforms. One ex-RCA engineer commented about the DINDI Israeli spies: "They were all a nice bunch of guys, even when they had their hands in your pockets."

June 2005 -- WHY NSA IS THE FORT KNOX OF THE U.S. INTELLIGENCE ESTABLISHMENT

Fort Meade Holds the Secrets that Countries from China to Israel Would Love to Get Their Hands On; Neo-Con Access to NSA Threatens to Destroy or Alter the Real Transcripts of History

For years, the National Security Agency has been able to tap the secret communications of America's enemies and allies. The result has been that the "Agency" has had a unique ear on the world's communications, one that has permitted it to archive the actual of series of events in recent years, not the news crafted by successive U.S. administrations for public consumption. Up until now. The assault of the Bush administration and its embedded neo-conservatives threaten to eliminate for future historians, the actual record of foreign policy, military, and intelligence events that have affected generation after generation of Americans. The secret relationship between NSA and an encryption firm called Crypto AG is but one of the secrets held at NSA's Fort Meade headquarters.

    The secret Crypto A.G. - NSA relationship remained relatively covert until March 1992 when Hans Buehler, Crypto A.G.'s Swiss marketing representative for Iran, was arrested in

Teheran on his twenty-fifth sales trip and charged with espionage by the Iranian military counter-intelligence service. His Iranian captors accused the tall, fiftyish businessman and former radio officer in the Swiss merchant marine, of spying for the "intelligence services of the Federal Republic of Germany and the United States of America." Buehler denied all of the Iranian charges.

Buehler, who spent nine months blindfolded in solitary confinement in a Teheran prison was questioned daily by his Iranian interrogators for five months. The Iranians claimed to know that Crypto A.G. was a "spy center" and that the company worked together with foreign intelligence services. They also claimed that Crypto's cipher machines were manipulated in some way to make it easy for them to be decrypted.

The Swiss authorities first believed that Buehler had been arrested in retaliation for the arrest in Switzerland of Zeynold Abedine Sarhadi, an employee of the Iranian embassy in Berne and a nephew of Iranian President Hashemi Rafsanjani. Swiss police had arrested Sarhadi in early 1992 for what they believed was his role in the assassination in 1991 of former Iranian Prime Minister Shahpour Bakhtiar in Paris. The Swiss were planning to hand Sarhadi over to the French authorities to face trial on murder charges. There was a connection between the detention of Buehler on espionage charges and the assassination of Bakhtiar but it was not a quid pro quo based on Sarhadi's arrest in Switzerland.

The Iranians had become aware that the Crypto A.G. cipher machines they were using may be yielding intelligence to Western intelligence agencies, particularly NSA and GCHQ. On August 7, 1991, one day before the discovery of Bakhtiar's body, British and American SIGINT operators had intercepted and decoded a message from the Teheran headquarters of the Iranian Intelligence Service, VEVAK, to Iranian diplomatic missions in London, Paris, Bonn, and Geneva, which inquired "Is Bakhtiar dead?" It was clear to the British and Americans that the Iranian government was behind the assassination and the Iranian intelligence service, VEVAK, now knew for certain that their encrypted communications had been broken by the West.

On December 6, 1994 a special French terrorism court convicted two Iranians of murdering Bakhtiar but it strangely acquitted Sarhadi. "Justice has not been entirely served [for] reasons of state," bitterly complained Bakhtiar's widow, Shahintaj. Observers of the Sarhadi trial believed that one "reason of state" may have been a tacit agreement between France, Switzerland, the BND, and NSA not to provide the valuable deciphered Iranian communications to the French court, thus preserving the relatively uncertain security of the Crypto A.G. cipher manipulation program.

The Iranians, had, for some time, suspected a problem with their Crypto cipher units. Based on previous Libyan and Syrian suspicions concerning the security of their Crypto A.G. equipment, the Iranians had ample reason to believe that their units had somehow been rigged. Iran first became suspicious about their cipher units when it was reported, in 1987, that the NSA had intercepted coded Iranian diplomatic cables between Teheran and the Hezbollah (Party of God) terrorist group in Lebanon via Iran's embassies in Beirut and Damascus. U.S.

officials revealed that the intercepts yielded "conclusive evidence that Iran ordered the kidnapping" of ABC News Beirut correspondent Charles Glass.

Iran's suspicions were heightened in January 1995 when it was reported that NSA intercepts of the communications of Iranian Interior Minister Ali Akbar Mohtashemi in 1988 implicated Iran, not Libya, in the terrorist bombing of PanAm Flight 103 over Lockerbie, Scotland in December of that year. The Iranian-financed bomb killed all 259 persons on board the ill-fated Boeing 747 and another eleven people on the ground. None other than Colonel Qaddafi, himself, confirmed the report that Mohtashemi was involved although it was not clear whether this was based on intimate knowledge that Qaddafi possessed or his faith in the veracity of the NSA intercepts. One intelligence summary prepared by the U.S. Air Force Air Intelligence Agency and released in redacted form pursuant to a Freedom of Information Act request by lawyers for the bankrupt PanAm airlines cites Mohtashemi as the master behind the Lockerbie bombing. The intelligence summary states:

"Mohtashemi is closely connected with the Al Abas and Abu Nidal terrorist groups. He is actually a long-time friend of Abu Nidal. He has recently paid 10 million dollars in cash and gold to these two organizations to carry out terrorist activities and was the one who paid the same amount to bomb PanAm Flight 103 in retaliation for the U.S. shoot-down of the Iranian Airbus. Mohtashemi has also spent time in Lebanon."

Other NSA intercepts apparently revealed that Mohtashemi transferred the ten million dollars used for the bombing of PanAm 103 to terrorists employed by the Syrian-based Popular Front for the Liberation of Palestine-General Command (PFLP-GC). This transfer was apparently made through a Greek bank in Athens. The PFLP-GC was paid for constructing the bomb that blew up the plane as well as arranging for the bomb to be placed on the jumbo jet. Sensitive money transfer orders from Iran would have almost certainly been encrypted. Someone in the West obviously possessed the decryption key.

Libyan cipher machines were also of particular interest to the Americans and Germans. Libyan leader Muammar Qaddafi was known to be supporting terrorist groups around the world and particularly some very violent factions in Europe. The German intelligence service (the Bundesnachrichtendienst or BND) apparently knew the Libyan encryption key settings through their secret arrangement with Crypto A.G. and, in turn, gave them to the Americans and the British. In April 1984 GCHQ intercepted and decoded messages sent from Tripoli to the Libyan People's Bureau in London. One coded message ordered the bureau's diplomatic staff to fire on an anti-Qaddafi demonstration on the street in front of the Libyan mission. Britain later used this information to charge the Libyans with the shooting death of a female British police officer.

One European source commented that "information from the files of the ex-East German regime, the Stasi files, may have also found their way into Iran, and in these the real background of the Crypto A.G. string-pullers could be noted." One former senior engineer of Crypto A.G. later remarked that the arrest of Buehler by Iran was directly related to the manipulation of Crypto's equipment. He further revealed that "the Iranians had probably suspected for some time that manipulated machines had been sent to them. I don't know whether Buehler was in the picture about the manipulations. Officially, no one in the firm was permitted to know, although some suspect it and some naturally know it."

Some Crypto A.G. engineers contend that NSA prevailed on Crypto A.G. to sell their cipher machines to Iran not only because NSA wanted to be able to listen in on encrypted Iranian government communications but also because they viewed Crypto A.G. as a ready, willing, and very cooperative re-engineering "pass through." Pakistan was allegedly granted American military credits with only one provision, that it buy its encryption equipment from Crypto A.G.

One former Crypto A.G. chief engineer stated that he knew that the German and American SIGINT agencies were involved in manipulating Crypto cipher machines and that NSA used one of its major contractors, Motorola, to perform the actual technical alterations. He also said that he was personally involved in the manipulation process. Juerg Spoerndli, another former Crypto A.G. engineer who was responsible for designing encryption equipment, said that in the late 1970s he weakened the strength of his cipher units. He stated he was "ordered to change algorithms under mysterious circumstances."

Spoerndli's contentions are supported by American cryptographic experts. One former Racal cryptographer confided that such NSA manipulation of commercial encryption equipment is widespread, affecting not only Crypto A.G. gear but also that of his old firm, Racal. This should come as no surprise considering that firm's close ties with GCHQ. The former Racal specialist claims that the NSA manipulation is very formal and consists of the following steps:

1. NSA schedules to have its personnel come to the site of the cryptographic company to conduct an inspection of new encryption equipment.

2. NSA cryptographic experts examine each cryptographic application including algorithms.

3. NSA approves each algorithm for use.

4. NSA technicians record encrypted sessions, including cryptographic key exchanges.

5. When NSA feels that it is able to decrypt the communications of the encryption unit in question, it permits export.

NSA ensures that its "tampered" products receive favorable treatment in the granting of U.S. Foreign Military Sales to the armed services of other countries. According to the Racal engineer, the NSA forced U.S. contractors to use Crypto A.G. equipment in the Saudi Navy Expansion Program, giving NSA a back door into future Saudi encrypted naval communications.

From the German side, Siemens Defense Electronics Group also provided technical assistance for the machine manipulation process. In fact, Crypto A.G. has been called a "secret Siemens daughter" by a previous director of the encryption firm. The manipulated cipher machines were apparently rigged so that when some 120 countries that were Crypto A.G. customers used them, the random encryption key could be automatically and clandestinely transmitted with the enciphered message.

The BND and NSA codebreakers then used the transmitted key to decrypt the message. In older, mechanical cipher machines an extra lever allows the secret key to be sent with the encrypted message. These messages were easily decrypted by NSA and BND. One previous Crypto A.G. employee contends that all developmental Crypto A.G. equipment had to be sent to the German Central Cipher Bureau (Zentralstelle für Chiffrierung [ZfCH]), now the Federal Information Security Agency (Bundesamt für Sicherheit in der Informationstechnik [BSI] which is also Department 62 of the BND) in Bad Godesburg near Bonn and NSA for approval.

In other cases, Crypto A.G. was apparently forced to market encryption equipment sent directly from the United States. One former Crypto A.G. engineer inspected one of the first prototype machines sent by the Americans. He remarked that he found the machine useless and when he emphasized to his superiors that he could improve the encryption process if he was given access to the mathematical functions, two American cryptographic "experts" refused to disclose the information. According to a confidential Crypto A.G. memorandum, one of the NSA "experts may have been Nora L. Mackabee, an NSA cryptographer who is now retired on a horse farm in Maryland's Howard County along with her husband Lester, another retired NSA employee. Between August 19 and 20, 1975, three Crypto A.G. engineers huddled with Ms. Mackabee (who is identified as representing "IA" -- most likely "intelligence agency") along with three Motorola engineers and one another American, Herb Frank, who one Motorola engineer recalled was probably from another U.S. intelligence agency based in northern Virginia but described him as a non-technical person who seemed to be making the administrative arrangements for Ms. Mackabee.

Many former Crypto A.G. engineers of the Zug firm have spoken about machine manipulations having taken place and one of them reported that his life had once been in danger. That particular engineer, who objected to the use of NSA equipment by Crypto A.G., disclosed that he was warned by a foreign intelligence service in the late 1970s not to demonstrate the operation of his equipment at a technical exhibition. He wisely took the agency's advice for a bomb subsequently exploded at the exhibition killing five people. It was later reported that the exhibition in question was held in Syria and the warning came from the Syrian intelligence service.

Crypto's secret deals with NSA have not been popular with the firm' engineers. At first Juerg Spoerndli was supportive of the machine manipulation. Spoerndli said "I was idealistic. But I adapted quickly . . . The new aim was to help Big Brother U.S.A. look over these countries' shoulders. We'd say. 'It's better to let the U.S.A. see what these dictators are doing." Spoerndli soon grew apprehensive over the manipulation. "It's still an imperialistic approach to the world.

I don't think it's the way business should be done," Spoerndli later concluded. Another former Crypto A.G. engineer, Ruedi Hug, was also critical of the deal. "I feel betrayed," Hug declared. "They always told us, 'We are the best. Our equipment is not breakable, blah, blah, blah . . . Switzerland is a neutral country.' "

During the Cold War, Switzerland may have been a neutral country in name only. A document released in 1995 by the UK Public Records Office indicates that Switzerland and NATO concluded a secret deal in 1956. The "Top Secret" document, dated February 10, 1956 with the reference PREM 11/1224, was written by the famous British World War II figure, Field Marshal Bernard L. Montgomery, affectionately known as "Monty." While Monty was a vice-commander of NATO, he discussed a secret alliance with Swiss Defense Minister Paul Chaudet. In peacetime, Switzerland would be officially neutral but in wartime it would side with NATO. Another U.S. document released in 1995 shows that Switzerland was important to U.S. national security. One Presidential Directive on National Security prepared for President Truman states that "Switzerland . . . delivers precision instruments and other materials (authors' emphasis) necessary for the armament of the USA and NATO countries."

The secret manipulation program yielded dramatic results on April 4, 1986, when NSA BND, and British GCHQ "outstations" in West Germany, West Berlin, and Cyprus, as well as SIGINT-gathering Direct Support Units on board the U.S. Navy Sixth Fleet's U.S.S. America and Coral Sea, picked up three encrypted messages between the Libyan Peoples' Bureau in East Berlin and its headquarters in Tripoli. Early in the morning of April 5th, the La Belle discotheque in West Berlin was bombed, killing Kenneth Ford, a twenty-one-year-old American Army Sergeant and a Turkish woman and injuring 230 people.

President Reagan was undoubtedly referring to the messages intercepted by NSA when he said the U.S. had hard evidence of Libyan involvement in the attack. One of these was a March 25th message from Tripoli to Peoples' Bureaus throughout Europe, including East Berlin. The message simply said, "Prepare to carry out the plan." The day before the bombing, NSA intercepted two additional messages from the Peoples' Bureau in East Berlin to Tripoli. The first stated, "We have something planned that will make you happy" and a second, which arrived in Tripoli almost simultaneously to the bomb's detonation in West Berlin, said, "An event occurred. You will be pleased with the result." That was all the proof President Reagan needed to order, on April 14, 1986, a retaliatory bombing raid on Libya's capital, Tripoli and its second largest city, Benghazi. Reagan said, "Our evidence is direct, it is precise, it is irrefutable."

NSA was clearly unhappy about the comments made not only by Reagan but those made by White House Press Secretary Larry Speakes; U.S. Ambassador to West Germany, Richard Burt; and NATO Commander, General Bernard W. Rogers about America's possession of "irrefutable proof," "very clear evidence," and "indisputable evidence" about Libya's involvement in the bombing. These officials were getting dangerously close to revealing the truth about the manipulation of Libya's Crypto A.G. cipher machines. President Reagan even disclosed the date of the first intercepted Libyan message concerning the Berlin attack -- March 25th. That, NSA felt, was disclosing pure COMINT, something if done by an NSA analyst would result in he or she facing a long jail term. In response to the administration revelations, NSA issued a classified advisory stating that such comments were "severely hampering" its ability to obtain information, in effect telling both the President of the United States, his press secretary, the American ambassador to Bonn, and the NATO commander to keep their mouths shut. NSA director Odom said the United States had suffered "just deadly losses" in the Libyan affair because of news leaks. NSA also created a new and more restrictive compartment under which communications intercepts were more severely restricted.' Odom undoubtedly did not want disclosure of the ultra-secret cryptographic bugging program to occur on his watch.

NSA restrictions aside, Ray Cline, a former deputy director of the CIA, claimed that decrypted Libyan messages were flashed by NSA and GCHQ to American and British military forces and government agencies. On April 15, the Libyans, who were quite aware of the SIGINT capabilities of the West, ordered one of its warships to fire two missiles at an American navigational station on the Italian island of Lampedusa, a small island southwest of Malta. The Libyans apparently believed the station was an American listening post. Whether or not this was true, Italian Prime Minister Bettino Craxi announced that the missiles had not destroyed the station as the Libyans claimed but had fallen short of their target, harmlessly falling into the Mediterranean Sea.

The NSA and GCHQ were cooperating in the secret Crypto A.G. manipulation program. Apparently, GCHQ was intercepting coded Egyptian traffic from Cairo's embassy in London as early as 1958. It also turns out that the Egyptians were using Crypto A.G. cipher machines. GCHQ cryptanalysts in Cheltenham were able to detect new settings on ciphers at the Egyptian embassy in London through a process called "leading the machine." Engulf was the code name assigned to the GCHQ special program that collected technical cryptographic intelligence on cipher machines, including those of Crypto A.G. NSA was still deciphering Egyptian government communications after President Anwar Sadat steered Egypt firmly into the western camp. During the transition between the Carter and Reagan administrations, outgoing CIA director Stansfield Turner told his successor, William Casey, that "the NSA had the Egyptian government wired electronically."

GCHQ's technical collection program benefited from the work of Britain's Secret Intelligence Service or MI6 in positioning listening equipment in key locations throughout GCHQ's area of coverage, especially in the Middle East. SIS microwave wiretaps in Libya during the 1960s enabled GCHQ and NSA to listen in on all the telephone conversations of Libya's King Idris. During the same time period., hidden microphones installed in China's new embassy in Mogadishu, Somalia and the Soviet embassy in Khartoum, Sudan, courtesy of less than attentive local security services in both countries, permitted the analysts at GCHQ and NSA to gauge the geopolitical intentions of both Communist countries in the volatile Middle East.

Aware that in the early 1980s the Irish government had purchased cipher equipment from Crypto A.G., the GCHQ began intercepting messages from the Irish embassy in London to the Foreign Ministry in Dublin. During sensitive bilateral negotiations that led to the signing of the Anglo-Irish Agreement in November 1985, GCHQ intercepted encrypted Irish government messages and passed the plaintext on to senior British officials in the Foreign Office, the Northern Ireland Office and No.10 Downing Street. The Irish government, being tipped off about the hole in their cryptographic security, began to send classified information between London and Dublin either by diplomatic courier or by Aer Lingus pilots.

The NSA, GCHQ, and BND may have also reaped the benefits of Crypto A.G. machines having gone to East Germany and the Soviet Union's KGB in the late 1980s. According to a German magazine report, a Swiss national named Edwin Bollier (Bollier was code named "Rubin" by the East German Stasi) had arranged to sell Crypto A.G. equipment to the East Germans who were honoring a request made by the KGB for the encryption gear. Bollier worked for Mebo, A.G., a Zurich-based company. The Stasi paid the coin-operated Swiss middleman 120,000 Deutsche Marks (at the time about $50,000) as a commission for obtaining the Crypto A.G. equipment.

"Rubin" had come to the attention of western intelligence agencies earlier when they "discovered" that he was the alleged source of the timers supposedly used by the Libyans in the bombing of PanAm Flight 103. Mebo, A.G. may have been a West to East pass-through company for more than just encryption equipment. The Stasi were particularly suspicious that "Rubin" might have been a double agent for the CIA. "Rubin" had earlier delivered special radio antennas, pulse coders, computer terminals, and a classified American voice recognition system called "Mark" to the Stasi's Department III, East Germany's chief SIGINT agency. The Stasi was amazed that "Rubin" could deliver such an espionage "toy" so fast from the United States. Stasi officials were convinced "Rubin" was a double agent for the Americans.

Former Stasi General Gerhard Höferer revealed that he was convinced that Bollier was "a double agent." An official of Germany's version of the FBI, the Bundeskriminalamt, agreed with the former Stasi general in stating "a man like Bollier must have had protectors in the West." When a German reporter for Der Spiegel pointedly asked Bollier if he had any contacts with the CIA, he brusquely replied, "no comment."

Department III seemed to know enough about the inner workings of the rigged Libyan Crypto A.G. units that they had no problem decoding Tripoli's diplomatic messages. The plaintext East German intercepts of Libyan traffic, released when the East German government collapsed, bolster the argument that Libya was involved with the La Belle bombing. The East German intercepts also point out that the East German regime, a known supporter of terrorist attacks against Western targets, simply allowed the attack to proceed without warning West Berlin officials. Not only did the Stasi know about Libya's plans for La Belle but it knew that the Libyans had two backup targets: the kindergarten at the John F. Kennedy School in West Berlin and a U.S. Army bus used by the school.

Regardless of whether the Soviet coup plotters were relying on foreign cryptographic devices to communicate their plans to depose Mikhail Gorbachev, President Bush ordered NSA-intercepted and decrypted plain text messages sent by the Kremlin plotters, principally KGB chairman Vladimir Kryuchkov and Defense Minister Dmitri Yazov, to be delivered to Russian

Republic President Boris Yeltsin. On his second visit to Washington in June 1991, Yeltsin was pulled aside at a Soviet embassy cocktail reception by a senior U.S. senator acting on the behest of deputy national security adviser Robert Gates. Yeltsin was asked his opinion of the COMINT the U.S. had passed to him concerning the planned coup against Gorbachev: Gates specifically asked Yeltsin, "Are we being overwrought about the coup?" "Absolutely not!" thundered Yeltsin in response, "there will be a coup before the end of the calendar year. Gorbachev doesn't believe it, but I'm preparing for it."

Former NSA director Odom, who had shown his disgust with Ronald Reagan's cavalier handling of COMINT material during the showdown with Libya and the president's subsequent release of COMINT in 1988 to prove that Sadaam Hussein ordered poison gas attacks on the Kurds, was not thrilled about the sharing of intercepted NSA "product" with, of all people, the Russians. Odom lamented to author Seymour Hersh that transferring such intelligence to the Russians resulted in "a terrible, terrible tradeoff." Odom bemoaned the situation saying "Now the Russians know what I know. That is such a huge loss for the future." Odom's strange reasoning would indicate that he thought that the Russians were totally unaware of the vulnerability of Soviet communications to NSA surveillance. Odom's tendency of hoarding important SIGINT to prevent "sensitive sources and methods" being revealed, would plague the Agency in future international crises, including the Gulf war and the Bosnia conflict.

The Swiss government apparently went along with the BND-NSA-Crypto A.G. manipulation operation so long as Crypto A.G. did not sell bugged units to Swiss government agencies. BND and NSA apparently agreed to this demand and Crypto received permission to sell "clean" encryption units, for example, to the Swiss army.

The procedure by which NSA and their BND counterpart manipulated the Crypto cipher units is considered clever from an engineering viewpoint. The manipulated equipment automatically broadcasts to NSA and the BND the user's cipher keys and computer settings within the encrypted text of the message. When they obtained the key settings, the NSA and BND could decrypt the message and read its contents. Although Crypto A.G. officially denied this, it seems to be a continuation of the original deal made between Friedman and Hagelin, Sr. in the 1950s.

NSA is so concerned about its own vulnerability of having its cryptographic units "bugged," it has instituted a special security program to protect U.S. government encryption gear. Code-named Quadrant, the program is designed to provide tamper-resistant components for NSA's crypto-equipment. This program protects components down to the micro-chip level -- any attempt to alter the chip results in its immediate internal destruction.

The rigging of encryption units by Western SIGINT agencies has apparently been extended to computer software components of encryption equipment through a process known as "red threading." According to a former Swiss government official, the Germans once tried to pressure the Swiss to allow a "red thread" Trojan horse program to be installed in the encryption software produced by a Swiss company. The company in question was not Crypto

A.G. However, the other major encryption manufacturer in Switzerland was Gretag Data Systems A.G., a firm once owned by AT&T and later owned by Information Resources Engineering (IRE), Inc. of Baltimore, Maryland. Interestingly and probably not coincidentally, IRE was staffed by a number of former NSA cryptographic engineers. A third Swiss encryption company, Info Guard, A.G., was fully acquired by Crypto A.G. on June 16, 1994. Info Guard, which had been fifty percent owned by Crypto A.G., primarily sold encryption units to banks in Switzerland and abroad.

In February 1995, Mohammed Abdallah el-Hosck, a former Libyan spy for the CIA said that he had turned over the secret key settings of Libyan cryptographic machines to the Americans while he was Libya's second-in-command of its People's Bureau in Lagos, Nigeria. El-Hosck claimed that Libya's embassy used a Swiss cryptographic machine called "Kretaj." Because of the similarities in Arabic between the pronunciation of the letters "g," "j," and "k" the machine must have been a Gretag cipher machine. The Libyans may have switched from Crypto A.G. ciphers to Gretag units following the revelations that the NSA was able to decode their traffic and prove their involvement in the La Belle disco bombing in 1986. The Libyans did decide to purchase encryption units from a Swiss company following the announcement from Washington that the Americans had broken their code. One senior American official said the fact that the Libyans were making their codes more difficult to crack would "make our job tougher." But NSA seemed to have the Gretag base covered as well.

The Libyan claimed that the Lagos embassy's cipher unit was the same size as a lap-top computer and that two plugs were inserted that would encrypt messages. El-Hosck claims that during one night in 1979 he allowed a CIA officer into the Libyan compound. The CIA agent reportedly copied the information contained in the Libyan plugs. According to one knowledgeable cryptographic machine expert, the "plugs" compromised by el-Hosck were actually EPROMs (electronically programmable read-only memory) devices. An EPROM contains a secret cryptographic key. The Libyans, in an effort to protect their cryptographic secrets from compromise, probably divided their encryption key into two parts, placing each part of the key on two different EPROMs. Each EPROM possibly contained a 100-character "group key" which was likely produced by a random key generator computer program in Tripoli and then sent to various Libyan diplomatic missions around the world. In addition to the group key, an additional key, smaller in length than the group key, would have been typed into the Gretag unit by a Libyan communications technician. This key, known as the "fundamental key," is usually changed periodically by the machine's user.

For NSA, el-Hosck only had to betray the Libyan group key, found on the EPROM device, because that gave the NSA codebreakers critical knowledge about the Libyans' key management procedures. The el-Hosck story pointed out that although it might be more efficient to place trap doors in cryptographic products, there was still a need for black-bag operations to provide foreign cryptographic material to the NSA codebreakers. But as cryptographic equipment became more sophisticated, with even the data on the EPROM keys becoming enciphered, the Trojan horse implants began to look more and more attractive.

After spending nine months in an Iranian prison, Hans Buehler was released when Crypto A.G. paid a one million dollar bail bond to the Iranians. Shortly after his return to Zurich, and while celebrating his wife's birthday, Buehler was summarily dismissed by Crypto A.G. Baffled by his employer's turnabout, Buehler began to look into the reasons why he was fired. Current and former Crypto employees were apparently so furious about Buehler's treatment, they began to tell him about their own first-hand knowledge of manipulated cipher equipment. One former high-level engineer for Crypto A.G. corroborated Buehler's suspicions. He said, "I hold proofs [sic] of the rigging of code machines. These proofs [sic] are in a safe place. Fifteen years ago, I saw American and German engineers doctoring our machines." When asked what he did with his "proofs" the unidentified former Crypto A.G. engineer told Swiss television: "It took me some time until I was certain about the manipulations. The proofs: technical documents . . . I put them in a bank safety deposit box. Then I informed the federal prosecutors' office in Berne. There were many conversations. Suddenly, these contacts were broken off and the affair petered out." When Swiss television asked the engineer why he did not publicly produce the "proofs," he stated, "My personal security is not what it should be." He was then asked if he was afraid of the consequences. He replied, "Yes. I consider that it's deadly dangerous to lift the veil. The same kind of thing could have happened to me that happened to Hans Buehler."

The engineer told another reporter "the schemes and the cipher keys were created by them [NSA and BND]. I immediately, discreetly, notified the Swiss prosecutors' office. There was an investigation. I was never able to find out the result. Today, the Buehler affair brings everything out in the open again. And, I'm afraid. What happened to Hans Buehler could happen to any other salesperson of Crypto A.G. It's not a question of attacking this company; it's a question of saving lives . . ."

When the Swiss media began to reveal the background of Buehler's story, Crypto A.G. responded by suing their former employee. Crypto A.G. management was obviously afraid that all the sordid details of their "cooperation" with foreign intelligence agencies would be revealed. They were clearly interested in squashing the story and muzzling its key player, Buehler. "I didn't know that the equipment was bugged," Buehler said, "otherwise the Iranians would have gotten it out of me by their many 'methods.'"

Nevertheless, the damage to Crypto A.G.'s credibility was already done. Many of Crypto A.G.'s customers began to distance themselves from the firm. As a result, Crypto's management began to reassure its customers about its stability and independence from Western intelligence services. In the fall of 1994, a concerned delegation from Indonesia was invited, at Crypto A.G.'s expense, to visit the company's headquarters in Steinhausen. Crypto A.G. was also forced to reassure the secrecy-conscious banking industry customers of Info Guard A.G. of the security of its equipment.

Some Crypto A.G. customers were no so easily placated. The Army Security Agency once had a slogan: "In God we trust, all others we monitor." Not so, however, with God's earthly emissaries. In addition to using ceremonial Swiss Guards to protect its small Roman enclave,

Vatican City also uses Swiss cipher machines to protect diplomatic communications transmitted from the Holy See to the many papal nuncios around the world. When informed of the details concerning the Hans Buehler incident, a Vatican official angrily responded by calling the perpetrators "bandits!"

Crypto A.G. may not be the only cryptographic firm with which NSA has struck "deals." It is known that the British benefited from Argentina's use of Crypto A.G. ciphers. During the Falklands War, British GCHQ operators were able to decrypt classified Argentine message traffic because the Argentineans were using rigged cipher machines. Former British Foreign Office minister Ted Rowlands publicly stated that GCHQ had penetrated Argentine diplomatic codes. However, Argentina was also using cipher machines manufactured by Datotek, a relatively small Dallas-based firm, once a subsidiary of AT&T. Apparently Datotek, like Crypto A.G., found most of its clients in the Third World (especially Latin America where Datotek machines were bought with U.S. Foreign Military Sales funds) and also, like its Swiss competitor, its machines most likely contained bugs. During the Falklands war, NSA reportedly provided Britain with plain text English translations of Argentine classified messages encrypted by Datotek machines.

There were reports that NSA had been able to decrypt the codes used by the Sudanese mission to the UN and the Sudanese foreign ministry in Khartoum. News of this surveillance surfaced following the terrorist bombing of the World Trade Center in New York in February 1993. After the FBI arrested eight men on June 24, 1993, Sudan immediately became suspect when it was discovered that the terrorist ringleader, Siddiq Ali and four others were found to be carrying Sudanese passports. ABC News reported on August 16, 1993 that NSA had been able to link Sudan to the bombing based on electronic intercepts of diplomatic traffic between New York and Khartoum. NSA intercepts apparently showed that a "critical link" existed between the bombers, the Sudanese mission, and the government in Khartoum.

Sudan's supplier of cryptographic equipment is allegedly PK Electronics, a somewhat secretive company based in Hamburg, Germany. PK Electronics is not a developer of cryptographic equipment but a re-seller of cipher machines from third party manufacturers. Once an order is placed with PK Electronics, it, in turn, orders the cipher units directly from the manufacturer.

As the trial of the terrorist bombers began in New York, the Justice Department strangely decided not to present the intercepts as evidence in their prosecution. NSA has traditionally balked at releasing its sensitive intercepts during any government trial, especially when sensitive methods like foreign cipher machine decryption are involved. Also, there were reports that the U.S. government had secretly come to an understanding with Sudan's military leader, General Omar Hassan Bashir, not to publicize Sudan's link to the bombing in return for a cooling of Khartoum's close relationship with Iran.

NSA's cryptographic machine rigging may not end with companies like Crypto A.G. and Datotek. According to one knowledgeable cryptographic industry expert, NSA's program to co-opt the services of encryption manufacturers probably extends to all those within reaches of

NSA operatives. American cryptographic companies would be definite candidates for such participation. The NSA program also likely extends to companies in NATO and pro-U.S. countries which have close relationships with GCHQ, NSA, and the BND. Neutral countries' firms would seem to be off-limits to NSA deals. However, it is believed that European neutral countries were approached by high-level American officials who stated that although it was understood that neutrals could not help the United States militarily during the Cold War, their assistance in cooperating in the cryptologic war against the Soviets would be an important, yet covert, contribution. Apparently this demarche paid off when NSA allegedly received support from cryptographic companies in Switzerland, Sweden, and Finland. According to the crypto industry expert, even if Crypto A.G. is finally exposed, "there are other Hagelins and Cryptos willing and able to step up to the bat."

Notes

The secret Crypto A.G. - NSA relationship: "The Case of Hans Buehler," Swiss Radio International, Sunday Supplement, broadcast May 14, 1994.

The Iranians claimed to know: Stefanovitch, VSD (14-20 April 1994), p. 50.

The Swiss authorities first believed: "Swiss Still Have No Access to Arrested National," Reuters, March 31, 1992.

The Iranians had become aware: Stefanovitch, VSD, 14-20 April 1994, p. 50.

On August 7, 1991: Res Strehe, Verschlüsselt ("Enciphered") (Zurich: Werd Verlag, 1994), p. 36.

On December 6, 1994 "Justice has not been . . .": "Indications but No Proof of Iranian State Terrorism," Neue Zuercher Zeitung (December 8, 1994).

The Iranians, had, for some time: "Sammelsurium von Erkenntnissen," Der Spiegel (April 21, 1986), p. 20.

"conclusive evidence that Iran": "NBC Says U.S. intelligence shows Iran ordered Glass' kidnapping," Boston Globe (July 2, 1987), p. 17.

Iran's suspicions were heightened: "Iran als Urheber des Lockerbie Desasters?" Neue Zürcher Zeitung (January 25, 1995), p. 1.

None other than Colonel Qaddafi: Patrick Cockburn, "Gadafy adopts plan to expel 30,000," Irish Times (February 21, 1995), p. 11.

"Mohtashemi is closely connected . . .": Air Intelligence Agency intelligence summary SECRET NOFORN WNINTEL message dated March 4, 1991 to various military commands involved with Desert Storm (O 041900Z MAR 91). "O" means the message had a precedence of Operational

Immediate and "1900Z" means 1900 hours Greenwich Mean Time. NOFORN stands for Not Releasable to Foreign Nationals while WNINTEL is the former acronym used for Warning Notice - Intelligence Methods and Sources Revealed.

transferred the ten million dollars; This transfer was apparently made: Wayne Madsen interview with Pierre Salinger, former ABC News Chief European Correspondent.

"information from the files": Interview with European cryptographic industry representative..

"the Iranians had probably suspected": Interview by Frank Garbely of former Crypto A.G. engineer, Swiss German Television, March 23, 1994.

Some Crypto A.G. engineers contend: "Crypto: Nur heisse Luft?" Tages Anzeiger (July 6, 1994).

Pakistan was allegedly: Martin Stoll, "Trieb die Crypto ein Doppelspiel," Tages Anzeiger (July 5, 1994).

NSA used one of its major contractors: Interview by Frank Garbely of former Crypto A.G. engineer, Swiss German Television, March 23, 1994.

Juerg Spoerndli; "ordered to change algorithms . . .": Scott Shane and Tom Bowman, "Rigging the Game," Baltimore Sun (December 10, 1995), p. 9A.

One former Racal cryptographer confided that such NSA manipulation of commercial encryption equipment; According to the Racal engineer, the NSA forced: Wayne Madsen interview with former Racal cryptographic engineer, November 30, 1994.

Siemens Defense Electronics Group: "Trojanische Ohren," Focus (No. 13, 1994), p. 38.

"secret Siemens daughter": "Geheimniskrämer," Bilanz (March 1988), p.147.

The manipulated encryption machines: Interview with former Crypto A.G. employee.

all developmental Crypto A.G. equipment: "Trojanische Ohren," Focus (No. 13, 1994).

Crypto A.G. was apparently forced: Interview by Frank Garbely of former Crypto A.G. engineer, Swiss German Television, March 23, 1994.

According to a confidential Crypto A.G. memorandum: Scott Shane and Tom Bowman, "Rigging the Game," Baltimore Sun (December 10, 1995), pp. 8A-9A. Another "IA," a Mr. Herb Frank, is also listed as a participant in the meeting.

Many former Crypto A.G. engineers: Interview by Frank Garbely of former Crypto A.G. engineer, Swiss German Television, March 23, 1994.

"I was idealistic."; "It's still an imperialistic approach"; "I feel betrayed . . .": Scott Shane and Tom Bowman, "Rigging the Game," Baltimore Sun (December 10, 1975), p. 9A.

A document released in 1995; "Switzerland . . . delivers precision instruments and other materials": "Montgomery memorandum casts shadow over Swiss neutrality," Statewatch (September-October 1995), p. 12.

It was later reported: Interview with former Crypto A.G. employee.

U.S.S. America and Coral Sea: "How U.S. Broke Libyan Codes," Financial Times (April 17, 1986).

"Prepare to carry out the plan"; "We have something planned that will make you happy"; "An event occurred. You will be pleased with the result": Joseph E. Persico, Casey: From the OSS to the CIA (New York: Viking,1990), p. 497.

"Our evidence is direct, it is precise, it is irrefutable.": Bob Woodward and Patrick E. Tyler, "Libyan Cables Intercepted and Decoded," Washington Post (April 15, 1986), pp. A1, A23.

"very clear evidence"; "indisputable evidence": Bob Woodward, Veil (New York: Simon and Schuster, 1987), pp. 444-445.

President Reagan even disclosed: "Spook Corner," The Economist (April 19, 1986), p. 24.

"severely hampering," Woodward, Veil, p. 445.

"just deadly losses": Norman Black, "Gen. Odom blames leaks for 'deadly' intelligence loss," Washington Times (September 3, 1987), pp. A1, A12.

NSA also created a new and more restrictive compartment: Woodward, Veil, p. 445.

NSA restrictions aside: "How US Broke Libyan Codes," Financial Times (April 17, 1986).

ordered one if its warships: "Tut, tut, mostly," The Economist (April 19, 1986), p. 24.

GCHQ was intercepting coded Egyptian traffic: Peter Wright, Spycatcher (New York: Viking Penguin, 1987), pp. 82-85.

"the NSA had the Egyptian government wired electronically.": Bob Woodward, Veil, p. 87.

microwave wiretaps in Libya during the 1960s; During the same time period: Tom Bower, The Perfect English Spy: Sir Dick White and the Secret War 1935-90, pp. 348-349.

Knowing that in the early 1980s: Conor O'Clery, "GCHQ breaks Irish cipher traffic; Irish coded messages broken by British," The Irish Times (January 24, 1987), pp. 1-2.

"Rubin"; 120,000 Deutsche Marks; "Rubin" had come to the attention of; "a double agent"; "a man like Bollier . . ."; "no comment": "Netz mit vielen Spinnen" Der Spiegel (April 18, 1994), pp.95-96.

Not only did the Stasi know about Libya's plans for La Belle: Leslie Colitt, Spymaster: The Real-Life Karla, His Moles, and the East German Secret Police (Reading, MA: Addison-Wesley Publishing Company, 1995), p. 117.

President Bush ordered NSA-intercepted and decrypted; On his second visit to Washington; "Absolutely not!"; "a terrible, terrible tradeoff" "Now the Russians know": Seymour Hersh, "The Wild East," Atlantic Monthly (May 16, 1994), pp. 84-86.

the president's subsequent release of COMINT in 1988: Christopher Andrew, For the President's Eyes Only (New York: HarperCollins, 1995), p. 501.

The Swiss government: Martin Stoll, "Trieb die Crypto ein Doppelspiel," Tages Anzeiger (July 5, 1994).

Quadrant: National Computer Security Center, Introduction to Certification and Accreditation (NCSC-TG-029, Version 1, January 1994), p. 41.

The manipulated equipment automatically broadcasts: Interview by Frank Garbely of former Crypto A.G. engineer, Swiss German Television, March 23, 1994.

"red threading": information from researcher of Swiss intelligence operations.

The other major encryption manufacturer in Switzerland: Encryption Products Database Statistics, Report of Trusted Information Systems, Inc. and the Software Publishers Association (October 31, 1994).

A third Swiss encryption company: Schweizerisches Handelsamtsblatt, No. 124, S. 3634, June 29, 1994.

In February 1995; The Libyan claimed: Bill Gertz, "Libyan defector wants millions for aiding CIA," Washington Times (February 21, 1995), pp. A1, A12.

The Libyans did decide; "make our job tougher": "Libyans Buy Message-Coding Equipment: Effort to Thwart U.S. Intelligence Leaks Leads to Swiss Firm," Washington Post (April 22, 1986), p. A8.

According to one knowledgeable: interview with cryptographic expert, March 3, 1995.

After nine months in an Iranian prison: Stefanovitch, VSD (14-20 April 1994), p. 50.

When asked what he did with his "proofs": Interview by Frank Garbely of former Crypto A.G. engineer, Swiss German Television, March 23, 1994.

The engineer told another reporter: Stefanovitch, VSD (14-20 April 1994), p. 50.

When the media in Switzerland: "Rendezvous: People and Places in Switerland," Interview with Hans Buehler by James Nason, Swiss Radio International transmission of July 18, 1994.

"I didn't know that the equipment was bugged,": Interview with Hans Buehler by Frank Garbely, Swiss GermanTelevision, March 23, 1994; also interview with Hans Buehler by Jacques Zanetta, Swiss French Television, November 26, 1993.

the damage to Crypto A.G.'s credibility: Interview with former Crypto A.G. employee.

"bandits!": Res Strehe, Verschlüsselt ("Enciphered"), p. 199.

Argentina's use of Crypto A.G. ciphers: Ibid., p. 137.

During the Falklands War: "America's Falklands War: A relationship sweet and sour," The Economist (March 3, 1984), p. 25.

Argentineans were using rigged cipher machines: Res Strehe, Verschlüsselt ("Enciphered"), p.137.

Former British Foreign Office minister Ted Rowlands: Duncan Campbell, "How we spy on Argentina," New Statesman (April 30, 1982), p. 5.

Argentina was also using cipher machines of Datotek: Interview with cryptographic industry expert.

It was originally reported: John McWethy, ABC World News Tonight, August 16, 1993.

Sudan's supplier: Wayne Madsen interview with ABC News correspondent John Cooley.

NSA's cryptographic machine rigging: Wayne Madsen interview with cryptographic industry expert.

"there are other Hagelins and Cryptos willing and able to step up to the bat.": Ibid.

August 3, 2005 -- "Clean up man" takes over NSA.

Army Lt. Gen. Keith Alexander took over as the Director of the National Security Agency on Aug. 1. Alexander, whose previous position was Deputy Army Chief of Staff for G-2, replaces Air Force Gen. Michael Hayden, the current Deputy Director of National Intelligence. Hayden, the longest serving NSA Director, was widely criticized within the agency for outsourcing critical intelligence functions to private contractors; transferring critical intelligence jobs to Georgia, Texas, and Colorado; and instituting personnel policies that were designed to purge NSA of many career government intelligence professionals. Alexander's three star rank surprised some at NSA who note that past NSA directors have usually arrived at the agency with 2 star rank and were subsequently promoted to three stars. It is also significant that Alexander, unlike a number of previous directors, does not have a strong signals intelligence (SIGINT) background. His experience is primarily in tactical intelligence.

August 17, 2005 -- Political purges continue at the National Security Agency (NSA).

NSA insiders report that politically-motivated purges orchestrated by the neo-conservative cabal at the Pentagon continue unabated at the signals intelligence (SIGINT) agency. Career NSA personnel who have been identified as non-conformists have been subjected to a psychologically abusive and Kafkaesque series of administrative and personnel actions, which ultimately lead to revocation of their security clearances and dismissal from the agency. The tactics involve the use of psychiatrists and psychologists who certify that targets for purges suffer from a myriad of personality disorders. Those subjected to such treatment have included personnel with over 16 years' experience in SIGINT and electronics intelligence (ELINT), foreign language capabilities (including Arabic and Urdu), and covert joint operations with the CIA in hostile environments. Contrary to earlier expectations, the new NSA Director, Lt. Gen. Keith Alexander, is continuing the draconian purge policies implemented by his predecessor, Gen. Michael Hayden, now the Deputy Director for National Intelligence. Alexander is also continuing the policy of purging career NSA personnel with a view to replacing them with less reliable contractors, including those who work for companies with ties to a hostile intelligence nation currently being investigated by the U.S. Attorney for Eastern Virginia. In addition, contractors are much less likely to question the misuse of raw SIGINT intelligence, including cherry picking SIGINT to bolster questionable Bush administration military actions and eavesdropping on opponents of those actions.

NSA personnel who are identified as targets of opportunity ultimately receive the following career-ending form letter:

NATIONAL SECURITY AGENCY

FORT GEORGE G. MEADE, MARYLAND 20755-6000

Date of notice

Employee's Name

Employee's Street Address

Employee's Town/City, State, Zip Code

Dear Mr./Ms.

This letter is to notify you of the NSA Access Appeals Panel's decision concerning your request for review of the revocation of your access to Sensitive Compartmented Information (SCI) made by the Associate Directorate of Security and Counterintelligence (ADS&CI). [L. Kemp Ensor]

After a thorough review and discussion of all the information contained in the investigative file, as well as your oral reply, the Panel decided to sustain the decision by Chief, Adjudications to revoke your access to SCI. The reason cited by the Panel for its decision is behavior that is inconsistent with the standards of Director Central Intelligence Directive (DCID) 6/4, Personnel Security Standards and Procedures Governing Eligibility for Access to Sensitive Compartmented Information.

As a result of the Panel's decision to sustain the revocation of your access to SCI, you no longer meet a mandatory condition of NSA employment. The Associate Directorate of Security and Counterintelligence [Ensor] and the Employee Relations office will complete your removal from NSA employment, effectively date.

This decision constitutes the final action by NSA of your due process under Executive Order 12968. If additional information concerning this matter is requested, please contact Security Information at (410) 854-4896.

signature

> BERNARD F. NORVELL
>
> Chairperson
>
> NSA Access Appeals Panel
>
> cc: NSA Access Appeals Panel (Case File)
>
> Q235, Security Information

August 23, 2005 -- In the spirit of the Soviet "psikhushka" psychiatric hospitals where anti-regime dissidents were sent, NSA is using psychologists to eliminate independent-minded intelligence analysts and other career employees.

Adverse psychiatric evaluations of experienced NSA professionals are being used by the neocons controlling the agency to gut America's signals intelligence and information security capabilities. Former NSA Director General Michael Hayden initiated this process and he was rewarded with the post of Deputy Director for National Intelligence where he can now extend his *psikhushkas* to other U.S. intelligence agencies.

WMR has received the following letter from a long-time NSA employee who is a victim of the psychiatric abuse:

> **NSA's Own Nest of Cuckoos**
>
> NSA's tribe of headshrinkers consists of a trio of psychologically tortuous on-the-payroll psychologists led by Dr. John Schmidt. Dr. Marianne Moran and Dr. Dina Wieczynski are his fledgling understudies who directly execute orders from both NSA's Office of General Counsel and NSA's Office of Security. These three psychologists hold all the cards for continued access to employment but many question if these doctors are abiding by the ethics of their profession. Most unsuspecting employees targeted by NSA's network of neoconservative officials often endure repeated brutal types of mental interrogations. Reminiscent of the witch trials in past centuries, former co-workers or acquaintances of these "marked" employees for termination are welcomed to falsify statements to Federal law enforcement agents assigned to NSA. Schmidt, Moran, and Wieczynski salivate in anticipation of their next victim to abuse. All three are conducting their own sadistic method of torture; Dr. Schmidt prefers to make female subjects sexually uncomfortable, but tends to take a harsher stand with males. Dr. Moran, like Dr. Wieczynski, appears to diagnose everyone with "personality trait" disorders, despite non-Agency doctors finding to the contrary. Based on a series of documents, Dr. Wieczynski appears to have mastered the art of psychic-evaluation, where the employee doesn't even have to be

present for an evaluation but she is able to give a complete "unbiased" analysis into the person's psyche. These talents are truly amazing considering the overwhelming number of agency-diagnosed employees with "personality trait" problems or, in essence, "sociopaths" who have freely wandered the halls of NSA over the past years. Particularly poetic is the fact that so many were never identified and rejected initially through the stringent security background investigations the agency conducts. On the other hand, the rising numbers of "insanity" cases could just reflect the Gestapo-like tactics generating massive paranoia throughout NSA. One former agency employee stated, "We are nothing more than lab rats for psychological testing at the whim of a hierarchy out of control . . . it is like being trapped in a fixed maze where there is no way to escape." How long will this career-fatal cat and mouse game continue?

August 24, 2005 -- WMR has received another scathing letter concerning the neocon pogrom at NSA. The following was recently received by mail with a Maryland postmark:

Headmistress of NSA Rules the Roost with an Iron Fist

Marie Vogelei is the chief of the secretive wing of NSA's Office of Security responsible for personnel disciplinary actions which result in the revoking of employees' clearances. Vogelei's department is ironically called Employee Relations and disguises itself officially under a branch of NSA's Associate Directorate for Human Resources. Employee Relations, formerly known as Adverse Action, changed their name in hopes of recreating a friendlier image by sponsoring propaganda seminars presented to agency managers encouraging naming names of so-called "problem employees." After years of promoting Backstabbing 101, it appears the agency has mastered the technique like skilled Samurai. The number of unemployed SIGINT spies has significantly risen under Warden Vogelei's watchful eye. Sources closest to her organization within the guarded palace walls whisper RUMINT (Rumor intelligence) the department of Employee Relations may be rapidly expanding personnel. Of course that is just until they end up having to fire their own staff. When will the game of duck-duck-goose end? Maybe NSA needs to hire Donald Trump to do the honors. Agency All Message reading, "Attention NSA: You're fired!"

The situation at NSA is getting worse by the day. The Bush administration of neocon traitors are dismantling America's intelligence infrastructure, one that has served this nation generally well since the end of World War II (not counting the 9/11 disaster, which has all the hallmarks of yet another Bush family treasonous action against the United States of America, an action the U.S. intelligence community was PREVENTED from stopping). This is another call to join WMR in a letter writing campaign to Congress seeking a stop the gutting of America's intelligence infrastructure.

September 4, 2005 – The Soviet-style "psikhushka" psychiatric abuse of NSA employees continues unchecked.

WMR is now able to report on yet another case of a senior NSA employee being fired from her job as a result of policy differences with a top Pentagon military officer. The NSA employee, who wishes to remain anonymous, was fired by the uncontrolled NSA Security Directorate after she had a policy difference with Marine Corps Colonel Robert A. Gearhart, Jr., the chair of the Pentagon's J6 Interoperability Policy Test Panel (IPTP) of the Joint Technology Architecture (JTA) program. The NSA employee was ordered to undergo a psychiatric examination by NSA's head shrink, forensic psychologist Dr. John Schmidt. She was ordered to see the NSA psychologist by NSA's Security Directorate, run by Kemp Ensor III. NSA Security and the Psychology unit maintain an organizational linkage that permits the immediate suspension of security clearances for "troublesome" employees. According to a For Official Use Only (FOUO) NSA Security organizational chart dated January 13, 2005, which was obtained by WMR, the Office of Personnel Security (Q2) is headed by Donna M. Pucciarella. The Q23 Adjudications branch, which is in charge of psychologically abusing NSA whistleblowers, is headed by William K. Zephir. His deputy is John B. Craven. Q234, "Special Actions" for Military and Special Access Processing, is headed by Michael J. Kilduff. WMR has spoken to two other NSA career employees who received similar treatment after they brought questionable practices to the attention of senior management at Fort Meade.

The fired NSA employee was about to disclose the fraudulent funneling of billions of dollars of Pentagon JTA funds to defense contractors in violation of Federal Acquisition Regulations and Federal law.

The financial chicanery involving illegal steerage of Pentagon money to defense contractors was discovered as part of the operations of the Information Technology (IT) Systems and National Security Systems (NSS) Interoperability Test Panel (ITP), which included the fired NSA employee as a voting principal chartered member. Other voting members of the panel include representatives from the US Army, the US Navy, the US Air Force, the US Marine Corps, the US Coast Guard, the Vice Director J6, the Defense Information Systems Agency (DISA), and the Defense Intelligence Agency (DIA). The firing of the NSA employee over her complaints about fraud, waste, and abuse in the Pentagon and NSA fits a pattern of reprisals taken against those NSA career employees who are witnessing the wholesale outsourcing of America's most sensitive intelligence operations to companies, some with ties to hostile intelligence nations.

December 1, 2005 – WMR will be at the US Courthouse in Greenbelt, Maryland today covering the trial of former National Security Agency (NSA) analyst Kenneth Ford.

He is charged with illegally possessing classified material. This case is yet another example of the out-of-control NSA Security Directorate, which is being used as a virtual Stasi to harass, terminate, and, now in the case of Ford, imprison anyone who crosses its path.

The Associated Press reports on this trial are extremely biased in favor of the government so their coverage of the case should be taken with a very small grain of salt. This is how the AP reported the first day of the trial: "A former National Security Agency employee admitted to backing his pickup truck up to an unguarded exit and hauling away boxes of classified material, an FBI agent testified Tuesday." The AP would seem to have found Ford guilty.

The government is charging Ford took classified material home to use on a resumé for a job in the private sector. Ford is also charged with making a false statement on a security clearance form for Lockheed Martin, a charge that almost never ends up in Federal court.

However, this case involves a jaded witness, Ford's one-time girlfriend, "Tonya Tucker," an individual who has a long rap sheet, aliases, and a history of informing for the FBI, according to informed sources. Knowledgeable sources also report that Ford worked as an analyst on communications intercepts involving two major events: 911 and the lead up to the Iraq War. It is obvious that the Bush Justice Department and Pentagon has gone to great lengths to see Ford out of commission for ten years in a Federal penitentiary.

For NSA, the Ford case represents a return to past institutionalized racism at the signals intelligence agency and yet another example of an unrestrained Security Directorate working with untrustworthy FBI agents.

December 3, 2005 -- EXCLUSIVE -- Intelligence "cooking" and retaliation also plagues IMINT (Imagery intelligence) community but with a healthy dose of contract fraud

WMR has already reported on tainted intelligence being created on the orders of the Bush administration in the SIGINT (signals intelligence) and HUMINT (human intelligence) communities. Largely ignored has been the effect of this policy in the IMINT (imagery intelligence) community. IMINT analysts carefully scan spy satellite and air reconnaissance photos taken of foreign airfields, weapons labs, shipyards, government office complexes, and other strategic and tactical sites.

MZM, the company involved in paying bribes to former California GOP Representative Randy "Duke" Cunningham, was also part of the cooking of intelligence on Iraq years prior to the US invasion, according to a former weapons expert at the National Ground Intelligence Center

(NGIC) in Charlottesville, Virginia. MZM was sold by owner Mitchell Wade to Veritas Capital and is now known as Athena Innovative Solutions, Inc.

According to a former IMINT and weapons analyst, who worked since 1988 for various intelligence agencies looking closely at Iraq, NGIC, which is comprised of US Army Intelligence and Security Command (INSCOM) intelligence analysts and personnel detailed from the National Geo-Spatial Intelligence Agency (NGA), had an all-too-cozy relationship with MZM. The firm's single source, non-competitive contract with NGIC paved the way for the cooking of some of the intelligence used to justify the invasion of Iraq.

After NGIC's deputy director, Bill Rich, Sr., retired, he was quickly hired by MZM, which had replaced Battelle as the prime contractor for NGIC. Soon after taking the job with MZM, Rich's son, who had no prior intelligence experience, was also hired by MZM, according to the former analyst. In addition, NGIC's retired Sergeant Major was also hired by the firm, according to the same source. The links between MZM and Cunningham were so close, members of Wade's family also reportedly steered money to Cunningham's campaign coffers.

Since the MZM-Cunningham scandal broke, the firm has been cut off from all work at NGIC. However, according to NGIC sources that has not affected Rich, who continues to work for a new NGIC contractor, Sparta, Inc., which, like MZM, is conveniently located in the University of Virginia Research Park, across the street from NGIC.

The weapons analyst said that NGIC purposely altered figures on the number of Russian helicopters in order to justify the Crusader gun system, which, at the time, was being built by United Defense, which, in turn, was owned by The Carlyle Group. After the analyst objected to the inflation by NGIC management of the numbers of working helicopters in Russia, he found himself subject to a security clearance investigation by US Investigations Services (USIS), a firm in which the Carlyle Group has a major financial stake, USIS's Iraq operations were under investigation by US Army Col. Ted Westhusing last June. During that investigation, Westhusing was reported to have shot himself in the head while in a trailer near Baghdad.

In a manner reminiscent of how the National Security Agency (NSA) treats whistleblowers, the NGIC analyst was forced to see the center's sole psychologist, someone who was on good terms with Deputy Director Bill Rich. The psychologist determined that the analyst suffered from a psychiatric problem even though his own HMO contradicted that evaluation. In June 2001, the analyst had his security clearance revoked and was terminated in 2002.

In August 2001, the analyst arranged to have some of his NGIC paperwork sent to him at home by NGIC security. However, when a clasped and taped enveloped arrived at his home, there were clear indications that sometime during the passage of the documents through four levels of NGIC management, including NGIC security, something was inserted into the files: a SECRET NOFORN WINTEL document [NOFORN is "no foreign dissemination" and WINTEL is "Warning - Intelligence Sources and Methods Revealed']. The analyst dutifully informed the FBI and the Army Criminal Investigation Division (CID) at Fort Monroe, Virginia about the incident.

However, the analyst was never asked to sign his statement about the incident. This is eerily similar to the planting of two boxes of classified documents in the home of former NSA analyst Kenneth Ford, who is currently on trial after being charged with the possession of classified material.

The intelligence cooking on Russian military aviation was so bad, according to the analyst, that NGIC plagiarized a September 1984 Defense Intelligence Agency (DIA) document and tried to post it in an intelligence report on INTELINK, the intelligence community-wide internal "Internet" for classified information. The only problem was that in "cutting and pasting" 1984 Russian helicopter threat information to justify the Crusader project, the term "Soviet Union" was left in the Fall 1999 intelligence report. The Soviet Union ceased to exist nine years earlier.

The NGIC analyst also was well aware as early as 2000 that the aluminum tubes discovered in Iraq and were later claimed by the Bush administration to be for nuclear centrifuges for an Iraqi nuclear weapons program were nothing more than artillery replacement barrels for the Italian "Medusa 81" artillery rocket that had been produced in Egypt. The analyst has personally briefed Dick Cheney, while he was Secretary of Defense, during Desert Shield in 1990 about the anti-aircraft gun barrels. The analyst was on loan to the Pentagon's National Military Joint Intelligence Center (NMJIC) from the Intelligence Threat Analysis Center (ITAC) at the Washington Navy Yard during Desert Storm and maintains that Cheney, whom he described as a "prick," knew what the aluminum tubes were for in 1990 and knew about them when he lied about their being part of Iraq's nuclear reconstitution program. Also present at the same 1990 intelligence briefing for Cheney was Pete Williams, the then-Pentagon press spokesman and currently an NBC TV news reporter.

NGIC altered the aluminum tube intelligence by ordering two individuals -- an artillery and cannon expert, respectively, to write a bogus intelligence report. The analyst who complained about this said that determination should have been made by NGIC's Technical Chemical Nuclear (TCN) branch, and not by the two individuals in question. However, the TCN experts realized that the tubes in question had nothing to do with a nuclear weapons program.

Moreover, the aluminum tubes used to justify the attack had actually been captured by US forces in Iraq during Desert Storm in 1991 and were conveniently used later to "prove" the existence of a nuclear program over a decade later.

In essence, NGIC tainted raw and refined intelligence received from its three primary providers -- INSCOM headquarters at Ft. Belvoir, Virginia; the Defense Intelligence Agency's (DIA) HUMINT collection databases (including translated intelligence) and NGA.

NGIC analysts and MZM contractors at the center also began altering intelligence databases containing threat data on various weapons systems, including helicopter production in Russia, Iraq, China, France, and Poland. When objections were raised to such tampering, the reply from NGIC/contractor management was "Congress is just a bunch of liberals and fags . . . we will tell them what they need to know." The analyst said that MZM, through bribery deals with

Cunningham (who served on the House Permanent Select Committee on Intelligence) and GOP Representatives Katherine Harris (FL) and Virgil Goode (VA), successfully influenced Congress by successfully tampering with intelligence coming from NGIC. MZM was also involved in providing unspecified "intelligence services" for the Bush White House and purchasing furniture for the White House.

Goode, who sits on the House Armed Services subcommittee for Military Construction, received money from MZM and shortly afterwards, the firm opened an office, complete with Sensitive Compartmented Information Facilities (SCIFs), in Goode's hometown of Martinsville, Virginia. However, an NGIC source said that all Goode received from MZM was $40,000, which compared to what they paid Cunningham, showed that Goode "sold his ass cheap."

December 4, 2005-- Another vicious Bush administration attack on a U.S. intelligence professional -- Greenbelt, Maryland

For former National Security Agency (NSA) analyst Kenneth W. Ford, what occurred on January 11, 2004 was like a scene out of the movie "Enemy of the State." Ford, a tall, slim, intelligent, and well-mannered four year member of the uniformed branch of the U.S. Secret Service who guarded President Bill Clinton and George W. Bush at the White House and even conversed with Clinton during late night walks with first pet "Buddy," found himself face-to-face in the basement of his Waldorf, Maryland home with abusive and threatening agents of the FBI and NSA. Ford's ordeal was not merely life imitating art, it was, and continues to be, a living nightmare.

Ford was being accused of illegally possessing a cache of classified NSA documents at his home. In reality, Ford had been set up by NSA's Security and Counterintelligence Directorate and FBI after they had contracted the services of a Florida woman with a long criminal record and an income stream that can only be attributed to her past use by the FBI as a professional confidential informant (CI).

Ford had been an up-and-coming NSA intern/analyst during the 9-11 attacks, Operation Enduring Freedom in Afghanistan, and the ramping up to the Iraq war and the war itself. As both an intern and a computer whiz, Ford worked in various parts of the massive signals intelligence complex: the Cyber Incident Analysis Division (CIAD) (X72) in the Information Assurance Directorate and in NSA main operations. He transferred from NSA's operations (Signals Intelligence) Directorate (SID), where he worked in the Iraqi section (called the "Iraqi shop"), to the Technical Exploitation Center (TEC), a highly classified building on the NSA campus dominated by a large white "golf ball" or radome on its roof. Two boxes, one containing his unclassified files, notebooks, VHS tapes, and office supplies and the other containing classified files and documents, were transferred by Ford's supervisor and NSA's internal classified material control personnel from Ops to TEC.

A longtime NSA intelligence specialist confirmed that the above NSA divisions exist and that CIAD, SID, amd TEC are unclassified. "In fact, CIAD answers the unclass phone with that name," said the source. Also confirmed was the existence of the "Iraqi shop," a name that bemuses many NSA professionals because of the factory-like terminology for a unit made up of Arabic and Kurdish linguists that closely examines communications intercepts from Iraq. Particularly since the rise of Sh'ia political dominance in Iraq, the "Iraqi shop" has worked closely with the "Iranian shop." Another source familiar with the Iraqi shop, Iranian shop, Turkish shop, Syrian shop, and other Middle Eastern intercept analysis units at NSA reports that in the two years prior to 9-11, NSA Director Michael Hayden's penchant for outsourcing critical NSA operations to private firms resulted in the termination, through forces retirements or outright firings, of 1000 experienced linguists, mathematicians, and computer specialists. In 1999, the Director of NSA's "I Group," which oversaw NSA's training and training evaluation programs, pushed for cross training of linguists -- including fluency in Iraqi Arabic by Standard Arabic speakers. The idea was not only rebuffed but the entire I Group was eliminated. Many of the linguists fired prior to 9-11 spoke Arabic and Farsi. Hayden, the longest serving NSA director (1999-2005), is now the Deputy Director for National Intelligence.

When Ford left TEC on January 5, 2005 for the private sector, he turned the boxes in to his supervisor. The government maintains that on his last day at work, Ford backed his pick-up truck to the TEC and loaded the boxes and drove off with them. However, that is plainly impossible at the facility, which does not permit any civilian vehicle to enter the loading dock area and which is covered by security guards who inspect outgoing materials. The area is also covered by security cameras. Ford contends that he drove his car, not truck, to work on his last day and that a security camera located in the entrance/exit area of the building would have clearly recorded that fact. NSA falsely testified that there were no security cameras installed at the super-secret building on Ford's last day at work.

At Ford's trial today at the U.S. Court House in Greenbelt, Maryland, presided over by US District Court Judge Peter Messitte, FBI agents with Evidence Response Team testified that they took possession of two boxes of classified material at Ford's home on the evening of January 11, 2004. However, none of the FBI agents could say how the boxes made their way from NSA's classified material custodians and internal mail handling system to the kitchen in Ford's Waldorf home. NSA does not seem to have the internal records that such a transfer of classified material within the agency would have normally generated. In addition, the FBI could not comment on how some of the documents from the boxes were found scattered about Ford's home -- in the kitchen pantry, in his bedroom, and, very curiously, in the suitcase of a mysterious house guest who is central to the case.

To answer that question, it is time to introduce one Tonya Tucker, a Florida resident with no visible means of support who met Ford through a web site called Blackplanet.com, which runs a dating service for African-American professional singles. Ford and Tucker knew each other for some nine weeks. But that is all the time it took for Ford to become ensnared in the same web of government deceit, corruption, and retaliation that has damaged or destroyed the careers of honest and hard working intelligence and law enforcement professionals in the NSA, CIA, FBI,

Defense Intelligence Agency, Army, Air Force, Homeland Security Department, and other agencies.

And like Ambassador Joseph Wilson and his wife Valerie Plame Wilson, who stood in the way of the neo-con efforts to trump up bogus weapons of mass destruction (WMD) intelligence against Saddam Hussein, Ford, although not as high ranking and high profile, was also deemed a threat to the Bush administration. Theoretically, if Ford were to have been assigned to the SID's "Iraqi shop" at NSA and authored an intelligence analysis report on Iraqi WMDs, which stated, contrary to the White House's claims, that they did not exist, that report would have ended up on the desks of the major perpetrators of the war -- Vice President Dick Cheney, his indicted Chief of Staff Lewis "Scooter" Libby, and other White House Iraq Group (WHIG) players. As an NSA source revealed, "during the 1980s, NSA COMINT [communication intercepts] were straight translations and transcriptions form the intercept." Because they sometimes tended to reveal sources and methods, in the early 1990s, NSA changed its standards to allow for "journalistic reporting." "Analysts are permitted to put their comments, mixing COMINT and unclassified information, in reports in the same way the CIA wrote its reports," said the source. The names of the analyst and the branch chief are contained in these reports, including any that might have been drafted by Ford and eventually sent to the White House.

Notwithstanding his important job at NSA, Ford quickly went from being an NSA analyst to an "Enemy of the Bush State." The retaliation was as sloppy as it was venal.

Tucker, who once told Ford she was "paid to lie," falsely claimed to be an attorney, an employee of the consulting firm Bearing Point, and a Defense Department contractor for SPAWAR (Space and Naval Warfare Systems Command) with a Top Secret clearance. NSA Special Agent Robert McCaslin confronted Ford on the night of his arrest with an allegation that he and FBI agents found a classified NSA document in Tucker's suitcase in Ford's home. How a classified document could have ended up in Tucker's suitcase is a mystery, considering she had no security clearance. It is also noteworthy that the FBI did not arrest Tucker for carrying a classified document in her suitcase from her hotel to Ford's residence. Also suspicious is the fact that while FBI agents were quick to seize the two boxes of classified material they failed to secure Tucker's suitcase, in which one of the classified documents was found stuffed in a FEDEX envelope. The FBI later said they simply "forgot" to seize the suitcase.

Tucker meets all the criteria for an FBI C.I. or confidential informant. While staying in Maryland, Tucker resided in a deluxe suite at the Homestead Suites hotel in Annapolis, where such rooms currently cost $128.99 per day. Tucker, who has been arrested for credit and check violations in Florida, paid for the room with an American Express card, then a VISA card, cash, and finally, a cashier's check. Two Sun Bank receipts from Florida were discovered in the same suitcase that contained one of the classified documents: one for $5000 deposited in the checking account of her father and the other for $270 deposited to her own account.

Tonya Tucker, is also known as Kayla Walker, Tonya Stewart, and seventeen other aliases. Tucker was arrested in Florida in December 2002 and placed on probation until 2007. However, the terms of that probation were suddenly revoked in 2003. Her rap sheet includes arrests for credit card and check fraud, possession of forged documents, grand theft, and larceny. Although there is no record of Tucker having worked for Bearing Point, phone records indicate she made two calls to Bearing Point's Bala Cynwyd, Pennsylvania office on January 9, 2004, two days prior to Ford's arrest. It is also significant that Tucker had in her possession the phone number of an agent of NSA's Security and Counterintelligence Associate Directorate (ADS&CI), a number that is not readily available to members of the public, let alone someone with a criminal record. In addition, Tucker's Homestead Suites records indicate that her bills were paid by a "Universal Technology Systems." A Google search shows the only company with a similar name is "Universal Systems & Technology" of Centreville, Virginia, a company that is contracted to the FBI, DIA, and the Justice Department, specializes in maritime and aviation security, and which has an office in Tucker's hometown of Orlando and another in Norfolk, Virginia, where Tucker traveled on occasion, according to sources close to the case.

Taking the witness stand on December 2, Tucker claimed she saw the word "classified" on documents she found in boxes in Ford's home. However, classified U.S. government documents are never marked "classified." They carry the labels Top Secret, Secret, or Confidential. If they contain Sensitive Compartmented Information (SCI), they will also carry lateral markings such as COMINT, BYEMAN, GAMMA, TK, VRK, and others. Tucker used an alias when she claimed to have phoned NSA. Tucker also admitted to making up information she told the FBI.

According to the government prosecutors, the documents contained in the two boxes planted in Ford's home were what one could expect to find on an NSA's employee's desk: Top Secret documents with header and footer classifications, along with lateral markings: TOP SECRET/COMINT/NOFORN, TOP SECRET/COMINT/X1, and SECRET/COMINT. Some of the documents, obviously over-classified, dealt with training courses, NSA's intern program, and such subjects as "Global Network," "Intern Checklist," and "NET-A." One document dealt with a classified NSA database known by its cover term PINWALE.

Assistant U.S. Attorney David I. Salem curiously placed a great deal of relevance on the issue of Ford having a paper shredder in his home as if that is unusual during a time when more and more people are buying shredders to destroy mail and other paperwork containing the type of personal information used for identity theft.

Ford, as required by NSA regulations, earlier reported a threatening e-mail sent to him at his America On Line address a month and a half before his arrest. The e-mail was sent by a "Dr. Takiya," who claimed to be a friend of Tucker. "Takiya" threatened Ford that his security clearance would soon be revoked.

Realizing that NSA's penchant for outsourcing to private contractors meant that he could increase his salary while continuing to do work for NSA, Ford opted to leave the agency on January 5, 2004 for Northrop Grumman. Arrested in January 2004 and not indicted until May of this year, in the interim Ford was fired by both Northrop Grumman and Lockheed Martin after their government clients exerted pressure on the firms. An NSA source revealed that upon retirement, NSA employees are handed a list prepared by Human Resources that contains a "list of suggested employers." Northrop Grumman and Lockheed Martin are included on that list.

An NSA source confided why it is believed Ford was set up in a trap by NSA Security and the FBI. The usual method to eliminate "problem" employees at NSA is to tag an NSA employee as "troublesome." That sets into motion a fixed schedule of Kafkaesque theatrics that include repeated visits to the NSA Psychology unit that practices a form of "junk psychiatry" that includes such tactics as "good cop, bad cop interviews" and the highly-discredited shrink card game known as the "Rorschach" test, which requires subjects to state what a series of ink blots resemble. The NSA source firmly believes that since Ford was an outstanding employee who also happened to be an African-American, the NSA "troublesome" game would not work. "If they fired Ford like they have other analysts, NSA Security would've come up against the agency's diversity goals and the Equal Employment Opportunity Commission and that would have caused real problems for them," said the source. That factor and the fact that Ford had left NSA for the private sector meant that Ford had to "be set up with a criminal act enabled by a broadened Patriot Act that allowed NSA Security and the FBI to manufacture a criminal case -- something that could be easily sold as a national security threat in a post-911 country," opined the source who has served three decades with the NSA.

One NSA employee said that a common practice among NSA employees is for them to hold on to each other's memos-for-the-record in case they are "set up" by NSA Security.

In addition to the charge of illegally possessing classified material, the government has also charged Ford with making a false statement on his Lockheed Martin security clearance application. The government maintains that Ford never mentioned his arrest by the FBI. However, a close perusal of a copy of the application form plainly shows that in answer to the question about ever having been arrested, Ford checked "Yes," with an explanatory statement of "2004/01/12 False Arrest. No police record, No charge." Further, Ford explained he was falsely accused by a woman who contacted the FBI.

The nightmare for Ford has extended to his parents, Kenneth Sr. and Gloria. Mr. Ford worked for the U.S. Postal Service at the Brentwood Postal Facility in Washington, DC, the trans-shipment point for the anthrax-laden letters that were sent to the Democratic leadership in the US Senate, a still unresolved bio-terrorist act that disrupted the legislature during the time the draconian USA-PATRIOT Act was being forced by the Bush administration. Two of Ford's co-workers in the processing section died as a direct result of anthrax inhalation.

Kenneth Ford, Sr. actually retired the same day -- October 15, 2001 -- that the anthrax letters came through Brentwood. However, he was still required to take Cipro because of possible exposure to the deadly bacteria. A number of Brentwood employees later became ill from the after effects of either anthrax exposure or adverse reactions to Cipro and other antibiotics. Mrs. Ford is also a longtime Federal government employee. The Fords cannot understand how the government could be so callous in setting up their son, their only child, in a carefully contrived and planned trap.

The Ford family joins a growing list of families -- the Wilsons, the Edmonds, the Tices, the Ritters, the Sheehans, and many, many others, who have greatly suffered merely for doing what is right for America and being good citizens.

> SIDEBAR:
>
> WMR has in the past reported on the severe abuses carried out by members of NSA's private security force, the Associate Directorate for Security and Counter-intelligence (ADS&CI). The virtually independent Stasi-like force has terrorized NSA's work force with psychological abuse, coercive tactics, sexual harassment, and frame ups. The American taxpayers are paying for the salaries of these individuals and their various toys that include Humvees with DVD players. In the public interest, it is time for America to get to know these folks much better. WMR has obtained a For Official Use Only (FOUO) organization chart of Q2 (NSA Personnel Security) from January of this year. Informed sources say the chart remains relatively up-to-date.

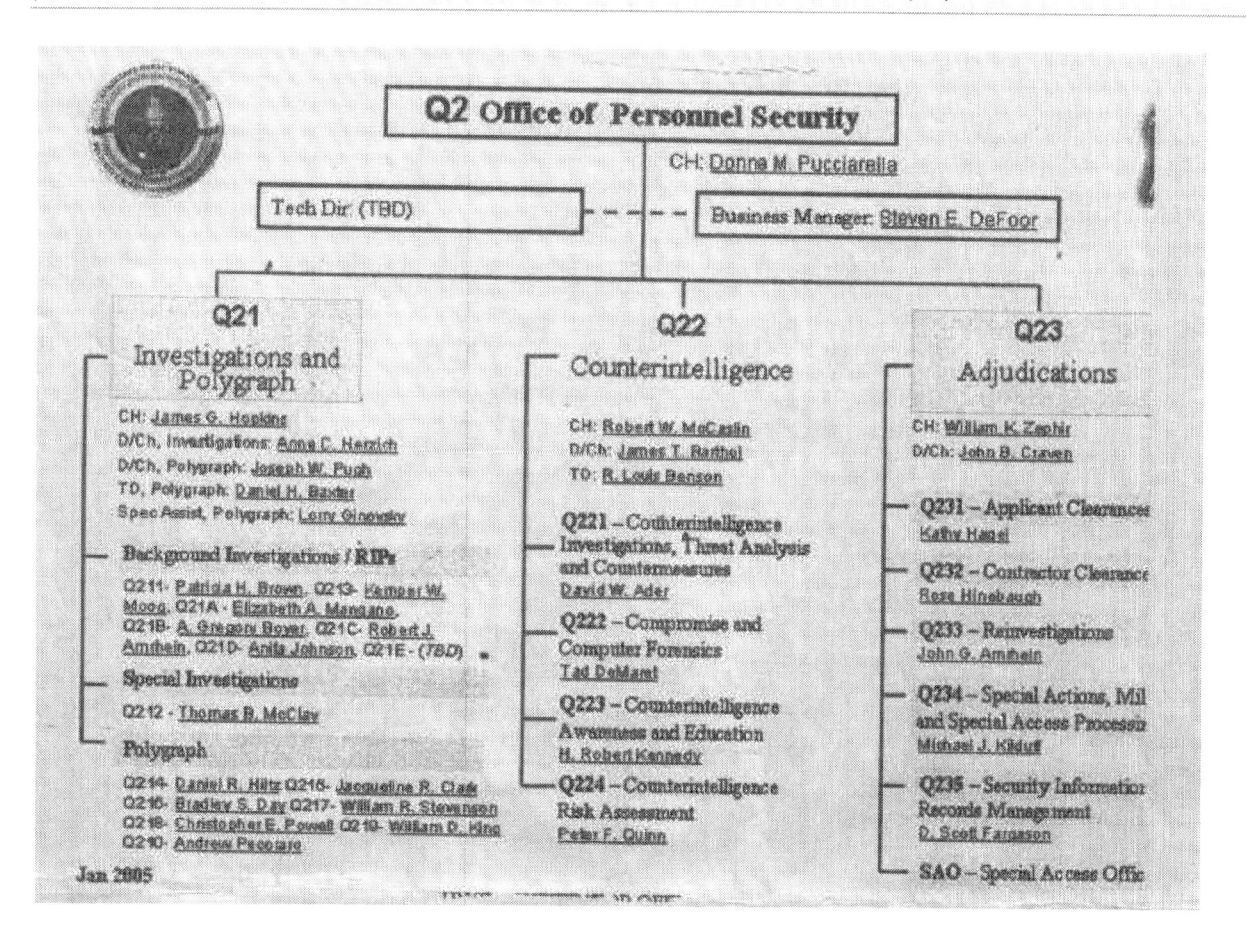

December 4, 2005 -- Current Deputy Director for National Intelligence helped lay groundwork for 9-11 intelligence failures. National Security Agency (NSA) insiders speak out about Hayden's and his NSA predecessors' climate of fear, retribution, and lack of priorities.

Much has been written about why NSA failed to report four important intercepts prior to 911 that would have alerted the United States that a major attack was to take place on September 11, 2001.

The intercepts of Al Qaeda communications were:

Sept. 10, 2001 - "The match is about to begin."

Sept. 10, 2001 - "Tomorrow is zero hour"

In addition, two other intercepts of Al Qaeda cells in the United States were also ignored:

Sept. 10, 2001 - "Watch the news."

Sept. 10, 2001 - "Tomorrow will be a great day for us."

WMR can report that because of poor management decisions made by then-NSA Director Air Force Gen. Michael Hayden, the NSA did not have the expertise or ability to adequately identify key intercepts that, if known and understood in time, could have prevented the 911 attacks. These intercept "takes" for the day sat unread in an area of the NSA basement known as the "Carillon pool" until it was too late.

The reasons why NSA was caught unprepared for 911 essentially go back a decade before Hayden's arrival as director. After the collapse of the Soviet bloc, NSA's Russian linguists and Soviet experts were considered the golden employees. Even though the threat changed and the Russian priorities were downgraded, the Russian experts were placed in top management positions in areas in which they had no experience. In what would be a fateful decision, Russian experts were put in charge of Middle East and Asian units, according to NSA sources. It was so bad, according to one source, that when an NSA branch manager, who only knew Russian, was placed in charge of China operations, he embarrassed himself and NSA when, during a Washington, DC briefing for old China hands from the CIA, DIA, and other agencies, he was unable to correctly pronounce Chinese names.

The decision to promote Russian experts to top management, rather than Arabic, Farsi, and other language experts, would eventually result in almost total ignorance of the warning signs that were developing in the Middle East in the early 1990s. Overworked, under-appreciated, and with no chance of promotion, many Arabic linguists began leaving NSA in the middle 1990s, just as a firebrand Islamic fundamentalist named Osama Bin Laden was making some disturbing comments from Sudan and later, Afghanistan.

By 1998, some 1000 top NSA specialists -- linguists, mathematicians, and computer programmers -- had left the agency. However, the old Russian experts remained and were promoted. One of them was Maureen "Mo" Baginski, a Russian linguist, who was appointed to head the NSA's important Signals Intelligence Directorate (SID). She would later be blamed by

Hayden and others for being partly responsible for the 911 failures at NSA. However, old NSA hands say that it was not fair to blame Baginski, since she "was out of her element" when dealing with the Middle East. Baginski is now a senior official of the FBI.

Making matters worse was the initiative to purposely drum out of NSA a number of experienced Middle Eastern and South Asian linguists as part of Hayden's reorganization program that emphasized outsourcing. One NSA linguist, fluent in Pashto (the language of the Taliban), Farsi, and 16 other languages was forced to retire a few years before 911. He was told by NSA managers that "minor languages" like Farsi and Pashto "never will be important to us." In fact, NSA paid little attention to "low density languages" that would later become critical. These included Uzbek, Urdu, Pashto, Dari, Farsi, and various Arabic dialects.

Attempts to convince Hayden that he had to beef up Middle Eastern language proficiency by training better instructors, concentrating on Middle Eastern dialects, and evaluating and upgrading language training programs went unheeded. Although Hayden paid plenty of lip service to these ideas, nothing ever happened. Eager to carry out his pet Groundbreaker and Trailblazer outsourcing projects, the NSA Director continued to sell the NSA store to private contractors.

Moreover, the NSA contracting firms, some of which were large Pentagon weapons system providers, convinced Hayden that China, not the Middle East, was the highest priority. As a result, by 2000, Groundbreaker/Trailblazer contractors such as Lockheed Martin and Boeing had successfully seen to it that China, not the Middle East, would be the focus of NSA's re-engineered signals intelligence systems. By hyping the "China threat," intelligence could be used to justify large defense programs in which the contractors had a vested interest. Chief among these was the Ballistic Missile Defense system being pushed by Donald Rumsfeld, who was not yet Defense Secretary but who championed "Star Wars II" as the head of the Rumsfeld Commission on missile defense. Of course, China was high on Rumsfeld's mind when his commission's report rhetorically asked, "What if China gave North Korea advanced missile technology (or even a completed missile)?"

Meanwhile, intelligence from NSA raw intercepts were being leaked to the media, including Parade magazine, in order to justify expensive defense systems to counter the "China threat." NSA analysts were appalled at the lackadaisical way important intelligence was being leaked. Sources for COMINT on China and other countries involved in weapons proliferation -- targeted telephone numbers and fax, computer, and other telecommunications links -- literally dried up overnight and continued to stay dark, according to one source.

Hayden's predecessor as director, Air Force General Kenneth Minihan, did try to stress multi-skills and multi-lingualism for NSA analysts in his National Cryptologic Strategy for the 21st Century (NCS21) reorganization plan. However, Minihan never did much to launch his NCS21 initiative. Minihan's plan specifically stated that NSA would:

"Invest in our people through education, training and career development to achieve and maintain required skill levels. Our overall occupational structure will be skills-based and constantly tuned to mission requirements and achieve information superiority."

However, Hayden scrapped NCS21, replacing it with GROUNDBREAKER and TRAILBLAZER.

NCS21 would have also helped curb the problem with the "stovepiping" of intelligence, which prevented intelligence like the September 10, 2001 NSA Al Qaeda intercepts from getting to those decision makers who needed it. One of NCS 21's stated goals was to:

"Work with the intelligence community to develop interactive databases to enable the policy maker to initiate a single request, search all available community databases, and receive the requested data."

Rather than integrating databases, Hayden's programs were discontinuing databases, particularly those that concentrated on the Middle East and South Asia.

As a result of the interplay between Hayden, the contractors, and Rumsfeld, NSA's intercept priorities were focused away from the Middle East to Chinese missile and other weapons systems. Repeated urging to beef up NSA's Middle Eastern and African capabilities were ignored, even after the 1998 U.S. embassy bombings in Kenya and Tanzania.

Many linguists were tossed out based on trumped up "security" problems. NSA Security is noted for running a virtual Gestapo-like operation at the agency. According to dozens of current and ex-NSA employees interviewed by WMR, anyone targeted for any reason by NSA management soon finds themselves the subject of interrogations, forced visits to the NSA psychologist, and finally clearance revocation and termination. The terminations of linguists with critical skills continued right up to September 2001.

Hayden's two reorganizations projects -- Groundbreaker and Trailblazer -- saw a number of NSA's language databases being terminated because of a lack of funding due to the outsourcing of critical operational responsibilities.

A few NSA analysts early on predicted that Islamic radicals encouraged by Saudi radical clerics would soon launch a major suicide terrorist attack on American soil.

The analysts based their prediction on a number of key events and dates. One was the September 12, 1994, suicide crash of a stolen Cessna plane flown into the South Lawn of the White House by Frank Corder. (President Clinton was then staying at Blair House, across Pennsylvania Avenue from the White House). The other was the undetected flying of a Cessna aircraft through heavily-fortified Soviet air defense systems by 19 year-old German pilot Mathias Rust in 1987. Rust landed his aircraft in Red Square, within yards of the offices of the top Soviet leadership.

The other significant date pointed to by NSA analysts was September 11. This was the last day of the siege by the Palestinian terrorist group "Black September" of Israeli athlete hostages at the 1972 Munich Olympics, a day and month that NSA Middle East experts pointed out was significant throughout the Islamic world. Eleven Israeli athletes were killed by their Black September captors. Black September took its name from the September 1970 massacre by King Hussein of Jordan of thousands of Palestinians in Jordan who attempted to stage a coup.

NSA managers who did not understand the nuances of the Middle East claimed that since the "U.S. eliminated Black September," nothing connected to the group or the month of September could be taken seriously.

But two decades later, NSA began to obtain tapes of incendiary speeches by Wahhabi Muslim Saudi clerics in mosques throughout the oil-rich kingdom. When the contents of the transcriptions of these tapes were compared to classified COMINT [Communications Intelligence] and information in articles in various Arabic language newspapers, alarm bells went off in the Middle East branches at Fort Meade, particularly after the February 26, 1993 terrorist bombing of the World Trade Center. A report never distributed outside of NSA reported that "Saudi extremists were contemplating 'kamikaze'-type attacks in the United States using aircraft." Ironically and eerily, the date of that report was September 11, 1993. Because the report was not totally based on SIGINT, it was rejected as flawed by NSA management.

Also ignored were clear indications that certain Israeli elements were engaged in suspicious activities prior to 9-11. Although NSA has traditionally been skeptical about Israeli intentions – ever since the 1967 unprovoked Israeli attack on the NSA ship USS Liberty and severe compromises of classified information from the Pollard affair and the DINDI/PIEREX joint NSA-Israeli activities in the 1980s – by the late 1990s, NSA gingerly handled intercepts of Israeli communications. It is such a touchy subject that the name tags of NSA linguists that carry their language expertise in one case have been altered. Hebrew linguists tags are denoted as "Special Arabic," an obvious attempt to demonstrate to those NSA employees without special access that the agency does not listen in on Hebrew communications.

Israel was suspected by some NSA and CIA analysts of helping to beef up China's missile and other weapons systems with sophisticated technology. Some of this technology was used to make improvements to the Chinese Silkworm anti-ship missile, the C-801 sea-skimming missile, and the EM-52 rocket-propelled anti-ship mine. These weapons systems were then offered by China to Iran.

There were attempts at the analyst level to try to share intelligence prior to 9-11. This was done through the Tech Track program, an analyst-led initiative to identify various subject area experts, particularly in the non-Russian areas, who could be called on for assistance. This program was showing success before NSA management stepped in and took it over. An attempt to eliminate the stovepiping of intelligence was quickly ended due to senior management interference.

Analysts figured out other clever ways to meet with other experts, both within the NSA and at other intelligence agencies. Not necessarily knowing the names of counterparts in other intelligence sections, subject area experts figured out a way to organize dinner meetings at Washington area restaurants by sending out notices on secure networks to particular intelligence branches and sections at the NSA, CIA, DIA, and other agencies. The analysts would identify one another based on the color of the neckties they agreed in advance to wear.

December 5, 2005 -- Nothing anonymous at NSA, including AA

NSA sources report that the NSA Security Directorate is so out of control it attempted to browbeat an NSA employee into turning over the names, addresses, and other personal details of members of his Alcoholics Anonymous support group to security. The problem began when the employee was stationed at the NSA base in Menwith Hill, UK. Having determined he had a drinking problem after many years of overseas assignments, the employee sought the help of the local British AA group. Successful in becoming sober and turning his life around, the employee and his wife, also an NSA employee, eventually returned to the United States where they were assigned to NSA headquarters at Fort Meade. However, security required the employee to undergo a security update and was asked whether he had developed any foreign contacts. When he answered yes and that the contacts were members of his British AA group, NSA Security demanded the names, addresses, and other information on the AA members. After the NSA employee said that AA's very name indicated that members were anonymous and revealing names of members would violate AA principles, Security accused him of failing to cooperate and suspended not only his, but his wife's security clearance. Both employees were assigned to the NSA motor pool at the Friendship Annex (FANX) of NSA for nine months, where on salaries of over $60,000 each they charged batteries and washed NSA staff vehicles.

December 14, 2005 -- Prosecution and defense closing arguments in the Kenneth W. Ford case.

The defense and prosecutors presented their closing arguments today to the jury at the US Court House in Greenbelt, Maryland, in the case of former NSA analyst Kenneth W. Ford. The government charged Ford with possessing two boxes of classified material at his Waldorf, Maryland home in January 2004 after a tip was phoned in to NSA Security by a dubious FBI informant with along criminal record named Tonya Tucker, aka Tonya Stewart, Kayla Walker and 17 other aliases.

Ford, a uniformed Secret Service officer at the White House during the Clinton and G. W. Bush administrations before transferring to the intern program at NSA, was also charged with making a false statement on a security clearance form for a civilian contractor job after he left NSA. An examination of the clearance form clearly shows that Ford answered "yes" to the question about being arrested in January 2004 but also noted that the arrest was based on false charges.

The Ford case hinges on strong evidence that the two boxes of classified documents were placed in Ford's home in a carefully-contrived plan to get back at Ford for his analytical reports while working for the NSA Signals Intelligence Directorate. Ford ended up on the White House radar screen after he began to be "published," meaning his reports, containing his name and office, made their way up the chain of command to the White House. In at least one case, Ford's report was at variance with White House contentions that there was concrete intelligence that Saddam Hussein possessed weapons of mass destruction. Today, in a speech at the Woodrow Wilson Center, President Bush took "responsibility" for faulty pre-war intelligence leading up to the Iraq war. However, Ford and his colleagues at NSA were well aware that the intelligence the White House was basing its decision on was faulty from the beginning.

From November 2002 to May 2003, Ford worked as an intern in the OPS-1 Building at NSA. This was the time period during which the White House was "fixing intelligence" for the case for war, according to the Downing Street Memo and other documents. It was therefore problematic when Ford's intelligence reports reached the White House containing his analysis that there was nothing to support the allegations of an Iraqi WMD threat.

In May 2003, Ford transferred to NSA's Technical Exploitation Center (TEC) as part of the normal rotation for interns. This is the point in time when NSA Security had possession of the two boxes later "discovered" in Ford's home by Tucker, the confidential informant, termed a "tipster" by the prosecution.

Ford's supervisor gave conflicting testimony at today's trial. First, she testified that Ford was not permitted to carry the documents between tours, that is from the OPS-1 Building to the TEC. She later stated that the documents would have been sent via internal NSA classified mail from OPS-1 to TEC. She did state that in some cases, NSA employees who are issued a "courier badge" are permitted to transfer classified documents internally at the NSA campus. Ford's supervisor could not recall whether Ford had ever applied for a courier badge. Nor was she aware that there were security cameras installed at NSA.

Ford's supervisor testified that she asked Ford to pick up the two boxes located on Ford's old desk in OPS-1 and take them to his new office. However, while she also testified that she never heard of Ford's new location, the TEC building, she admitted she wrote Ford's name and the address of the TEC building on the box containing classified material, something that would have been normal if the box was sent to TEC via NSA internal classified mail. However, Ford's supervisor also testified that she did not mail the documents to Ford's new address. Ford's supervisor also admitted that a number of people had access to Ford's documents during the two month period they were in OPS-1 after Ford's departure.

The supervisor, identified only at Kathleen "M," also stated that while she recognized some of the documents found in the boxes as those associated with a training course Ford took while assigned to OPS, she did not recognize many of the other documents that were discovered in the boxes.

Ms. "M" also testified that NSA Security controls do not preclude someone simply removing two boxes of classified material from NSA. The NSA complex, complete with guards, fences, gates, security cameras, special sensors, security representatives assigned to every work section, and random searches of vehicles and personal belongings, is one of the most heavily-protected facilities in the United States. Sources close to NSA report that it would be in keeping with past NSA Security Directorate practices to have "coached" the witness prior to testimony.

Former NSA analyst and whistleblower Russ Tice testified on behalf of Ford and stated that it was virtually impossible to wantonly carry two boxes of classified material out of NSA without being checked by NSA guards and recorded by video cameras. US Attorney David I. Salem contended that Tice, a 17-year veteran of the NSA, Defense Intelligence Agency, Naval Information Warfare Activity, Marine Corps Intelligence, and US Air Force, was "not an expert" on NSA security procedures.

WMR has previously reported on an analyst at the National Ground Intelligence Center in Charlottesville, Virginia having discovered that security at the center slipped a "Secret" document into an envelope mailed to him at home after he left the center. The analyst immediately notified the FBI and the Army Criminal Investigation Division (CID) upon discovering the document, however, the CID never took an official statement from the ex-analyst.

The NGIC analyst had blown the whistle on the nature of the Iraqi aluminum tubes, which the Bush administration contended were for Iraqi nuclear centrifuges. The analyst had personally briefed then-Defense Secretary Dick Cheney in 1990 that the tubes were Egyptian "knock offs" used as replacement barrels for an Italian-made rocket launcher. Moreover, US troops captured and took possession of the barrels during Desert Storm.

December 17, 2005 -- Note on NSA spying story in yesterday's *New York Times*.[1] WMR reported on May 15, 2005:

"May 15, 2005 -- According to National Security Agency insiders, outgoing NSA Director General Michael Hayden approved special communications intercepts of phone conversations made by past and present U.S. government officials.

It is noteworthy that in the fictional movie 'Enemy of the State,' it was under the authority of a 'training mission' that renegade NSA officials targeted U.S. civilians for eavesdropping. United States Signals Intelligence Directive (USSID) 18, the NSA's 'Bible' for the conducting of

---

[1] The December 16 story, titled "Bush Lets U.S. Spy on Callers Without Courts," by James Risen and Eric Lichtblau, was the first mainstream media report on warrantless wiretapping by the NSA.

surveillance against U.S. persons, allows 'U.S. material,' i.e., listening to U.S. persons, to be used for training missions. However, USSID 18 also requires that all intercepts conducted for such training missions are to be completely destroyed after completion of the training operation. In the case of Bolton and other Bush administration hard liners, the material in question was not deleted and was transmitted in raw intercept form to external agencies for clearly political purposes – a violation of the Foreign Intelligence Surveillance Act and USSID 18, which only allows such raw training mission intercepts to be transmitted when evidence of criminal activity is uncovered during the training mission. Unlike signals intelligence (SIGINT) data stored in the ANCHORY (formerly known as the SIGINT On-line Intelligence System or "SOLIS") database, training intercepts are completely off-the-books and, in the case of raw intercepts provided to Bolton and others, the NSA and its Signals Intelligence Directorate (SID) can claim 'plausible deniability' in stating that only 'official' intercept transcripts were provided to users outside the agency. Because they are to be destroyed after completion of training missions, the training intercepts do not appear in any agency logs and cannot be obtained by the Senate Foreign Relations Committee unless they are subpoenaed directly from Bolton and his colleagues.

December 22, 2005 -- He who lies most, lies worst.

President Bush is contending that a government leak about Osama Bin Laden using his satellite phone in 1998 resulted in the Al Qaeda leader avoiding the phone or "going dark," to use an National Security Agency (NSA) term. That, Bush maintains, resulted in an intelligence failure.

Once again, Bush is just plain lying (along with being misinformed). It was no secret that Bin Laden stopped using his satellite phone in 1996 after Chechen President Dzhokar Dudayev was killed by a Russian air-to-ground missile as he was talking on his satellite phone. In that case, Dudayev erred by keeping his conversation longer than two minutes, ample time for a joint Russian-US operation to pinpoint his location using an overhead U.S. communications intelligence satellite. The editor reported and spoke in detail on that operation in 1996:

("DID NSA HELP RUSSIA TARGET DUDAYEV?" by Wayne Madsen, Covert Action Quarterly, Summer 1997:

Strong evidence suggests that the US, in violation of its ban on assassination, used the world's most sophisticated satellite technology to help Russia target the Chechen leader, and boost both Yeltsin's and Clinton's election chances.)

and was once berated by a senior Pentagon officer for referring to the public news reports concerning it in an address to a seminar in Tyson's Corner, Virginia. Also, from Wayne Madsen, "Report Alleges US Role in Angola Arms-for-Oil Scandal," CorpWatch, May 17, 2002:

"Jardo Muekalia, who headed UNITA's Washington office until it was forced to close in 1997, says the military forces that ultimately succeeded in assassinating [Jonas] Savimbi were supported by commercial satellite imagery and other intelligence support provided by Houston-based Brown & Root, Cheney's old outfit. Both the State Department and Pentagon vehemently deny any US government role in the killing of Savimbi.

But the US frequently uses such intelligence wizardry to help track down troublesome leaders. In 1996, according to US and British intelligence sources, the NSA may have passed on location data to the Russians on the location of Chechen President Dzhokar Dudayev (he was struck by an air-to-surface missile while talking on his satellite phone). In 1999, the New York Times reported that Turkey captured Kurdish Workers' Party leader Abdallah Ocalan after his cell phone location data was tracked by U.S., British, and Israeli intelligence agents."

From *Network World*, "The Terrorist Network," by Sharon Gaudin, Nov. 26, 01:

"Chechen leader Dzokhar Dudayev knew he needed to limit the time he spent using the satellite phone given to him by his Islamic allies in Turkey. It was the spring of 1996, and the survivor of two Russian assassination attempts was wary of Russia's ability to home in on his communication signal - and his location.

But on the evening of April 21, Dudayev, baited by Russian President Boris Yeltsin's offer of peace talks, called an adviser in Moscow to discuss the impending negotiations.

This time, Dudayev stayed on the phone too long.

American spy satellites, trained on Iraq and Kuwait, were quickly turned north to the Caucasus mountains and Chechnya, according to a former communications specialist with the U.S. National Security Agency (NSA). The satellites pinpointed the Chechen leader's location to within meters of his satellite phone signal, and the coordinates were sent to a Russian Sukhoi Su-25 fighter jet.

Dudayev was killed by two laser-guided air-to-surface missiles while still holding the phone that gave him away.

This deadly lesson, which the U.S. has never officially confirmed, was not lost on Osama bin Laden, a purported Chechen ally who fed money and weapons to their fight against the Russians. That lesson was complete when bin Laden subsequently received word that U.S. spy satellites, perhaps the very same that located Dudayev, had eavesdropped on his own satellite phone conversations. And members of the NSA played the tapes for visitors.

'Bin Laden knows what has happened and he's a smart man,' says Wayne Madsen, a security consultant and former communications specialist with the U.S. Navy and the NSA. 'He's learned his lesson... and he knows technology is a double-edged sword so he's using it carefully.'

Today bin Laden is believed to school his soldiers in high-tech tools of communication. E-mail, online dead drops, satellite phones, cell phones, encryption and digital camouflage called stenography (see story, next page) are all tools of Al Qaeda, bin Laden's terrorist network. Those high-tech tools enable members of Al Qaeda to communicate with terrorist cells (or groups) hidden around the world.

But bin Laden himself uses none of it.

Instead, he has fallen back on ancient methods of communication, denying the U.S. and its allies the chance to track electronic footprints, satellite signals or even the radiation emissions from cellular phones. A grid of trusted human couriers, foot soldiers melding in with civilians, crisscross Afghanistan and flow into neighboring countries carrying written and whispered messages that are then electronically shot around the world."

Bush is actually trying to stop the flood of leaks from NSA and other intelligence agencies by disgruntled analysts and other professionals by making noise about "leaks." Its a desperate move on Bush's part. It was Bush who alienated the US Intelligence Community and now Bush will pay the political price for his arrogance and demoralization of the "INT" agencies: Sigint, Humint, Imint, and Elint.

December 24, 2005 -- NSA snooping of web dates back to 1995 (Factoring in telecommunications industry mergers, it is not difficult to determine what companies are involved in domestic surveillance today)

Wayne Madsen, in an article written for the June 1995 issue of *Computer Fraud & Security Bulletin* (Elsevier Advanced Technology Publications), wrote that "according to well-placed sources within the Federal Government and the Internet service provider industry, the National Security Agency (NSA) is actively sniffing several key Internet router and gateway hosts."

Madsen says the NSA concentrates its surveillance on destination and origination hosts, as well as "sniffing" for specific key words and phrases. He claims his sources have confirmed that the NSA has contracted with an unnamed private company to develop the software needed to capture Internet data of interest to the agency. According to Madsen, the NSA monitors traffic primarily at two Internet routers controlled by the National Aeronautics and Space Administration (NASA), one in College Park, MD (dubbed "Fix East") and another at NASA Ames Research Center in Sunnyvale, CA ("Fix West"). Other NSA Internet sniffers, he said, operate at busy routers knows as Mae East (an East Coast hub), Mae West (a West Coast hub), CIX (reportedly based in San Jose), and SWAB (a northern Virginia router operated by Bell Atlantic).

Madsen says the NSA may also be monitoring traffic at network access points, the large Internet gateways operated by regional and long-distance service providers. The NAPs allegedly under surveillance are in Pennsauken, NJ (operated by Sprint), Chicago (run by AmeriTech and Bell Communications Research), and San Francisco (Pacific Bell). "Madsen claims the NSA has deals with Microsoft, Lotus, and Netscape to prevent anonymous email." "One senior Federal

Government source has reported that NSA has been particularly successful in convincing key members of the US software industry to cooperate with it in producing software that makes Internet messages easier for NSA to intercept, and if they are encrypted, to decode," Madsen wrote.

"A knowledgeable government source claims that the NSA has concluded agreements with Microsoft, Lotus and Netscape to permit the introduction of the means to prevent the anonymity of Internet electronic mail, the use of cryptographic key-escrow, as well as software industry acceptance of the NSA-developed Digital Signature Standard (DSS)."

December 26, 2005 -- Colin Powell says Bush's use of NSA to conduct warrantless wiretaps acceptable.

On December 25, former Secretary of State Colin Powell told ABC News This Week that the Bush administration's use of NSA to spy on U.S. citizens without a Foreign Intelligence Surveillance Court warrant was legitimate. However, Powell, himself, was the target of such eavesdropping by NSA. While he was Powell's deputy undersecretary for international arms control, unconfirmed US ambassador to the UN John Bolton, on the orders of Dick Cheney, instructed NSA to conduct domestic eavesdropping on phone calls between Powell and New Mexico Governor Bill Richardson. Of primary interest to Bolton and Cheney was Powell's green light to Richardson to conduct diplomatic back channel nuclear talks with North Korea's UN ambassador in New York.

From WMR, May 15, 2005: "Intelligence community insiders claim that a number of State Department and other government officials may have been subject to NSA "training" surveillance and that transcripts between them and foreign officials likely ended up in the possession of Bolton and his neo-conservative political allies, including such members of Vice President Dick Cheney's staff as David Wurmser (a former assistant to Bolton at State), John Hannah, and Lewis "Scooter" Libby.

Possible affected individuals include: . . . New Mexico Governor Bill Richardson and his telephone conversations with Secretary of State Powell and North Korea's deputy UN ambassador Han Song Ryol . . ."

December 28, 2005 -- NSA spied on its own employees, other U.S. intelligence personnel, and their journalist and congressional contacts.

WMR has learned that the National Security Agency (NSA), on the orders of the Bush administration, eavesdropped on the private conversations and e-mail of its own employees,

employees of other U.S. intelligence agencies -- including the CIA and DIA -- and their contacts in the media, Congress, and oversight agencies and offices.

The journalist surveillance program, code named FIRSTFRUITS was part of a Director of Central Intelligence (DCI) program that was maintained at least until October 2004 and was authorized by then-DCI Porter Goss. FIRSTFRUITS was authorized as part of a DCI "Countering Denial and Deception" program responsible to an entity known as the Foreign Denial and Deception Committee (FDDC). Since the intelligence community's reorganization, the DCI has been replaced by the Director of National Intelligence headed by John Negroponte and his deputy, former NSA director Gen. Michael Hayden.

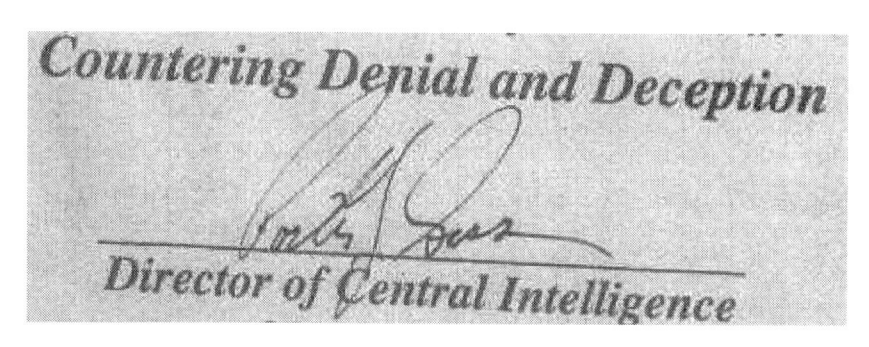

NSA FIRSTFRUITS

Countering Denial and Deception

Director of Central Intelligence

Washington, DC

NIC

FIRSTFRUITS was a database that contained both the articles and the transcripts of telephone and other communications of particular Washington journalists known to report on sensitive U.S. intelligence activities, particularly those involving NSA. According to NSA sources, the targeted journalists included author James Bamford, the *New York Times'* James Risen, the *Washington Post's* Vernon Loeb, the *New Yorker's* Seymour Hersh, the *Washington Times'* Bill Gertz, UPI's John C. K. Daly, and this editor [Wayne Madsen], who has written about NSA for *The Village Voice, CAQ, Intelligence Online*, and the Electronic Privacy Information Center (EPIC).

In addition, beginning in 2001 but before the 9/11 attacks, NSA began to target anyone in the U.S. intelligence community who was deemed a "disgruntled employee." According to NSA sources, this surveillance was a violation of United States Signals Intelligence Directive (USSID) 18 and the Foreign Intelligence Surveillance Act of 1978. The surveillance of U.S. intelligence personnel by other intelligence personnel in the United States and abroad was conducted without any warrants from the Foreign Intelligence Surveillance Court. The targeted U.S. intelligence agency personnel included those who made contact with members of the media, including the journalists targeted by FIRSTFRUITS, as well as members of Congress, Inspectors General, and other oversight agencies. Those discovered to have spoken to journalists and oversight personnel were subjected to sudden clearance revocation and termination as "security risks."

In 2001, the Foreign Intelligence Surveillance Court rejected a number of FISA wiretap applications from Michael Resnick, the FBI supervisor in charge of counter-terrorism surveillance. The court said that some 75 warrant requests from the FBI were erroneous and that the FBI, under Louis Freeh and Robert Mueller, had misled the court and misused the FISA law on dozens of occasions. In a May 17, 2002, opinion, the presiding FISA Judge, Royce C. Lamberth (a Texan appointed by Ronald Reagan), barred Resnick from ever appearing before the court again. The ruling, released by Lamberth's successor, Judge Colleen Kollar-Kotelley, stated in extremely strong terms, "In virtually every instance, the government's misstatements and omissions in FISA applications and violations of the Court's orders involved information sharing and unauthorized disseminations to criminal investigators and prosecutors . . . How these misrepresentations occurred remains unexplained to the court."

After the Justice Department appealed the FISC decision, the FISA Review court met for the first time in its history. The three-member review court, composed of Ralph Guy of the 6th U.S. Circuit Court of Appeals, Edward Leavy of the 9th Circuit, and Laurence Silberman [of the Robb-Silberman Commission on 9/11 "intelligence failures"] of the D.C. Circuit, overturned the FISC decision on the Bush administration's wiretap requests.

Based on recent disclosures that the Bush administration has been using the NSA to conduct illegal surveillance of U.S. citizens, it is now becoming apparent what vexed the FISC to the point that it rejected, in an unprecedented manner, numerous wiretap requests and sanctioned Resnick.

December 30, 2005 -- More on FIRSTFRUITS

The organization partly involved in directing the National Security Agency program to collect intelligence on journalists -- FIRSTFRUITS -- is the Foreign Denial and Deception Committee (FDDC), a component of the National Intelligence Council. The last reported chairman of the inter-intelligence agency group was Dr. Larry Gershwin, the CIA's adviser on science and technology matters, a former national intelligence officer for strategic programs, and one of the primary promoters of the Iraqi disinformation con man and alcoholic who was code named "Curveball." Gershwin was also in charge of the biological weapons portfolio at the National Intelligence Council where he worked closely with John Bolton and the CIA's Alan Foley -- director of the CIA's Office of Weapons Intelligence, Nonproliferation, and Arms Control

(WINPAC) -- and Frederick Fleitz -- who Foley sent from WINPAC to work in Bolton's State Department office -- in helping to cook Iraqi WMD "intelligence" on behalf of Vice President Dick Cheney and Scooter Libby. In addition to surveilling journalists who were writing about operations at NSA, FIRSTFRUITS particularly targeted State Department and CIA insiders who were leaking information about the "cooking" of pre-war WMD intelligence to particular journalists, including those at the *New York Times*, *Washington Post*, and CBS 60 Minutes.

The vice chairman of the FDDC, James B. Bruce, wrote the following in a 2003 article in *Studies in Intelligence*, "This committee represents an interagency effort to understand how foreign adversaries learn about, then try to defeat, our secret intelligence collection activities." In a speech to the Institute of World Politics, Bruce, a CIA veteran, was also quoted as saying, "We've got to do whatever it takes -- if it takes sending SWAT teams into journalists' homes -- to stop these leaks." He also urged, "stiff new penalties to crack down on leaks, including prosecutions of journalists that publish classified information." The FDDC appears to be a follow-on to the old Director of Central Intelligence's Unauthorized Disclosure Analysis Center (UDAC).

Meanwhile, WMR's disclosures about FIRSTFRUITS have set off a crisis in the intelligence community and in various media outlets. Journalists who have contacted WMR since the revelation of the FIRSTFRUITS story are fearful that their conversations and e-mail with various intelligence sources have been totally compromised and that they have been placed under surveillance that includes the use of physical tails. Intelligence sources who are current and former intelligence agency employees also report that they suspect their communications with journalists and other parties have been surveilled by technical means.

2006

<u>January 5, 2006 -- More details emerge on NSA spying on journalists and politicians.</u>

On January 3, 2006, NBC's Andrea Mitchell interviewed James Risen, one of the New York Times reporters who broke the story on NSA eavesdropping of U.S. citizens. WMR reported on May 10, 2005 that NSA had a special system that eavesdropped on journalists:

> May 10, 2005 WayneMadsenReport.com
>
> Spying on Unfriendly Journalists
>
> The inquisition side of NSA is the one that Hayden and his advisers do not want the public to see. In fact, NSA maintains a database that tracks unofficial and negative articles written about the agency. Code named FIRSTFRUITS, the database is operated by the Denial and Deception (D&D) unit within SID. High priority is given to articles written as a result of possible leaks from cleared personnel.
>
> According to those familiar with FIRSTFRUITS, Bill Gertz of *The Washington Times* features prominently in the database. Before Hayden's reign and during the Clinton administration, Gertz was often leaked classified documents by anti-Clinton intelligence officials in an attempt to demonstrate that collusion between the administration and China was hurting U.S. national security. NSA, perhaps legitimately, was concerned that China could actually benefit from such disclosures.
>
> In order that the database did not violate United States Signals Intelligence Directive (USSID) 18, which specifies that the names of "U.S. persons" are to be deleted through a process known as minimization, the names of subject journalists were blanked out. However, in a violation of USSID 18, certain high level users could unlock the database field through a super-user status and view the "phantom names" of the journalists in question. Some of the "source" information in FIRSTFRUITS was classified—an indication that some of the articles in the database were not obtained through open source means. In fact, NSA insiders report that the communications monitoring tasking system known as ECHELON is being used more frequently for purely political eavesdropping having nothing to do with national security or counter terrorism.
>
> In addition, outside agencies and a "second party," Great Britain's Government Communications Headquarters (GCHQ), are permitted to access the journalist database. FIRSTFRUITS was originally developed by the CIA but given to NSA to operate with CIA funding. The database soon grew to capacity, was converted from a Lotus Notes to an Oracle system, and NSA took over complete ownership of the system from the CIA.

> Tens of thousands of articles are found in FIRSTFRUITS and part of the upkeep of the system has been outsourced to outside contractors such as Booz Allen, which periodically hosts inter-agency Foreign Denial and Deception meetings within its Sensitive Compartmented Information Facility or "SCIF" in Tyson's Corner, Virginia. Currently, in addition to NSA and GCHQ, the National Geospatial-Intelligence Agency (NGA), the Defense Intelligence Agency (DIA), and National Reconnaissance Office (NRO) routinely access the database, which is, in essence, a classified and more powerful version of the commercial NEXIS news search database.
>
> In addition to Gertz, other journalists who feature prominently in the database include Seymour Hersh of *The New Yorker*; author and journalist James Bamford, James Risen of *The New York Times*, Vernon Loeb of *The Washington Post*, John C. K. Daly of UPI, and this journalist [Wayne Madsen].
>
> NSA abhors negative publicity. Anytime the agency is the subject of unwanted media attention, [NSA Director Michael] Hayden sends out an email known as an "All Agency." The memo reiterates NSA's long standing "neither confirm nor deny" policy regarding certain news reports:
>
> "NSA personnel must refrain from either confirming or denying any information concerning the agency or its activities which may appear in the public media. If you are asked about the activities of NSA, the best response is 'no comment.' You should the notify Q43 [Public Affairs] of the attempted inquiry. For the most part, public references to NSA are based upon educated guesses. The agency does not normally make a practice of issuing public statements about its activities."
>
> ---
>
> Note: Although FIRSTFRUITS, like other intelligence cover terms, are not supposed to have any connections with the systems or programs for which they provide cover, the term "first fruits" has an interesting history:
>
> "Speak unto the children of Israel, and say unto them, When ye be come into the land which I give unto you, and shall reap the harvest thereof, then ye shall bring a sheaf of the first fruits of your harvest unto the priest . . . " - Leviticus 23:9

The NBC transcript originally read:

"Mitchell: Do you have any information about reporters being swept up in this net?

Risen: No, I don't. It's not clear to me. That's one of the questions we'll have to look into the future. Were there abuses of this program or not? I don't know the answer to that

Mitchell: "You don't have any information, for instance, that a very prominent journalist, Christiane Amanpour, might have been eavesdropped upon?"

Risen: "No, no I hadn't heard that."

Inexplicably, NBC then deleted the last two paragraphs from its original transcript.

New information provided to WMR expands on our initial reports about the Bush administration using NSA to spy on politicians, including phone conversations between then-Secretary of State Colin Powell and New Mexico Governor Bill Richardson concerning diplomatic back channels to North Korea's UN ambassador. Informed sources also report that Arizona Republican Senator John McCain was also subject to NSA eavesdropping. Of particular interest to the White House was McCain's actual commitment to Bush during the 2004 presidential campaign, evidence his Indian Affairs Committee collected on GOP lobbyist Jack Abramoff's tribal casino activities, and details of McCain's medical condition. McCain is recovering from skin cancer. McCain has also been assured by senior GOP officials that in the event Dick Cheney steps down as Vice President, McCain would be rewarded for his past support for Bush with the Vice President's slot.

January 8, 2006 -- According to a report in today's Swiss newspaper *Sonntagsblick*, Swiss intelligence intercepted a November 10, 2005, fax from Cairo to the Egyptian embassy in London confirming the presence of secret CIA detention centers in Eastern Europe. The fax was intercepted by the Swiss military's Onyx satellite interception system, which has intercept ground stations in cantons Valais, Schaffhausen, and St. Gallen.

Swiss signals intelligence operations are handled by the Division Conduite de la Guerre Electronique (CGE), a part of the armed forces Groupe Renseignements (Intelligence Group's) Office Federal des Troupes de Transmissions (OFTT).

The Egyptian fax confirms that 23 Iraqi and Afghan nationals were transferred to the Mihail Kogalniceanu airbase near Constanta, Romania. The Egyptian fax also confirmed the presence of CIA detention centers in Kosovo, Bulgaria, Ukraine, and Macedonia. The Swiss signals intelligence intercept confirms WMR's November 11 and 28, 2005 reports about CIA prison facilities in all these locations. Swiss authorities claim they will open an investigation into the leak of the Secret Swiss intelligence report.

January 13, 2006 -- The name has been changed to protect the guilty.

The National Security Agency's (NSA) illegal database code-named FIRSTFRUITS, which contains transcripts of the communications of and articles written by U.S. journalists about NSA has undergone a name change. Inside sources report that because of the "compromise" of the system, the name of the database has been changed from FIRSTFRUITS. However, the database continues to be maintained under a new cover term.

January 25, 2006 -- Bush at NSA Headquarters in Fort Meade, Maryland today.

According to NSA sources, NSA personnel pre-selected to attend President Bush's speech today at the headquarters were told to applaud and show visual support for the president. NSA Security will be at the event in force to detect any rumblings from the gathered employees or other signs of displeasure with Bush.

February 4-5-6, 2006 -- Former NSA analyst Kenneth Ford was accepted into a fast track internship program at NSA in November 2002

A former White House Secret Service officer, Ford, a young African American with three college degrees, was what NSA wanted as a future senior executive at America's signals intelligence agency. That was until Ford's first internship assignment brought him face-to-face with what the Bush administration was cooking up for Iraq. After having transferred from NSA's Information Assurance X72 branch to start his internship in the Signals Intelligence Division (SID), Ford found himself assigned to the all-important "Iraqi shop," the branch responsible for analyzing communication intercepts of Iraqi military, civilian government, diplomatic, and commercial traffic for signs of weapons of mass destruction activity or proliferation.

In April 2003, Ford, a GS-9 who had been learning about the secretive world of signals intelligence through classroom and on-the-job training, was assigned the task of scouring the databases of intercepts, looking for anything that might indicate the presence of WMDs. The White House was clearly nervous about its earlier claims that Saddam Hussein possessed WMDs. By May 2003, with U.S. forces in Iraq, it was clear that there were no stockpiles of WMDs as had been claimed by President Bush, Vice President Cheney, and Defense Secretary Rumsfeld, among others in the administration. Ambassador Joseph Wilson visited Niger in February 2002 to investigate claims that Iraq had attempted to obtain yellowcake uranium in that country. Wilson discovered the claims were false. In March, Cheney, not content with Wilson's findings in his reports to the CIA and State Department, stated on Meet the Press that Saddam was "trying once again to produce nuclear weapons."

But those weapons were never found. The Bush administration's WMD claims, the original basis for invading Iraq, were discovered to have been without merit. However, Cheney and his staff, including indicted Chief of Staff Lewis "Scooter" Libby engaged in what the Vice President called a "work up" on Joe Wilson. That "work up" also saw Wilson's wife, a covert CIA officer who worked on WMD proliferation issues, outed by the White House along with her entire Brewster Jennings & Associates cover company network.

It was clear that the neo-cons conducted a "slash and burn" campaign against those in the intelligence community who did not agree with the contention that Iraq possessed WMDs. In May 2003, Ford was directed to draft an intelligence report on what Iraqi SIGINT revealed about WMDs. His report stated that while Iraqi intercepts that contained the words "diode oscillators" could have had a military use and, more remotely, could have been used along with detonators, there were many other non-military uses for such devices. Ford also spoke to an NSA expert on counter-proliferation about the Iraqi WMD claims. In fact, Ford was a key liaison between the Iraqi shop and the Counter-proliferation branch at NSA. NSA's counter-proliferation expert agreed that the oscillators mentioned in the Iraqi intercepts had many uses other than being components for nuclear weapons. Ford's report with his findings, along with his name as the original drafter, went up the chain of command, was reviewed by senior NSA staff, and ultimately found its way to the office of Vice President Cheney. It was at that point in time Ford became a target for an administration that was hell bent on purging every level of the U.S. intelligence community of anyone who in the least way showed any degree of independence from the Bush administration's party line.

Something strange occurred within the Iraqi shop in March 2003, the same month the U.S. launched its invasion of Iraq. There was a sudden influx of private contractor linguists into the branch. After he took over as NSA Director in 1999, Gen. Michael Hayden began the process of contracting out NSA support jobs to contractors but operational responsibilities were to have been maintained by career NSA civilians. However, in the case of the Iraqi shop, contractors with Arabic and Kurdish linguistic abilities arrived on the scene. NSA sources report that the contractors were to cook SIGINT analysis on Iraq in the same manner that other WMD intelligence on Iraq had been doctored, on Cheney's orders, by the CIA, Defense Intelligence Agency, and the National Geo-spatial-Intelligence Agency.

Without his knowledge, the Bush administration laid an insidious trap for Ford -- a trap that would end his hopes of a professional career at NSA and eventually land him into a court room facing trumped up charges of illegally removing two boxes of classified documents in broad daylight from a well guarded building within the NSA campus at Fort Meade, Maryland. The Florida informant, Tucker, reportedly "tipped" the FBI and NSA to the presence of classified documents in Ford's home. In fact, it was Tucker who brought one classified document into Ford's home, given to her by Thompson that was later used as an excuse for the FBI and NSA agents to enter Ford's home on January 11, 2004. Ford was detained in his home for seven hours, not permitted to drink any water, was denied bathroom privileges, witnessed his home being ransacked by FBI and NSA agents, and was then forced by Thompson to sign a confession without the presence of any other witness. Ford, fearful for his life, wrote a statement which was then supplemented by an additional statement written by Thompson. Later, the FBI claimed it seized two boxes of classified documents in Ford's home, even though no photos were taken of the boxes or other documents purported by the FBI and NSA agents to have been found in the house. For two days, Thompson waited in a car parked outside Ford's home to wait for the proper time for his informant Tucker to plant the one classified document that would begin the frame up. Sources report that Thompson has since been transferred by the FBI to Indiana.

Ford wrote in a letter to his attorney that during his seven hour ordeal with the FBI and NSA agents ransacking his home, "people were walking around my home and me as if I were 'a piece of crap.' The phone was ringing continuously and I was not allowed to answer it. Thoughts were going around my head of them shooting and killing me. They could always have said I resisted them. I was scared." For two of the seven hours, the agents were in Ford's home without a search warrant and there is evidence from phone records of Thompson's informant Tucker that the FBI entered Ford's home previously in a "sneak and peek" operation to place a wiretap on Ford's telephone.

The efforts to which the Bush administration went to frame Ford point to the importance the White House gave to making examples. A number of Justice Department, FBI, NSA, and private contractor personnel were tasked with setting up Ford, who never had so much as a speeding ticket. For someone with such a clean record, Ford had to be charged with something spectacular. The trouble began in earnest in November 2003 after Ford was approached by FBI confidential informant Tucker who misrepresented herself as a successful lawyer. Ford then received a threatening e-mail on November 25, which he dutifully reported to NSA Security only to be told not to worry about it. The email said that his security clearance should be "revoke."

According to sources close to the case, the agents and officials tasked by senior U.S. government officials to carry out the frame up of Ford were FBI Special Agents Michael Thompson and Frederic Marsh; NSA Security Counterintelligence Agent John McCaslin (who were all part of the group that planted a single classified document inside Ford's home); "Tonya Tucker," (aka Tonya Stewart) a Florida confidential informant with a long rap sheet, many aliases, and apparently previously known to Thompson in Florida; Kathleen "M," Ford's branch chief at the Iraqi shop who had custody of the classified materials Ford was later charged with taking home; officials of Northrop Grumman, an NSA contractor who agreed in December 2003 to hire Ford after an NSA-sponsored job fair, but who later were involved in the frame up by stating that Ford had "confessed" to them; Maryclaire Rourke, the Justice Department's Branch Chief for Counterintelligence, and David I. Salem, the Assistant U.S. Attorney for Maryland. Salem and Rourke worked together to keep the Ford case alive. McCaslin alleged that two training course materials containing PowerPoint slides from www.navigators.com were classified NSA documents. As part of Ford's internship program, he attended the course to get up to speed on Voice over IP (VOIP) technology. Part of the tasking for NSA's Iraqi shop was to listen in on Iraqi communications using the Internet-based technology.

Tucker, who had no visible means of support and who used a company ID badge from Bearing Point, was in touch with NSA long before she met Ford. Her phone records indicate several calls to NSA, identified in the phone records as the "Waterloo, Maryland" exchange. "Waterloo" is a cover term used by the phone companies for NSA. There were several calls to "Waterloo" numbers prior to and after Ford's arrest. On January 8, 2004, just prior to Ford's arrest, Tucker placed calls to phone number, 410 782 1000, registered to an unidentified customer in Elkridge, Maryland, in the vicinity of NSA headquarters. On January 9, Tucker placed seven calls to TASC, an intelligence agency contractor in Fairfax, Virginia. After Ford's arrest, on January 12, Tucker made several calls to the "Waterloo" (NSA) number, 410 854 6466, and additional calls were made to TASC in Herndon, Virginia. Up until January 31, 2004, Tucker continued to make calls to unidentified government phone numbers in Maryland. Tucker was pre-briefed to tell the FBI that Ford planned to sell classified documents to an unknown foreign diplomat at a pre-arranged meeting at Dulles Airport in Virginia.

Although Tucker had an extensive rap sheet, she appeared to have a close working relationship with a number of U.S. intelligence agencies and contractors. She also had three years of her seven-year Florida parole status waived so that she could travel to Washington, DC to sting Ford. Tucker had been convicted of grand theft, illegal possession of a credit card, petit theft, forgery, and credit card fraud.

Salem, a resident of Columbia, Maryland, a town that is a stone's throw from NSA, originally succeeded in having Federal Judge Alexander Williams removed from the Ford case. Williams was problematic for the Bush administration. As an African American, it was feared Williams would be sympathetic to Ford. Salem also threatened to bring espionage charges against Ford's private attorney who had been granted a Top Secret/Special Background Investigation clearance for the case. The defense attorney was pressured to withdraw from the case. When he refused, Salem took the low road of threatening him with indictment for a security breach. There were also questions concerning the relationship between Salem and Ford's original attorney, Federal Public Defender for the Southern Division of Maryland, John Chamble. Salem had originally attempted to add a charge of aiding and abetting against Ford. The charge was that Ford aided and abetted a known criminal, Tonya Tucker, in furtherance of her crimes. However, since Tucker was the chief government informant, Salem apparently decided that bringing up Tucker's role would expose the activities of FBI agent Thompson and other government functionaries in the affair. In addition, Thompson was coached by Salem to studiously avoid any mention of Ford's work in the Iraqi shop. Thompson only mentioned Ford's work in X72 and at the Technical Exploitation Center (TEC), the unit to which Ford was transferred after his internship in the Iraqi shop. However, Thompson was coached by Salem to studiously avoid any mention of the Iraqi shop, where the classified "evidence" used against Ford originated.

Salem's case further began to crumble after U.S. Magistrate Judge Jillyn Schultz, on August 25, 2004, ordered that Ford "be permitted to secure employment in a classified capacity" with the caveat that "employer must be notified of pending charges." After Ford began a job with Lockheed Martin, he explained the arrest on his security questionnaire and stated it was based on false charges. With the Bush administration seeking to ruin him financially and jail him, Ford did not last long at Lockheed. One of Salem's charges was that Ford "lied" on his Lockheed security questionnaire, a felony.

It took Salem two years to bring Ford to trial, a clear violation of the Speedy Trial Act. Apparently, when the neo-cons want to string out a prosecution phase because of the lack of a case, they are successful as they were in the case of Ford. However, when it serves their interest to delay a defense trial, as they have done in the case of Scooter Libby, they are successful as well. In any case, the neo-cons have compromised the U.S. justice system.

Salem also successfully had Ford's pre-trial officer removed from the case after she showed sympathy with Ford's plight. Salem's case appeared shattered on May 16, 2005 when U.S. Judge Peter Messitte dismissed the two Ford indictments of unauthorized possession of national defense information and making a false statement, without prejudice. The "without prejudice" caveat was key. Salem was able to bring back the indictment before the same judge just one week later. Salem's case was slipping away but the higher ups in the Bush administration expected results. And results they would get.

As a result of Salem's serious prosecutorial misconduct, during Ford's November 2005, witness after witness for the government perjured themselves without fear of recrimination. The jury was salted with at least one tainted member.

One member of the federal jury that convicted Ford on one count, each, of retaining classified material and lying on a security questionnaire for a Federal contractor turned out to have been a one-time program manager for Northrop Grumman, an NSA contractor. That fact should have disqualified him from the jury, however, it is clear that jury intimidation and tampering was also ordered up by the Bush administration.

Salem succeeded in getting his conviction of Ford last November. Ford faces sentencing on March 1 at the U.S. Courthouse in Greenbelt, Maryland and up to 15 years in prison. However, Salem and his associates must now face their own investigation, one that is focused on prosecutorial misconduct, perjury, and criminal conspiracy to violate the civil rights of a U.S. citizen. After the neo-cons seized control of the United States in 2001, what happened to Ford could happen to any U.S. citizen.

February 6, 2006 -- NSA Security, long an out-of-control entity, is now conducting a witch hunt at the agency.

Working with the FBI, NSA Security agents are ruthlessly questioning potential sources of the leak about Bush's illegal NSA wiretapping program. Director of National Intelligence John Negroponte and CIA Director Porter Goss have stated that they want journalists subpoenaed by a grand jury to testify about their sources. As far as this journalist is concerned, Messrs. Negroponte and Goss can take a long walk off a short pier.

March 3, 2006 -- NSA Security emulating East German Stasi in every respect.

NSA sources report that the agency's out-of-control security directorate, in its pursuit of "leakers," is now attempting to have the families of NSA personnel to inform on them. While it is illegal to compel someone to testify against their spouse, that is not a problem with NSA Security, which has been visiting the homes of NSA employees in an attempt to persuade the spouses of NSA employees to reveal information about leaks. The visits have been intimidating, according to those who were approached by the NSA Security personnel. In addition, WMR has also learned that the psychiatric abuse committed against NSA employees by NSA psychiatrists working in concert with NSA Security is now the subject of full-blown ethics investigations by the Maryland Psychiatric Society, the Maryland Board of Physicians, and Maryland Psychological Association. The investigation may result in the loss of state licenses for NSA psychiatrists and psychologists who have engaged in abusive practices.

According to congressional Democrats, in the event that the Democrats assume control of one or both houses of Congress next year, there will be investigations of the NSA Security Directorate that could result in referrals to the Justice Department for criminal indictments against NSA and contractor personnel who have engaged in illegal surveillance and other criminal acts.

March 30, 2006 -- US Judge Peter Messitte today sentenced former NSA "Iraqi shop" signals intelligence analyst Ken Ford Jr., to six years in prison and no fine as a result of his politically-motivated conviction for allegedly removing two boxes of classified materials from NSA during broad daylight without detection. In fact, the documents were planted in Ford's home in retaliation for his SIGINT report casting doubt on the White House contention that Iraq possessed weapons of mass destruction. That report, which contained Ford's name as preparer, eventually ended up on the desk of Vice President Dick Cheney. As a result, Ford became a target of the neo-con cell operating from within Cheney's office and the White House Iraq Group (WHIG), the same cabal that compromised Valerie Plame Wilson's covert identity and mission.

Ford was given six years on the first count of unauthorized removal of classified information and three years (to be served concurrently) for making a false statement on a government security clearance form for a classified job with Lockheed Martin filled out nine months after his arrest. In fact, Ford stated on the form that his arrest was wrongful but that was construed by Assistant US Attorney David Salem as a false statement.

Tomorrow, WMR will provide a more detailed report on this case and the prosecutorial misconduct and false statements made by Salem before Judge Messitte during today's sentencing hearing. Today was a dark day for the U.S. system of jurisprudence -- years after Jim Crow, the virtual "lynching" of innocent African Americans blatantly continues in a concerted effort by agenda-laden judges and crooked prosecutors with out-and-out political motives.

March 31, 2006 -- In yesterday's sentencing hearing for former NSA analyst Ken Ford, Federal Judge Peter Messitte mentioned the defense's contention that the classified NSA documents Ford was accused of removing from NSA had been planted in Ford's home. Messitte also stated, "no one knows how he [Ford] ended up with these documents." Messitte also referred to Florida resident Tonya Tucker [one of many aliases], the government's confidential informant who initiated the sting against Ford, as a "curious figure." Yet, even with such doubts about the case against Ford, Messitte sentenced Ford to six years in prison.

In fact, the prosecution engaged in gross and illegal misconduct for the duration of the trial and pre-trial. The prosecutor, Assistant US Attorney David Salem, relied on false affidavits, perjured testimony, and a tainted jury -- complete with a government jury plant who did not identify himself as a former employee of NSA contractor Northrop Grumman -- and coached witnesses to get his conviction against Ford, the only U.S. intelligence employee who has been jailed as a result of his expressed doubts about Iraqi weapons of mass destruction. Ford prepared a May 2003 NSA signals intelligence report, based on intercepts of Iraqi communications and interviews with NSA counter-proliferation specialists, that disproved the Bush administration's theory about Iraqi WMDs. That report eventually ended up in Vice President Dick Cheney's office. The same type of retaliatory "work up" used on Ambassador Joe Wilson and his covert CIA wife was launched against Ford. However, as a young GS-9 and African American, Ford was much more vulnerable to being set up in a criminal sting than the more savvy and experienced members of the US Intelligence Community.

When Ford's defense attorney, Spencer Hecht, argued that former CIA Director John Deutch and Clinton National Security Adviser Sandy Berger received very lenient sentences for the same crimes for which Ford was convicted, Salem defended their actions, stating, "they took the [classified] documents for the continuation of their work." Salem said that Deutch, who took home a classified CIA laptop computer and then connected it up to American On Line and reportedly surfed pornographic web sites and collected data transfer programs known as "cookies," remained as CIA director. He also said that Berger, who took classified documents from the National Archives, needed them for his testimony in Congress about the Millennium bombing plot. Salem also stated that Deutch and Berger continued to have security clearances when they took home classified documents. Deutch received a reprimand and Berger received a $10,000 fine and three years of probation. Contrary to what Salem said about Berger's clearance, Berger had a National Archives clearance, which is not the same as the multi-compartmented clearance he possessed as National Security Adviser. However, Salem argued that in Ford's case, his alleged removal of classified documents was the same as an individual transmitting them to a foreign power. He said, "anyone could have walked into Ford's kitchen and seen the documents."

Salem also perpetuated several other frauds upon the court during the sentencing hearing. He stated "there are no security procedures at NSA that would prevent an employee from removing documents." Salem said there was "no guard . . . no working camera" at the Technical Exploitation Center (TEC) building where Ford allegedly removed documents in broad daylight. Adding two arguments not brought up in the trial, Salem alleged that Ford took documents from NSA "on more than one occasion" and in response to the defense argument that the documents were planted, he stated, "the government may have additional evidence not reported to the court before." Salem also contended that Ford removed "thousands of pages of

Top Secret documents" from NSA. However, under questioning from Messitte, Salem downwardly re-estimated the number of Top Secret pages from "thousands" to well below a thousand, since many of the pages alleged to have been removed were unclassified, confidential, and secret.

Ford's attorney requested that Ford remain free from prison pending the appeal of the verdict. However, Messitte ordered a prison report date of May 15, 2006.

The Ford case ample evidence that the federal judiciary and Justice Department are as infested with neo-cons as the intelligence community, Pentagon, State Department, and White House. Ken Ford received a six year sentence one day after GOP lobbyist Jack Abramoff, someone who spied for South Africa in the 1980s, ripped off Native American tribes, engaged in bribery of members of Congress, illegally funneled charity proceeds to right-wing settlers on the West Bank of Palestine, and is under investigation for a gangland murder in Florida, received a five year and 10 month prison term.

Salem's perpetuation of fraud against the court came one day after his one-time counterpart in Detroit, former Assistant US Attorney Richard Convertino was indicted by a Federal grand jury for conspiracy, obstruction of justice, and making false statements. Convertino and State Department security officer Harry R. Smith III were indicted for their misconduct in four North African immigrants who were charged with being members of a "sleeper operational combat cell." The convictions of the North Africans was dismissed in 2004 as a result of Justice Department prosecutorial misconduct. Convertino contends he was acting on orders from Washington and is being unfairly targeted in a Bush administration reprisal.

Salem's court antics also followed news from the US Attorney's office in Philadelphia that it was investigating Transportation Security Administration attorney Carla J. Martin for illegally coaching witnesses in the Zacarias Moussaoui case in Alexandria, Virginia. US Judge Leonie Brinkema called Martin's witness coaching, "the most egregious violation of the court's rules on witnesses in all the years I've been on the bench."

All the misconduct elements present in the Convertino and Martin cases were practiced by Salem in his vendetta against Ford. If the US Attorney's office in Detroit can bring charges against Convertino and the US Attorney's office in Philadelphia can investigate Martin (the US Attorney's office in Alexandria was forced to recuse itself), then some US Attorney's office outside of Maryland would be acting well within legal bounds to investigate Salem for prosecutorial misconduct in a politically-charged and motivated case.

April 7, 2006 -- Class action lawsuit against AT&T in AT&T-NSA cooperation deal "big" according to NSA insiders.

In January, the Electronic Frontier Foundation (EFF) sued AT&T for secretly permitting NSA to conduct warrantless "dragnet surveillance" of domestic and international communications, including those of U.S. citizens. EFF's filings in the case include sworn affidavits from retired AT&T technician Mark Klein and former Federal Communications Commission (FCC) communications expert J. Scott Marcus and several internal AT&T technical documents. The Bush Justice Department weighed in on the case and objected to the technical documents being introduced as evidence, claiming they may be classified. The documents have been introduced and remain under court seal by the U.S. Court for the Northern District of California.

AT&T's history of cooperating with NSA is a long one. One of the AT&T technical documents may regard how AT&T cooperated by routing long line cables through NSA facilities for wiretapping purposes. In the case of NSA headquarters at Fort Meade, Bell Long Line cables from Washington, DC to New York were run into special NSA intercept centers where certain diplomatic lines, such as those between the Soviet, and later the Russian embassy in Washington and the Russian UN Mission and Consulate in New York were tapped, along with those of other "hostile intelligence" diplomatic missions. The system was code named "Occupier." However, recent revelation from NSA indicate that the tapping of cable and RF spectrum communications has expanded well past Occupier and similar intelligence and counter-intelligence communications targeting systems to include law-abiding American citizens and legal residents.

NSA source are emphatic that NSA's surveillance programs have broken a number of U.S. laws and that the Bush administration, itself, is in violation of the law.

As a historical note, the following was written by this editor about NSA's future surveillance plans in 1994:

Voice and data broke free from their copper wire coaxial restraints and are now being transmitted via satellites, microwave, and fiber optic links; through complex Integrated Services Digital Networks (ISDNs) and broadband transport mechanisms; controlled by corporations and other private institutions through Private Branch Exchanges (PBXs); and over cellular telecommunications grids. The Puzzle Palace and its friends at the FBI and other federal law enforcement agencies became afraid that technology was overrunning their ability to listen in on communications. And there were even newer, more sophisticated systems being developed that would make communications surveillance ten times more difficult -- satellite switching of communications (an orbiting version of the local telephone exchange building), personal communications services, and personal communications numbers. The last two offerings would permit an individual to be reached on his own telephone number practically anywhere in the world through a complex network comprising all or part of the new technologies but one which would primarily bounce signals off of low earth orbit satellites.

The plan to put the nation's telecommunications network under constant electronic surveillance could not be accomplished unless manufacturers of telecommunications equipment built their products with an eavesdropping capability. The promoters of digital surveillance thought this could be accomplished by "using a manufacturer's designed feature which would route identified targeted information to a specific switch where the court-ordered intercept can occur."

As for the burgeoning national data networks like Compuserve, Prodigy, and the biggest one of them all, INTERNET, the FBI and NSA tele-surveillance experts reasoned that on-line computer hosts, network servers, communications bridges, data routers, and inter-network gateways could be tapped by using pre-existing data monitoring capabilities provided by software tools known as Message Transfer Agents (MTAs) and Network Management Centers. These computer monitoring services could be re-programmed to route particular messages on an ad hoc basis to a government computer to conduct court-ordered surveillance of data communications.

INTERNET monitoring became more important for NSA as various groups that the Agency traditionally monitored: foreign political parties, secessionist movements, human rights organizations, environmental groups, trade unions, and religious sects began using the world-wide grid to communicate with their compatriots and with one another. Not only were these groups using sophisticated forms of encryption like PGP -- "Pretty Good Privacy (PGP)" -- but also anonymous remailers to hide their identities. Of special concern to NSA were reports that Iran's Shi'ite mullahs had been trained on using the INTERNET to communicate with people around the world from the Iranian religious center at Qom. NSA feared that INTERNET could potentially become an avenue for planning terrorist attacks.

NSA was forced to keep up with this newest form of communications for its various international targets. NSA began using its own connections to the INTERNET to perform network monitoring. Some INTERNET users have also reported the presence of "ghost hosts" on the network. Apparently, these computer systems serve no other purpose than to momentarily capture network traffic, copy it, and quickly relay the data packets without any significant degradation of performance.

During 1994, the Zapatista National Liberation Front, which was fighting Mexican troops over land rights in Mexico's southern state of Chiapas, began distributing electronic messages on the INTERNET. These messages provided news on the rebellion as well as calls for assistance from supporters around the world. In the past, such guerrilla groups used clandestine radio broadcasts to accomplish the same task. NSA's web of receivers were successful in not only intercepting the broadcasts for their intelligence value but also in conducting radio direction-finding to pinpoint the location of the broadcasts. NSA would not have this luxury with INTERNET. Through its tangled web of servers and anonymous re-mailers, the originators of such messages could hide in the nebula of cyberspace. NSA required much more control over the systems that comprised INTERNET. One division of NSA's Collection Group, K2 division -- Global Network Programs-- was dedicated to capturing intelligence from computer networks, especially INTERNET. Divided into five branches, two are specifically targeted against computer networks: K24 (end-to-end systems) and K25 (facsimile and data network systems).

NSA sources say that AT&T's participation in the Bush administration's domestic communications surveillance is at the heart of the illegality of the program.

April 20, 2006 -- Today, Director of National Intelligence John Negroponte is delivering a speech at the National Press Club in which he will pat himself on the back for the great job his bureaucracy of 1500 is doing to streamline intelligence to those who need it. However, a senior U.S. intelligence professional scoffs at Negroponte's so-called "accomplishments." The official sent along the diagram below that shows DNI as just another bloated, idle, and expanding bureaucracy. According to the official, some of Negroponte's and his deputy Gen. Michael Hayden's "accomplishments" include:

1. Parametric data linking signals intelligence (SIGINT) and electronic intelligence (ELINT) to overhead imagery intelligence (IMINT) is virtually non-existent.

2. SIGINT and ELINT databases have no tools to ensure the data is usable for field activities and "war fighters."

3. Analysts concentrate on SIGINT message texts and not on the frequencies and other parametric data. This has caused a number of "friendly fire" incidents in Iraq and Afghanistan and the failure to adequately recognize threat frequencies from the cordless and cellular phones used to detonate improvised explosive devices (IEDs) in Iraq.

4. It now takes one year to get updated technical data to field military units from the National Security Agency (NSA) and the National Air & Space Intelligence Center (NASIC) at Wright-Patterson Air Force Base.

5. The management at NSA's Weapons and Space Data Services branch is largely incompetent -- some of the databases they rely on are 35 years old. For example, they contain data on the armed forces of the USSR, Czechoslovakia, East Germany, Yugoslavia, South Yemen, and Rhodesia -- nations that no longer exist.

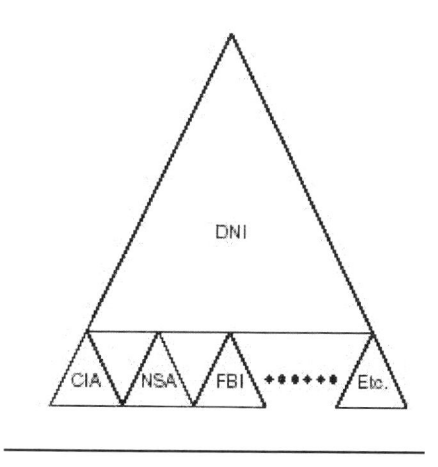

May 7, 2006 -- WMR reported extensively on Michael Hayden's management, scandal, and morale problems at the National Security Agency (NSA).

The Bush administration, always anxious to reward misconduct and mismanagement, now wants Hayden to bring his baggage to a decimated Central Intelligence Agency (CIA). Based on Hayden's past at the NSA, Langley should stand by for psychiatric abuse, more Gestapo-like tactics from imported security personnel from Fort Meade, contractor fraud, FBI "sting" set ups like that which befell NSA Iraqi shop SIGINT analyst Ken Ford, Jr. -- the author of a SIGINT report that stated reports of Iraqi WMDs were not backed up by intercepts of Iraqi communications -- and a general disregard for the law. There will also be harassment by Hayden of retired and former CIA officers who continue to speak out. This was a hallmark of Hayden's tenure at NSA where he subjected former NSA officers and journalists to whom they spoke to special surveillance from an intelligence database code-named FIRSTFRUITS.

May 11, 2006 -- In the wake of today's *USA Today* report that the National Security Agency has secretly collected phone call records on tens of millions of Americans from AT&T, Verizon, and Bell South, WMR can report that the Senate Armed Services Committee will soon hold a classified hearing in the Sensitive Compartmented Information (SCIF) hearing room in the Hart Office Building on the Special Access Programs (SAPs) under which these illegal domestic surveillance programs were conducted by NSA and the Department of Defense. George W. Bush's selection as the next CIA Director, Gen. Michael Hayden, was NSA Director at the time the illegal surveillance programs were launched.

May 24, 2006 -- Note from Fort Meade to Langley [in reference to Michael Hayden becoming CIA director] -- from an Intel Community colleague: "From NSA to the CIA, be very afraid. Prepare to be assimilated by the dark side." Signed, "The Unknown SIGINTer."

June 27, 2006 -- Republican Rep. Peter King (NY), the chairman of the House of Representatives Homeland Security Committee, has called for the U.S. Attorney General to prosecute *The New York Times* under the Espionage Act for revealing the existence of a secret program by the Bush administration to spy on international financial transactions involving the Belgium-based Society for Worldwide Interbank Financial Telecommunication (SWIFT), an international clearinghouse consortium of 7800 banks in over 204 countries that electronically wires trillions of dollars between banks on a daily basis. King told Chris Matthews yesterday on MS-NBC, "the *New York Times* is putting its own arrogant elitist left wing agenda before the interests of the American people, and I'm calling on the Attorney General to begin a criminal investigation and prosecution of the *New York Times* — its reporters, the editors who worked on this, and the publisher."

However, WMR has learned that the monitoring of SWIFT by the National Security Agency (NSA), via links with the Financial Crimes Enforcement Network (FINCEN), a Treasury Department financial monitoring activity located in Tyson's Corner, Virginia, and CIA financial monitoring systems connected to SWIFT mainframe gateways in La Hulpe, Belgium; Culpeper, Virginia; and Zouterwoude, Netherlands, is nothing new and predates 9-11 by almost two decades. The Bush administration has expanded the program to monitor transactions involving smaller monetary transfers.

In fact, during the 1980s and 90s, the NSA and CIA collected intelligence on financial transactions between the United States and Ireland and Northern Ireland involving Irish terrorist groups supported by Peter King. The group Irish Northern Aid (NORAID) funneled money to the Irish Republican Army (IRA) that was used to buy weapons used to blow up civilians and members of the British government, military, and police. King was an active supporter of NORAID, a tax-exempt front for the IRA. Martin Galvin, King's friend and former NORAID chief, rejected the Northern Ireland Good Friday agreement and supports the agenda of the terrorist "Real IRA."

During the 1980s, NSA's British counterpart, the Government Communications Headquarters (GCHQ), intercepted a number of King's phone calls from the United States and from within Britain, in which his political and financial support for the IRA was discussed. GCHQ relied on Canada's Communications Security Establishment (CSE) to monitor King's domestic phone calls in New York and Long Island since U.S. law, including the Foreign Intelligence Surveillance Act (FISA), prohibited the surveillance of King by NSA assets. King's financial and political support for the IRA coincided with the terrorist group's alliances with Palestinian, Lebanese, Latin American, Basque, Corsican, German, and Breton terrorist groups and the Libyan government of Muammar el Qaddafi. NSA signals intelligence (SIGINT) intercepts demonstrate that Libya and Lebanese terrorist groups targeted Americans in terrorist attacks during the 1980s, while King supported their Irish compatriots with money and weapons.

If Mr. King wants the *New York Times* prosecuted for espionage, he should be prepared to be prosecuted for aiding and abetting acts of terrorism against American citizens and the citizens of America's allies.

July 28, 2006 -- National Security Agency (NSA) whistleblower Russell Tice subpoenaed to testify. Release from the National Security Whistleblowers Coalition:

Government Begins its Witch Hunt Targeting Whistleblowers

On Wednesday, July 26, Russell Tice, former National Security Agency (NSA) intelligence analyst and a member of National Security Whistleblowers Coalition (NSWBC), was approached outside his home by two FBI agents who served him with a subpoena to testify in front of a federal grand jury. NSWBC has obtained a copy of the subpoena issued for Mr. Tice's testimony and is releasing it to the public for the first time. The subpoena directs Mr. Tice to appear before the jury on August 2, 2006 at 1:00 p.m. in the Eastern District of Virginia. Mr. Tice "will be asked to testify and answer questions concerning possible violations of federal criminal law."

In response to the subpoena, Mr. Tice issued the following statement: "This latest action by the government is designed only for one purpose: to ensure that people who witness criminal action being committed by the government are intimidated into remaining silent." He continued: "To this date I have pursued all the appropriate channels to report unlawful and unconstitutional acts conducted [by the government] while I served as an intelligence officer with the NSA and DIA. It was with my oath as a US intelligence officer to protect and preserve the U.S. Constitution weighing heavy on my mind that I reported acts that I know to be unlawful and unconstitutional. The freedom of the American people cannot be protected when our constitutional liberties are ignored and our nation has decayed into a police state."

On December 22, 2005, the National Security Whistleblowers Coalition made public a request by Tice to report to Congress probable unlawful and unconstitutional acts by the government while he was an intelligence officer with NSA and DIA. In a press release, NSWBC urged the congress to hold hearings and let Mr. Tice testify. Mr. Tice, a responsible veteran intelligence officer, tried to use the so-called appropriate channels, including the United States Congress, to responsibly and lawfully disclose government wrongdoing.

"What we are seeing here is a government desperate to cover up its criminal and unconstitutional conduct. They now are going beyond the usual retaliation against whistleblowers who courageously come forward to report cases of government fraud, waste, abuse, and in some cases such as this one, criminal actions. Their old tactics of intimidation, gag orders, and firing, have not stopped an unprecedented number of whistleblowers from coming forward and doing the right thing. Desperate to prevent the public's right to know, they now are getting engaged in a witch hunt targeting these patriotic truth tellers." stated Sibel Edmonds, the Director of National Security Whistleblowers Coalition.

In addition, the timing of the subpoena appears to be more than a little suspect. On July 25, 2006, Judge Matthew Kennelly upheld the government's assertion of the state secrets privilege in Terkel v. AT&T. The crucial issue in the case was whether or not the government's program of surveillance had been publicly acknowledged, and Kennelly wrote "the focus should be on information that bears persuasive indication of reliability." If there were reliable public reports of the program then the fact of the program's existence could not be a state secret. Kennelly found that there were no reliable sources of public information about the contested program's existence sufficient to thwart the government's need for secrecy. In other words, the existence of the program had not been conclusively established, and the government therefore had a right to prevent probing into the matter. This stops a case that represented a serious threat to the Bush administration.

Professor William Weaver, NSWBC Senior Advisor, stated: "Russ Tice is the only publicly identified NSA employee connected to the *New York Times* in its December 2005 story publicizing warrantless Bush-ordered surveillance. Tice is also publicly perceived as someone who could authoritatively establish the existence of the program at issue in Terkel; Tice could remedy the defect in the plaintiff's case cited by Kennelly that allowed the government's assertion of the state secrets privilege to be successful. Later, on the same day Kennelly's opinion was filed, the Department of Justice sent out Tice's subpoena. The date on the subpoena is July 20th, before Kennelly's decision was filed, but the issue in the Terkel case was so pregnant that it would be easy for the government to anticipate the ruling and only issue the subpoena to Tice if necessary. It has now become necessary, and the government seems to be moving to put pressure on Tice not to reveal information that would confirm the electronic surveillance program at issue in Terkel by threatening him with investigation and possible indictment."

****

Ed. note: The venue of the grand jury that has subpoenaed Tice, the Eastern District of Virginia in Alexandria, is noteworthy. It indicates that Tice may merely be a witness and not a target in the investigation. NSA and DIA, where Tice worked, are in Maryland and the District of Columbia, respectively. Any case involving those agencies would be normally handled by the District Courts for Southern Maryland and the District of Columbia, respectively. However, when Porter Goss was CIA director, he stated he wanted to prosecute journalists who published what he considered classified information. The CIA is headquartered in Virginia and the US District Court for Eastern Virginia is considered a "rocket docket" for CIA legal matters.

It should also be noted that Tice was a witness for the defense in the Bush administration prosecution of former NSA "Iraqi shop" signals intelligence analyst Kenneth W. Ford, who was convicted in a joint FBI-NSA set-up operation for removing classified documents in broad daylight and under heavy security from an NSA facility to his home. That case was tainted by David Salem, a federal prosecutor with close links to neo-con operatives in the Bush administration. Ford authored an NSA signals intelligence report that called into question the presence of weapons of mass destruction in Iraq. That report ended up on the desk of Vice President Dick Cheney where it earned him the wrath of Cheney, Scooter Libby, and other neo-cons who were part of the White House Iraq Group (WHIG). Ford was sentenced to six years at the Federal Penitentiary in Lewisburg, Pennsylvania. The WHIG was the same group that targeted CIA non-official cover officer Valerie Plame Wilson and her husband, Ambassador Joseph Wilson.

Former NSA Director Gen. Michael Hayden, who oversaw the harassment of NSA employees during his tenure at Fort Meade, Maryland, is now CIA Director at headquarters in Langley,

Virginia. Any CIA-initiated national security investigations would normally end up in the hands of the US District Court for Eastern Virginia, especially if the target(s) is(are) residents of the court's eastern Virginia jurisdiction. Tice is a resident of Maryland.

U.S. Department of Justice

Criminal Division

Washington, D.C. 20530

July 25, 2006

Mr. Russell Tice

Re: 06-4 / 06GJ376 / 06-2206

Dear Mr. Tice:

A subpoena has been issued for your appearance before a federal grand jury in the Eastern District of Virginia. It is the policy of the Department of Justice to provide the following basic information to ALL persons concerning their appearance before the grand jury. The subpoena directs you to appear on August 2, 2006 at 1:00 p.m.

The grand jury consists of sixteen to twenty-three persons who inquire into federal crimes which may have been committed in this judicial District. Only authorized persons may be present in the grand jury room while evidence is being presented. This means that the only persons who may be present while testimony is being given are members of the grand jury, attorneys for the government, the witness under examination, an interpreter when needed, and for the purpose of taking the evidence, a stenographer or operator of a recording device.

You will be asked to testify and answer questions concerning possible violations of federal criminal law. The public, through the grand jury, has a right to every person's evidence except where the privilege against self-incrimination would apply.

In testifying before the grand jury, you will be expected to answer all questions asked of you, except to the extent that truthful answers to questions would tend to incriminate you. An untruthful answer to any question may be the basis for prosecuting the untruthful witness for perjury. Anything that you say may be used against you by the grand jury or may later be used against you in court. You may consult your attorney before testifying; you may have your attorney outside of the grand jury room; and if you desire, you will be afforded a reasonable opportunity to step outside the grand jury room to consult with your attorney before answering any question.

If you have any questions concerning the general subject matter of your appearance, your travel arrangements, or other questions, you may contact the undersigned at (202) 353-9350.

Very truly yours,

Steven A. Tyrrell

Enclosures

<u>Aug. 1, 2006 – Israeli firm to provide eavesdropping services for Malta's security services.</u>

The Malta Communications Authority has awarded the New York City-based and Israeli-owned company Verint (formerly Comverse Infosys) a contract to install a communications intercept system for the Malta security services. Comverse Infosys was the subject of Drug Enforcement

Administration and Department of Justice concerns about its access to sensitive communications prior to 9/11.

Israel's interest in Malta is noteworthy. According to former FBI Turkish-Azeri-Farsi translator Sibel Edmonds, Malta, in addition to Cyprus and Dubai, are banking linchpins in a global drugs and weapons smuggling network involving Turkish criminal syndicates. In the case of A Q Khan's nuclear smuggling network, these Turkish networks intermeshed with similar smuggling networks based in Israel.

Aug. 30, 2006 -- Post card from Denmark

Danish Army Major Frank Grevil was once the only chemical weapons expert in the Danish Intelligence Service (Forsvarets Efterretningstjeneste or "FE"). That was until he realized the neo-con Danish government -- that governs with the support of the extreme right-wing People's Party (which maintains National Socialist beliefs) -- was making false claims about the chemical weapons threat from Saddam Hussein's Iraq and Grevil decided to do something about it.

After Denmark became the only Nordic country to blindly follow the United States into war in Iraq, Grevil understood he possessed the "smoking gun" intelligence proving that the claims made by Prime Minister Anders Fogh Rasmussen and his government -- that Iraq could deliver a chemical weapons punch to Denmark -- were patently false.

It was 2004 and Grevil was witnessing Danish troops increasingly becoming mired down in George Bush's and Tony Blair's Iraq fiasco. After comparing Rasmussen's public comments on the "threat" of Saddam's using chemical-laden missiles or aircraft to launch an attack on Denmark, Grevil spoke to a couple of Danish journalists about certain FE threat assessment intelligence reports that proved Rasmussen's claims to be spurious. One of the reports stated that there was "no reliable information on operational weapons of mass destruction" in Iraq.

As early as 2002, Grevil had been preparing threat assessments on Iraq that contradicted the Iraq WMD claims of the government. After Denmark helped the U.S. and Britain in the March 2003 invasion and occupation of Iraq and the Parliament began raising questions about intelligence in early 2004, only to be stonewalled by the government, did Grevil feel it was time to inform the public through the media about the Danish government's "Big Lie." In February 2004, Grevil provided copies of the threat assessments to the journalists that proved the government had lied about the Iraqi WMD threat. In March 2004, the Copenhagen police charged Grevil with disclosing classified information and in November 2004, the City Court of Copenhagen found Grevil guilty and sentenced him to 6 months in prison (the prosecutor wanted a one year sentence). Grevil appealed the verdict. The High Court for Eastern Denmark later upheld the conviction but reduced the sentence to four months.

Before taking the bold step of delivering the actual threat assessments to the media, Grevil urged the journalists -- Michael Bjerre and Jesper Larsen of *Berlingske Tidende* to ask the government to disclose the reports -- which were identified by their subjects and titles. After the government stonewalled the journalists, Grevil printed out the relevant reports from the FE's Intranet and handed them to the journalists (both of whom and their editor, Niels Lunde, are now facing criminal prosecution for publishing extracts of the reports).

The revelations in the assessments showed the Danish government to be lying about the so-called chemical weapons delivery threat from Saddam. For such claims to have had any merit, Saddam would have had to possess an intercontinental ballistic missile delivery system (he did not) or an air force capable of evading the air defense systems of some 8 or 9 countries to deliver the chemical attack on Denmark. That means Saddam would have had to had sophisticated planes that could have flown unimpeded across Turkey, Ukraine, Romania, Serbia, Austria, Hungary, Poland, and Germany to deliver a chemical knock out attack on Denmark. Again, the government's claim was false on its face.

The Danish government reacted to the media revelations in typical neo-con fashion. After Grevil was identified as the source of the leak, the neo-con media began to publicly humiliate him and speculated that he had accomplices in the FE. Grevil conceded that far from being some sort of left-winger, he actually supported some of the principles of the governing Conservative Party. But for the blood thirsty neo-cons, that was of no consolation or concern. They wanted to make an example of someone and Grevil was their man.

In Grevil's first trial, various classified documents were submitted as evidence by the defense, the very same documents that, on appeal, the prosecution tried to suppress. The entire judicial process represented an illegal alliance between the supposed independent judiciary, the FE, and the Rasmussen government. The FE and its Danish government interlocutors also barred from testifying on behalf of Grevil, Pentagon Papers whistleblower Daniel Ellsberg and former International Atomic Energy Agency director general and chief Iraq WMD inspector Hans Blix. The six person jury that found Grevil guilty in a 5 to 1 vote was composed of three professional jurors and three lay people. One of the lay jurors was later discovered to have been a one-time activist for the Center Democrat Party, which later merged with the governing Conservative Party.

Since his conviction was upheld on appeal in September 2005, Grevil has yet to hear from the government about reporting to prison. The government is perhaps stung by the fact that Grevil and his actions are supported by some 65 percent of the Danish public, far greater than Rasmussen's public support. The Danish government has also been stung by the fact that Grevil's case has caught the attention of the European Court of Human Rights in Strasbourg and his case may go before that court. A ruling against the Danish government by Strasbourg would mean Grevil's reinstatement, back salary, and other compensation.

In addition to the merits involving Grevil's decision to call the government on its phony reasons for sending Danish troops to die in Iraq, is the fact that the government violated the Danish Public Security Act, which was enacted in an effort to discourage the over-classification of government information with the intent of withholding important information, including intelligence information, from the public. The documents revealed by Grevil to the media, while proving the Danish government was lying about the Iraqi WMD "threat," came nowhere close to disclosing sensitive sources or operations, as alleged by the FE and the prosecutors.

The Public Safety Act states that it is the content and context of classified information, not the classification stamp or stamps, which should determine the sensitivity of the information. If the information is in the public interest what is revealed cannot be used in a prosecution.

The neo-con reaction to the Grevil case was a mirror image of what occurred with other national security whistleblowers in the United States and Britain. After some embarrassing intelligence disclosures were made by CIA, National Security Agency, Defense Intelligence Agency, Britain's Government Communications Headquarters (GCHQ), and MI-6, draconian purges of Iraq war naysayers were conducted across the board. The same occurred in the FE. There is reason to believe that the FE also purged from its ranks or demoted its solitary experts on nuclear weapons proliferation, biological weapons, and missiles. The Rasmussen government and FE were determined to make an example of Grevil as a warning to other intelligence analysts that the same fate would confront them if they spoke out. Based on the fear that came over the agency after the Grevil indictment, the government's plan was extremely effective.

After never adjusting to the realities of the post-Cold War era, the FE is still organized as a NATO Baltic front line intelligence service geared up for the defense of the Baltic Straits from military action from a non-existent German Democratic Republic and USSR, as well as a non-existent Warsaw Pact Poland. The FE's signals intelligence (SIGINT) capabilities (for example, from its SIGINT station at Aflandshage near Copenhagen) are targeted against commercial satellite communications traffic. The FE's SIGINT unit has little or no capability to target Middle East communications. The FE's small budget has resulted on its over-reliance on hugely sanitized and overly-analyzed and edited intelligence from the CIA. The FE continues to emphasize outmoded language skill sets -- Russian, German, and Polish -- while paying scant attention to the more critical Arabic, Farsi, Urdu, Tamil, Turkish, and Kurdish.

There have been suggestions from within the FE for it to build its own ship-based SIGINT platforms that would independently collect intelligence from the Persian Gulf, Arabian Sea, and other hot spots involving Danish interests. However, the Danish government is content with its very junior status to the Americans and the FE's chief, Rear Admiral Jørn Olesen (who is an office admiral, not a seagoing one) appears satisfied to periodically visit CIA Headquarters in Langley, Virginia and lunch with the CIA Station Chief at the U.S. embassy in Copenhagen where he is regaled with small talk and niceties.

The relationship between Rasmussen and Bush is similar to that between Olesen and his CIA counterparts. Some Danish intelligence professionals are alarmed at the close personal relationship between the American President and the Danish Prime Minister. It is assumed that the Bush administration has promised Rasmussen some future international position, such as Secretary of NATO or the UN in return for his sycophantic embrace of Bush and his policies.

As with Bush, Rasmussen also demonstrates as obsessive compulsive disorder. For example, he is known at luncheons and dinners to meticulously wipe off individual grapes and other fruits before eating them, a ritual that is very noticeable to others present. On a visit to Bush's Crawford Ranch in Texas, Rasmussen and Bush avidly went bicycling together. The "gay" rumors about Rasmussen are not merely confined to the gossip tabloids and general public. Rasmussen's "slant" is also discussed among the intelligence community, always on guard against possible blackmail scenarios involving senior government officials.

The Grevil case in Denmark is alarmingly similar to other national security whistleblower cases in the U.S., Britain, and Australia, complete with tainted evidence, political show trials, public humiliation at the hands of the neo-con media (in Denmark, this came from the same media elements that inflamed Muslims by publishing unflattering cartoons of the Prophet Mohammed), withholding of critical evidence, and an overall disregard for the rule of law).

Neo-cons like Bush, Blair, and Rasmussen, rather than believing their future years out of office will feature corporate board rooms and lucrative speaking gigs, may want to think otherwise -- that is if powerful former and current members of the intelligence community and military have their way. A number of intelligence professionals are now looking at both the Nuremberg War Crimes documents and the documents released by the West German government in 1953 on the secret deliberations by the German high command's and German Abwehr military intelligence's Project Valkyrie to depose Adolf Hitler in a coup at his Wolfschanze lair in 1944 and put other pro-Hitler Nazis on trial by German special tribunals. Both sets of documents are being examined in an effort to establish legal and moral baselines for bringing insane war criminals to justice. Such intelligence interest in Nuremberg and Valkyrie would indicate that Bush, Blair, Rasmussen, Australia's John Howard, Dick Cheney, Donald Rumsfeld, and other leading neo-cons may have more than lucrative corporate board memberships and speaking circuits to worry about after they leave office. A courtroom and prison cell in The Hague may await them all.

2007

April 17, 2007 -- Our sources inform us that a possible fire today has knocked out classified communications services at the US State Department's Communications Annex facility (State Communications Annex - SA26 - in Beltsville, Maryland), just outside of Washington, DC. Also affected by the outage is the joint National Security Agency-Central Intelligence Agency Special Collection Service (SCS) (F6) ("CSSG") located in a building off Springfield Road and located adjacent to SA-26, which is located at 8101 Odell Road. The SCS relies on the State Department backbone secure satellite communications for its links to covert listening posts and devices around the world. Agencies affected by the communications outage are the State Department, NSA, CIA, and Department of Defense. The State Department has been forced to use its backup facility. a CIA facility located at Brandy Station in northern Virginia.

Last October, a 6-alarm fire broke out on the roof of Nathan Hale Hall on NSA's Fort Meade, Maryland complex. Among other units, the building housed the 902nd Military Intelligence Unit, which maintains the Threat and Local Observation Notice database used to surveill threats to Army bases and personnel. "Threats" included peace and veterans groups.

April 30, 2007 -- A tale of two trials: influence peddling, judge shopping, and dirty prosecutors

On May 2, US Federal Judge Peter Messitte will again take up the case of Ken Ford's request for access to government documents, including trial transcripts, in order to facilitate his appeal for conviction of possessing classified National Security Agency documents at his Waldorf, Maryland home. The government, through US Attorney for Southern Maryland Rod J. Rosenstein and the original prosecuting attorney, Assistant US Attorney for Southern Maryland David Salem, is arguing that release of the transcripts contain classified information and, therefore, must be withheld under the provisions of the Classified Information Procedures Act.

Ford was set up in a clumsy Justice Department, FBI, and NSA Security Division operation to punish him for his May 2003 signals intelligence (SIGINT) analysis report that concluded, based on intercepts of Iraqi communications, there was no truth to the Bush administration's claim that there were weapons of mass destruction in Iraq. Ford's report, with his name and that of his supervisor on it, ended up on Vice President Dick Cheney's desk. From that time on, Ford was a marked man for the neo-con cabal operating within the White House, Justice Department, Pentagon, and US Intelligence Community senior staff.

The Bush administration, using an FBI confidential informant with documented ties to two intelligence contractors, TASC and Bearing Point, planted a classified document in Ford's home after she had struck up a relationship with the NSA analyst and former uniformed Secret Service officer who guarded President Bill Clinton. Ford was convicted in December 2005 of possessing classified information and making a false statement to a government agent. In March 2006, Ford was sentenced to six years in prison. Messitte refused to allow Ford to remain free pending an appeal of his conviction.

Just as the case with other U.S. Attorneys around the country who were "loyal Bushies" and kept their jobs while a number of other U.S. Attorneys were fired for political reason, the US Attorney's office for Southern Maryland is rife with political malfeasance, especially in the Federal Public Defender's Office. The Ford case was highlighted by judge shopping, suborning perjury from witnesses, jury tampering, witness badgering, questionable fraternization between the chief prosecutor and the public defender, and using the Classified Information Procedures Act (CIPA) to withhold evidence from the defense.

Compare the Ford case to the case of the two former American Israel Public Affairs Committee (AIPAC) officials, Steve Rosen and Keith Weissman, charged with illegally receiving classified information from convicted former Pentagon intelligence official Larry Franklin. Unlike the Ford case, the Rosen-Weissman case involved the passing of classified CIA information to a foreign intelligence agency – Israel's Mossad. Last month, US Federal Judge for Eastern Virginia T. S. Ellis ruled against prosecutors who also wanted to invoke the CIPA provisions to withhold classified information from the defense team representing Rosen and Weissman, both of whom are charged with violating the 1917 Espionage Act. The Rosen-Weissman lawyers are viewed as trying to "graymail" the prosecution by forcing a delay in the trial or withdrawal of charges by forcing the disclosure of classified information.

The Rosen-Weismann team are arguing that the government seeks to try their clients based on "secret evidence" and the Coalition for Jewish Concerns (AMCHA) is arguing that by perpetuating the "myth" that that a powerful lobby of those who are loyal to Israel first and America second controls the reins of government, the prosecutors in the AIPAC case are emulating the prosecutors of French Jewish Army officer Alfred Dreyfus who was convicted of treason based on secret evidence. In reality, Ken Ford is the actual new Alfred Dreyfus. Dreyfus was targeted because he was Jewish, Ford was partly targeted because he was a rising African American intelligence professional in a world that is largely composed of conservative white males.

It will be interesting to see whether Judge Messitte follows the precedent set by Judge Ellis in the AIPAC case. If Messitte rules for the government and agrees to keep the transcripts from the Ford trial secret and refuses to allow Ford's release from prison to prepare his appeal, then prosecutors Rosenstein and Salem, with their close links to groups aligned with AIPAC and like-minded organizations, can be accused of the very cabalism, a perception that AMCHA called a "myth" in its arguments against the use of secret evidence in the Rosen-Weissman case in Virginia.

May 4-6, 2007 -- On Wednesday, US federal Judge Peter Messitte decided not to break with the precedent set by US Judge T. S. Ellis in the American Israel Public Affairs Committee (AIPAC) Espionage Act case and ruled that federal prosecutors must make sanitized court transcripts from the trial of former NSA analyst Ken Ford, Jr. available to Ford's defense attorney. The Ford defense argued that the transcripts are necessary for Ford's appeal of his conviction for allegedly possessing classified materials at his Waldorf, Maryland home. Ford was the target of an FBI/NSA set up by a vindictive White House unhappy that his SIGINT analysis report on Saddam Hussein's government's communications failed to reveal the presence of weapons of mass destruction in Iraq. Messitte gave the CIA two weeks to redact classified portions of the transcripts and make them available to Ford's defense attorney. Assistant US Attorney David Salem, a key player in the set up of Ford, said that classified portions of the transcript would never be made available to Ford's defense attorney.

In the AIPAC espionage case, Judge Ellis ruled against prosecutors who wanted to invoke the Classified Information Procedures Act (CIPA) to keep classified information from the defense team for former AIPAC officials Steven Rosen and Keith Weissman. The Ford prosecutors tried the same CIPA gambit but faced a similar decision from the bench. However, the prosecutors appear determined to redact as much transcript information as possible in order to negatively impact Ford's appeal.

May 18-20, 2007 -- WMR's first series of articles, upon our inception in 2005, covered the misuse by the Bush administration, particularly Vice President Dick Cheney and State Department Arms Control Assistant Secretary John Bolton, of the National Security Agency (NSA) to conduct illegal domestic eavesdropping, particularly against Secretary of State Colin Powell, New Mexico Governor Bill Richardson, and Democratic members of the Senate Foreign Relations Committee, including ranking member Joe Biden. WMR reported that NSA's then-Director, General Michael Hayden, authorized domestic eavesdropping under the cover of NSA "training exercises," permitted under United States Signals Intelligence Directive 18 but illegal under the Foreign Intelligence Surveillance Act (FISA) if transcripts of the intercepts were maintained and not destroyed. We reported that the transcripts were sent to Bolton and Cheney.

Recent revelations by former Deputy Attorney General James Comey that in 2004 he, then-Attorney General John Ashcroft, and FBI Director Robert Mueller refused to authorize the White House's plans for NSA domestic eavesdropping are further indications that our well-placed NSA sources witnessed wholesale violation of FISA and internal NSA regulations prohibiting warrantless domestic wiretapping. Then-White House Counsel Alberto Gonzales and Chief of Staff Andrew Card attempted to have Ashcroft, who was barely conscious and recovering from surgery in George Washington University Hospital, authorize the illegal eavesdropping. Ashcroft refused the White House pressure as did Comey.

June 18, 2007 -- NSA officials deride U.S. Constitution.

Our National Security Agency (NSA) sources report that at a recent conference at the Fort Meade signals intelligence agency, several speakers commented that the U.S. Constitution is standing in the way of NSA "doing its job." The comments by NSA officials on the heels of the Senate and House Judiciary Committees threatening to subpoena Justice Department documents on NSA's domestic electronic surveillance program is noteworthy.

Under the tutelage of Generals Michael Hayden and Keith Alexander and as a result of pressure from the Bush White House, NSA has whittled away the regulations designed to prevent unwarranted eavesdropping on American citizens. Those regulations, which implemented the Foreign Intelligence Surveillance Act within NSA, were enshrined in United States Signals Intelligence Directive (USSID 18). Many veteran NSAers, who were schooled to studiously follow USSID 18 provisions, have been purged under the Hayden-Alexander tenure of NSA.

June 25, 2007 -- U.S. intelligence remains in Uzbekistan

Although the government of Uzbekistan expelled U.S. military forces from the Karshi-Khanabad airbase, also known as "K2," in 2005, WMR has learned that a U.S. intelligence presence, approved by the Uzbek government, remains covertly within the strategic energy-rich nation that borders on Afghanistan.

U.S. intelligence assets include special signals intelligence units of the National Security Agency (NSA), which have also reportedly been sent to Tajikistan and Kyrgyzstan to employ "close in" eavesdropping systems against mostly Islamist targets in the region.

In the past, the 205th Military Intelligence Battalion, headquartered at Fort Shafter, Hawaii, deployed SIGINT units to Uzbekistan in support of Operations NOBLE EAGLE and ENDURING FREEDOM.

June 29 - July 1, 2007 -- The CIA's "Family Jewels" file shows that things have not changed much since the 1960s and 70s

The "Family Jewels" documents recently released by the CIA show that not much has changed since the 1960s and 70s. American journalists were being physically surveilled and wiretapped, government employees thought to be leakers were also under surveillance and subjected to polygraphs, and U.S. domestic communications were being wiretapped as part of "testing."

However, the CIA also acquired from AT&T "routing slips" of "overseas telephone calls between persons in the US and persons overseas and telephone calls between two foreign points routed through US switchboards." The CIA domestic wiretapping operation lasted for approximately six months. In February 1972, AT&T "call slips" were obtained for three of four months for US-China telephone calls. Since interception was not involved, the operation was deemed legal.

Domestic microwave communications were intercepted as part of a "communications link loading study."

In September 1972, "hearability" tests of certain high frequency long-distance commercial circuits between the US and South America were conducted by the CIA. On January 30, 1973, the tests were aborted after it was determined they were illegal.

The CIA routinely provided support, including technical assistance, to metropolitan police departments in their efforts to surveill anti-Vietnam War groups. Liaison was established between the CIA and the Montgomery County, Maryland; Fairfax County, Virginia; Arlington County, Virginia; Washington, DC Metropolitan; Miami; New York City; New York State; Los Angeles; and San Francisco police departments and the San Mateo County Sheriff's Office. Through the CIA's contact with the Law Enforcement Assistance Administration (LEAA), it had contact with police departments, large and small, throughout the country.

The CIA maintained support and training links with foreign police agencies through the International Police Academy.

CIA support and training for foreign police officers was conducted through the International Police Academy through the US Agency for International Development (USAID).

The CIA was concerned about a Ramparts magazine article in January 1972 that stated that the CIA's Bob Kiley and Drex Godfrey were working to improve police organizations throughout the country. The information was contained in a December 21, 1971, memo written by DDP Thomas H. Karamessines.

CIA mail covers, in cooperation with the FBI, conducted mail surveillance, beginning in 1953, of incoming and outgoing Russian and "other selected" mail at Kennedy Airport in New York. The operation was code named SRPOINTER. It was part of an overall project called HTLINGUAL. A similar operation was conducted in San Francisco for China incoming and outgoing mail. The operation was code-named Project WESTPOINTER.

A CIA black bag breaking and entering was conducted at the home of a CIA employee, a defector, in Silver Spring, Maryland. The operation was REDFACE I.

The CIA participated in a domestic CIA and National Security Agency communications intelligence (COMINT) collection project, which they deemed as "illegal," which was code-named LONG SHAFT.

A May 30, 1973 CIA memo from CIA Inspector General William V. Broe points to a "high degree of resentment" among "many Agency employees" over being asked to participate in a domestic spying operation code-named MHCHAOS. Americans who traveled to the following locales were targeted by MHCHAOS: Paris, Stockholm, Brussels, Dar es Salaam, Conakry, Algiers, Mexico City, Santiago, Ottawa, and Hong Kong.

The program to reptriate Bay of Pigs Cuban Brigade prisoners from Cuba was code-named Project MOSES.

The CIA cooperated with the Bureau of Narcotics and Dangerous Drugs (BNDD), the forerunner of the Drug Enforcement Administration (DEA), in Project TWO-FOLD. The CIA also funded foreign travel on behalf of the Cabinet Committee on International Narcotics Control during the Nixon administration.

The CIA's collection of data on dangerous drugs from U.S. pharmaceutical and other firms was code-named Project OFTEN.

After a leak of information concerning the Strategic Arms Limitation Talks (SALT) to the New York Times' William Beecher, President Richard Nixon ordered an investigation of the leak and the CIA arranged with the State Department's Security chief G. Marvin Gentile to polygraph one Defense Department official and three from the Arms Control and Disarmament Agency. After Murrey Marder of the *Washington Post* reported that the FBI polygraphed the four government officials, FBI Director J. Edgar Hoover was incensed and said it was another government agency that was responsible. The documents released show that Hoover was right -- the CIA was the agency involved.

A July 10, 1970, account in the CIA documents refers to an inquiry from Rep. Richard Ichord, the chairman of the House Internal Security Committee about a leak concerning Cambodian leader Lon Nol's selling of rice to the "Communists" and his attempted deal making with Hanoi. General Lon Nol was put in charge of Cambodia by the CIA after a coup ousted Prince Sihanouk.

A December 10, 1970, account states that the Deputy Director for Central Intelligence found no links between the Black Panthers and the "fedayeen" as had been alleged by FBI director Hoover.

A July 8, 1971, account states that Nixon's assistant John Ehrlichman phoned the Deputy Director for Central Intelligence and informed him that the White House was appointing Howard Hunt as a security consultant.

A July 16, 1971, account states that the President's Foreign Intelligence Advisory Board (PFIAB) members, Franklin Lincoln, Dr. William Baker, and Frank Pace were conducting a damage assessment from the release of the Pentagon Papers.

An August 13, 1971, account states that information in the *New York Times'* Tad Szulc's article, "Soviet Move to Avert War Seen In Pact With India," contains "highly classified" CIA Clandestine Service material, an indication that a CIA mole was close to Soviet Foreign Minister Andrei Gromyko.

Another Szulc article was the subject of an August 16, 1971, account. Szulc's "Attempted pro-Soviet coup in Yemen is Reported," was also reported by the CIA to contain information from a classified TSCS Clandestine Service report.

An August 19, 1971, account states that White House staffer John Lehman wanted to know what four volumes of the secret Pentagon Papers had been turned over to Beacon Press for publication by Alaska Senator Mike Gravel.

A December 20, 1971, account states that Jack Anderson's Washington Post column, "Hussein: Help or I'll Go on a Ghazou," contains information from an Exclusive Distribution (EXDIS) message from King Hussein of Jordan to President Nixon.

A December 28, 1971, account complains about another Anderson column the previous day. In it, there was material from three SALT EXDIS memos, a State Department Limited Distribution (LIMDIS), and two CIA Clandestine Service TDCSs.

A January 12, 1972, account states that the White House's Lawrence Houston noted that Nixon had nominated Henry Peterson to become Assistant Attorney General for the Criminal Division. It is noted that Peterson was helpful in the "Itkin case." Herbert Itkin was a New York labor lawyer who had worked by Sen. Joseph McCarthy and CIA director Allen Dulles and soon became an FBI informer on the mob, while at the same time was a liaison between the CIA and the mob. Iktin made CIA payments to gangsters in Britain and the Caribbean in return for information and other "services."

A February 7, 1972, account indicates that Lawrence Housotn would take no action in the near future with respect to the Hans Tofte case. Hans Tofte was a CIA officer and a native of Denmark. The Chinese spekaing Tofte helped build the OSS's and CIA's clandestine network in Korea, China, and Japan. Tofte was a major CIA spy in Japan and Korea during the Korean war. Tofte also tried to send a one-man hit team into North Korea to assassinate North Korean leader Kim Il Sung. Tofte also had close links to Nationalist Chinese leader Chiang Kai shek and the CIA's airline chief Gen. Claire Chennault.

In 1966, a number of Secret CIA documents stamped SECRET were found in Tofte's closet. It turned out he had other classified documents scattered in other locations. Tofte had also been a CIA source for journalists and authors. Tofte was fired from the CIA on September 15, 1966 and he died under mysterious circumstances in 1987.

A November 3, 1972, account states that the CIA director flat out denied to the Washington Star News' David Kraslow that the CIA was asked to report on the Democratic Party and that led to the Watergate incident "and others."

A December 13, 1972, account reports that the *Washington Evening Star News'* Thomas B. Ross suspected the CIA was involved in the Watergate break-in because a passport bearing the name Edward Hamilton was fond in the possession of burglar Frank Sturgis.

A January 15, 1973, account stated that Watergate burglar Eugenio Martinez had been on the CIA payroll until June 17, 1972, and was used to report on "Cuban exile matters." June 17 was the day of the last Watergate burglary.

A February 7, 1973, account states that former CIA director Richard Helms was appearing that day before the Senate Foreign Relations Committee chaired by Senator J. William Fulbright on CIA police training, the ITT affair in Chile (which included CIA break-ins involving Howard Hunt's burglar team of the Chilean embassy in Washington), and the Watergate break-in. CIA director James Schlesinger states that he lobbied Senators Hubert Humphrey, Gale McGee, and Hugh Scott to make "appropriate public statements following Mr. Helms appearance."

The CIA stated in a barely-readable memo from Western Hemisphere chief Theodore Shackley that Jack Anderson's report that Howard Hunt broke into Chilean diplomatic missions in Washington and New York on behalf of ITT had "no foundation." The break-in of the Chilean Chancery in Washington occurred on May 13, 1972, around two weeks before the first Watergate burglary. Papers and radios were searched. Chile under President Salvador Allende had been negotiating terms over acquiring Chile's telecommunications neywork from ITT control. The CIA documents show that State's Security chief Marvin Gentile was in the loop on the Chilean embassy break-in. State's Security is responsible for security of foreign embassies along with the Executive Protection Servcie of the Secret Service.

A December 12, 1972, account notes an inquiry from the New York Times' David Burnham about a CIA information processing briefing for twelve members of the New York Police Department.

A January 18, 1973, account stated that Representative Lucien Nedzi briefed CIA officials on a conversation the congressman had with Seymour Hersh of the *New York Times* on what the reporter had discovered about domestic CIA activities. The briefing occurred during an agency briefing with Nedzi prior to the congressman's trip to Finland, Leningrad, Sofia, and Athens.

A March 6, 1973, account states that Hugh Sidey of *Time* was going to write that Howard Hunt was employed by a CIA proprietary company called Robert R. Mullen Company. The CIA admits the company provided "cover" for "one or two officers overseas."

The documents also show close liaison between the Bay of Pigs CIA operatives, those arrested for the 1972 break-in of the Democratic National Committee at the Watergate, and mobsters associated with the assassination of President John F. Kennedy, particularly Johnny Roselli. The documents show the involvement of Robert Maheu, Howard Hughes' chief adviser, and a New Yorker named Sam Gold, in establishing links between the CIA and the "Cuba crowd." One of the "Cuba crowd" was Juan Orta, a Cuban who had access to Castro and who was to poison him. After Orta got "cold feet," the mission went to Dr. Anthony Verona, a ringleader of the exiled Cuban "junta" in Florida.

In Spring 1972, Bay of Pigs operative E. Howard Hunt phoned the CIA's External Employment Assistance Branch's Frank O'Malley and asked him if any CIA lockpickers who were retiring or resigning from the agency might be available. The call was between Match and May 1972. In May 1972, Hunt and his colleagues were arrested for the break-in at the Watergate.

Hunt was also apparently acting as a recruiter for the Republican Party in 1971. A retired CIA officer living in Winter Haven, Florida said Hunt tried to recruit him as Security Officer for the GOP and that "money was not a problem." The ex-CIA agent was asked to provide a "positive and counteraudio program" for the Republican Party.

Hunt and ex-CIA agent James McCord's recruiting efforts are documented in the report, including an attempt to hire an ex-CIA employee from Halifax Security Company of Chicago prior to the Watergate break-in.

A June 20, 1972, CIA account states that Watergate burglar Bernard L. Barker was hired by the CIA in 1960 and terminated in 1966. There is also an acknowledgment that Hunt and McCord were CIA employees.

A May 23, 1972, CIA memo concerned a report by CBS News' Dan Rather on Watergate that contained information from a classified report. The report indicated that CIA employees had leaked classified information to Rather.

Another May 23, 1972, CIA memo concerned beacons furnished to U.S. ambassadors in the event they were kidnapped.

A June 26, 1972, account says that the CIA director concurred with the FBI's Freedom of Information Act release to Bernard Fensterwald of three photos acquired of Lee Harvey Oswald in Mexico and which were previously furnished to the Warren Commission. The Oswald photos are actually those of an Oswald imposter, said to have been a CIA mercenary who worked in the Congo in the early 1960s.

A January 22, 1973, account of Howard Hunt's previous night's appearance on TV was noted by General Vernon Walters. The CIA Executive Director was concerned about Hunt's statement that he felt he was no longer bound by his CIA secrecy agreement.

A May 23, 1973, memo states that a CIA Deputy Director for Plans (DDP) official in charge of narcotics matters knew Watergate burglar leader G. Gordon Liddy and was "probably involved with Hunt." The DDP officer was also linked to the CIA's Lou Conein of the White House.

Conein surfaces in a June 1, 1973 "Eyes Only" memo on controversial expenditures of CIA funds. It says that "when Lou Conein received his summons to report to the Joint General Staff Headquarters on 1 November 1963 a large amount of cash went with him.' Written by the CIA's IG Walter Elder, the memo informs Colby, "My impression is that the accounting for this and its use has never been very frank or complete." Conein's transfer to the Pentagon was only three weeks before President Kennedy's assassination in Dallas and the day before President Ngo Dinh Diem's assassination in Saigon.

The same memo states that McCone was not satisfied with the use of Agency funds for the improvement of the economic viability of West Berlin and an investment program in Mali.

The memo also reveals that in the Bay of Pigs invasion a number of members of the Alabama Air National Guard officers lost their lives and there was surprise at the CIA that this received little attention.

The memo also questions McCone's use of a KC-135 in July 1964 to fly Aristotle Onassis and Maria Callas from Rome to Athens. McCone also is said to have pressured the publisher of "The Invisible Government" to change a few things. The publisher refused and Elder writes, "I doubt that this old saw will ever sing again." In retrospect, the CIA in the future would try and prevent the publishing of other books in their entirety or without substantial editorial changes.

In a May 23, 1973, memo to CIA employees, William Colby, on behalf of Director Schlesinger, requested all contacts between CIA employees and the following: H. R. Haldeman, John D. Ehrlichman, John Dean. Egil Krogh, David Young, E. Howard Hunt, G. Gordon Liddy, James W. McCord, Charles W. Colson, John J. Caulfield, Eugenio Rolando Martinez Careaga, Juan Rigoberto Ruiz Villegas, Bernard L. Barker, Virgilio Gonzales, and Frank Anthony Sturgis.

A May 8, 1973, memo to Schlesinger and Colby states that Sy Hersh stated to the CIA, "I have information that Cushman [then Deputy DCI General Robert Cushman] knew exactly what he was okaying when he gave approval to assist Hunt." The memo is called "Sy Hersh's provocative teaser for the day."

When columnist Jack Anderson caught wind of the assassination attempts against Castro and published the story in *Washington Merry-Go-Round*, Anderson was routinely targeted for CIA surveillance. Other journalists surveilled included Michael Getler of the Washington Post, and Seymour Hersh of the *New York Times*. The Anderson surveillance and that directed against his assistants Brit Hume, Leslie Whitten, and Joseph Spears, was code named CELOTEX II, The Getler surveillance was CELOTEX-I.

A June 1, 1973 CIA memo states that then-CIA director John McCone, on March 7, 1962, agreed to tap the phones of columnists Robert S. Allen and Paul Scott uner pressure from Attorney General Robert F. Kennedy because classified information was appearing in their columns.

The same memo states that Robert Kennedy and President Kennedy approved McCone injecting the CIA's Cord Meyer into the labor dispute between the AFl-CIO's George Meany and the United Auto Workers' Walter Reuther. Reuther, who was considerably to the left of Meany and was anti-Vietnam War and an ally of Martin Luther King, Jr., died in an airplane crash on May 9, 1970.

Surveillance of ex-CIA employee and whistleblower Victor Marchetti was code named BUTANE.

The CIA satellite surveillance of crop production and futures market estimates for "industrial exploitation." The program was called HILLTOP.

The National Reconnaissance Office (NRO) conducted satellite surveillance and analysis for "political leverage, industrial exploitation, and civil damage suits." The program was code-named RIVER BOAT.

Just as Bush, today, has effectively abrogated anti-political assassination Executive Order 12333, instituted as a result of CIA director William Colby's revelations about political assassinations in the 1960s, the CIA, then, oversaw assassination programs against a number of world leaders, including Fidel Castro of Cuba, Patrice Lumumba of Congo, and Rafael Trujillo of the Dominican Republic.

A CIA memo states, "In November 1962, Mr. [redacted] advised Mr. Lyman Kirkpatrick that he had, at one time, been directed by Mr. Richard Bissell to assume responsibility for a project involving the assassination of Patrice Lumumba, then, Premier, Republic of Congo. According to [redacted] poison was to have been the vehicle as he had been instructed to see Dr. Sidney Gottlieb in order to prepare the appropriate vehicle." Frank Carlucci was the CIA's number two man in Congo and he has often been linked to the Lumumba assassination.

The documents reveal the CIA's involvement in civilian departments and agencies of the government. For example, Commerce Secretary Peter Peterson's secretary is revealed to have been a CIA employee. The CIA also maintained joint projects with the Atomic Energy Commission, Treasury Department, Customs Bureau, Alcohol and Tobacco Tax Division of the Internal Revenue Service, Secret Service, Federal Aviation Agency, National Institute of Health, Arms Control and Disarmament Agency, Environmental Protection Agency, National Aeronautics and Space Administration, Department of Agriculture, Coast Guard, U.S. Army, Navy, and Air Force.

The CIA concluded that none of its U-2 reconnaissance aircraft were on the East Coast during the 1972 Democratic and Republican Conventions in Miami and the Watergate break-in.

The CIA was asked repeatedly by the Nixon administration for intelligence linking planned demonstrations at the 1972 Republican National Convention, which was first scheduled for San Diego and then switched to Miami and the Democratic National Convention in Miami to foreign intelligence agencies.

A February 23, 1972, CIA memo linked John Lennon to two anti-war groups involved in anti-war demonstrations at the GOP convention in San Diego: Project Yes and the Election Year Strategy Information Center (EYSIC). Lennon was shot by Mark David Chapman in New York on December 8. 1980. The CIA concluded there is "little new evidence of foreign plans or efforts to inspire, support, or take advantage of actions designed to disrupt or harass" any of the 1972 conventions. Three months before the GOP was to hold its convention in San Diego, it moved it to Miami after it was revealed that ITT lobbyist Dita Beard offered $400,000 in sponsorship money to the San Diego convention in return for the Nixon Justice Department dropping an anti-trust suit against the firm. The Democrats also held their convention in Miami.

A June 23, 1972, CIA report said that the agency's two stations in Miami, JMCOBRA and JMFALCON, would coordinate convention security with the US Secret Service. However, it indicated there was no intelligence suggesting Cuban intelligence disruption but did warn against possible problems from Latin American exiles (likely Cuban right-wing groups).

Another CIA program, said to have "sensitive domestic overtones" was the Deputy Directorate for Science and Technology Office of Research and Development's (DDS&T/ORD) "VIP Health and Behavior Prediction System." Another project conducted remote physiological measurements, remote cardiographs on "naive subjects."

Other CIA research and development funds were spent on Radar People Detector (with Aerospace Inc.) and an adhesive restraint, non-lethal incapacitation system for civilian crowd control and riot control.

Two CIA projects, "Restless Youth" and another dealing with "Black Radicalism in the Caribbean," dealt with radicalism among America's youth, particularly the anti-Vietnam Students for a Democratic Society (SDS), and America's young blacks. Interest in the subject was shown by President Lyndon Johnson, Walt Rostow, his national security adviser, and former Deputy Defense Secretary Cyrus Vance, and later, by Vice President Spiro Agnew, Nixon's national security adviser Henry Kissinger, Nixon counselor Patrick Moynihan, and White House staffer Lawrence Houston.

In June 1970, a CIA Office of Counterintelligence officer named Archer Bush was asked to write a memo on links between militant blacks in the US and the Caribbean, with a specific focus on Stokely Carmichael.

The CIA's Foreign Broadcast Information Service (FBIS) was tasked with monitoring foreign radio reports about statements and speeches by American POWs in Hanoi, Jane Fonda, and former

Attorney General Ramsey Clark. FBIS linguists were also loaned to other agencies, like the FBI, for domestic signals intelligence (SIGINT) analysis.

The CIA's National Photographic Interpretation Center (NPIC) was tasked in January 1972, with performing image enhancement on tapes of Jack Anderson's TV show. The purpose was to identify serial numbers on CIA documents in Anderson's possession.

One CIA memo dated May 8, 1973, indicates the CIA was particularly uncomfortable with the work of Dr. Sidney Gottlieb, the Technical Services Department chief who has been linked to poisoned assassination weapons and LSD experiments. In the memo to CIA director Schlesinger, Ben Evans states, "Carl Duckett [DDS&T chief] brought this up and said he is very uncomfortable with what Sid Gottlieb is reporting and thinks the Director would be ill-advised to say he is acquainted with this program. Duckett plans to scrub it down with Gottlieb but obviously cannot do it this afternoon."

> MEMORANDUM FOR: Mr. Colby
>
> Carl Duckett brought this up and said he is very uncomfortable with what Sid Gottlieb is reporting and thinks the Director would be ill-advised to say he is acquainted with this program. Duckett plans to scrub it down with Gottlieb but obviously cannot do it this afternoon.
>
> Ben Evans
> 8 May 1973
> (DATE)
>
> 00213

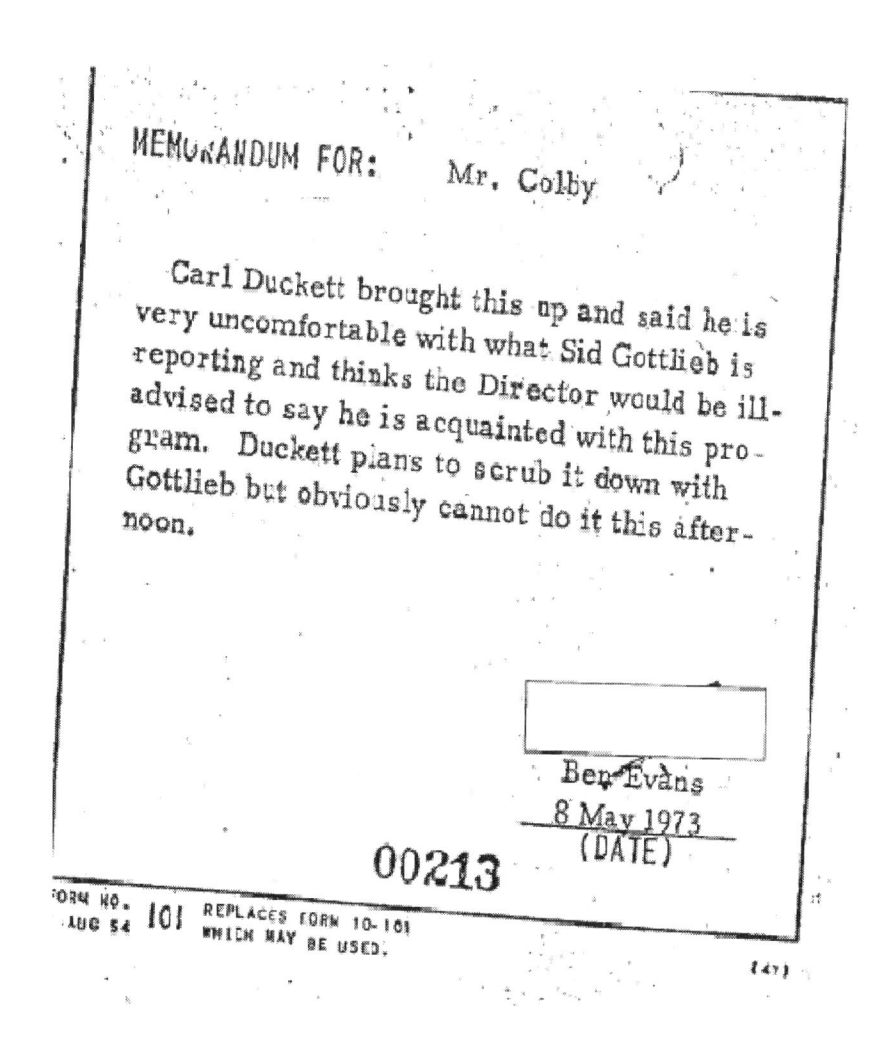

There was also considerable information contained in the Family Jewels concerning Robert Vesco, a fugitive who headed a CIA proprietary firm called Investors Overseas Service (IOS), a company with which President Nixon's brother Donald and his son, Donald, Jr., was involved.

Donald, Jr. also worked for Vesco's International Control and was based in the Bahamas. Nixon's other brother, Edward, was a director of Vesco's company. Vesco had also donated handsomely to Nixon's 1972 campaign, in cash. In 1971, then-White House Counsel John Dean requested information from the CIA regarding the Vesco project. Nixon's brother Donald worked for Marriott Corporation and was linked to Howard Hughes' top assistant Noah Dietrich. Donald offered Marriott's airline catering service to Aristotle Onassis' Olympic Airlines of Greece.

Vesco fled a Securities and Exchange Commission (SEC) investigation and asked for asylum in Cuba. He was later jailed by the Cubans for thirteen years.

A 1972 CIA memo indicates that a CIA program code-named BKHERALD had something to do with the Vesco project. It also stated that Vesico was President of International Control Corporation of Fairfield, New Jersey. The founder of IOS was Bernie Cornfeld, an international fugitive. Costa Rica's President Jose Figueres was also linked to IOS. Vesco had lived for a while in Costa Rica, Nicaragua, Antigua, and the Bahamas.

A May 7, 1973, CIA memo states that Schlesinger ordered the Deputy Director of Intelligence Dr. Edward Proctor to produce a crash project to produce a paper on Vesco. The memo also refers to a "high-level American intercession" on behalf of Vesco. Former director Helms was asked if this was relevant information and he said it was not.

A May 7, 1973, CIA memo states that T.G. Barreaux of the SEC contacted the CIA about the Vesco matter. After a meeting between Barreaux and the CIA, the CIA provided Barreaux with one piece of information about a banking transaction by Vesco.

A July 23, 1971 memo describes a phone call between the CIA's deputy director Gen. Bob Cushman and "someone in the White House" about Vesco. The person in the White House wants to know about a Ray Finkelstein, a Belgian-born Brazilian linked to two IOS principals: Gilbert Straub and Bernie Kornfeld [sic].

A May 8, 1973, CIA memo, states that John Dean contacted the CIA about Vesco and IOS, particularly embarrassing information relating to the fact that Nixon's nephew worked for IOS. The CIA passed six reports to Dean via his deputy Fred Fielding, the current White House Counsel for George W. Bush.

The same memo stated that Assistant Attorney General for Internal Security Robert Mardian had been deeply involved in the "split between Bill Sullivan and Mr. Hoover." Hoover accused Sullivan, his chief of FBI Intelligence, of passing files to Mardian without Hoover's permission and Hoover fired him. Hoover died on May 2, 1972, weeks before the Watergate break-in.

Nixon reinstated Sullivan to the FBI after Hoover's death and wanted to make him director but he ultimately went for L. Patrick Gray. Sullivan became a critic of the FBI's COINTELPRO program designed to infiltrate various political groups in the country. Sullivan died on

November 9, 1977 from an "accidental" gun shot while he was deer hunting in New Hampshire. Sullivan was due to provide the House Committee on Assassinations with information about the JFK and King assassinations.

A March 1972, CIA report describes the type of non-official cover firms the CIA used in the past. This definition correctly describes the Brewster Jennings & Associates weapons of mass destruction cover company exposed by the Bush-Cheney White House in 2003: "As a part of CIA operations abroad, arrangements are made with a number of U.S. entities to serve as the ostensible sponsor of individuals abroad. This can include business entities controlled by the CIA or proprietaries. While they may exist within the U.S., their purpose is to conduct or support operations abroad."

The French have a saying, "the more things change, they more they stay the same."

<u>July 27-29, 2007 -- Neocon intelligence cooking adversely affected one of the most classified programs at NSA</u>

In the lead up to and aftermath of the U.S. military attack on Iraq, the Bush administration tasked practically every classified intelligence system and element in the U.S. intelligence community to produce tainted and cooked intelligence to support the administration's false claims that Iraq possessed weapons of mass destruction and had dealings with "Al Qaeda."

WMR has learned that the intimidation of the U.S. intelligence community extended into one of the National Security Agency's most classified programs -- the remote viewing largely inherited from previous programs at the CIA and Defense Intelligence Agency (DIA).

The NSA picked up the remote viewing from the CIA's "Stargate" program after it was officially terminated after an American Institutes for Research study concluded the program should be abandoned in 1995.

Remote viewing uses specially-cleared psychics to locate WMDs, kidnapped persons, covert intelligence agents, and terrorists. The U.S. government's interest in remote viewing began with the CIA's Project Scanate in 1970.

The problem for the Bush political operatives assigned to the NSA is that the remote viewers, gifted with extrasensory abilities, knew the administration was lying about WMDs and other topics. The remote viewers, who conduct their special form of surveillance deep within the bowels of the NSA Fort Meade complex in a highly-secured room where there is always a two-person control on remote viewing sessions, began to suffer various forms of administrative sanctions by the NSA Security department.

October 29, 2007 -- SPECIAL REPORT -- United Flight 93 shot down by Air Force jets scrambled from Andrews

According to U.S. intelligence sources, the archives of the National Security Agency (NSA), available to cleared users via the INTELINK network, contains an archive of Flash precedence and Sensitive Compartmented Information (SCI) NSA intelligence messages known as "CRITICs."

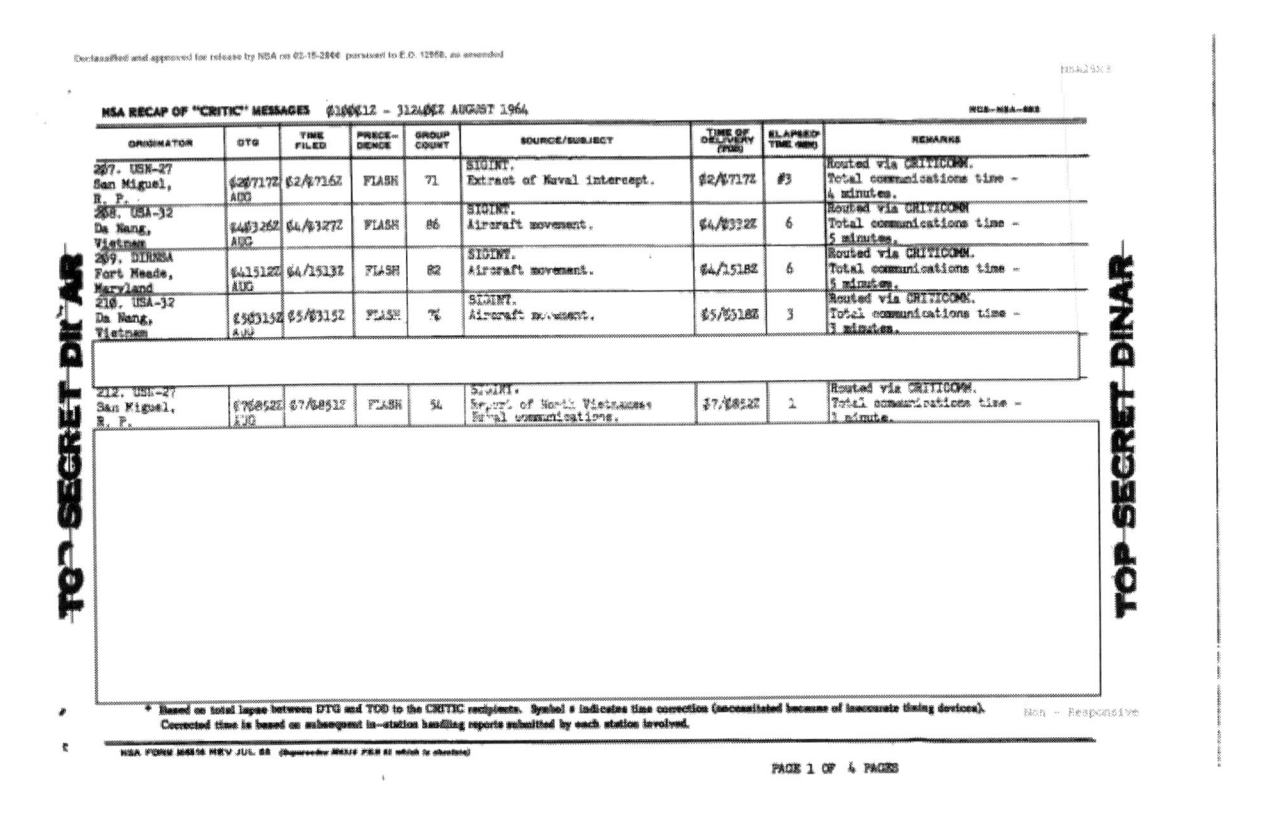

Above: Example of a CRITIC from 1964.

One such CRITIC from September 11, 2001, which includes a number of follow-on intelligence reports, concerns United Airlines flight 93, downed over Shanksville, Pennsylvania. However, the CRITIC is at odds with the official account of the fate of United 93, which is that passengers and crew attacked the hijackers and forced the plane to crash into the ground.

Then-Homeland Security Secretary Tom Ridge, a former Governor of Pennsylvania, added to the legend of the passengers and crew on United 93 in stating, "The passengers and crew did whatever they humanly could--boil water, phone the authorities, and ultimately rush the cockpit to foil the attack." A Hollywood movie, "United 93," put the legend ascribed to the flight on the big screen.

United 93, a Boeing 757 with 44 people on board, took off from Newark International Airport at 0841 Eastern Daylight Time on September 11.

The NSA CRITIC, according to sources who have seen it, is about five or six sentences, and paraphrasically states:

"Two F-16s scrambled from Andrews Air Force Base at [likely 1336 Zulu]. Civilian airline hijacked. Over state of Pennsylvania civilian airliner was "intercepted" at (Latitude and Longitude of intercept]."

Several follow-up CRITICs are appended to the first United 93-related CRITIC. One follow-up CRITIC mentioned a possible fifth hijacked plane flying south from Canada that was near the Canadian-U.S. border. Another CRITIC states the plane "intercepted" over Pennsylvania was "confirmed civilian."

A number of NSA analysts have seen the CRITICs in question and it is well-known within the signals intelligence (SIGINT) community that United 93 was shot down by two U.S. Air Force interceptors on the morning of September 11 over Pennsylvania.

Furthermore, according to U.S. Army and Navy sources, the debris of United 93 was brought by trucks to Andrews Air Force Base. One senior Navy officer on duty at Andrews during the morning of 9/11, told his wife and son (the son was also serving in the military), "We shot down the plane."

On December 2, 2005, WMR reported: "Cheney order to shoot down United Flight 93 confirmed again. Vice President Dick Cheney ordered two U.S. Air Force fighters to shoot down United flight 93 over Shanksville, Pennsylvania on September 11, 2001, according to an intelligence officer who was monitoring the flow of intelligence between the Pentagon and the White House that morning. After the target was identified as United flight 93, Cheney gave the order to engage the target and shoot it down. There have been previous reports that Cheney ordered the shoot down."

On May 27, 2005, WMR reported: ". . . the career NSA operational personnel may be getting squeezed not so much for policy and management differences but because of what they know about the lies of the Bush administration. In addition to the obvious lies about Iraqi WMDs, many personnel are well aware that what occurred on the morning of 9/11 was not exactly what was reported by the White House. For example, President Bush spoke of the heroic actions of the passengers and crew aboard United Flight 93 over rural Pennsylvania on the morning of 911. However, NSA personnel on duty at the NSOC that morning have a very different perspective. Before Flight 93 crashed in Pennsylvania, NSA operations personnel clearly heard on the intercom system monitoring military and civilian communications that the "fighters are engaged" with the doomed United aircraft. NSOC personnel were then quickly dismissed from the tactical area of the NSOC where the intercom system was located leaving only a few senior personnel in place. NSA personnel are well aware that Secretary of Defense Donald Rumsfeld did not 'misspeak' when, addressing U.S. troops in Baghdad during Christmas last year, said, 'the people who attacked the United States in New York, shot down the plane over Pennsylvania.' They believe the White House concocted the 'passengers-bring-down-plane' story for propaganda value.'"

The most recent revelations from the intelligence community bolster the case that the Bush administration created a series of myths, eagerly amplified by the corporate news media, regarding the events of 9/11.

October 31, 2007 -- NSA "Went Dark" on Caucasus Region Hours before Beslan attack

According to sources at the National Security Agency (NSA), hours before a group of Chechen separatists took 1200 children and adults hostage at a school in Beslan, in the Russian republic of North Ossetia-Alania, NSA intercepts of INMARSAT (International Maritime Satellite) and cell phone traffic in the region "went dark." Analysts at NSA and the Medina Regional SIGINT Operations Center (MRSOC) in San Antonio, Texas had been monitoring cell phone and INMARSAT phone traffic in Beslan but all communications intercepts of traffic suddenly ceased.

After seizing the school, the attackers, claimed to have been Chechen Islamist terrorists, confiscated all the cell phones of all the adults. They also insisted that all hostages speak Russian and not Ossetian or else they would be killed. After a three-day siege, Russian security forces stormed the school. 396 people, the majority of whom were child hostages, were killed in the siege. Seventy percent of the victims were Muslims. President Vladimir Putin's aide Aslambek Aslakhanov said the attackers were not Chechens because they only spoke Russian. Freed hostages said the terrorists spoke Russian with heavy foreign accents.

Russia linked some of the hostage takers to Islamist exiles in London, where the now much-adored former KGB agent Alexander Litvinenko was assisting Russian-Israeli mobster/tycoon Boris Berezovsky to help Chechen and other anti-Russian forces to help topple the Putin government in Moscow. Litvinenko later died from polonium poisoning, an act blamed on Putin but appears to have been a Russian-Israeli mafia hit designed to eliminate an uncomfortable witness to dubious and illegal activities by the Russian-Israeli mafia based in London, Tel Aviv, and New York.

A Russian parliamentary commission, headed by Alexander Torshin, later concluded that there was evidence of involvement of a "foreign intelligence agency" in the Beslan incident. The agency was not named.

The fact that the NSA's sophisticated surveillance platforms "went dark," in an unprecedented manner, on unencrypted South Ossetia and Caucasus regional communications shortly before the Beslan incident indicates that high-level parties knew of the attack in advance and did not want NSA intercepts to yield the identities of the terrorist planners and leaders.

Such an infiltration of NSA and targeted satellite and cellular communications systems in Russia could have only come from within the Bush administration, the telecommunications industry, and/or that of NSA's SIGINT partner, the United Kingdom's Government Communications Headquarters (GCHQ). The Beslan tragedy was not only used to detract from Putin's strongest suit, domestic security, but was used by the neocons to try to entice Russia into the American-British wars and planned "anti-terrorism" wars against Iraq, Iran, Syria, and other countries.

November 1, 2007 -- NSA linguists and analysts being assigned to Iraqi combat duty as "Army Augmentees

It is not just Foreign Service officer Jack Crotty and his fellow diplomats at the State Department who are being drafted for duty in Iraq. Yesterday, Crotty, speaking on behalf of his colleagues, told Foreign Service Director General Harry Thomas that they considered Condoleezza Rice's plan to draft Foreign Service Officers for Iraq duty a "potential death sentence."

But the Foreign Service is not alone in being angry about being drafted for dangerous duty in the Iraq quagmire Bush and his neocon pals have plunged the United States.

Linguists and analysts at the National Security Agency (NSA) are leaving in droves because many are receiving orders to combat assignments in Iraq to supplement battle-weary Army personnel. Many enlisted NSA personnel are deciding not to re-enlist in order to avoid Iraq duty.

The NSA military personnel, from Army, Air Force, Marine Corps, and Navy units are referred to as "Army augmentees." A Russian linguist was recently transferred to Army augmentee duty in Iraq from an Air Force activity at NSA. A Chinese linguist decided not to re-enlist rather than face duty in Iraq.

For example, members of the 12th Aerospace Expeditionary Force, which comprises Air Force NSA personnel, may get a deployment card to Iraq if the AEF "bucket number," in this case 12, comes up as the next AEF required to send personnel to Iraq. In that case, Air Force signals intelligence personnel face the risk of ending up in combat duty in Iraq.

WMR previously reported that Hebrew linguists at NSA are being targeted for replacement, and possible re-assignment to Iraq, if they do not show enough loyalty to Israel. It is also apparent that the identities of these linguists have been shared by top level U.S. intelligence officials with members of Israeli intelligence as some have been threatened abroad by foreign *agents provocateurs*.

November 2-4, 2007 -- NSA and Maryland: Unholy Alliance

WMR has previously reported on the close association between the National Security Agency (NSA) at Fort Meade, Maryland and agencies of the state of Maryland.

For example, NSA has recruited some of its psychologists from the Maryland correctional system. The NSA psychologists have been used to harass NSA employees and were used to concoct phony medical reasons for NSA employees to lose their security clearances, a step before employment termination.

NSA has been purging a number of its civilian and military employees for reasons that they have refused to go along with the cooking of intelligence and their anti-war stances.

NSA Office of Security has also established close links to Maryland state police, Anne Arundel County police, and Baltimore police political surveillance units that have targeted anti-war groups active in the Fort Meade area.

WMR has now learned that NSA's tentacles now extend into the Maryland Department of Labor where state employees have denied unemployment benefits to NSA employees who have been terminated. Maryland Department of Labor unemployment interviewers have been known to ask probing questions of ex-NSA personnel to try and get them to reveal classified information. The ruse is designed to place the ex-employees into positions where they could not only be denied unemployment benefits but be prosecuted for revealing classified information.

November 2-4, 2007 -- NSA signals intelligence yields clues about future nuclear war

According to National Security Agency (NSA) sources, the nuclear weapons "shop" at the agency has amassed signals intelligence (SIGINT) indicating that Russia possesses a greatly-refined electro-magnetic pulse (EMP) nuclear weapon designed to create an EMP shield that would prevent the use of aircraft, computers, most telecommunications devices, and even land vehicles in a targeted region.

The nuclear weapon is released in the atmosphere and temporarily disrupts computer and other electronic equipment for a pre-determined period of time. However, in the event of a conflict, both opposing sides would be similarly affected during the time the atmosphere is rendered unstable for advanced equipment.

The United States also possesses such weapons. In the event of a U.S. attack on Iran, it is anticipated that the United States would use such a weapon in the initial phase of a strike on Iran: a non-lethal "shock and awe" tactic. However, it is also likely that U.S. forces could also be targeted with a similar EMP shield nuclear weapon if Russia decides to respond militarily to an attack on Iran.

In effect, the next war might leave no smoking guns or mushroom clouds.

November 19, 2007 -- NSA not interested in WMD proliferation by Russian-Israeli-Ukrainian Mafia

While the *New York Times* is reporting that the security of Pakistan's nuclear weapons is a top U.S. intelligence priority, with the revelation that the Bush administration seriously considered sharing America's own nuclear security "permissive action links" (PALS) technology with Pakistan but decided against it, WMR has been told by knowledgeable U.S. intelligence sources that the trafficking of nuclear materials and components by individuals and entities that are part of the global Russian-Ukrainian-Israeli Mafia (RUIM) is not being monitored by the National Security Agency's (NSA) worldwide signals intelligence (SIGINT) system.

None of the NSA SIGINT "shops" -- centers that are tasked with different surveillance missions and regional targets -- are charged with listening in on the communications of potential threats to U.S. and allied national security posed by RUIM trafficking in WMD. These NSA "shops" include the Russian nuclear shop, the Israel shop, and those concentrating on the former Soviet "stans" in Central Asia. The SIGINT shops would normally be looking at the nuclear smuggling activities of emigré Russian and Ukrainian WMD smugglers.

For example, there were no CRITICs, top priority NSA intelligence messages, generated in the matter of Alexander Litvinenko and his polonium-210 poisoning in London. Litvinenko, who was linked to both Russian-Israeli exiled oligarch Boris Berezovsky and Chechen guerrillas allied with "Al Qaeda."

WMR previously reported that former CIA counter-proliferation agent Valerie Plame Wilson's covert network of Brewster Jennings & Associates non-official cover (NOC) agents, as well as sources and contacts, were rolled up by the neocons in the White House and State Department to protect Bush administration officials, including Vice President Dick Cheney, who have secret business dealings with members of the RUIM global network. The turning off of NSA's "ear" on the weapons of mass destruction smuggling activities of the RUIM is another indication of White House meddling in critical intelligence gathering functions.

WMR reported on June 1, 2005, that "although [NSA] contractors are required to have the same high level security clearances as government personnel at NSA, there are close connections between some NSA contractors and countries with hostile intelligence services." The primary country then in question was Israel.

December 4, 2007 -- Intelligence still being cooked by neocons

A new U.S. National Intelligence Estimate (NIE) has stated, contrary to corrupted and false intelligence emanating from neocon circles in Washington and Israel, Iran stopped its nuclear weapons program in 2003 and that the program has not resumed.

The NIE should put an end to neocon disinformation about Iran's rapid nuclear weapons acquisition program but the neocons and the Bush White House continue to rattle sabers at Iran.

On December 2, 2007, the Rupert Murdoch-owned *Times of London* engaged in further disinformation. The paper quoted Prof. Uzi Even, a nuclear scientist who helped start the Israeli nuclear weapons facility at Dimona, that the secretive Israeli strike on a facility in Syria in September destroyed a nuclear bomb plant being constructed with the help of the "DPRK." The reference "DPRK" is a formal diplomatic reference to North Korea.

A U.S. intelligence source, familiar with all signals intelligence (SIGINT) intercepts of the nuclear proliferation threat in the Middle East, stated that there is absolutely no intelligence that any precursor or primary nuclear weapons components were ever transported to Syria from North Korea, Iran, Russia, or any other source.

The National Security Agency (NSA) maintains a SIGINT center or "shop" devoted to monitoring nuclear weapons proliferation. SIGINT satellites, ground outstations, and mobile units did not detect any communications -- Arabic, Korean, Russian, Farsi, Turkish, or Hebrew -- on Syrian nuclear acquisition or activity up to the time of the Israeli (or U.S. or joint U.S./Israeli) attack on the site Syria claims was a desertification research center but may have been a conventional missile assembly plant with no nuclear connection.

December 31, 2007 - January 1, 2008 - No evidence of Pakistani or U.S. SIGINT intercepts of "Al Qaeda" in Pak tribal regions

WMR's intelligence sources are scoffing at the Pakistani Interior Ministry contention that it could prove that former Prime Minister Benazir Bhutto was assassinated on the orders of "Al Qaeda's" chief in South Waziristan, Baitullah Mehsud. The Interior Ministry claims that it recorded an "intercept" of Mehsud's communications in which Mehsud allegedly congratulated his followers for the attack on Bhutto in the heavily-garrisoned city of Rawalpindi.

Bhutto's political party and Mehsud both rejected the claims about the communications intercepts of Mehsud and said the Pervez Musharraf regime was behind the assassination of Bhutto.

U.S. National Security Agency (NSA) sources have told WMR that signals intelligence (SIGINT) intercepts of Al Qaeda and Taliban leaders are rare in Afghanistan, Pakistan, and elsewhere.

Not only is cell phone coverage spotty to non-existent in remote areas like Waziristan but ever since the 1996 NSA intercept of Chechen President Dzokhar Dudayev's satellite telephone call to Moscow, which was passed in to Russian security authorities who triangulated his position and killed him with an air-to-surface missile, Al Qaeda and Taliban leaders, including Osama Bin Laden, have refrained from using electronic communications. mindful of U.S. intelligence's capability to lock in on the locations of cell phone and sat phone signals.

This editor wrote about this in *Covert Action Quarterly* in 1997:

"During the evening of April 21, Dudayev went outside his headquarters, a small house near the village of Gekhi Chu, some 20 miles southwest of Grozny, the Russian occupied Chechen capital. At 8:00 p.m., he phoned [Duma Deputy Konstantin] Borovoi in Moscow to discuss [Boris] Yeltsin's latest olive branch. 'Soon, it could be very hot in Moscow,' he told Borovoi. "Do you live in the center?' In the center and even next to the Interior Ministry, Borovoi responded. 'You should probably move out for the time being,' Dudayev warned. Dudayev may have been telling Borovoi that a Chechen attack on the Interior Ministry was imminent. 'That's out of the question,' Dzhokar Mussayevich, Borovoi responded, using the familiar Russian term of address. Then Dudayev said, 'Russia must regret what it is doing.' Borovoi's line suddenly went dead. This time, Dudayev had stayed on the phone too long.

Just seconds before what were to be the Chechen's last words, a Russian Sukhoi Su-25 jet, armed with air-to-surface missiles, had received his coordinates. It locked on to Dudayev's phone signal and fired two laser-guided missiles. As one exploded just a few feet away, shrapnel pierced Dudayev's head. He died almost immediately in the arms of one of his bodyguards.

The Russians had previously tried some less advanced methods to kill Dudayev and failed. On one occasion, Dudayev had been given a knife with an electronic homing device embedded in the handle but it was discovered before Russian aircraft could lock in on the signal.

Suspicion centered on the US and the National Security Agency's Vortex, Orion, and Trumpet, the world's most sophisticated (SIGINT) spy satellites.

They were partially designed to intercept the mobile telephone systems used by the big brass in the Soviet and Warsaw Pact high commands. The NSA SIGINT birds were, therefore, extremely useful against the kind of telephone Dudayev had been given by his Turkish friends."

The familiar stock footage of Bin Laden coming out of an Afghan cave holding a satellite phone handset was made long before the Dudayev assassination by the Russians.

Not only did Bin Laden heed the lesson of Dudayev's death but so did Shamil Basayev, the Chechen guerrilla commander who was often linked to "Al Qaeda." Before his assassination in 2006 by Russian Federal Security Bureau agents in a remote car bombing attack, locating Basayev was hampered by his avoidance of using any telecommunications. NSA failed to record one intercept of Basayev while he was being hunted by Russian and American intelligence agencies.

However, Pakistani Inter Services Intelligence (ISI) agents in Afghanistan and the Pakistani tribal regions in the northwest of the country have not been so reticent in using telecommunications. According to WMR's source in NSA, U.S. SIGINT operators in Afghanistan and elsewhere have routinely intercepted communications of ISI agents dealing with the provision of arms and ammunition to Taliban and "Al Qaeda" forces in Afghanistan that use the weapons against U.S. and other NATO military forces in the country. The knowledge of ISI's and the Musharraf regime's involvement in arming the killers of American troops has resulted in a general belief by experienced U.S. SIGINT analysts that anything coming from the Musharraf government relating to Bhutto's assassination can be completely disregarded as falsehoods.

2008

February 28, 2008 -- Creative financing at NSA continues to enrich SAIC

The signals intelligence (SIGINT) outsourcing bonanza began under then-National Security Agency director General Michael Hayden who was rewarded for his efforts at enriching defense contractors like Science Applications International Corporation (SAIC), Booz Allen Hamilton, and others by being appointed CIA director by President George W. Bush.

Hayden's outsourcing mania at Fort Meade has not only continued under his successor, General Keith Alexander, but has grown.

WMR has learned that SAIC in currently raking in tons of cash from NSA's signals intelligence budget. The intelligence giant's most recent jackpot is a $100 million sole source contract that lacks even the most basic contracting controls, including a concept of operations plan.

The SAIC project, known as RT10 (Real Time 10) is a program to enhance NSA's real time signals intelligence collection. WMR has also learned that RT10 includes many aspects that violate the Foreign Intelligence Surveillance Act (FISA) restrictions on domestic surveillance within the United States. However, without any contract oversight, SAIC and NSA's director and Chief Scientist, who are patrons of the RT10 project, SAIC and its sub-contractors are free to spend the taxpayer's money on a project that may either skirt or violate US domestic eavesdropping laws.

Furthermore, WMR has learned that in order to fund RT10 "off-the-books," NSA has re-allocated ("raided" is the term used by NSA insiders) money from other, more critical SIGINT programs, including tactical SIGINT collection systems used in battlefield environments like Iraq and Afghanistan, and electronic intelligence (ELINT) programs used to monitor weapons systems in the "electronic battlefield."

For example, before the outsourcing craze and "raiding" of other projects to fund "pet projects," ELINT intelligence updates averaged about 70 per month. After the budget cuts, they now average 100 per year. Those cuts put US and allied military personnel in extreme jeopardy since they have to deal with intelligence, including fire control radar, early warning data, and "identification friend or foe" (IFF) data, that is outdated and possibly incorrect, increasing the likelihood of more "friendly fire" incidents.

March 28-30, 2008 -- NSA pulling over and detaining drivers

WMR has learned that the National Security Agency's security personnel are pulling over drivers who mistakenly exit Balitmore-Washington Parkway into an unmarked entrance into the Fort Meade complex. It should be noted that a number of Maryland public roads transverse the Fort Meade military base and there is an NSA cryptology museum that is open to the general public. Its property also adjoins the NSA campus.

NSA security personnel inspect driver's licenses, registration, and insurance papers of all drivers pulled over. The drivers stopped have no intention of trying to enter NSA or any other "U.S. government property."

In the case of foreign nationals or green card holders, NSA has been detaining such individuals even if their driver's documents are in order. Immigrants' rights groups are complaining about NSA's checkpoint operations.

April 11-13, 2008 -- Prosecutor malfeasance revealed in trial of NSA analyst

WMR has learned from knowledgeable sources that in the 2006 trial of former National Security Agency (NSA) "Iraqi shop" signals intelligence (SIGINT) analyst Ken Ford, Jr. for allegedly removing classified material from the NSA, federal prosecutor David Salem permitted falsified evidence to be produced at the trial. Ford's name appeared as the analyst on an NSA SIGINT report that ended up on the desk of Vice President Dick Cheney. The report concluded that, based on NSA intercepts of the communications of Saddam Hussein's government, the presence of weapons of mass destruction in the country could not be supported by the intelligence. Cheney, in Cheney fashion, ordered a retaliation against Ford. Salem is linked to the neocons and Israel Lobby in Washington.

On March 31, 2006, WMR reported the problems with the evidence presented against Ford: "In yesterday's sentencing hearing for former NSA analyst Ken Ford, Federal Judge Peter Messitte mentioned the defense's contention that the classified NSA documents Ford was accused of removing from NSA had been planted in Ford's home. Messitte also stated, "no one knows how he [Ford] ended up with these documents."

WMR has learned how the evidence was manufactured against Ford who was sentenced to six years in prison by Messitte after his conviction by a tainted and pressured jury.

FBI Special Agent Michael L. Thompson testified that one of Ford's fingerprints, his little finger -- was found on the second page of a document allegedly removed from NSA. Thompson testified that Ford's prints were not found on any of the other thousands of pages of documents Salem referred to n the trial. Later, the FBI fingerprint expert testified under defense cross-examination that she was given only one document to analyze.

With only one document to analyze, how did Thompson know Ford's fingerprints were not on any of the other documents? WMR has learned that Thompson made copies of documents in Ford's NSA workplace and that Thompson had a preexisting relationship with Kathleen Mitchell, Ford's supervisor in the "Iraqi Shop," from which all the papers cited by Salem originated.

The document that allegedly contained Ford's print was placed into evidence at the trial. The document was supposedly the paper handed to Ford at his Waldorf, Maryland home by NSA Security Agent Robert McCaslin. However, the document in question was unreadable. It cannot be determined if the document is from NSA or a badly-copied page from the phone book. Salem dubiously told the court that the document was severely damaged during fingerprint analysis. Salem used as evidence a photograph allegedly of the "smoking gun" document taken not in Ford's home, but at an FBI facility. Salem offered only his words as evidence of this document being in Ford's home and perjured himself about the authenticity of the document while appearing before the court.

Salem also contended that classified NSA information was found in Ford's computers. It is believed that Salem oversaw the placing of classified NSA information or "false flag" classified data on the computer of Tonya Tucker, the dubious FBI confidential informant who helped entrap Ford. In a letter, dated July 31, 2004, from NSA Security Agent McCaslin to Salem, it was stated that Ford's electronic equipment at work and at home was inspected by NSA and found to be clean. This letter was not allowed into the trial as evidence. Ford's defense attorney did not receive a copy of the letter until August 2005, over a year later. The letter was received anonymously in the mail at the office of Ford's attorney.

Salem's behavior in the Ford case is similar to that of US Attorneys Leura Canary and Alice Martin in the prosecution of Alabama's former Democratic Governor Don Siegelman. Judge Messitte's malfeasance in the case is a carbon copy of that of Judge Mark Fuller in the Siegelman case. The U.S. Attorneys who refused to go along with political prosecutions by the Bush regime were fired. Those who agreed to political prosecutions remain in place. They include Maryland's very slimy David Salem.

UPDATE: The current status of the Ford appeal: Ford's attorney received the rest of the trial transcripts in mid-May, 2007. He filed an appeal brief with the 4th circuit Appeals Court on October 16, 2007. The government filed a nonsensical brief 35 days later. They asked for and received a two-week extension. The defense filed its responding brief on December 20, 2007. It is now in the process of waiting for an oral argument.

April 15, 2008 -- NSA's treasure trove of financial data

Although the U.S. government has relied on some dubious sources, particularly the Israeli intelligence-connected Search for International Terrorist Entities (SITE), for intelligence on the financing of terrorist groups, within the bowels of the National Security Agency (NSA) is found a little-known intelligence collection operation known as the "Follow the Money (FTM) shop."

This unit, with links to the Treasury Department's Financial Crimes Enforcement Network, the Internal Revenue Service (IRS), FBI, CIA, and the Federal Reserve, tracks all suspicious money movements worldwide, including those involving the financing of terrorist groups. The FTM shop maintains databases on contributions to various groups, payments of kidnapping ransoms, charity fronts, "hawala" or Islamic banking activity, Internet gambling activities, and government funding of covert operations.

Since 9/11, NSA's FTM shop has had direct access to the Society for Worldwide Interbank Financial Telecommunication (SWIFT), the global network that transfers funds between banks. Some banks, particularly Rabobank of the Netherlands, have reportedly permitted direct access by U.S. intelligence to its banking computers.

The FTM shop also tracks the activities of the Russian-Israeli Mafia, particularly in the Balkans and Eastern Europe. During the 1990s, one particular financing ring was the one established by leading neocons Richard Perle and Douglas Feith at Riggs Bank in Washington, DC. The fund, called the Bosnia Defense Fund, collected hundreds of millions of dollars for Bosnia's Muslim government from such countries as the United Arab Emirates, Egypt, Malaysia, Saudi Arabia, Iran, Kuwait, Turkey, Jordan, and Brunei. Official U.S. involvement in the fund is indicated in an April 15, 1996 State Department financial document that references the "Bosnia Federation Defense Fund."

19X6166			Bosnia Federation Defense Fund
19X6166.1			Bosnia Federation Defense Fund
19X6166.2			Bosnia Federation Defense Fund
19X6166.3			Bosnia Federation Defense Fund
19X6166.4			Bosnia Federation Defense Fund
19X6166.5			Bosnia Federation Defense Fund
19X6166.8			Bosnia Federation—General Contract Account
19X6166.9			Funds of Bosnia Federation for Training and Equipment

The "bleeding" of Bosnia Defense Fund proceeds from the Bosnian Central Bank in Sarajevo to groups linked to "Al Qaeda" was recorded not only by Riggs Bank overseers and FINCEN but also NSA's FTM shop. Former NATO Commander Wesley Clark, a strong supporter of Hillary Clinton's presidential bid, praised Perle and Feith for their work for the Bosnian government at the 1995 Dayton Peace Conference.

However, if Clark were to have walked into the NSA FTM shop he would have seen extensive wire diagrams with the names of individuals -- including the leading players in the Bosnia Defense Fund, banks such as Riggs and the Bosnian Central Bank, the Feith and Zell law firm in Washington, and various cell phone numbers. The presence of Serbo-Croatian linguists in the FTM shop ensured that detailed translated telephone transcripts of conversations connected with the money flows to Bosnia were also contained in the top secret, sensitive compartmented intelligence database.

Similar information on other established money trails are found in the databases of the FTM shop, including Rep. Peter King's (R-NY) past fund raising activities on behalf of the Irish Republican Army, once designated a terrorist group by the U.S. government.

One entity that was of interest to the FTM shop was the General Council of Islamic Banks led by Saudi billionaire Saleh Abdullah Kamel, the chairman of Dallah al Baraka Group (DBG) and a major shareholder in Al Shamal Bank in Sudan, the one-time bank of choice of Osama Bin Laden. DBG was suspected by the U.S. government of links to Al Qaeda and two 9/11 hijackers via an intermediary named Omar al Bayoumi. After 9/11, convicted GOP lobbyist Jack Abramoff signed Kamel up as a client, in part to restore the image of Saudi Islamic banking.

However, at the NSA FTM shop, Abramoff showed up in the databases along with his Saudi clients.

Today, type in the names "Viktor Bout," "Boris Berezovsky," "Leonid Nevzlin," or "Pierre Falcone" in the search engines of the FTM databases, and the real picture of who the chief players are in the bogus neocon-contrived "global war on terror" becomes evident.

In one small corner of the NSA labyrinth is a unit that, from a follow the money standpoint, connects the financial dots. And in some cases, the dots show irrefutable links between top Jewish neocons such as Feith and Abramoff and various Saudi and other Muslim financiers who have popped up on shady financial activity radar screens across the U.S. intelligence and law enforcement communities. It is only the American people who are kept in the dark about these shady relationships.

April 16, 2008 -- Flight 93 shot down by Air Force jets

WMR has received another confirmation, bringing the total number to three, that United Flight 93, hijacked on the morning of September 11, 2001, was shot down over rural Pennsylvania by U.S. Air Force jets scrambled from Andrews Air Force Base in Maryland. There are also reports that one F-16 scrambled from Langley Air Force Base in Virginia returned to base minus one air-to-air missile but the National Security Agency CRITIC report specified the interceptors that downed United 93 took off from Andrews.

The third confirmation, as were the first two, is from a National Security Agency (NSA) source.

In fact, a number of personnel who were on watch at the Meade Operations Center (MOC), which is a floor below the NSA's National Security Operations Center (NSOC), were aware that United 93 was brought down by an Air Force air-to-air missile. Personnel within both the MOC and NSOC have reported the doomed aircraft was shot down.

The 9/11 Commission, which is now known to have been influenced by Bush adviser Karl Rove and its Executive Director Phil Zelikow, never interviewed the on-duty signals intelligence personnel who were aware that United 93 was brought down by Air Force jets. The cover-story is that passengers on board the plane struggled with hijackers and flew the plane directly into the ground near Shanksville, Pennsylvania. Investigators have stressed that the 8-mile debris field left by the doomed aircraft proves the government's story is a hoax.

May 30 - June 1, 2008 -- America's decimation of Iraq's auto mechanics

The United States military has indiscriminately targeted anyone in Iraq who has uttered words relating to auto repair or auto mechanics, according to a National Security Agency (NSA) Arabic linguist who revealed that the auto mechanics and repairmen were automatically targeted because the US military decided they could be installing bombs in vehicles.

On March 16, WMR reported that an ex-Marine testified at Winter Soldier in suburban Washington, DC that his unit mortared a tire shop in Al Qaim by mistake and without compensation to its owner.

The incident in Al Qaim reflected a widespread assault on anyone involved in the automotive repair and maintenance business in Iraq.

The NSA source reported that key words like "alternator," "battery," and "transmission" would result in intercepts of Iraqi cell phone and land line calls being transmitted to U.S. assault units who would target the location of the phone calls with rocket and mortar attacks, resulting in the deaths of the mechanics and anyone in close proximity to them, including their families.

The orders to attack anyone communicating any automotive-related words and phrases were issued by senior Defense Department echelons and the NSA, under both Generals Michael Hayden and Keith Alexander, carried out NSA's collaboration in the program.

The NSA source said the United States has eliminated an entire class of entrepreneurs in Iraq, hard working, intelligent, self-taught, and self-made businessmen whose only concerns were keeping their automotive repair businesses financially solvent.

June 30, 2008 -- The "X Files" scene at Fort Meade

It was a scene right out of the TV series the "X Files." WMR has received eyewitness accounts of one of the strangest incidents that ever transpired at the National Security Agency (NSA) headquarters at Fort Meade, Maryland.

It was late 1988 and Admiral William Studeman, who was later the Deputy Director of Central Intelligence under both George H. W. Bush and Bill Clinton, had just taken up residence at the official home of the Director of NSA (DIRNSA), located on Butler Avenue at Fort Meade. However, the residence of DIRNSA is no ordinary military base residence -- it is a virtual annex of NSA and includes a highly-secured Sensitive Compartmented Information Facility (SCIF) in which is located an encrypted Secure Telephone Unit (STU-III) connected to NSA headquarters and a safe that contains Special Compartmented Information (SCI) documents that involve America's most sensitive sources and methods for collecting communications intelligence.

During the day, while Studeman's mother was staying at the house, a knock came on the front door. Answering the door, Mrs. Studeman was met by a well-dressed African-American man who greeted her, entered the house, quickly brushing by her, and went upstairs.

After going into the kitchen, Studeman's mother asked a Navy petty officer, who doubled as a mess cook, who the man was and why he came into the house. The petty officer reflexively opened a kitchen drawer, grabbed a gun, and quickly pushed the NSA director's mother into a closet instructing her not to leave until further notice.

Within short order there was the sound of helicopters over the home. Soon, Studeman's mother saw a man wearing a gas mask open the closet door and he quickly put a gas mask on her. Before being whisked from the home for a few hours, the admiral's mother saw an armored personnel carrier in the front of the house, along with a SWAT team. Upon returning to the house, the director's mother saw broken window glass and one of the doors in an upstairs room was completely gone.

Studeman later told his mother that the episode was merely a "drill." However, she believed the man who whisked past her at the front door never survived the "drill" or whatever transpired that day.

July 8, 2008 -- US spy plane incident with China more serious than reported

The April 1, 2001, incident between a U.S. Navy EP-3E signals intelligence (SIGINT) aircraft and two Chinese J-8 fighters 70 miles off Hainan island was worse than reported by the media at the time. According to National Security Agency (NSA) sources, the Navy aircraft, after being intercepted by the two Chinese fighters, was forced to land at Lingshui airbase on Hainan by one of the two Chinese aircraft. The other Chinese fighter crashed after it collided with the wing of the EP-3E SIGINT aircraft. The nose and a propeller of the US Navy plane was damaged in the collision.

NSA intercepts of the incident reveal that the plane, piloted by Shane Osborn, who later received the Distinguished Flying Cross for "heroism," did not land at Hainan voluntarily but was forced down by the other Chinese jet. In addition, the EP-3E flight crew was not able to destroy much of the plane's classified equipment and other material because of the threat it would be shot down if the Chinese pilot saw material being thrown from the plane into the South China Sea. This editor described the standard emergency destruction protocols for aircraft such as the EP-3E and P-3 anti-submarine warfare aircraft on *The News Hour* with Jim Lehrer on April 3, 2001.

Reports at the time stated that the US Navy plane conducted an emergency landing on Hainan without Chinese authorization. According to the NSA intercepts of Chinese communications, the original story about the unauthorized landing now appears to be false. China retained possession of the "black boxes" from the EP-3E aircraft that would have shown that China demanded the aircraft land on Hainan or be shot down.

Based on NSA intercepts of the event, it now appears that the Chinese not only obtained classified SIGINT and electronic intelligence (ELINT) material but also extremely classified and sensitive cryptographic keying material. In effect, the worst case scenario as described by this editor on *The News Hour* played out: "if they [the Chinese] got those keys, that means they could decode all past U.S. intelligence, military communications around the world, not just in that area [Southeast Asia] but in other places as well."

The forcing down of the EP-3E aircraft may represent the worst compromise of US classified information since North Korea captured the NSA spy ship, the *USS Pueblo*, on January 23, 1968. In that case, classified information, including cryptographic keying material, ended up in the hands of not only the North Koreans, but the Soviets.

NSA intercepts of the Hainan incident also reveal that before the US crew was released on April 11, 2001, Secretary of State Colin Powell warned Beijing of U.S. military action against China if it did not immediately release the crew and plane. The plane was later dismantled by a Lockheed Martin crew sent to Lingshui airbase and was flown out on a Russian-built Antonov 124 transport plane.

The Washington Post and *New York Times* hailed George W. Bush's handling of the spy plane incident with China. However, based on the NSA intercepts, the forcing down of the Navy plane with its treasure trove of classified information represented the most damaging compromise of US classified material since 1968. The NSA director at the time, Air Force General Michael Hayden, was promoted to Deputy Director of National Intelligence and Director of the CIA.

July 24, 2008 -- United 93 shoot down reference again appears in news

At the first military commission trial yesterday in Guantanamo, Cuba, Navy Lieutenant Commander Timothy Stone, one of the prosecutors, told the jury that accused Al Qaeda terrorist Salim Hamdan, a Yemeni citizen, was guilty of knowing about the 9/11 attacks because he overheard a conversation between Osama Bin Laden and Al Qaeda number two man Ayman al Zawahiri concerning details of the attacks. According to a Reuters report from the court room, Stone stated: "If they hadn't **shot down** the fourth plane it would've hit the dome." The reference was to United 93, which crashed near Shanksville, Pennsylvania. Chief prosecutor Colonel Lawrence Morris later said that Stone was merely quoting Hamdan, however, Morris would not even concede that the "dome" reference was to the U.S. Capitol building.

Whether or not Stone was himself referring to the shootdown of United 93 or whether he was quoting Hamdan, who was, in turn, quoting either Bin Laden or Zawahiri is immaterial. The shootdown of United 93 is backed up by evidence in U.S. intelligence files, including those found in the super-classified CRITIC database maintained by the National Security Agency (NSA). There is little doubt that the prosecutors in Guantanamo had some form of access to CRITIC and other intelligence in preparing their case against Guantanamo detainees like Hamdan.

The fate of United 93 serves as an example of the lying conducted by the Bush administration in order to advance its perception management campaign to inflate and perpetuate the cleverly-constructed U.S. government propaganda surrounding the 9/11 attacks.

August 5, 2008 -- Incarcerated former NSA Iraq analyst is refused appeal without a hearing

Yesterday, in a stunning development, US Fourth Circuit Court of Appeals in Richmond, Virginia let stand, without ever hearing an oral argument, the December 15, 2005 conviction by the U.S. Court for the southern district of Maryland of former National Security Agency (NSA) "Iraqi shop" signals intelligence analyst Ken Ford, Jr.

The judgment, rendered by Judges Harvie Wilkinson III, a Republican appointed by Ronald Reagan; Blane Michael, appointed by Bill Clinton (Wilkinson and Michael are jogging partners); and William Traxler, also appointed by Clinton and who leans to the right, simply stated: "In accordance with the decision of this Court, the judgments of the District Court are affirmed." After a dubious trial, in which false statements were introduced by Assistant U.S. Attorney David Salem, improper collusion between Salem and presiding U.S. Judge Peter J. Messitte, a tainted jury member employed by an NSA contractor, and an FBI confidential informant with a long criminal record, Ford was found guilty of one count of violating the Espionage Act and one count of lying on a federal form.

In denying an appeals hearing, the Fourth Circuit ruled: "we affirm the district court's dismissal without prejudice of the original indictment against Ford, and Ford's subsequent conviction and sentence. We dispense with oral argument because the facts and legal contentions are adequately presented in the materials before the court and argument would not aid the decisional process."

On April 30, 2007, WMR summed up the government's flimsy case against Ford and revealed the political purposes of his being set up in a sting operation:

"Ford was set up in a clumsy Justice Department, FBI, and NSA Security Division operation to punish him for his May 2003 signals intelligence (SIGINT) analysis report that concluded, based on intercepts of Iraqi communications, there was no truth to the Bush administration's claim that there were weapons of mass destruction in Iraq. Ford's report, with his name and that of his supervisor on it, ended up on Vice President Dick Cheney's desk. From that time on, Ford was a marked man for the neo-con cabal operating within the White House, Justice Department, Pentagon, and U.S. Intelligence Community senior staff.

The Bush administration, using an FBI confidential informant with documented ties to two intelligence contractors, TASC and Bearing Point, planted a classified document in Ford's home after she had struck up a relationship with the NSA analyst and former uniformed Secret Service officer who guarded President Bill Clinton. Ford was convicted in December 2005 of possessing classified information and making a false statement to a government agent. In March 2006, Ford was sentenced to six years in prison. Messitte refused to allow Ford to remain free pending an appeal of his conviction.

Just as the case with other U.S. Attorneys around the country who were 'loyal Bushies' and kept their jobs while a number of other US Attorneys were fired for political reason, the US Attorneys office for Southern Maryland is rife with political malfeasance, especially in the Federal Public Defender's Office. The Ford case was highlighted by judge shopping, suborning perjury from witnesses, jury tampering, witness badgering, questionable fraternization between the chief prosecutor and the public defender, and using the Classified Information Procedures Act (CIPA) to withhold evidence from the defense."

The FBI and NSA also provided a laptop computer containing "NSA papers" on their dubious confidential informant, one Tonya Tucker from Florida. Salem, the prosecuting U.S. attorney, later inexplicably traveled to Alabama to "confiscate" the computer from Tucker. However, there is no connection between Tucker, a resident of Florida and temporary resident of Maryland during her government-sponsored entrapment of Ford, and the state of Alabama. Tucker later revealed that she was upset with Salem for confiscating the laptop because, as she stated, "there are NSA papers on it." The government never proved that Ford retained the large amount of classified information, either paper-based or computer-based, as they originally attempted to allege. Given the malfeasance of the federal judiciary, particularly U.S. Judge Mark Fuller, and the US Attorney's offices in Alabama in the political prosecution of former

Alabama Democratic Governor Don Siegelman, Salem's involvement in retrieving a government computer with NSA data from Alabama is highly suspicious.

Salem falsely stated during Ford's trial that "there was a deliberate removal of thousands of documents, thousands of pages of documents from NSA." However, Salem and the government could never prove that Ford removed any documents from NSA and a number of NSA employees told WMR that it is virtually impossible to remove the number of documents alleged by Salem without either NSA's approval or interception by NSA security. In fact, former NSA analyst and whistleblower Russ Tice testified to that fact during Ford's trial. Tice's testimony and credibility was challenged by Salem.

Salem, during his arguments, also defended the actions of then-CIA director John Deutch and Clinton National Security Adviser Sandy Berger in removing classified information from secured locations. The following is what Salem stated during Ford's sentencing hearing on March 30, 2006: *"And let me just briefly, you know, Sander [sic] Berger and at least John Deutsch [sic], these individuals, I don't profess to know the facts of them. I really don't know, and I didn't have time to, you know, go through and see carefully what happened, who decided to charge what, and what the back channel situation was, but ultimately in each of these instances, individuals took documents related to their work for continuing their work. That is to say they may have taken the documents from a secure location, brought it to some unsecure location and then intended -- brought it back or were caught and brought it back, but they took it on behalf of their work.*

Of course, Mr. Deutsch [sic], being the head of the CIA, took it. He was still the director of the CIA and had those documents. Sandy Berger took those documents, he thought, to testify on the Hill to -- about his job, that is to say specifically, I think, with respect to classified cases or classified information with the Hill was questioning him about, and he took those documents out of the archives, a couple of which he put, I guess, in his clothing and ultimately -- but he was using those documents for his position, for his job."

Salem said the Deutch/Berger cases were different from the case against Ford. In Deutch's case, a criminal referral was made to the Justice Department regarding Detuch's removal of a classified computer from the CIA to his home, but Attorney General Janet Reno declined prosecution. The media reported that Deutch's classified Macintosh computer was used to surf porn web sites from his home. President Clinton gave Deutch a full pardon on his last day in office. Salem was incorrect about Berger. Berger removed from the National Archives five classified documents on the 2000 Millennium bombing plot in preparation for his testimony before the 9/11 Commission. Berger pleaded guilty to a count of removing and retaining classified material, was fined $50,000, sentenced to two years of probation and 100 hours of community service and lost his security clearance for three years and his law license.

Salem and Messitte studiously avoided discussion of the indictment of two American Israel Public Affairs Committee (AIPAC) officials for receiving classified information in violation of the Espionage Act at Ford's trial. The reason was simple. In the case against former AIPAC officials

Steve Rosen and Keith Weissman for receiving highly-classified documents from convicted former Pentagon analyst Larry Franklin in violation of the Espionage Act, there was a documented foreign intelligence agency involved, that of Israel. In Ford's case, the FBI alleged that the former NSA analyst was planning to sell classified documents to an unnamed foreign intelligence agency at Dulles International Airport. There was no record of Ford ever having gone to Dulles, no foreign intelligence agency or even nation identified, and no proof that Ford had ever communicated with a foreign intelligence service or government. There is a reason that Salem and Messitte, as well as Salem's boss, US Attorney for Maryland Rod Rosenstein wanted to avoid discussion of Deutch, Berger, Rosen, and Weissman and thr reason had nothing to do with espionage.

On March 31, 2006, WMR reported :*"Salem also perpetuated several other frauds upon the court during the sentencing hearing. He stated 'there are no security procedures at NSA that would prevent an employee from removing documents.' Salem said there was 'no guard . . . no working camera' at the Technical Exploitation Center (TEC) building where Ford allegedly removed documents in broad daylight. Adding two arguments not brought up in the trial, Salem alleged that Ford took documents from NSA 'on more than one occasion' and in response to the defense argument that the documents were planted, he stated, 'the government may have additional evidence not reported to the court before.'"*

Salem's fellow Assistant U.S. Attorney Mary Claire Rourk alleged during the trial that Ford removed two boxes of classified document from the TEC building in his pickup truck. However, under questioning by Ford's defense attorney, Ford's supervisor Jackie Welch said Ford was not driving a truck as alleged by the government.

"Q. Okay. On that particular day, do you recall what color car or vehicle Mr. Ford was driving?

A. It was a car. I remember it being a light-colored car with a tan interior."

Q. . . . it was not a truck?

A. It was not a truck."

The most egregious element of the prosecution of Ford is the fact that Salem, according to trial insiders, sought to have the criminal case against Ford removed from the jurisdiction of U.S. Magistrate Judge for Maryland William Connelly, an African-American who may have given Ford, also an African-American, a fairer trial, and judge-shopped for a magistrate who would be more supportive of the government's prosecution of Ford. The case is similar to the conflicts-of-interest inherent in U.S. Judge Mark Fuller, a former GOP operative, in trying the case against Governor Siegelman in Alabama.

It is interesting to note Salem's use of the term "back channel" in his defense of the actions of Deutch and Berger. WMR has learned what "back channel" to which Salem may have been referring and it has nothing to do with national security but religion, a factor that should not enter into a judicial proceeding in the United States in any manner. Salem, according to trial insiders, insisted that the case against Ford be reassigned from African American U.S. Judge Connelly to Judge Peter Messitte, because Messitte is Jewish, as is Salem and Rosenstein. Trial observers pointed out several cases in which Messitte assisted and even coached Salem in his prosecutorial tactics from the bench during the trial. The case against Ford, therefore, contains many racist overtones and elements of a criminal conspiracy involving U.S. attorneys and a federal judge. Minus the racist element, these were the same factors involved in the case against Governor Siegelman.

The "Jewish factor" in drumming up support for the illegal U.S. war against Iraq has recently been cited by a number of respected individuals, including *Time* magazine's Joe Klein, who contended in a recent column that "Jewish neocons" have placed the national security interests of Israel over those of the United States. For the record, Klein is Jewish. Former conservative Republican Representative John Hostettler of Indiana, in a new book, contends that Jewish political appointees in the Pentagon and increased donations to Republicans by Jewish donors helped propel the United States into war with Iraq. Hostettler was one of only six Republicans to vote against the 2002 Iraq war resolution. Professors John Mearsheimer of the University of Chicago and Stephen Walt of Harvard, authors of the book, The Israel Lobby," have written, "Jewish Americans have set up an impressive array of organizations to influence American foreign policy, of which AIPAC is the most powerful and best known." The Jewish magazine, *Forward*, stated: "As President Bush attempted to sell the . . . war in Iraq . . . America's most important Jewish organizations rallied as one to his defense. In statement after statement community leaders stressed the need to rid the world of Saddam Hussein and his weapons of mass destruction."

On March 30, 2006, WMR reported: "the [classified] documents were planted in Ford's home in retaliation for his SIGINT report casting doubt on the White House contention that Iraq possessed weapons of mass destruction. That report, which contained Ford's name as preparer, eventually ended up on the desk of Vice President Dick Cheney. As a result, Ford became a target of the neo-con cell operating from Cheney's office and the White House Iraq Group (WHIG), the White House group that compromised Valerie Plame Wilson's covert identity and mission."

There is no question as to the vindictiveness of Cheney in lying the United States into the Iraq war. Author Ron Suskind's new book, "The Way of the World," is to reveal that Cheney ordered the CIA to prepare a back-dated forged letter, dated July 1, 2001, from the head of Iraq's intelligence service, Tahir Jalil Habbush al-Takriti, to Saddam Hussein, showing that lead hijacker Mohammed Atta trained for the 9/11 mission in Iraq, with Saddam's approval. Cheney, according to Seymour Hersh, also contemplated using US Navy SEALS, dressed as Iranians in false-flagged speed boats, to attack U.S. Navy ships in the Persian Gulf to precipitate a U.S. military attack on Iran.

The fact that Cheney and Justice Department officials selectively worked with three tainted officers of the court -- two federal prosecutors and one federal judge -- to illegally make an example of Ken Ford, who concluded Saddam Hussein did not possess weapons of mass destruction, is a travesty of American justice. Unfortunately, the Fourth Circuit in Richmond has perpetrated the injustice against Ford and should be held accountable for its actions. But that may not come any time soon. Ford's parents have asked Senator Charles Schumer, a member of the Senate Judiciary Committee, and House Judiciary Committee Chairman John Conyers to review their son's case in the same manner that other political prosecutions by the Bush/Cheney White House are now being reviewed. They never received a response. Nor did they receive any support from either the Reverends Jesse Jackson or Al Sharpton after pleas to advance the cause of Ford as a victim of a political crime. Ford remains incarcerated at the Lewisburg Federal Penitentiary in Pennsylvania, never receiving his day in appeals court.

August 15-17, 2008 -- Intercepts reveal Georgian sneak attack on South Ossetia

United States and British signals intelligence (SIGINT) intercepts of Caucasus region communications, including the cell phone calls of Georgian, South Ossetian, and Russian government and military officials, reveal that Georgia was involved in a sneak attack on the evening of August 8 against South Ossetia and its Russian peacekeepers, WMR has learned from American intelligence sources.

The National Security Agency (NSA) maintained a series of SIGINT intercept stations in Georgia that were directed at Russian communications. In addition, Georgian communications, including satellite communications, were under surveillance from the NSA SIGINT station at Menwith Hill in England, as well as Britain's Government Communications Headquarters (GCHQ) in Cheltenham, also in England.

The SIGINT "take" from the Georgian assault on South Ossetia does not square with media reports of Russian "aggression" against Georgia. Once again, a split has developed between seasoned U.S. intelligence professionals and Bush administration officials who are offering up propaganda suited to the purposes of the neocon Mikheil Saakashvili regime in Tbilisi. A similar split occurred prior, during, and after the U.S. invasion of Iraq when the intelligence did not square with the propaganda emanating from the Bush White House. In recent years, such a gulf between intelligence reality and White House policy has also developed with regard to Iran's nuclear program.

Ironically, as the Bush administration seeks to restore the days of the Cold War, Russia has a number of U.S. intelligence professionals agreeing with its stance and statements on South Ossetia.

August 18, 2008 -- NSA continues surveillance of journalists; WMR editor subject of espionage investigation

On May 10, 2005, WMR reported on the existence of a highly-classified database at the National Security Agency (NSA), formerly code-named "FIRSTFRUITS," that monitored journalists who reported on the activities of the eavesdropping agency, as well as other intelligence matters. A few weeks later, according to an executive-level source at the NSA, and confirmed by a related source within NSA's "Q" Directorate, the Directorate for Security and Counterintelligence, this editor has been a subject of a national security investigation since June 2005 that remains ongoing. The investigation of this editor is classified at the level SECRET/COMINT (NOFORN). COMINT is "Communications Intelligence" and NOFORN denotes "Not Releasable to Foreign Nationals/Governments/Non-US Citizens."

According to National Security Agency/Central Security Service Policy 1-27, dated March 20, 2006 and signed by NSA Chief of Staff Deborah Bonanni, the investigation of the public disclosure of the unconstitutional and illegal FIRSTFRUITS surveillance system would be coordinated by the NSA, Department of Defense, Director of National Intelligence, and the Department of Justice.

Since the disclosure of FIRSTFRUITS, NSA changed the cover name but the system remains in existence. Not only does the follow-on to FIRSTFRUITS contain articles about NSA written by journalists, it has been expanded to include information gleaned from wiretaps on journalists, including sources with whom they communicate by phone, email, fax, and Voice-over-IP (VOIP), including Skype, which the NSA has managed to bring under easier surveillance due to some recent advances in VOIP surveillance technology, according to NSA sources.

This editor has, thanks to dozens of NSA sources, managed to report on the poor morale; overbearing Stasi-like conduct of NSA security personnel, including the wrongful prosecution and conviction of NSA Iraqi shop analyst Ken Ford, Jr.; contract mismanagement and fraud conducted by then-NSA Director General Michael Hayden; outrageous treatment of NSA whistleblowers by the NSA security and psychological staffs that work in the same fashion that the old Soviet KGB and psychiatric hospitals treated dissidents; and the outsourcing of sensitive signals intelligence contracts to companies with dubious links to foreign intelligence agencies, most importantly, those of Israel.

Federal investigators are apparently using the terms "espionage" and "treason" with regard to the investigation that includes this editor. The maximum penalty for espionage and treason, according to U.S. Sentencing Guidelines, is death.

On January 12, 2006, this editor first reported on the criminal investigation being carried out by the Bush administration: *"Informed intelligence sources have informed this editor that he has, since October 2005, been under an active federal criminal investigation as part of the Bush administration's probe of leaks about illegal NSA surveillance of U.S. citizens.*

To reiterate what I've stated before: I refuse to cede my First Amendment rights and will not cooperate with ANY grand jury asking questions about sources and I will refuse to turn over notebooks or other materials to any investigators, warrant or not. I'm willing to become a political prisoner rather than succumb to the fascist thugs in the Bush administration. WMR is working on a number of investigations involving The Carlyle Group, the Fellowship Foundation, and illegal surveillance. We will continue to publish until the Bush administration makes their move to shut us down. Again, your support has helped us to gain enough of a media presence to make the Bush administration nervous."

This publication, not intimidated by NSA, the FBI, or other Bush administration entities, will continue to report on the misuse of America's intelligence agencies for political purposes and the repeated violations of the U.S. Constitution by illegal surveillance of citizens, including First Amendment-protected journalists. WMR has learned today that our colleague, New York journalist Joe Lauria, who has written a series of articles on the Turkish/Israeli intelligence network exposed by former FBI translator Sibel Edmonds, is now also the subject of an FBI "leaks" investigation.

The FIRSTFRUITS journalist surveillance system was renamed after our exposure of its existence. According to our NSA source, who was involved in another operation designed to scan the media and academia for leaks, a program called "Cryptologic Insecurities," FIRSTFRUITS exists within a new strategic program by NSA to surveill journalists, which may be the subject of a classified United States Signals Intelligence Directive (USSID 304P), dated June 7, 2007. One term used by NSA with regard to journalists in the FIRSTFRUITS follow-on surveillance system is the Orwellian-sounding "media control."

There is also reason to believe that additional journalists are now subject to FIRSTFRUITS surveillance and include Eric Lichtblau of the *New York Times*, Christiane Amanpour of CNN, and Lauria.

WMR has also learned that NSA has drastically cut the number of Hebrew and Russian linguists, with the Hebrew linguists suffering the greatest cuts. The result of this decision is that the two languages used most by international organized criminal syndicates that are part of the Russian-Israeli Mafia are virtually free to conduct their weapons, diamond, and drug smuggling operations, as well as financial fraud, without being subject to NSA surveillance.

Perhaps the fact that there exists a cabal within the U.S. District for Maryland a few officials who have conspired to wrongfully prosecute NSA employees is not coincidental to the purge of Hebrew and Russian linguists at NSA. A triumvirate has emerged that suggests illegal collusion to prosecute NSA whistleblowers that includes U.S. Attorney for Maryland Rod Rosenstein, his assistant David Salem, and US Judge Peter Messitte, who, according to U.S. intelligence sources, carries, in addition to his U.S. passport, a passport issued by Portugal.

WMR has also learned that an NSA signals intelligence mission codenamed "SALAMANDER," partly devoted to monitoring communications in Georgia, may have been misused to provide the neocon Georgian government of Mikheil Saakashvili with intelligence gleaned from NSA intercepts of Saakashvili's political opponents, including alleged phone calls with Russian embassy officials in Tbilisi. Those targeted in the wiretaps include Labor Party leader Shalva

Natelashvili, Freedom Party leader Konstantin Gamsakhurdia, the late Georgian opposition financier Badri Patarkatsishvili, and Conservative Party leader Zviad Dzidziguri. The provision of U.S. SIGINT to a nation like Georgia, which is well outside the normal American "second party" and "third party" SIGINT partners, represents a dramatic departure from traditional U.S. intelligence management and may have provided sensitive sources and methods information to the Georgian government, one which includes a number of dual Georgian-Israeli nationals.

August 25, 2008 -- Russia captures U.S. intelligence-collection vehicles

On August 18, Russian troops who captured the Georgian Black Sea port of Poti destroyed a Georgian naval vessel and captured 21 Georgian soldiers. The Russians also captured another prize, five U.S. Marine Corps Humvees that were providing signals intelligence and electronic warfare assistance to Georgian forces. Along with the Humvees and their classified equipment, the Russians also obtained important and highly-classified encryption codes used by the United States and NATO to scramble their military and diplomatic communications. U.S. intelligence sources told WMR that the Russians obtained an intelligence windfall from the capture of the Humvees.

White House spokesman Gordon Johndroe called for Russia to immediately return the vehicles. The Pentagon refused to admit how many Humvees had been seized by the Russians and stated the vehicles were at Poti awaiting shipment back to the United States. However, there are other reports that the Humvees were involved in fighting between Georgian troops and Russian troops in Abkhazia. The Humvees have reportedly been transported to Moscow where their equipment and communications codes will be analyzed.

On August 15, three days before the Humvees were captured, WMR reported: "the National Security Agency (NSA) maintained a series of SIGINT intercept stations in Georgia that were directed at Russian communications." On August 8, WMR reported that NSA had issued orders for SIGINT equipment in Georgia to be destroyed: "WMR has learned that the 'Georgia shop' at the 'National Security Agency (NSA) Texas complex, the former Medina Regional Security Operations Center in San Antonio, has issued orders that in the event of a full-scale Russian invasion of Georgian territory, all signals intelligence (SIGINT) equipment stationed in Georgia and which has been aimed at intercepting Russian communications in the Caucasus region, is to be destroyed and NSA personnel evacuated." The NSA order apparently did not reach the Marine Corps Reserve unit in Poti.

The Humvees belonged to a Marine Corps Reserve unit and are reportedly Special Operations Forces (SOF) Intelligence Vehicles that contain satellite communications equipment and intelligence analysis workstations via which ground personnel can access intelligence databases, including those that contain imagery intelligence from reconnaissance Unmanned Aerial Vehicles (UAVs) and orbiting satellites.

It appears that the Marines were engaged in an intelligence cover mission officially billed as a program to train Georgians to drive Humvees before their deployment to Iraq. The cover mission was officially called the Georgian Stability and Sustainment Operation and was based out of the Krtsanisi Training Center, about 6.5 miles outside of Tbilisi.

White House warnings and State Department demarches are unusual in a case involving normal Humvees lost in a battle zone. The high-level interest in the Humvees seized indicates that the Bush administration, as with the U.S. Navy EP-3E Aries electronic intelligence plane forced to land by China in 2001 after it collided with a Chinese MiG fighter, has been responsible for the compromise of yet more classified signals intelligence and cryptographic material.

August 26, 2008 -- SIGINT employed against global pedophile rings

WMR has learned from sources close to Britain's Government Communications Headquarters (GCHQ), the National Security Agency's (NSA) British counterpart headquartered in Cheltenham, England, that the British signals intelligence (SIGINT) agency has not only broken the 256-bit AES (Advanced Encryption Standard) used in Voice-over-IP (VOIP) Skype communications but has successfully managed to monitor Skype voice and text chats of individuals involved in international pedophilia networks.

One of the international networks monitored by GCHQ was reportedly involved in the May 2007 abduction from a Portuguese resort of Madeleine McCann, a British youngster who was just days away from her fourth birthday.

In addition to GCHQ's success in breaking Skype's AES encryption, German and Austrian police have reportedly installed "black box" interception units at telecommunications switches and the Frankfurt IPX Internet router to snag Skype communications and subject them to brute force decryption attacks.

Pedophiles who use encryption to mask their exchange of pornographic images were stung last March when police, using the Microsoft-developed Child Exploitation Tracking System (CETS), broke a major international ring of pedophiles in New Zealand, Australia, Germany, Austria, the Netherlands, the United States, Canada, Britain, and Belgium. Police targeted heavily-encrypted graphic images in their worldwide investigation.

August 27, 2008 -- Is the "echo" a sign of cell phone tapping?

The complaints are coming mostly from journalists and political activists, however, they all ring of the same problem: some twenty percent of cell phone calls are met with the receiver hearing his or her own voice coming back in an echo. And its a new phenomenon. The caller can hear the person called repeating "Hello" over and over again but the receiver can only hearing his or her own voice being pinged back.

The "echoing" is not limited to particular cell phone service providers or cell phone types. Customers of AT&T, Verizon, and T-Mobile are reporting the same problem with phones from Nokia, Samsung, Nokia, Motorola, and Ericsson.

Technicians report that echoes occur when there is not a complete connection or if there is a third party connection on the call. While echoing has been a minor problem in the past, the frequency of complaints is increasing and affecting journalists and political activists from Washington, DC to New York City and California to Texas.

Government agencies are already able to remotely activate a cell phone and use the microphone to listen in on conversations. The only way to prevent this surveillance is to agree to "batteries out" conversations, something that is employed more and more among journalists while talking to sources as well as others concerned about high-tech snooping from "roving bugs." Similarly, removing the battery from a cell phone also disables the Global Positioning System and cell tower triangulation capabilities used by law enforcement and intelligence agencies to track the location of the user, according to U.S. intelligence sources.

WMR has learned that the Bush administration, in its final months in office, has made several strategic and tactical moves to ensure that the wireless industry comes into full compliance with government eavesdropping policies and technical compliance with them. The echoing of cell phone calls appears to coincide with these Bush administration moves and is an indication that the policy has been given priority over the technology.

August 29-31, 2008 -- U.S. signals intelligence re-focusing on Russia

Companies that make up the U.S. military-intelligence complex stand to make billions of dollars from a renewed Cold War with Russia, according to U.S. intelligence community sources.

After the fall of the Berlin Wall and the Soviet Union, Cold War-era intelligence agencies, such as the National Security Agency (NSA), only reluctantly gave up intelligence systems aimed at the former Soviet Union and former eastern bloc. In fact, only as late as 2004 did the NSA scrap its arcane BLACKSTONE system, which monitored Russian high frequency communications, including ground communications between Russian military units and the communications of Russian airlines like Aeroflot, Siberian Airlines, and Transaero, many of which fly planes manufactured by Boeing and Airbus. In addition, NSA could have easily picked up the phone to Continental Airlines if it had questions about Aeroflot. Aeroflot is a code-sharing partner of the Houston-based U.S. airline.

Russian linguists and electronic intelligence specialists who mastered in everything from Soviet radar signals to the flight schedules of Soviet and Russian civilian aircraft found themselves looking for new employment.

Some Cold War-era NSA operations were turned toward new targets. For example, the SALAMANDER system began focusing on the tense Caucasus region, the area that has recently seen armed conflict between Russian and U.S.-backed Georgian troops, and even Ukrainian troops in Iraq that were members of the U.S. "Coalition of the Willing." Apparently, the neocons in the Bush administration were suspicious when, in 2003, the relatively pro-Russian Ukrainian Prime Minister Viktor Yanukovych sent the largest non-NATO contingent of troops to assist the United States in its Iraq occupation. Therefore, Ukrainian troops' communications were subjected to NSA eavesdropping by SALAMANDER and translated copies of Ukrainian communications were analyzed by U.S. counter-intelligence personnel.

It was soon discovered that some Ukrainian *Sluzhba Bezpeky Ukraiyiny* (SBU) -- Ukrainian Security Service -- agents in Iraq were not only feeding intelligence to Russia but also to their old friends in the security services of Iran, China, and members of Saddam Hussein's old Mukhabarat intelligence service. The neocons were so anxious to bolster the "international" credentials of its coalition force, it gladly took into its ranks intelligence agents who were passing secrets to the supposed "enemy." Ukraine's neocon-supported President Viktor Yushchenko quickly withdrew Ukraine's troops from Iraq in 2005.

U.S. intelligence contractors like Booz Allen, SAIC, and Northrop Grumman will particularly cash in on new and expanded signals intelligence (SIGINT) systems that target more modern Russian communications, including cell phones and other wireless networks. NSA's CANDLESTICK system specifically targets Russian cell phone calls, while CHRYSALIS is designed to identify particular frequencies of interest to U.S. eavesdroppers.

It is not only Russia that is subjected to the enhanced "hearing aid" for Uncle Sam's "Big Ear." The new progressive governments of Latin America are also being subjected to signals intelligence surveillance at levels not seen since the Reagan years of the *contra* wars in Central America. NSA Spanish language-intercept systems with odd code names like PINK FLAMINGO and BIRD BATH, are not only eavesdropping on the "usual suspects" like Colombian drug cartels, but also focusing in on the communications of the governments of Venezuela, Nicaragua, Bolivia, Ecuador, Uruguay, Paraguay, Argentina, Chile, and Guatemala. These same SIGINT systems, in addition to others, were used in the abortive U.S.-backed coup d'etat against Venezuelan President Hugo Chavez in April 2002.

However, the Russians will have a leg up on a new U.S. intelligence onslaught. WMR's initial report that Russia captured U.S. intelligence equipment and other material from abandoned sites and vehicles in Georgia is now being widely reported in the Russian and Western media.

According to ITAR-TASS, Russia also has in its possession the passport of an American, Michael Lee White of Texas, who was attached to the Georgian 3rd Mechanized Infantry Brigade in Tskhinvali, South Ossetia. White's birth date is listed as June 12, 1967 and the passport was issued in Houston on October 11, 2001. The passport contained a current visa for Kazakhstan.

September 15, 2008 -- "Einstein" replaces "Big Brother" in Internet surveillance

WMR has learned from government sources that the Bush administration has authorized massive surveillance of the Internet using as cover a cyber-security multi-billion dollar project called the "Einstein" program.

Billed as a cyber-security intrusion detection system for federal computer systems and networks, WMR has been told that the actual intent of Einstein is to initially monitor the email and web surfing activities of federal employees and contractors and not in protecting government computer systems from intrusion by outsiders.

In February 2008, President Bush signed a directive that designated the National Security Agency (NSA) as the central administrator for the federal government's computer and network security.

Although Einstein is primarily a program under the aegis of the Computer Emergency Readiness Team (US-CERT) of the National Cyber Security Division of the Homeland Security Department, WMR has learned that it has the personal support of Director of National Intelligence (DNI) Mike McConnell, a former NSA director. Einstein is advertised as merely conducting traffic analysis within the dot (.) gov and dot (.) mil domains, including data packet lengths, protocols, source and destination IP addresses, source and destination ports, time stamp information, and autonomous system numbers. However, WMR has learned that Einstein will also bore down into the text of email and analyze message content. In fact, most of the classified budget allotted to Einstein is being used for collecting information from the text of messages and not the header data.

In fact, WMR has learned that most of the classified technology being used for Einstein was developed for the NSA in conducting signals intelligence (SIGINT) operations on email networks in Russia. Code-named PINWALE, the NSA email surveillance system targets Russian government, military, diplomatic, and commercial email traffic and burrows into the text portions of the email to search for particular words and phrases of interest to NSA eavesdroppers.

The DNI and NSA also plan to move Einstein into the private sector by claiming the nation's critical infrastructure, by nature, overlaps into the commercial sector. There are classified plans, already budgeted in so-called "black" projects, to extend Einstein surveillance into the dot (.) com, dot (.) edu, dot (.) int, and dot (.) org, as well as other Internet domains. Homeland Security Secretary Michael Chertoff has budgeted $5.4 billion for Einstein in his department's FY2009 information technology budget. However, this amount does not take into account the "black" budgets for Einstein proliferation throughout the U.S. telecommunications network contained in the budgets for NSA and DNI.

In anticipation of the regulatory problems inherent in domestic email surveillance by the NSA, the Bush administration has ensured that the Federal Communications Commission (FCC) and industry associations have been stacked with pro-surveillance loyalists to ensure that Einstein is widely accepted and implemented.

September 16, 2008 -- "Einstein" being extended to the South Pacific

The National Security Agency's (NSA) "Einstein" Internet surveillance technology is set to be extended to the nations of the South Pacific if New Zealand's NSA counterpart, the Government Communications Security Bureau (GCSB) gets its way.

One nation, the Cook Islands, is suspicious of the offer to connect it, via submarine cable, with the South Pacific Information Network (SPIN). There is a provision that the laws of New Zealand govern the operation of the system. Cook Islands is a self-governing associated territory of New Zealand. New Zealand, under the UKUSA signals intelligence (SIGINT) alliance of the United States, Britain, Canada, Australia, and New Zealand, is responsible for collecting SIGINT from the Pacific island nations.

SPIN and another Pacific cable system, ASH, have termination points in Hawaii. The SPIN system will connect Niue, French Polynesia, Vanuatu, Solomon Islands, New Caledonia, Papua New Guinea, Fiji, Australia, Tonga, Wallis and Futuna, Samoa, and American Samoa.

September 19-21, 2008 -- NSA believes that spying on journalists is not an urgent matter

After WMR and this editor became aware that the National Security Agency (NSA) was conducting a national security investigation of which this editor is a subject, we filed a Freedom of Information Act (FOIA) request with NSA. The request, dated August 19, 2008, requested "any and all documentation, including but not limited to written letters, memoranda, phone call logs, and any and all NSA correspondence with external agencies and departments, and any and all electronic records (electronic mail and text messages), between the dates of May 10, 2005 and the present that include the name 'WAYNEMADSEN' or 'WAYNEMADSENREPORT' or 'WAYNEMADSENREPORT.COM.'"

WMR requested media status, previously granted to us by the Department of State, as well as expedited processing of the request. While we were recognized as media and after having first been informed by phone by NSA that our FOIA request would be expedited, we were informed in an August 29, 2008 letter that expedited processing was denied and our request would be placed in "the normal processing queue," which means we will wait our turn behind FOIA requesters who want information on everything from microwave chip implants in their back sides and dental fillings to people who claimed to have had a ride on an alien spaceship and want NSA's records on their "excellent adventures."

NSA does not believe that our revelations on NSA spying on journalists and maintaining an illegal database for such spying rises to the level that "the information is urgently needed by an individual primarily engaged in disseminating information to inform the public about actual or alleged Federal Government activity. Urgent need means that the information has a particular value that will be lost if not disseminated quickly."

NATIONAL SECURITY AGENCY
CENTRAL SECURITY SERVICE
FORT GEORGE G. MEADE, MARYLAND 20755-6000

> Your request for expedited treatment has been denied because it does not meet the FOIA's criteria for expedited treatment. We will process your request in our normal processing queue. If you do not agree with this assessment of your request, you may file an appeal as indicated below.

WMR maintains that violation of the First Amendement right of freedom of the press is certainly of "value" that must be disseminated to the public as quickly as possible.

WMR intends to appeal the NSA's reversed decision.

It would appear that NSA does not want us peering too deeply into the "onion" of surveillance that has a number of new and old layers. One curious twist to this story is that one of the NSA investigators who is pursuing the national security probe of this editor happens to share a very unique name with a former CIA employee who was fired by the CIA in 1978 after his fingerprints were discovered on a cracked open safe belonging to the House Assassinations

Committee. The committee was looking into the killing of President John F. Kennedy and Dr. Martin Luther King.

House committee chief counsel G. Robert Blakey demanded that CIA director Stansfield Turner and his deputy, Frank Carlucci, explain why the CIA officer, tasked with courier duties for CIA documents requested by the committee, had rifled through the autopsy photos of President Kennedy. The CIA officials explained it was no big deal but fired the CIA employee anyway. Later, the employee told a Jack Anderson's staffer said that nothing was stolen from the safe but neither confirmed nor denied breaking into it himself.

September 30, 2008 -- NSA reverses decision on WMR FOIA request

The National Security Agency (NSA) has reversed itself and will grant WMR expedited processing of its Freedom of Information Act (FOIA) request on all agency written and electronic records containing information on "WAYNEMADSENREPORT," 'WAYNE MADSEN" OR "WAYNEMADSENREPORT.COM."

Previously, NSA granted WMR media status in our FOIA request but rejected our media expedited processing request. In a September 25, 2008 letter, NSA stated: "Since you are a member of the media, we have interpreted your request to be for information related to you in that capacity, especially with regards to any media activities relating to NSA." WMR believes that NSA files contain evidence that the signals intelligence agency has been conducting warrantless eavesdropping on journalists and that this highly-classified code word program lies at the heart of the parts of the program deemed illegal by Attorney General John Ashcroft, Deputy Attorney General James Comey, and FBI Director Robert Mueller. The parts of the program that were illegal were refused re-certification by Ashcroft and Comey in the now famous March 2004 hospital confrontation between a bed-ridden Ashcroft with Comey by his side and White House Counsel Alberto Gonzales and Chief of Staff Andrew Card.

NSA's letter also states that its expedited processing has discovered material responsive to our request and it "is not voluminous or complex." Our request has been placed in a "first-in, first-out processing queue for Non-Personal Easy cases."

There is an interesting caveat that possibly points to the surveillance of journalists. This editor, along with a New York-based journalist, have received a similarly-worded paragraph in our respective responses from NSA to our FOIA requests: "If . . . you were seeking what you may believe to be intelligence or surveillance records on you, please be aware that NSA/CSS targets unspecified persons or entities involved in terrorism as part of the nation's efforts to prevent against terrorist attacks."

WMR previously reported on the existence of a classified surveillance system, once code-named "FIRSTFRUITS," that was directed against journalists who write about signals intelligence and intercept issues. According to United States Signals Intelligence Directive 18 (USSID 18), U.S. persons are not to be targeted by NSA surveillance unless a warrant has been issued by the Foreign Intelligence Surveillance Court (FISC). The Bush warrantless surveillance program bypassed the FISC and permitted sweeping surveillance of Americans, known as "U.S. persons" in USSID 18. The NSA letter caveat that "unspecified persons or entities" are targeted as part of the counter-terrorism powers granted to NSA following 9/11 indicate that these persons and entities likely include journalists and their sources.

October 31-November 1, 2008 -- NSA has mental patients working as security agents

Under the tutelage of Generals Michael Hayden and Keith Alexander, the National Security Agency (NSA) has been turned into a virtual Pavlovian village where mentally off-balanced security agents conduct purges of NSA employees suspected of disloyalty, not in a national security sense, but against the George W. Bush-Dick Cheney neocon regime in Washington.

On October 24, Bush visited the Fort Meade NSA complex. Bush's illegal domestic communications surveillance program has placed the signals intelligence agency under Hayden and Alexander into a political storm and both agency directors face possible criminal indictments for violating the law and the Constitution.

Bush's visit to NSA was clouded in mystery. NSA employees, including active duty military personnel, who were walking outside before Bush's motorcade pulled up to the NSA main headquarters building were told by NSA police to cross the main street from the headquarters and wait behind the Eagle Fitness Center during Bush's arrival and under no circumstance were they permitted to look at the motorcade. NSA police officers were similarly instructed that while on the street they were not allowed to look at the motorcade. One NSA employee likened Bush's visit to the arrival of an Egyptian Pharaoh when the mere mortals were told not to gaze upon the "Shrubbery Pharaoh."

WMR has also learned that NSA employees have been plagued by a number of NSA Security Office agents who appear to be mentally unbalanced. For example, some agents who work for the Q Group act like "Agent Smith," the computer-generated G-man in the movie "The Matrix." Others are described as suffering from hallucinations and using coercion and physical threats against NSA employees. Other agents have accused NSA personnel of contributing to the collapse of Fannie Mae by defaulting on mortgages. This abuse has resulted in the plummeting of morale at NSA with many linguists and cryptologists working under conditions described as Kafkaesque. One reason for the abuse may be to intimidate NSA personnel to ensure they do not reveal any information about the illegal NSA domestic surveillance program authorized by Bush and Cheney.

In the past, WMR has reported on NSA Security working closely with NSA's Human Resources Department, particularly the psychological services unit, to pull employee clearances after accusing them of mental problems. Most of NSA's psychologists have dubious credentials and some were hired away from Maryland's prison system.

It would appear that based on the odd behavior of some NSA security agents that it is the NSA security group that is in severe need of psychological and psychiatric assistance from NSA's staff of shrinks.

November 7-9, 2008 -- Construction firm does well under Michael Hayden

During Michael Hayden's seven year tenure as National Security Agency (NSA) director and subsequent stints as deputy Director of National Intelligence and Central Intelligence Agency (CIA) director, his meteoric career rise has paralleled the good fortunes of the Greeley, Colorado-based construction company Hensel Phelps. The firm's introduction into the world of building intelligence facilities began in 1996 when it opened a separate profit center in Chantilly, Virginia, in the heart of Washington, DC's military-intelligence complex. It has been an impressive climb for a company founded in 1937 in Greeley by local builder Hensel Phelps. Like another favorite U.S. government construction firm, Bechtel, Hensel Phelps is employee-owned.

From its corporate history, Hensel Phelps appears to have done quite well in securing Air Force contracts. Hayden retired as an Air Force general earlier this year under pressure from Defense Secretary Robert Gates. The firm received major contracts at Tinker Air Force Base, Oklahoma; Cape Canaveral Air Station, Florida; Hollomon Air Force Base, New Mexico; and the White Sands Missile Range, New Mexico. Outside of the Air Force, Hensel Phelps has secured major contracts for the headquarters of the U.S. Army Forces Command (FORSCOM) and U.S. Army Reserve Command (USARC) at Fort Bragg, North Carolina; the Brigade Combat Team Complex No. 3 (BCT-3) at Fort Bliss, El Paso, Texas; a major Defense Department medical training center at Fort Sam Houston, Texas; the National Maritime Intelligence Center at the Office of Naval Intelligence, Suitland, Maryland; and the Military Department (MILDEP) Investigative Agencies Headquarters at Marine Corps Base in Quantico, Virginia.

Other major national security contracts include the Non-Proliferation and International Security Center, Los Alamos, New Mexico.

Among the most lucrative contracts received by Hensel Phelps is the construction of the new Defense Information Systems Agency (DISA) center at Hayden's old home base of Fort George G. Meade in Maryland. With 4300 employees and contractors and 1,070,000 square feet of office space, the DISA headquarters will complement the sprawling headquarters of NSA, Hayden's old command. The co-location of the two activities will also essentially bring the Pentagon's civilian computer and communications system infrastructure under the de facto control of the NSA, now the world's largest surveillance and espionage agency.

But perhaps nothing rivals the huge new NSA/Central Security Service complex at Fort Gordon, code-named SWEET TEA and part of the follow-on signals intelligence reorganization first proposed by Hayden as NSA director, code named TURBULENCE. For Hayden and NSA, the code word is apt. The two previous reorganization programs, GROUNDBREAKER and TRAILBLAZER were mired in cost overruns and charges of sweetheart, as opposed to SWEET TEA deals between Hayden and his top advisers and intelligence contractors like SAIC, CSC, and Booz Allen. The latter is where current National Intelligence Director, retired Admiral Mike McConnell, himself a former NSA director, served as a corporate head honcho.

SWEET TEA will accommodate some 4,000 personnel in 500,000 square feet of space. The $1 billion facility will be dedicated to monitoring communications in the Middle East and Europe. Other construction projects of NSA/CSS Texas in San Antonio and NSA/CSS Hawaii are designed to boost NSA's global eavesdropping capabilities. NSA Texas concentrates on Latin America while NSA Hawaii will be tuning in on Asia.

Hensel Phelps has done well under Hayden's tutelage over the intelligence community. One question remains: Has Hayden also done well?

December 12-14, 2008 -- Collection of personal and biometric data now a new "INT"

Traditionally, intelligence services have employed a number of intelligence collection methods to gather information. Human intelligence or "HUMINT" collects information from human intelligence assets; signals intelligence or "SIGINT" collects electronic signals; imagery intelligence or "IMINT" is dedicated to the collection of images from satellite and other reconnaissance platforms, and the list goes on.

However, there is a new "INT" on the block: "Identity Intelligence" or "I^2." I^2 collects personally-identifiable data on individuals from biometrics such as fingerprints, facial recognition, gait analysis, human identification-at-a-distance, DNA, retina and iris scans, hand geometry and other personal data collection systems; financial data from automatic teller machine and credit and debit card transactions; and global positioning system data captured from the use of cell phones and Blackberry devices. When coupled with Geospatial intelligence (GEOINT), I^2 can be displayed on large scale and work station electronic maps in intelligence fusion centers that have been popularized by movies such as "Body of Lies" and "Quantum Solace."

WMR was the first to report that many of the massive thefts of personal data were being carried out by a super-secret unit within the U.S. intelligence community that wanted to collect personal data after the Total Information Awareness (TIA) system of the Defense Advanced Research Projects Agency's Information Awareness Office and its then-chief, Iran-contra figure Admiral John Poindexter, were hauled on the carpet by Congress over the privacy-invasive system. Congress de-funded TIA but it re-emerged in a more clandestine environment within the National Security Agency (NSA) and Homeland Security Department, funded covertly with money laundered through the Department of Energy and its research laboratories.

Some I^2 systems are apparently being integrated in geo-spatial systems in order to find individuals in even remote locations. Operation Enduring Freedom - Trans Sahara (OEF-TS) and its military component, the Trans-Sahara Counter Terrorism Initiative (TSCTI), which targets nomadic peoples in the Sahara Desert who are thought to be "terrorists," employs I^2 and GEOINT under classified programs with such cover names as CREEK SAND and AZTEC ARCHER.

I^2 is such a hot new area of intelligence, and the CIA is sponsoring an Identity Intelligence Conference for only properly cleared personnel.

It is also apparent that I^2 is being actively supported by a number of high-tech firms, including Microsoft, Oracle, and Google.

2009

February 4, 2009 -- SPECIAL REPORT. NSA's meta-data email surveillance program exposed

WMR has learned details of one of the most important components of the National Security Agency's warrantless wiretapping program code named "STELLAR WIND." The highly-classified STELLAR WIND program was initiated by the George W. Bush administration with the cooperation of major U.S. telecommunications carriers, including AT&T and Verizon.

The interception of text communications by STELLAR WIND was a major priority of the NSA program.

The major NSA system for intercepting text communications is called PINWALE. On September 15, 2008, WMR first reported on how PINWALE was used to target Russian e-mails, "Code-named PINWALE, the NSA email surveillance system targets Russian government, military, diplomatic, and commercial email traffic and burrows into the text portions of the email to search for particular words and phrases of interest to NSA eavesdroppers."

WMR has learned additional details of PINWALE. The system is linked to a number of meta-databases that contain e-mail, faxes, and text messages of hundreds of millions of people around the world and in the United States. Informed sources have revealed to WMR that PINWALE can search these meta-databases using various parameters like date-time group, natural language, IP address, sender and recipients, operating system, and other information embedded in the header. When an NSA analyst is looking for Farsi or Arabic e-mails, the sender and recipients are normally foreign nationals, who are not covered by restrictions on eavesdropping on U.S. "persons" once imposed on NSA by United States Signals Intelligence Directive 18 (USSID 18). However, STELLAR WIND and PINWALE negated both USSID 18 and the Foreign Intelligence Surveillance Act of 1978 by permitting NSA analysts to read the e-mails, faxes, and text messages of U.S. persons when PINWALE search parameters included searches of e-mails in English. When English language text communications are retrieved, analysts read the text message content to determine whether it contains anything to do with terrorism. However, rather than being deleted, the messages are returned to the meta-databases.

Text message records in PINWALE, a system developed by NSA contractor Booz Allen Hamilton, are contained in three major meta-databases code-named LIONHEART, LIONROAR, and LIONFUSION.

Not only are text communications between U.S. persons in the United States and recipients abroad contained in the PINWALE meta-databases but text messages between U.S. persons within the United States are also held in the databases.

WMR reported on May 10, 2005, that Booz Allen is also the major contractor for an NSA database code named "FIRSTFRUITS" that tracked not only the articles of journalists but contained intercepts of their communications, ". . . part of the upkeep of the [FIRSTFRUITS] system has been outsourced to outside contractors such as Booz Allen."

The involvement of the telecommunications companies in STELLAR WIND and PINWALE was revealed when former AT&T technician Mark Klein leaked AT&T documents on the program 2006. AT&T's interception entailed NSA snooping equipment being placed within AT&T centers in San Francisco; Bridgeton, Missouri; San Diego; San Jose; Atlanta; Seattle; and Los Angeles.

The Obama administration recently appealed a decision by U.S. Judge Vaughn Walker of the U.S. Court for the Northern District of California who ruled that a lawsuit brought by the Al Haramain Islamic charity (Al Haramain v. Bush), in which the charity charges that it was the subject of illegal warrantless wiretapping under STELLAR WIND, could proceed.

WMR has previously reported that STELLAR WIND may have been used to prosecute Democratic governors and other Democratic officials around the country. WMR has received confirmation that when NSA analysts monitoring e-mails and other text messages, encountered information from PINWALE meta-databases that did not involve terrorism or foreign counterintelligence issues but did involve other possible criminal matters, NSA lawyers would determine whether such information should be turned over to Department of Justice criminal prosecutors. However, with information passed to WMR that NSA directors Michael Hayden and Keith Alexander were in total lockstep with the Bush-Cheney political agenda, with Alexander once boasting to a group of NSA employees that "I am a Rumsfeld man," there is the real possibility that PINWALE data ended up in the hands of U.S. Attorneys like Patrick Fitzgerald in his vendetta against deposed Illinois Rod Blagojevich and Alice Martin and Leura Canary in their Bush White House-directed political prosecution of former Alabama Governor Don Siegelman.

If Fitzgerald's legal brief against Blagojevich contains PINWALE-derived wiretap information it would explain why he has been unsuccessful in finding a grand jury in Chicago to indict Blagojevich. WMR was specifically told that e-mails between Washington and Chicago would be contained in PINWALE and that is something that could pose a problem for Fitzgerald in explaining where all his intercepts of Blagojevich originated. It may also explain why the Obama administration does not want details of STELLAR WIND to be exposed in Al Haramain v. Bush.

February 5-9, 2009 -- NSA signals intelligence system compromised to Israelis

WMR has learned that a super-classified National Security Agency (NSA) signals intelligence intercept system code-named SUPERCODING was compromised to Israeli intelligence agents shortly before Israel's surprise attack on Lebanon in July 2006.

The compromise occurred when the shipment of a SUPERCODING hardware unit from NSA headquarters in Fort Meade, Maryland to Camp Arifjan in Kuwait was changed from a classified restricted access shipment to a general postal shipment. After the SUPERCODING unit was received at Camp Arifjan, there were unmistakable signs that the hardware unit, which contains TOP SECRET Handle Via COMINT Channels Only software, was tampered with after being delivered to Israeli intelligence for use in the Israeli attack on Lebanon. The compromise of SUPERCODING took place prior to Israel's attack on Lebanon on July 12, 2006.

SUPERCODING is a signals intelligence (SIGINT) system that scans the full-spectrum of Iranian communications, from low frequency cell phone and walkie-talkie communications to higher frequency microwave and satellite communications.

NSA sources believe that Israel briefly stole the SUPERCODING system in order to copy its data for use in intercepting communications between Iran and Hezbollah in Lebanon.

Current Director of NSA General Keith Alexander was in charge of the agency at the time of the SUPERCODING compromise. His predecessor, General Michael Hayden, was deputy director for National Intelligence under director for National Intelligence John Negroponte.

The compromise of SUPERCODING, containing detailed intelligence on Iranian communications, frequencies, and sources of intelligence may represent the greatest breach of U.S. intelligence by Israel since the espionage committed by Israeli spy Jonathan Pollard.

February 9-10, 2009 -- Hayden's version of GPS: Saddam's tanks in Kazakhstan in 2003

WMR has learned that National Security Agency (NSA) intelligence was so bad in the weeks leading up to the March 2003 attack on Iraq, NSA high-frequency detection finding (HFDF) systems placed Iraqi tanks deep within Kazakhstan, a former Soviet republic in central Asia.

High-frequency detection finding, HFDF, which is also pronounced "Huff-duff," uses antenna arrays to triangulate fixes on communications and electronic emitters. A mainstay of NSA during the Cold War years, HFDF has become an antiquated signals intelligence method, being replaced by more sophisticated satellite and other airborne reconnaissance systems.

One antiquated NSA system, code named MEDIATOR, which then-NSA director General Michael Hayden insisted on keeping operational, was so poor it triangulated fixes on signals emanating from Saddam Hussein's tanks in Iraq in Kazakhstan and even beyond, in Russian central Asia. WMR previously obtained a list of NSA systems and MEDIATOR is found listed between two other NSA systems, MEDIASTORM and MEDIEVAL.

Hayden went on from NSA diretor to be the Deputy Director of National Intelligence and the CIA director.

February 15-16, 2009 -- More political chicanery involving NSA wiretaps?

Sen. Roland Burris (D-IL), appointed by ex-Illinois Democratic Governor Rod Blagojevich, impeached and convicted by the Illinois legislature, has admitted to money conversations with Blagojevich's brother, Robert Blagojevich.

In a February 4 affidavit to the Illinois House impeachment committee, Burris wrote that "there were several facts that I was not given the opportunity to make during my testimony to the impeachment committee."

Burris admitted he had three phone conversations with Robert Blagojevich, one in October and two after the election in November. The calls sought campaign contribution assistance from Burris. At least one of the phone calls may have been wiretapped by the FBI, according to some published reports. Republicans on the Illinois House impeachment committee are pressing for a perjury investigation of Burris.

However, the real story is U.S. Attorney for Northern Illinois, Patrick Fitzgerald, recently reappointed by President Barack Obama, undoubtedly with the support of White House Chief of Staff Rahm Emanuel, Rod Blagojevich's successor in the U.S. House of Representatives.

WMR reiterates its earlier reports that Fitzgerald is likely using illegal NSA wiretaps obtained under the National Security Agency's (NSA) illegal STELLAR WIND eavesdropping program. It now appears that the program is continuing under the Obama administration and stored intercepted phone calls are being used by the Obama White House against Burris in yet another attempt by Emanuel to purge his enemies from public office.

NSA sources have informed WMR that the two major communications links being monitored by STELLAR WIND are those that link Detroit and Chicago to the rest of the country and the world, particularly the circuits to Washington, DC. The official reason is the large number of Arab-Americans and Muslims living in both metropolitan areas. However, WMR is told that "conversations involving politics and politicians" were collaterally handed over routinely to the Justice Department, of which Fitzgerald is a part.

The Blagojevich prosecution and that of Detroit Mayor Kwame Kilpatrick, for which the latter saw the introduction as evidence of some 14,000 pager text messages between Kilpatrick and his chief of staff Christine Beatty, with whom he was alleged to be carrying on an extramarital affair, likely involved the handing over of NSA STELLAR WIND, PINWALE, LIONFUSION, LIONHEART, LIONROAR, and OCEANARIUM voice and text intercepts. These would have been obtained by Fitzgerald in the cases of Blagojevich and now Burris, and by Michigan's Republican Attorney General Mike Cox in the Kilpatrick case.

Kilpatrick resigned on September 18, 2008 and served a 99-day prison sentence for obstruction of justice involving the sex scandal. Senate Majority Leader Harry Reid is now investigating the charges that Burris was involved with the Blagojevich brothers in the "pay to play" scandal.

Kilpatrick's mother is Rep. Carolyn Kikpatrick (D-MI), who helped former Rep. Cynthia McKinney in conducting an informal 9/11 hearing in the House of Representatives in 2005. This editor served as one of the questioners of witnesses at the hearing.

It can be expected that Rep. Kilpatrick "got the message" in the indictment and jailing of her son, the former mayor, and she will no longer press the 9/11 truth cause. It is also apparent that Emanuel has his sights trained on Burris and he is looking forward to ensuring that Emanuel's ally, Governor Pat Quinn, stands ready to appoint, if necessary, Burris' replacement, someone who will toe the Emanuel and American Israel Public Affairs Committee (AIPAC) line.

April 13-14, 2009 -- Peep perps at NSA

WMR can provide a psychological profile of some of the people that the Obama administration permits to eavesdrop indiscriminately on the phone calls and emails of American citizens through the continuation of the Bush administration's "Stellar Wind" warrantless wiretapping program.

Last week, at the entrance to the cafeteria at the National Security Agency (NSA) headquarters in Fort Meade, Maryland, there was a display of marshmallow "Peeps," the candy chicks that appear every Easter. The purpose of the display was for staff to judge the best entry. Several of the Peep entries had, according to our NSA sources, been subjected to violence by firearms and other instruments, and had "blood" on them.

General Keith Alexander, the NSA director, is hoping for a high cyber-warfare position in the Obama administration. His agency's antics should be welcomed by Obama's Chief of Staff Rahm Emanuel, the Israeli-American ballet fairy who relished after the 1996 presidential election of taking a steak knife and plunging it into the dinner table uttering 'Dead! ... Dead! ... Dead!' after stating the name of every politician he thought had betrayed President Clinton. Perhaps Alexander can deliver some Peeps to Emanuel for a grizzly demise from a steak knife.

June 2-3, 2009 – Suspicions surround "suicide" of Israeli SIGINT service officer

Israeli military police are investigating the reported suicide death by an alleged self-inflicted gun shot wound to the head of Israeli Military Intelligence Unit 8200 department head 43-year old Major Aviya Moshe.

Major Aviya Moshe, a department head in Military Intelligence's 8200 unit, was found dead in his office at Unit 8200 headquarters in Herzliya, north of Tel Aviv, early Sunday morning. Moshe committed suicide, shooting himself with his personal handgun. *Ha'aretz* reported there were no indications that Moshe was exhibiting behavior that would prompt him to commit suicide.

There has been some speculation in the Lebanese press that Moshe's death could be linked to the roundup of Israeli spies in the Lebanese military. Lebanese authorities have, to date, charged 21 people, including two Lebanese Army colonels. An additional nine people have been detained on suspicions of spying for Israel.

The latest colonel arrested, Shahid Toumieh, was described by *As Safar* newspaper as a "signal code" officer, a position similar to that of Moshe in Israeli military intelligence. Lebanon says three of those charged with spying for Israel have fled across the border to Israel. It is believed that all the Lebanese charged with spying for Israel were providing intelligence on Lebanese Hezbollah to Israeli intelligence. Some of those detained by Lebanon were found with sophisticated communications equipment that may have originated with Israel's Unit 8200, the Israeli equivalent of the U.S. National Security Agency (NSA) that conducts electronic and signals intelligence (SIGINT) gathering. Unit 8200 is also known as the Central Collection Unit of the Intelligence Corps.

In 2003, a Unit 8200 officer, identified only as "Lieutenant A," was court-martialed for refusing to carry out the targeting of a civilian target in the West Bank city of Nablus. The lieutenant believed that by carrying out the order, innocent civilians would be killed in an Israeli aerial attack against the target and he believed that following such an order that would cause random casualties would be a violation of international law.

Many Herzliya officers have gone on to founding Israel's major telecommunications and software high-tech surveillance companies, including Check Point, ICQ, Amdocs, and Comverse Infosys.

June 25-26, 2009 – New Cyber-Command at NSA, Fort Meade, Maryland

Special to WMR:

[Ed. Note: On June 23, Defense Secretary Robert Gates ordered that the new U.S. CyberCommand will be a part of the U.S. Stategic Command (Stratcom) and will come under the command of the Director of the National Security Agency (NSA). The CyberCommand will be at NSA's headquarters in Fort Meade, Maryland.] We received the following from an NSA source:

"Subject: New Cyber Command and NSA

If this is indeed correct, the assertion that StratCom will be in control of this new CyberCom is complete and utter hogwash. As StratCom has neither the expertise nor technical resources to conduct this mission, the default control of CyberCom will fall, by design, into the lap of NSA. This was similarly true of StratCom being given responsibility for military space after the demise of US Space Command, which effectively ceded control of space to the Air Force. Are we to believe that CyberCom being headquartered not at Omaha, NE, but rather at Fort Meade, MD, right next to NSA; and with NSA's current director, Lieutenant General Keith Alexander, promoted to a four star general, as its head, is a coincidence? NSA has coveted control of cyber operations for some time and already exerts considerable influence in the mission field. Illegally, NSA has tapped into all domestic e-mail traffic within the United States. To allow them the ability to subject all U.S. domestic computer communications to offensive cyber-attacks and the many other aspects of digital 'information warfare' should make all of America shudder in fear. Of course this supposedly will be subject to congressional oversight, federal statutes, executive orders, and agency regulations, and we all now know how steadfastly NSA is committed to these safeguards and to our constitutional liberties. With NSA now pulling the wool over our new president's eyes, in conjunction with their contempt for congressional oversight, I am truly horrified of the prospect that NSA will usher us into a new dystopia where we will soon learn the mandatory newspeak language that will alter the concluding line of our national anthem from '... the land of the free and home of the brave" to, '... the land of the fear and the home of the depraved.'

This development indicates that SecDef Robert Gates is truly a creature of his former master.

Be afraid America, be very afraid, as NSA will soon be the number one 'clear a present danger' to your freedom and liberty.

Lord help us!"

July 3-5, 2009 -- NSA Security running amok to plug leaks about 9/11

WMR has learned that the National Security "Q" Group, responsible for security, has grown to an immense security and counter-intelligence force, with an estimated one thousand government employees, contractors, and paid informants. NSA's Security force is reportedly primarily tasked with plugging any leaks of classified or other information that points to U.S. government involvement with the terrorist attacks on September 11, 2001. NSA Security has doggedly pursued a number of NSA employees, some in "sting" operations, others in frequent polygraphs and repeated security interviews where threats are made by thuggish NSA security agents with and without the presence of FBI agents, and others in constant surveillance operations at their homes, churches, and other locations away from the Fort Meade, Maryland headquarters of the agency.

The most egregious NSA Security operation against an NSA employee was the 2004 arrest of NSA analyst Ken Ford, Jr. Ford became a target of opportunity for NSA Security and the FBI after Vice President Dick Cheney noted his name on an NSA signals intelligence report on Saddam Hussein's government that stated that there was no proof from interceptions of Iraqi communications that Saddam Hussein possessed "weapons of mass destruction." Cheney and other neocons in the Bush White House arranged for a "sting" operation to be mounted as retribution against Ford. Ford was charged with taking classified papers home from NSA headquarters, something that is quite impossible considering the stringent security in place at one of the most-secured complexes in the world.

Ford was convicted by a tainted jury and sentenced to seven years in federal prison. Ford, who is African-American, originally had an African-American federal trial judge. However, the judge was replaced by a pro-Iraq war U.S. judge, Peter Messitte, who set out to ensure a guilty conviction of Ford in cahoots with U.S. Attorney for Maryland Rod Rosenstein, and Assistant U.S. Attorney for Southern Maryland David Salem, both Bush appointees. Nothing was done by the judge or prosecutors to dismiss from the jury a contractor whose company had major contracts with NSA. The trio of Messitte, Rosenstein, and Salem have also "rocket-docketed" a number of cases, resulting in slam dunk convictions, against Arab- and Iranian-Americans in the southern district of Maryland.

NSA's Security chief is Kemp Ensor III. Ensor has built up what amounts to a massive law enforcement and intelligence agency in Maryland that operates as a virtual independent operation that answers to no one. Maryland's congressional delegation has shown little interest in oversight over the security operation.

In fact, WMR has learned that many NSA employees, aware of the political and other misuse of their agency by the Bush-Cheney administration, avidly backed Barack Obama for President hoping that the past era when NSA complied with te Foreign Intelligence Surveillance Act (FISA) and the Fourth Amendment of the Constitution would be restored. However, many NSA employees are bitterly disappointed that Obama has done nothing to curtail not only the widespread surveillance of the communications of law-abiding Americans but the constant "Stasi-like" harassment and surveillance conducted by Ensor's team of agents and confidential informants. WMR has also learned that NSA Security has been authorized to work directly with Washington area local police department intelligence divisions to carry out its surveillance of not only NSA employees and contractors, but journalists who report on the activities of NSA. Two police departments mentioned in this respect are the Alexandria, Virginia and Anne Arundel County Sheriff departments.

One senior-level NSA official recently found himself sitting in front of NSA Security questioners asking why he gave his NSA business cards to some students at a university. It turns out the official was trying to recruit students for NSA employment. When the official asked why there was a problem in his handing out his business cards, the answer by NSA Security was that some of them, all American citizens, had "Russian last names."

Even former NSA employees and contractors are being subjected to continual NSA Security surveillance and harassment at their work places and other locations, according to WMR's sources. Some have lost their jobs as a result of pressure from NSA Security.

WMR has in the past reported on NSA surveillance of journalists.

Since the revelation of the NSA journalist monitoring database, FIRSTFRUITS, which later added communications intercepts of journalist phone calls, emails, and faxes to its database, NSA Security has, according to information received by WMR, conducted physical surveillance of journalists it deems to be threats to the operations of the agency. The top targeted journalists, who make up a virtual "rogues' gallery" at NSA Security, complete with photographs and other personal information, are: former *Baltimore Sun* and current *Wall Street Journal* reporter Siobhan Gorman, *Washington Times* reporter Bill Gertz, former Baltimore Sun and current *New York Times* reporter Scott Shane, *Baltimore Sun* reporter Phil McGowan, author James Bamford, *New York Times* reporters James Risen and Eric Lichtblau, and this editor, Wayne Madsen.

In addition to the aforementioned, Firstfruits also contained the names of former *Washington Post* reporter Vernon Loeb, *New Yorker* journalist Seymour Hersh, and UPI's John C. K. Daly.

Ironically, NSA Security allegedly has its own connections in the news media. A *Washington Times* source revealed that the paper's writer of the "Inside the Beltway" column, John McCaslin, has a relative inside NSA Security -- Robert McCaslin, the chief of NSA Security counter-intelligence and the chief "sting" agent against Ford. Robert is, according to the *Washington Times* source, is the brother of the paper's columnist.

NSA Security is also able to utilize the agency's most sophisticated electronic surveillance systems to monitor the activities of journalists. The cell phones of journalists are routinely used as listening devices, even when turned off. And what was considered a sure-fire method of avoiding having a cell phone used as a transmitter, removing the batteries in what has become known as "batteries out" conversations, is no longer safe. Even when the batteries are removed, the global positioning system (GPS) chip in cell phones continues to have enough residual power that two to three pings from satellites can give away a person's location and what other uniquely-identifiable cell phone are at the same location.

The bottom line is that a number of NSA personnel who were on duty in the months leading up to 9/11, the day of the attacks, and subsequent weeks and months are aware of undeniable facts that point to a massive cover-up by the Bush-Cheney administration of the circumstances surrounding 9/11, including what actually befell United Airlines flight 93 and who was issuing direct military orders from the White House.

The Obama administration, rather than lessen the pressure on the NSA personnel, has turned up the heat and is resorting to even more draconian methods to ensure silence. The word from inside NSA is that a state of fear exists and the mission of the agency, to conduct surveillance of foreign communications to provide threat indications and warnings to U.S. troops and policy makers and protect sensitive U.S. government communications from unauthorized eavesdropping is suffering as a result.

August 28-30, 2009 -- NSA Q Group employs more Soviet-style security measures

WMR's National Security Agency (NSA) sources report that the agency's Q Group personnel security department, acting in concert with the dubious NSA medical unit, has adopted a new approach to dealing with NSA employees who express opposition to illegal surveillance policies and draconian internal security procedures.

NSA Security, headed up by Kemp Ensor III, and NSA medical worked in tandem to deny security access to employees determined to be mentally unfit to have access to classified information at NSA.

However, due to the attrition of highly-qualified personnel, the security-medical duo is now prescribing Prozac and Zoloft for NSA employees who refuse to fall into line. NSA is abuzz with the new requirement for employees to take what they call "happy pills."

The sexual harassment scene has also reportedly changed at Fort Meade. In the past, sexual harassment at NSA involved older male managers preying on young female employees. That has now changed in what has become an environment of "do ask and do tell." WMR has been informed that there is an increase in complaints about sexual harassment from new young male hires about being forced into "kinky rendezvouses" with older male managers.

December 14, 2009 -- Obama "surges" against world's fourth smallest country

After ordering a troop surge of 30,000 American military personnel to Afghanistan, President Obama authorized the National Security Agency (NSA) to mount "surge" surveillance of the telecommunications of the delegations at the Copenhagen Climate Change Summit of small island states, particularly the South Pacific atoll nation of Tuvalu, the world's fourth smallest nation that is in danger of sinking under the Pacific due to rising sea levels from melting polar ice. U.S. intelligence sources report that such a "surge" in surveillance would have involved the re-prioritization of NSA signals intelligence (SIGINT)-gathering assets, including electronic espionage satellites and ground stations in a network that extends from outside of Copenhagen; to Menwith Hill, England; and allied stations in New Zealand and Australia.

In January 2003, the Bush administration mounted a similar "surge" against the missions of countries on the UN Security Council to ascertain how they would vote on the UN Security Council resolution authorizing U.S. and British military action against Iraq.

On September 25, 2008, WMR carried the following report:

At a seminar held at American University in Washington on September 24, former United Kingdom Government Communications Headquarters (GCHQ) linguist Katharine Gun and former London *Observer and* current *New Statesman* reporter Martin Bright revealed that the Bush and Tony Blair governments were plotting to blackmail ambassadors to the UN in the "surge" surveillance of the telephones and e-mail of UN delegations in January 2003. Bush and Blair wanted to ensure the support of six UN Security Council members whose votes were needed for the resolution authorizing U.S. and British military action against Iraq.

The surge surveillance request was contained in an email sent to GCHQ from NSA's Frank Koza, NSA's chief of staff of the Regional Targets section of the agency. Gun, a Mandarin Chinese translator for GCHQ, realized that what was being requested of GCHQ would lead to an illegal war against Iraq. Gun leaked the email to the British media by hiding a copy in her handbag and taking it out of the GCHQ building in Cheltenham. When the email appeared in *The Observer*, GCHQ security mounted an investigation of each of the 100 employees of the agency who had access to the January 31, 2003 document. Gun eventually admitted to taking the email and was arrested by Special Branch Metropolitan London police officers who traveled from London to Cheltenham to make the arrest. Gun had criminal charges against her suddenly dropped when it became apparent that her trial on the leak of the Top Secret Code Word NSA directive to GCHQ would embarrass the Blair government . . . Since 2003, it has been discovered that the United States and United Kingdom wanted to intercept the office and home communications of the UN ambassadors of Pakistan, Chile, Angola, Guinea, Cameroon, and Mexico, six non-permanent members of the Security Council, to gather information that could be used to blackmail the ambassadors into voting for the US/UK Iraq war resolution. Ultimately, the Security Council refused to back the resolution . . . Since 2003, it has been discovered that the United States and United Kingdom wanted to intercept the office and home communications of the UN ambassadors of Pakistan, Chile, Angola, Guinea, Cameroon, and Mexico, six non-permanent members of the Security Council, to gather information that could be used to blackmail the ambassadors into voting for the US/UK Iraq war resolution. Ultimately, the Security Council refused to back the resolution."

President Bush threatened UN Security Council member Chile with the scuttling of a free trade agreement and member Angola with cancellation of U.S. Millennium Account funding.

Bush's successor, Obama, by ordering a similar "surge" on the phone calls, e-mails, and text messages of the leaders of small island states, appears prepared to use similar strong-armed tactics against nations that want rigorous action taken by the world's richest nations to stem the effects of climate change.

On December 12, *The Canberra Times* let the surveillance operation against the small island states slip out of the bag when it reported that NSA's Australian counterpart, the Defense Signals Directorate (DSD) in Canberra, was participating in the surge along with NSA and Britain's Government Communications Headquarters (GCHQ). The paper quoted an unnamed Australian intelligence official as stating that the "intelligence sharing and liaison arrangements" between Australia, the UK, and US [which also includes Canada's Communications Security Establishment (CSE) and New Zealand's Government Communications Security Bureau (GCSB)] were used to collect signals intelligence on not only small island states but also non-government environmental organizations represented at the Copenhagen summit.

The surge surveillance also concentrated on NGOs that were seeking to influence climate change negotiations through their close association with delegations from small island states, particularly tiny Tuvalu. Leaders like Obama, British Prime Minister Gordon Brown, and Australian Prime Minister Kevin Rudd were reportedly trying to find out about various delegations' negotiating positions in order to try to drive wedges and divisions between small countries and NGOs. In fact, a leaked e-mail containing a draft proposal by Danish Prime Minister Lars Lokke Rasmussen suggested that Denmark, Britain, and the United States were secretly conspiring to reduce the greenhouse gas emission targets while putting more pressure on developing countries. Denmark assisted NSA and its partners in the electronic surveillance of delegations in Copenhagen from the Danish Defense Intelligence Service (*Forsvarets Efterretningstjeneste*) listening station at Aflandshage, south of Copenhagen. From the Danish base, intercepted signals are transmitted to the NSA base in Menwith Hill, the GCHQ in Cheltenham, and NSA headquarters at Fort Meade, Maryland.

NSA's and its partners' ability to listen in on the communications of Pacific island leaders is made easier by special arrangements made between the spy agencies and cell phone service providers like Vodafone, previously implicated in NSA surveillance operations in Greece, India, and Montenegro, which allow the eavesdroppers to bypass rudimentary encryption features provided to heads of state and government. NSA director, General Keith Alexander, paid a "secret" visit to New Zealand's GCSB headquarters in Wellington in July where he was hosted by Air Marshal Sir Bruce Ferguson, GCSB's chief. Alexander's presence in New Zealand was discovered by an observant journalist in Wellington. In September of this year, a Radio New Zealand reporter allegedly "found" a notebook lost by a Treasury Department official. The notebook contained information about the modernization and reorganization of the New Zealand intelligence services, including GCSB.

Alexander was reportedly, in part, discussing the surge operations against the South Pacific states of the Cook Islands, the Federated States of Micronesia, Kiribati, the Marshall Islands, Nauru (the world's third smallest nation), New Caledonia, Niue, Palau, Papua New Guinea, Polynesia, Samoa, the Solomon Islands, Tonga, Tuvalu, and Vanuatu during the preliminary Pacific Islands Forum in Cairns, Australia in early August of this year and later in Copenhagen. GCSB analysts work alongside NSA personnel at Fort Meade and San Antonio, Texas. Since coming to office, Obama has ordered the Pentagon to restore close military and intelligence links with New Zealand and U.S. Defense Secretary Robert Gates and New Zealand Defense

Minister Wayne Mapp have met to seal a deal on closer defense links frayed in the 1980s over the ban on U.S. Navy nuclear-armed and nuclear-powered ships visiting New Zealand.

Tuvalu was at the top of America's surge policy because it delegation was the most active in opposing Rasmussen's proposal hammered out with Obama and Brown. Tuvalu led a walkout of developing nations a day after the Copenhagen climate summit commenced.

Tuvalu's lead negotiator in Copenhagen is Ian Fry, an Australian environmental lawyer. Tuvalu's Prime Minister Apisai Ielemia planned to travel to Copenhagen to sign a strong final agreement to limit greenhouse gas emissions. The allied signals intelligence surge against small island states and NGOs would have re-prioritized assets directed against insurgents in Afghanistan, Pakistan, and Iraq to target the emails and cell phone calls of Fry and Ielemia, according to an NSA source. But Fry and Ielemia are not alone in having their private communications intercepted and processed through UK-USA SIGINT alliance collection computers in Waihopai and Tangimoana, New Zealand and via the SIGINT Production Unit at GCSB headquarters at the Freyberg Building in Wellington; Geraldton, Australia; Kunia, Hawaii; Cheltenham, England; and Fort Meade, Maryland. Transcripts of the phone calls, e-mails, and text messages of leaders from Cook Islands Prime Minister Jim Marurai and Fiji's Prime Minister Voreqe Bainimarama to Kiribati's President Anote Tong and Papua New Guinea's Prime Minister Michael Somare. Somare's stance at Copenhagen would have been of interest to the SIGINT analysts after his blistering attack on Obama's climate policies at the recent Commonwealth Heads of Government summit in Trinidad.

Those in Copenhagen targeted by Obama's "E-surge" in Copenhagen also likely included environmental activist clerics Nobel Peace Prize Laureate Archbishop Desmond Tutu of South Africa; the Archbishop of Canterbury Rowan Williams; Reverend Tofiga Falani, the President, Congregational Christian Church of Tuvalu; Swedish Lutheran Archbishop Anders Wejryd; and Lutheran Bishop Sofie Petersen of Kalalit Nunaat (Greenland).

NSA's surge surveillance of the Copenhagen climate summit is not the first time the spy agency has targeted world leaders gathered for a conference. In 1993, President Clinton authorized a surge surveillance operation directed against the Asia-Pacific Economic Cooperation summit in Seattle, including the placement of audio and video surveillance equipment in hotel rooms by joint NSA-CIA Special Collection Service ("F-6") teams In 1995, a similar operation was directed against the Summit of the Americas in Miami.

2010

January 26, 2010 -- NSA outsourcing signals intelligence and surveillance jobs

At a news conference yesterday at the National Press Club in Washington, author James Bamford, who has written a number of books on the National Security Agency (NSA), said the NSA was continuing to outsource eavesdropping and other electronic surveillance tasks to companies like Science Applications International Corporation (SAIC), Boeing, and L-3. Bamford spoke at a press conference sponsored by the Electronic Privacy Information Center (EPIC) on the privacy dangers posed by airport body scanners.

March 4, 2010 -- More details emerging of NSA's next generation Internet surveillance

The Obama administration is continuing to expand a National Security Agency-run Internet surveillance program first started by the Bush administration.

The surveillance project, known as Einstein, was previously reported by WMR to be a surveillance program and not, primarily, a network security countermeasure as billed by NSA and the Bush administration.

Speaking at the RSA Security conference in San Francisco on March 3, Greg Schaffer, assistant secretary of Homeland Security for cybersecurity and communications, tipped attendees off on the future plans of the NSA and Homeland Security Department to extend Einstein 3 surveillance to non-government networks, including the Internet.

Einstein was a personal pet project of Bush's Homeland Security Secretary Michael Chertoff. With Chertoff continuing to advise the Homeland Security Department and Secretary Janet Napolitano, the Obama administration is continuing to embrace the Internet surveillance policies adopted by the Bush administration. Napolitano is also continuing Chertoff's policies by keeping most of the details about Einstein, both versions 2 and 3, classified.

The NSA and the Obama administration are claiming that Einstein 3 does not read the content of e-mail messages, however, much of the details of the system are not only classified but AT&T, which was instrumental in conducting highly-classified warrantless wiretaps of Internet traffic on behalf of the NSA as part of STELLAR WIND, is involved in testing Einstein 3.

The history of NSA's expansion of its surveillance capabilities suggests that it is being as disingenuous about Einstein 3 as it was about previous forays into private telecommunications surveillance, including the Clipper and Capstone encryption key escrow systems that allowed

NSA to possess the decryption keys to listen to and read scrambled private phone calls and e-mail messages, respectively.

NSA often will state we want to do "A" but not "B." In fact, NSA always wants to do "A" and "B," with plans to do "C."

April 16-18, 2010 -- SPECIAL REPORT. The hidden hands behind the Thomas Drake indictment

There is much more to the Obama administration's indictment on April 15 of former NSA senior executive Thomas Drake by the US Attorney for Maryland, Rod Rosenstein, a Bush holdover who has brought similar politically-motivated criminal charges against other NSA personnel. Drake is charged with ten criminal counts, including leaking classified information to a newspaper. WMR can confirm the paper is *The Wall Street Journal* and the reporter at the *Journal* who received Drake's information is Siobhan Gorman, who was also subject to electronic surveillance by the NSA and FBI while she was with the *Journal* and previously, *The Baltimore Sun*. Other charges brought against Drake, who continued to work for the NSA as a contractor after stepping down as an NSA executive, include obstruction of justice and making false statements to a federal law enforcement official.

Since leaving his executive position with the NSA, Drake has served as President and Chief Operating Officer of National Technologies Associates, Inc. of Alexandria, Virginia. The firm has revenues of $50 million and employs 600 people. Before NSA, Drake was an information technology and management consultant with Coastal Research & Technology, Inc. (CRTI).

While at NSA, Drake worked in the Signals Intelligence Division (SID), the group responsible for eavesdropping on foreign communications and, since the advent of warrantless domestic surveillance, domestic U.S. communications, as well.

WMR can report that as part of the Drake investigation, Gorman and the *Wall Street Journal* were subject to STELLAR WIND, warrantless wiretapping, as late as last year. The surveillance began when Gorman wrote a series of articles between 2006 and 2007 on NSA contracting cost overruns and mismanagement, information that was first reported by WMR in 2005.

Drake's prosecution by the Obama administration represents a continuation of a "witch hunt" by NSA and its Stasi-like Security unit, the "Q Group," to plug all leaks from the signals intelligence and cyber-warfare agency even if the information provided to the media concerns criminal conduct like contract fraud, sexual misconduct, illegal surveillance of American citizens, and illegal "sneak an peek" break-ins of the homes of NSA employees and contractors by NSA Q Group personnel and FBI agents.

In 2008, NSA and FBI surveillance of current and former NSA and Justice Department employees who were suspected of leaking information to the press about the NSA's super-classified STELLAR WIND warrantless digital surveillance program, called the "Terrorist Surveillance Program" by the Justice Department, was stepped up.

On March 10, 2008, Gorman wrote an article for the Journal titled, "NSA's Domestic Spying Grows As Agency Sweeps Up Data." Gorman wrote:

"According to current and former intelligence officials, the spy agency now monitors huge volumes of records of domestic emails and Internet searches as well as bank transfers, credit-card transactions, travel and telephone records. The NSA receives this so-called 'transactional' data from other agencies or private companies, and its sophisticated software programs analyze the various transactions for suspicious patterns. Then they spit out leads to be explored by counterterrorism programs across the U.S. government, such as the NSA's own Terrorist Surveillance Program, formed to intercept phone calls and emails between the U.S. and overseas without a judge's approval when a link to al Qaeda is suspected."

The previous year, as WMR reported in May 12, 2009, former Justice Department prosecutor Thomas Tamm's home was invaded by a SWAT team of federal agents.

In 2008, one of WMR's sources discovered that his home had been broken into and anything that could store digital data had been stolen: laptops, digital cameras, USB thumb drives, etc. Moreover, relatives of the individual discovered that the lock to their home had been drilled out in what was an obvious "black bag" sneak and peel operation.

That same year, this editor discovered that the lock to his apartment door at Potomac Towers in Arlington, Virginia had been drilled out by a circular saw drill bit that drilled around the lock cylinder. When the apartment maintenance man was called to check the lock, he discovered the fragments of the lock pins scattered on the floor at the base of the door. He stated at the time that he had never experienced anything like it in the past.

FBI and NSA surveillance of people affiliated with NSA continued through last week, with this editor and one of his sources being tailed in 2009 in the suburban Maryland suburbs of Washington, DC and an additional tail of a source being conducted last week in Annapolis, Maryland.

The indictment of Drake in reminiscent of the case brought against former NSA signals intelligence (SIGINT) analyst Ken Ford, Jr. in 2006. In March 2006, Ford was sentenced to six years in prison in a case replete with prosecutorial and judicial misconduct by Rosenstein, Assistant U.S. Attorney David Salem, and US Judge Peter Messitte. On April 30, 2007, WMR reported: "Ford was set up in a clumsy Justice Department, FBI, and NSA Security Division operation to punish him for his May 2003 signals intelligence (SIGINT) analysis report that concluded, based on intercepts of Iraqi communications, there was no truth to the Bush administration's claim that there were weapons of mass destruction in Iraq. Ford's report, with his name and that of his supervisor on it, ended up on Vice President Dick Cheney's desk. From that time on, Ford was a marked man for the neo-con cabal operating within the White House, Justice Department, Pentagon, and US Intelligence Community senior staff."

At one point during Ford's trial, Messitte called Ford to his bench and asked him if he had spoken to this editor. Ford replied that he had not, whereupon Messitte asked, "Is Mr. Madsen in the court room?" I was not present at the time but I was later told by an informed source that Messitte was prepared to call me to the stand to be asked about the sources of my stories on the case. Such a development would have required me to invoke my First Amendment rights, as the press is the only occupation identified by name in the Bill of Rights as being protected. There was a risk of a contempt ruling and possible federal prison had I been present during Messitte's "kangaroo court" proceedings.

Ford continues to serve his six year sentence at Lewisburg federal prison in Pennsylvania. Attorney General Eric Holder was sent a letter by Ford's parents on November 18, 2009, calling for the appointment of a special prosecutor in the case against their son. To date, Holder has not responded to the letter.

The letter follows:

November 18, 2009

SENT CERTIFIED MAIL / E-MAIL / FACSIMILE

RETURN RECEIPT

Honorable Eric H. Holder. Jr.

Attorney General of the United States

Honorable David W. Ogden

Deputy Attorney General of the United States

950 Pennsylvania Avenue, N.W.

Washington, D.C. 2053 0-0001

United States v. Kenneth Wayne Ford. Jr.

Criminal Case No(s): 04-cr-l l8JKS, 05-cr-0098PJM and 05-cr-0235PJM

Messrs. Holder and Ogden:

In the interest of justice, we, the parents of Kenneth Wayne Ford, Jr., ("hereafter Mr. Ford") request an immediate appointment of Special Counsel to investigate unwarranted prosecutorial misconduct, vehement malicious persecution and prosecution of Mr. Ford under the Espionage Act §793 (e) - Gathering, Transmitting or Losing Defense Information. On Wednesday, September 23,2009, President Obama mandated that DOJ establishes New State Secrets Policies and Procedures.1

President Obama's implementation of State Secrets and Policies encompasses matters in this case. Prosecutors knowingly and willfully engaged in conduct involving dishonesty, fraud, deceit and misrepresentation throughout this case and trial. Mr. Ford was convicted under 793(e) - Espionage and 1801 - Making A False Statement On A Government Form. Mr. Ford was sentenced to 6 years in prison for Count 1 and 3 years in prison, to be served concurrently with Count 1, for Count 2. After imprisonment, Mr.

----

1 "It sets out clear procedures that will provide greater accountability and ensure the state secrets privilege is invoked only when necessary and in the narrowest way possible..." Attorney General Eric Holder September 23, 2009

Ford is to be on probation for 3 years. He also was ordered to pay a $200.00 assessment. Mr. Ford began serving this unjust prison sentence on May 16. 2006. He has been in prison for over 3 years and 6 months for doing absolutely nothing, except being a patriotic American and a good person.

Not only is Mr. Ford innocent, but nothing happened. This case is totally fabricated by the FBI and all involved, specifically the prosecutors and judge know it. Mr. Ford is a victim of a hate crime, a malicious prosecution and a tragic rush to jail an innocent man. See North Carolina v. Seligmann 06-cr-4332-33 (Dismissed 4/712007), Franks v. Delaware, 438 U.S. 154 (1978) and Brady v. Maryland, 373 U.S. 83 (1963). These cases demonstrate that 'false' arrest can happen to anyone - as in the matter of distinguished Harvard professor Henry Louis Gates, Jr., one of the nation's pre-eminent African-American scholars, falsely arrested in his own home.

A. Prosecutors Willfully Withheld Exculpatory Evidence From Defense

DOJ prosecutors repeatedly invoked state secret privileges, suppressed evidence as classified and deliberately withheld from Mr. Ford's defense exculpatory FBI Search Warrant Affidavits for well over 19 months. Ultimately, these search warrant affidavits were suppressed from Mr. Ford's trial. We have recently discovered that these affidavits have never been filed and are not apart of Mr. Ford's official court file.

On December 15, 2005, United States Attorney For The District of Maryland Rod J. Rosenstein and Criminal Division Assistant Attorney General Alice Fisher issued a press release in Mr. Ford's case, which stated in part, that: (Though there was conflicting evidence of what Ford intended to do with the classified information - the jury's verdict demonstrates that it was satisfied that Ford had unauthorized possession of the information". With the admission of Rosenstein that there existed "conflicting evidence" in Mr. Ford's case and the fact that the judge removed the required elements of 'belief... and intent...' from the jury instructions, should have rendered the indictment defective. (See Exhibit A - Rosenstein Press Release dated 12/15/2005)

FBI Special Agents Michael L. Thompson and Frederick C. Marsh both submitted sworn search warrant affidavits to a federal judge alleging that a Tonya Tucker had contacted the NSA to report Ford's alleged espionage. (Ford had known Tucker for 9 weeks - from 11/13/2003 to 1/11/2004 - and decided that she definitely was not his type. He later realized Ms. Tucker is a FBI confidential informant and was placed into his life by Special Agent Michael L. Thompson.) Defense counsel subpoenaed cell phone records of Tonya Tucker from Sprint, which clearly listed the voice call details of Date, Time. Phone Number. Destination, etc. (Tucker's alleged cell phone calls were described in the Thompson affidavit and completely identified in the Marsh affidavit.

From this, we were able to subpoena thru our attorney, her cell phone records.) Sprint records affirmed that Tonya Tucker Did Not contact NSA on January 5.2004. January 9. 2004. January 10. 2004 and January 11, 2004 from her cell phone number 407-616-5683 listed on the Sprint telephone record print-out and on page 5 of 12 of FBI Special Agent Frederick C. Marsh's sworn search warrant affidavit, which he wrote was "in support of the sworn search warrant affidavit" submitted the previous day, to the same judge, by FBI Special Agent Michael L. Thompson.

With the introduction of the subpoenaed cell phone records, it is apparent the Thompson and March search warrant affidavits are perjured and fabricated. Both agents are therefore subject to penalties of perjury. Also. very importantly. the cell phone (It should be noted here that prosecutors told the jury that Ms. Tucker was a friend of Mr. Ford's and simply was a "tipster".) (See Exhibit B - FBI Affidavits and Tonya Tucker's Cell Phone Records)

Mr. Ford, as required by NSA regulations, earlier reported a threatening e-mail sent to him on Tuesday, November 25th2003 at his "AOL" address a month and a half before his arrest. The e-mail was sent by a "Dr. Takiya", who claimed to be a friend of Tonya Tucker. Based on newly discovered evidence on September 1.2009, it was confirmed that Ms. Tucker is the author of the e-mail. Ms. Tucker signed her name onto an internet guest book August 15, 2006 with the e-mail address of Msunique_2@yahoo.com, which is the same e-mail address of the treat letter sent to Kenneth Wayne Ford, Jr. on Tuesday, November 25 .2003.

The e-mail threatened Ford that his security clearances would soon be revoked. She said she knew people at NSA who had clearances just like he did. Ford reported the e-mail the very next day to NSA Head Security Officer Anne Mennis. She ignored the email, not taking it seriously at all.. Ultimately, the admission of the e-mail as exculpatory evidence to Mr. Ford was suppressed from the trial by the judge. (See Exhibit C - Threatening E-Mail / Newly Discovered Evidence).

Newly discovered evidence of a newsletter dated March 31. 2006, states that FBI Special Agent Dave Evans was the lead FBI supervisor in the case against Mr. Ford. The defendant, Mr. Ford, was never aware that FBI Special Agent Dave Evans existed. (We, his parents, discovered this newsletter on the internet in 2008.) FBI Special Agent Evan's newsletter was titled, Maryland Man Sentenced For 'Stealing Secret Documents'. However, indictments alleged that Mr. Ford was charged with 'Unauthorized Possession of National Defense Documents" - not theft of secret documents.

FBI Special Agent Evans also said that: "As it turned out, our tipster was and didn't even make the drive to the airport." Nonetheless, the prosecutors continued to prosecute and incarcerate an innocent man.

FBI Special Agent Evans also stated that: (Our agents ultimately determined ultimately ended up in." Nonetheless, prosecutors indicted and incarcerated Mr. Ford with knowledge that 6'qonflicted evi4ence" existed in this case. (See Exhibit D – FBI Special Agent Dave Evans' Newsletter dated 3/31/2006)

Certainly, the defense has a right to depose and cross-examine the FBI Special Agent who was the lead supervisor in this case. Prosecutors withheld FBI Special Agent Evans from the defense. They also withheld Special Agent Frederick C. Marsh from the defense. The Marsh affidavit was suppressed during the suppression hearing by the judge, Judge Peter J. Messitte, before the trial began on 11/29/2005. Thus, that which brought Mr. Ford into the legal system and ultimately into a federal courtroom for prosecution, was not allowed into the trial. The jury was unaware of the affidavits. (The defense did not get them until 19 months after Mr. Ford's arrest. Please keep in mind Mr. Ford has been totally under arrest the entire time since 1/11/2004 to the present.) To date, those affidavits have never been filed. They are not listed on the docket page of the case and they are not physically in the court file. It was represented and testified to the jury by DOJ prosecutors and FBI Special Agent Michael L. Thompson that he was the lead agent and only agent assigned to the Ford Case.

B. Even If Papers Had Been Present – The Text of §793 Is Vague And Should Not Have Been Applied In This Case

First, the statutes require that a defendant transmit information relating to the national defense. There are no allegations that Mr. Ford ever transmitted, sold, stole, secreted, purloined, paid for or otherwise obtained classified information inside or outside the government - by any illegal means. Legislative history of $793 makes plain that [Congress was concerned with spying].

The government never charged Mr. Ford with spying, injury to the United States on behalf of a foreign nation or communication to any person not entitled to receive classified information.

Due process requires that a criminal statute provide a person of ordinary intelligence fair notice that his contemplated conduct is forbidden. See Thomas v. Davis, 192 F.3d 445,45514n Cir. 1999). If a law is "vague or highly debatable, a defendant - actually or imputably - lacks the requisite intent to violate it." See United States v. Mallas. 7 62 F .2d 36r , 363 14'n cir.1985). criminal prosecution for the violation of an unclear duty itself violates the clear constitutional duty of the government to warn citizens whether particular conduct is legal or illegal. See U.S. v. Rosen and Weissman 05-cr-225.

A statute cannot be construed so as to delegate to prosecutors and juries the "inherently legislative task" of determining what type of possession of national defense information are so reprehensible as to be punished as crimes. See United States v. Kozminski. U.S. 93 1,949 (1988) (rejecting construction of criminal statute that would *delegate to prosecutors and juries the inherently legislative task of determining what type of coercive activities are so morally reprehensible that they should be punished as crimes").

Second, the canon of strict construction of criminal statutes and the rule of lenity ensure fair warning by resolving ambiguity in a criminal statute as to apply it only to conduct clearly covered. Lanier, 520 U.S. at 266. Third, due process bars courts from applying a novel construction of a criminal statute to conduct that neither the statute nor any prior judicial decision has fairly disclosed to be within its scope. Each of these three elements is based on the fact that it must have been reasonably clear the time that the defendant's conduct was criminal."

United States Attorney for the District of Maryland Rod Rosenstein confirmed by his own statement that: "Though there was conflicting evidence of what Ford intended to do with the classified information – the jury's verdict demonstrates that it was satisfied that Ford had unauthorized possession of the information."

Therefore, one would conclude that it was apparently not 'reasonably clear' that Ford's alleged conduct was criminal. Our son was incarcerated based on "unclear conflicting evidence'. An egregious miscarriage of justice at the highest level is evident throughout this case.

Each of these three manifestations is based on the notion that it must have been "reasonably clear at the time that the defendant's conduct was criminal". Elements applied to Mr. Ford's case affirm that reasonable clarity was severely lacking. Courts have ruled that §793 (d) and (e) apply only to the transmission of tangible information. In fact, these rulings were the basis of Special Counsel Patrick Fitzgerald's explanation as to why he did not bring charges under the Espionage Act §793 against either the government officials who leaked the name of CIA agent Valerie Plame to the press or the reporters who subsequently reported that name to millions of readers around the world.

The following exculpatory evidence, which would have exonerated our son, was suppressed from the trial and jury: 1) FBI Form 302 Statement by Tonya Tucker (FBI Confidential

Informant), 2) Tonya Tucker's threatening e-mail to Mr. Ford and 3) Special Agents Thompson's and Marsh's Search Warrant Affidavits. Special Agent Marsh's affidavit clearly affirmed on January 11, 2004, page 6 of 12 that: "A review of criminal history records reflect that TUCKER has a number of arrests, including arrests for Driving while suspended, Criminal trespassing, Robbery, among others."

Courts have repeatedly ruled that the government may not excuse its presentation of false testimony by claiming that: (a) it did not know, (b) it did not understand what other agencies knew, or (c) it believed the testimony. It cannot use these excuses because they are not the law and the facts do not support them. See Mesarosh. et al v. United States, 352 U.S. I (1956); Giglio v. United States, 405 U.S. 150 (1972); and United States v. Mason, et al., 293 F.3d, 826 (5th Cir.2002). Fourth Amendment violations enumerated in the matter of Franks v. Delaware were repeated violations perpetrated on Kenneth Wayne Ford, Jr. by the United States Department of Justice (DOJ). In the matter of Franks v. Delaware, the Court held that: "Where the defendant makes a substantial preliminary showing that a false statement that a hearing be held at the defendant's request."

Federal prosecutors in Mr. Ford's case willfully applied national security standards of the suppression of evidence and discovery. DOJ prosecutors willfully enforced national security clearances upon defense counsel with full knowledge that DOJ did not obtain mandatory FISA applications and approvals.

Prosecutors ignored strict procedural requirements in accordance to the Foreign Reform Act of 2000"). Prosecutors clearly violated Title VI §603, 605 and 607. This case should never have been prosecuted. Title VI $608 provides, in part, that: "If any provision of this title (including an amendment made by this title), or the application thereof, to any person or circumstance, is held invalid, the remainder of this title (including the amendments made by this title), and the application thereof. to other persons or circumstances shall not be affected thereby."

C. Background

Kenneth Wayne Ford, Jr. is now 38 years old. He is the cream of the crop of young American citizens. He is an African-American and is highly educated. Mr. Ford graduated from DeMatha Catholic High School in Hyattsville, Maryland in 1990. He then went to the University of Miami in Coral Gables, Florida and graduated from there in 1995 with a Bachelor of Business Administration in Management and Organization degree. Mr. Ford served 4 years in the Uniformed Division of the Secret Service, where he received two cash awards in consecutive years for outstanding service. While in the Secret Service, Mr. Ford continued his education and enrolled into Strayer University. To his credit, he graduated in 2001, summa cum laude" earning a Bachelor of Science in Computer Networking degree. Later, Mr. Ford enrolled in the Masters program at Strayer University, earning in 2004, a Master of Science in Information Technology degree.

In 2001, Mr. Ford accepted employment at NSA as a Signals Intelligence Analyst. While employed at NSA, he received a cash award for outstanding service. Later, he was recognized with a large plaque - his name listed, among others, for outstanding work on a particular project. It was disclosed in the trial by a State Department officer that Mr. Ford had security clearances that less than 150 people in the entire country hold. Mr. Ford has worked extremely hard all his life, as he was not born with a silver spoon in his mouth, inherited wealth or privilege. He has spent over 23 years acquiring an education. He would never do anything to jeopardize his life or his accomplishments. After Mr. Ford's conviction, Mr. Lambert, the probation officer assigned to formalize his pre-sentencing report, commented to me (his mother) and included in his report that "Kenneth has not even had a traffic ticket."

D. Case Overview

On Sunday, January 11. 2004. FBI Special Agent Michael L. Thompson and NSA Security Officer Robert McCaslin arrived at Mr. Ford's home at approximately 5:50 p.m. and fabricated that they wanted to talk to him about his former position. Mr. Ford invited them in because he was led to believe they wanted to get his expertise on a work-related situation. About ½ hour later, their attitudes changed and Mr. Ford realized they were unjustly accusing him of espionage. Simultaneously, with these accusations, they began searching his home - 2-1/2 hours before the search warrant arrived. FBI Special Agent Frederick Marsh arrived with a search warrant and about 23 additional agents.

During the course of this ordeal, Mr. Ford was threatened by Special Agent Michael L. Thompson's unnecessary withdrawal of his gun. He was terrorized for 7-1/2hows as the agents rampaged his home. He was not allowed to leave his residence, contact his parents or answer his telephone. He was denied food and water. He was not allowed to use his own bathroom until Thompson took him away from his home -7-1/2 hours later. See Title 18, Part I, Chapter 113C - Torture - "an act committed by a person acting under the color of law specifically intended to inflict severe physical or mental pain or suffering (other than pain or suffering incidental to lawful sanctions) upon another person within his custody or physical control." (See Exhibit E -Letter by Kenneth W. Ford, Jr. Documenting Events)

E. DOJ Triple Jeopardy Indictments

The government's 1st indictment, and 2nd case number, was filed on 3/4/2005. U.S. District Court Judge Peter J. Messitte dismissed the case without prejudice on 5/162005. The 2nd indictment, and 3rd cse number, dated 5/23/2005, contained the exact charges and language as the ls indictment. The 3rd indictment, which we had no knowledge of until recently, is dated 11/28/2005. The docket indicates that there was a superseding indictment, arraignment and plea of not guilty all on the same day – 11/28/2005. It indicates Mr. Ford appeared before Judge Messitte and gave a plea of 'not guilty' to each of the two counts against him. This is untrue. Mr. Ford never appeared before Judge Messitte or any other judge on 11/28/2005. His trial started the next day, 11/29/2005. It is impossible to appear for an arraignment one day and be tried by jury the very next day.

It should be noted here that on March 30, 2006, at the end of Mr. Ford's 2nd sentencing hearing, Judge Messitte dismissed the original indictment. He and Prosecutor Salem signed papers to that effect. Judge Messitte said several times during the trial, Mr. Ford was being prosecuted on the superseding indictment. (Of course, this is impossible.) Apparently, at some point, Judge Messitte and Mr. Salem realized this. Consequently, this dismissal has never been filed, is not in Mr. Ford's court file and is not on the docket. (See Exhibit F - Indictments, Docket Listings of 1//28/2005 Superseding Indictment, Arraignment and Not Guilty Plea and Transcript Page of Dismissal of Original Indictment) Also See $3434 - Presence of Defendant - (Rule) 3

Also, there appears on all three indictments: 'Aiding and Abetting (1S U.S.C. §2)'. Mr. Ford was never charged with this crime. It does not appear anywhere else in the indictment nor was it addressed in the trial to the jury. In addition to the indictments being illegal, these acts make the indictments themselves faulty.

The 1st count was cited under Federal Criminal Code 793(e) - Espionage. FBI Receipt For Property Seized / Form 597 listed all items seized from Mr. Ford's residence. Ironically, there was not one (1) document identified as 'classified papers' prosecutors falsely alleged were taken from Mr. Ford's residence.

At the trial, FBI Special Agent Bridget Bigham, Seizing Agent, testified that she was told to put a classified sticker on a Fed Ex envelope found in a suitcase which belonged to career criminal Tonya Tucker. (The envelope is listed by FBI Special Agent Bigham as #9 on the FBI Form 597.) (See Exhibit G - FBI Form 597) Special Agent 3

----

3 In United States v. Randall, f 71 F.3d 195, 203 (4th Cir. 1999) The Supreme Court ruled that the Fifth Amendment's grand jury guarantee does not permit a defendant to be tried on charges that are not made in the indictment against him, and therefore, 'after an indictment has been returned its charges may not be broadened through amendment except by the grand jury itself. See United States v. Randall, 471 U,S. 130, 143 (1985). See United States v. Brady, 456 U.S. 152; and United States v. Young, 470 U.S. 1, 16 (1985).

Bigham testified she did not look at the papers while in Ford's home. She further testified the alleged papers seized were not photographed in Ford's home as required by procedures, but were photographed days later at an FBI facility. (See Exhibit H - Excerpt of Agent Bigham's Transcript Testimony)

DOJ prosecutors testified during the trial that it did not have any 'surveillance evidence' nor 'any eyewitness accounts' of Mr. Ford allegedly removing classified documents from NSA. Prosecutors should have dismissed all charges against Mr. Ford.

The 2nd count was Title 18 U.S.C. $ 1801 - Making A False Statement On A Government Form. Mr. Ford accepted employment with Lockheed Martin. Prosecutor David Salem had already gotten him fired from Northrop Grumman and after working for 3 weeks at Lockheed Martin, Salem was successful in getting him fired from there also. Ford truthfully provided Lockheed Martin a 1-1/2 page written account of alleged charges against him. At the trial, Judge Messitte allowed Prosecutor Salem to severely redact Ford's written statement. Salem told the judge the statement "prejudiced him". (See Exhibit I - E-Mail Dated 10129/2004 to Lockheed Martin) AUSA David I. Salem and DOJ National Security Division Trial Attorney Mariclaire D. Rourke testified that Mr. Ford backed his pick-up truck to the loading dock and loaded these papers into his truck.

In contradiction of their testimony, Mr. Ford's former NSA supervisor, Ms. Jacqueline Welch ("hereafter Jacqueline W") testified that she in fact had seen Mr. Ford on the day in question - December 19, 2003 - standing in the parking lot beside his 'cream-colored 4 door sedan (car)'. Former Counsel on redirect, ascertained whether or not she knew the difference between a 'pick-up truck and a car . She affirmed that she did. Jacqueline W further testified that she never knew Mr. Ford had a pick-up truck. At that point, DOJ's over zealous prosecutors' alleged pick-up truck was referred to as a 'vehicle'. (See Exhibit J - Excerpt of Jacqueline W's Testimony)

Special Agent Michael L. Thompson admitted under oath that there were no fingerprints belonging to Mr. Ford found on any of the thousands of sheets of classified papers allegedly found in Mr. Ford's home. Once again, none of these alleged papers were listed on the FBI's official seized evidence Form 597. (See Exhibit K - Excerpt of FBI Special Agent Michael L. Thompson's Testimony)

F. Argument

Mr. Ford is the only American citizen in the history of the Espionage Act, to be charged, prosecuted and convicted under the statute without meeting the requirements of the statute. The United States Court of Appeals for the 4th Circuit recently upheld the requirements that in order to charge under the Espionage Act of 1917 - §793(e) one has to have the belief that what one is doing will harm the United States and/or help a foreign entity and one must have the intent to harm the United States and/or help a foreign entity. See United States v. Rosen and Weissman, 557 F.2d 192 4th Cir.2009).

Judge Peter J. Messitte, during the suppression hearings, willfully discarded the requirement that the government had to prove the "belief" 'element. Judge Messitte, while charging the jury, willfully eliminated the need for the government to prove the element of "intent."

Under the federal sentencing guidelines, espionage (Federal Criminal Codes §793(d) and (e) cannot be sentenced unless there is the element of transmittal. So, effectively, since a transmittal is a prerequisite for sentencing under §793(e), then without it, there cannot be a charge. The government never alleged Ford transmitted anything. As a matter of fact, NSA Security Officer Robert McCaslin sent a letter to Prosecutor David Salem dated 713112004 saying Ford's electronic equipment at work and at home were analyzed by NSA and were found to be clean. The letter was not allowed into the trial.

Subsequently, the "CIPA" Intelligence Authorization Act for 2001- Title VI §607 - Coordination Requirements Relating to the Prosecution of Cases Involving Classified information was totally ignored by Assistant United States Prosecutor David I. Salem and Dept. of Justice Trial Attorney Mariclaire D. Rourke.

The National Security Procedure Statute 9-90.020, provides that DOJ prosecutors had no authority to make decisions in this case. "CIPA" $607 - $1.1 of Executive Order No. 12958, provides that a Senior Official, the President of the United States, must be notified prior to prosecution. In this case, that President was former President George W. Bush, Jr. - another statutory mandate ignored and violated in the matter of Kenneth Wayne Ford, Jr. $793(e) 'unauthorized possession' is contradictory to the National Security Act which provides that NSA employees have a life-time obligation and commitment regarding NSA classified documents.

G. Violation of Dept. of Justice Guidelines/National Security Procedures

DOJ's USAM guidelines regarding National Security Procedures §9-90.020 clearly dictates that the authority to conduct prosecutions relating to the national security lies with the Justice. USAM unequivocally states, in part that:

All prosecutions affecting, involving or relating to the national security, and the responsibility for prosecuting criminal offenses, such as conspiracy, perjury and false statements, arising out of offenses related to national security, is assigned to the Assistant Attorney General of the National Security Division or higher authority. See 28 C.F.R. S 0.61 The Counterespionage Section of the National Security Division, under the supervision of the Assistant Attorney General or higher authority, conducts, handles, and supervises prosecutions affecting, involving or relating to the national security." DOJ trial attorney Mariclaire D. Rourke and AUSA David I. Salem did not have authority to prosecute a National Security Espionage case against Kenneth Wayne Ford, Jr.

We recently reviewed Mr. Ford's court file. Although there are a few orders, from 8/2005 to 1112005, appearing in the case file that indicate the Assistant Attorney General was in compliance with that particular order, it is with great concern that we ask you to investigate this. We have no proof or certification that the Assistant Attorney General's alleged involvement with this case was authentic. As in other things involving Mr. Ford's case, we suspect this too is a fabrication.

H. DOJ Violated FISA Court Statutes

FISA Court specifically prescribes procedures for the physical and electronic surveillance and collection of "foreign intelligence information" between "foreign powers" and "agents of foreign powers" (which may include American citizens and permanent residents suspected of being engaged in espionage and violating U.S. law on territory under United States control).

FISA allows a federal officer, authorized by the President of the United States acting through the Attorney Gener4l to obtain from a judge appointed by the FISA Court, search warrants and approval of electronic surveillance of a foreign power or an agent of a foreign power for the purpose of obtaining foreign intelligence information. Mandated strict FISA Court procedures were ignored by the FBI, DOJ Prosecutors and U.S. District Court of Maryland Judge Peter J. Messitte, who is not an appointed FISA Court Judge.

Specifically, FISA requires that where the target of the search or surveillance is a "United States person" - a U.S. Citizen or permanent resident alien - the judge must find that the Executive Branch's certification that a significant purpose of the search or surveillance is to obtain foreign intelligence information is not "clearly erroneous". See 50 U.S.C. §1805 and 1824. Also see Brady v. Maryland, 373 U.S. 33 (1963); Strickler v. Greene, 119 S.T. 1936 (1999).

The elements of violations are: (1) the evidence must be favorable to the accused, either because it exculpates the defendant or because it impeaches the government; (2) the evidence must have been suppressed by the government, either willfully or inadvertently; and (3) prejudice must have been ensued. See Franks v. Delaware, 438 U.S. 154 (1978); See Brady v. Maryland, 373 U.S. 83 (1963); See USA v. Rosen & Weissman 05cr-225 (E.D.Va.)

We are not elected or high level corporate officials. We are "grass roots" people who are honest and hard working. President Obama stated at the 2009 NAACP 100th Anniversary celebration, that: "America is a place where, if you work hard, you can achieve success." A grave injustice has been done to a good American citizen (Kenneth Wayne Ford, Jr.). American citizens rely upon the United States Department of Justice to follow the rule of law.

In good faith, the initiation of a formal procedural investigation and the appointment of a Special prosecutor on behalf of our son, Kenneth Wayne Ford, Jr., is warranted and specifically should include an investigation of prosecutorial misconduct, violations of national security procedures, violations of FISA Court procedures, violations of issues in applying states secrets rules and the willful suppression of exculpatory affidavits and other exculpatory evidence in this case.

We are available at any time that is convenient to you to discuss this case. The elements in this letter by no means cover all the infractions against Mr. Ford. There were just too many illegal things done to put in a letter.

We seek an immediate vacation of Mr. Ford's conviction, full restoration of his revoked clearances and an immediate apology from the Department of Justice (DOJ).

Thank you.

Sincerely,

Kenneth W. Ford, Sr.

Gloria D. Ford

EXHIBITS

1) Exhibit A - Rosenstein Press Release dated December 15, 2005

2) Exhibit B - Affidavits by SA Michael L. Thompson & SA Frederick C. Marsh and Tonya Tucker's Subpoenaed Cell Phone Records

3) Exhibit C - Tonya Tucker's threatening e-mail to Mr. Ford/Newly Discovered Evidence

4) Exhibit D - FBI Special Agent Dave Evans' Newsletter dated 3/31/2006

5) Exhibit E - Letter from Kenneth Wayne Ford, Jr. / Document of Events

6) Exhibit F - DOJ's Double Jeopardy Indictments; Docket of 11/28/2005

Indictment; Transcript Page of Dismissal of Original Indictment

7) Exhibit G - FBI Form 597 (Seized Items) w/ Computerized Listing Of Items

8) Exhibit H - Excerpt of Agent Bridget Bigham's Testimony

9) Exhibit I - E-Mail dated 10/29/2004 from Kenneth W. Ford, Jr. to Lockheed Martin

10) Exhibit J - Excerpt of NSA Jacqueline Welch's Testimony

11) Exhibit K - Excerpt of FBI Special Agent Michael L. Thompson's Testimony

President Obama, who prides himself as a constitutional scholar, having taught constitutional law at the University of Chicago, is about to become the subject of a major constitutional case in the indictment of Thomas Drake. Drake was not only exposing high level contract fraud involving two NSA directors -- Generals Michael Hayden and Keith Alexander -- but also allegedly involved a constitutionally-protected entity -- the press -- in making details of the fraud known to the American taxpaying public. Not since Watergate have the American people been subject to runaway surveillance by the NSA and FBI.

Obama, who supported retroactive immunity from prosecution for telecommunications companies that swept up the digital communications of all American after proclaiming he was against it, will be the person on trial in the Drake case. And Obama may very well end up like Richard Nixon if the government does not impose restrictions on the public's right to know through imposition of the draconian Classified Information Procedures Act and the State Secrets Privilege.

As one NSA insider tersely put it: "I truly believe that NSA has some illegally wiretapped information (big-time dirt) on Mr. Obama, and NSA has been using it (via blackmail) against him ever since he flip-flopped on the vote for retroactive immunity for the telecommunication firms that insisted they did nothing illegal when they joined in with the Bush administration in comprehensive, 'sea to shining sea' warrantless wiretapping of all domestic U.S. communications."

April 22, 2010 -- NSA domestic electronic surveillance targeted everyone

WMR has learned from U.S. intelligence sources that the Justice Department's Terrorist Surveillance Program (TSP), the warrantless domestic wiretapping program largely conducted by the National Security Agency (NSA), was a mere bureaucratic contrivance developed by the Justice Department to legally cover the NSA from constitutional oversight hearings by Congress and law suit actions from telecommunication customers over what amounted to total surveillance of the American people.

The NSA operation, code named STELLAR WIND, and known only to a few top officials in the Bush administration, targeted massive collected digital databases of phone calls, emails, faxes, pages, and other digital communications. The data, known as meta-data, was searched by NSA signals intelligence analysts for key words and phrases using a Google-like search engine.

The STELLAR WIND program was overseen by Vice President Dick Cheney's chief counsel David Addington. In a new twist, intelligence sources report that the plans for STELLAR WIND were put into place long before the 9/11 attacks. Qwest chairman Joseph Nacchio claimed that he and his firm were pressured by NSA six months prior to 9/11 to participate in a program to conduct warrantless surveillance of Qwest customers. Nacchio and Qwest believed the program was illegal and demanded court warrants. Nacchio was later indicted and convicted for insider trading, a move Qwest sources claim was government retaliation for Nacchio's refusal to participate in the wiretapping program. It is now been revealed to WMR that the program in question was, in fact, STELLAR WIND.

On February 25, 2010, WMR reported: *"WMR has learned from sources who worked in senior positions for the telecommunications company Qwest that its former Chairman and CEO Joseph Nacchio was threatened with retaliation after he refused to participate in an unconstitutional and illegal National Security Agency (NSA) wiretapping program after he met with NSA officials on February 27, 2001, some six months before the 9/11 attacks. Nacchio refused to turn over customer records without a court order -- something NSA did not possess at the time it made its request.*

After Nacchio refused NSA's request on the grounds that it was illegal, sources close to Nacchio reported his legal problems with the Department of Justice and the Securities and Exchange Commission began in earnest. First, Qwest lost out on several lucrative federal government contracts and second, Nacchio was indicted and convicted in 2007 of 19 counts of insider stock trading. Nacchio was sentenced to six years the Schuykill federal prison camp in Minersville, Pennsylvania where he is now assigned prisoner number 33973-013."

WMR has learned additional technical details about STELLAR WIND. The NSA was able to conduct key word and key phrase differentiation between various American accents by using sophisticated algorithms. The software used by NSA could determine the spoken word "car" in a Bostonian accent as opposed to the spoken word "car" in a Midwestern or Southern accent. The NSA algorithms could also determine spoken words in New York, Philadelphia, Hispanic, Asian, New Orleans, French Canadian, African American, Tidewater Virginian, and Native American accents, as well as others.

TARGETING JOURNALISTS

In addition to STELLAR WIND's warrantless tracking and analysis of meta-data containing all the communications of Americans, another super-classified code-named NSA program monitored the communications of U.S. journalists. At least 150 U.S. journalists were subjected to NSA surveillance. There is some evidence that the surveillance was also conducted prior to 9/11.

A U.S. intelligence source confirmed that among the journalists monitored were "Sy Hersh, James Bamford, Wayne Madsen, Siobhan Gorman, James Risen, Bill Gertz."

NSA's "Q Group" security branch maintains a file on many of the surveilled journalists. WMR has learned that the files include the driver's license photos of journalists, including the Virginia Department of Motor Vehicles license of this editor. The FBI is an active participant in the NSA journalist surveillance program. The Stasi-like electronic and physical surveillance continues to this day.

Of particular interest to NSA analysts were the satellite-borne communications of U.S. journalists reporting from foreign locations, including Afghanistan, Iraq, Iran, Cuba, Venezuela and other countries.

WHO ELSE HAS BEEN UNDER TOTAL SURVEILLANCE?

Although NSA's surveillance of journalists would appear to be a major and egregious violation of the Constitution, there is evidence that STELLAR WIND had another, more sinister, off-shoot. The most sensitive program conducted warrantless electronic surveillance of elected officials at the federal, state, and local levels, as well as federal and state judges. WMR has previously reported that the communications and transactional data of Governors Bill Richardson of New Mexico and former Governor Eliot Spitzer of New York were subjected to NSA surveillance. The surveillance of the two governors has been confirmed by extremely knowledgeable sources.

The future for NSA's warrantless total surveillance programs appears rosy. NSA is building a $2 billion, 120 acre meta-data facility at Camp Williams in Utah and another similar data repository in San Antonio, Texas. Data storage capabilities are also being expanded at NSA headquarters at Fort Meade, Maryland and at NSA's huge signals intelligence collection facility at Menwith Hill, UK. The Congress has made no move to question the NSA's warrantless spying on Americans and President Obama flipped his position when he backed retroactive immunity for telecommunication firms that illegally participated in STELLAR WIND and its affiliated surveillance programs before and after 9/11.

May 11, 2010 -- U.S. intelligence turns up surveillance ears on Turkey and Brazil

WMR has learned from U.S. and Middle East intelligence sources that the Obama administration has authorized an increase in signals intelligence (SIGINT) gathering directed against Turkey and Brazil. Both nations are acting as intermediaries with Iran to hammer out a deal to swap uranium for Iran's low-enriched uranium used for its nuclear power generating needs for nuclear fuel from abroad.

As the UN Security Council debates applying new sanctions on Iran, Turkey and Brazil, which are opposed to new sanctions, are quietly negotiating between Tehran and Russia and China to ensure that there will be at least one permanent member Security Council veto of a sanctions resolution.

Brazilian President Luiz Inacio Lula da Silva is due to visit Tehran next week for the G15 Summit with the nuclear fuel for uranium deal seen as high on his agendas in talks with Iranian officials. Iranian parliament speaker Ali Larijani, the nation's former chief nuclear negotiator, recently met with Turkish President Abdullah Gul in Istanbul. The nuclear swap deal was also high on the talk's agenda.

The independent initiatives of Turkey and Brazil has rankled the Obama administration and frequent dictator of its Iran foreign policy, Israel, which favor strong crippling sanctions on Iran.

The National Security Agency's (NSA) Regional Targets Section has applied a tactic on Turkey and Brazil used on the eve of the UN Security Council vote on authorizing military action on Iraq -- "surge" surveillance of the telephones and e-mail of the Turkish and Brazilian UN delegations conducted in January 2003. The surge surveillance is also being directed against key Turkish and Brazilian ministries and the nation's respective embassies in Moscow and Beijing. Turkey and Brazil are current non-permanent members of the Security Council.

Concerning the 2003 surge surveillance by NSA, on September 25, 2008, WMR reported: ". . . it has been discovered that the United States and United Kingdom wanted to intercept the office and home communications of the UN ambassadors of Pakistan, Chile, Angola, Guinea, Cameroon, and Mexico, six non-permanent members of the Security Council, to gather information that could be used to blackmail the ambassadors into voting for the US/UK Iraq war resolution. Ultimately, the Security Council refused to back the resolution."

Similar to the 2003 action by the Bush administration, the Obama administration is also turning up surveillance on other UN Security Council members' UN missions to ascertain their vote on Iranian sanctions. These include Japan, Uganda, Lebanon, Mexico, Nigeria, Gabon, Austria, and Bosnia-Herzegovina.

There are strong indications that Uganda and Lebanon will vote no on sanctions with a possibility that Japan and Austria will join them in opposition or abstain. Turkey is suspected of using its influence in Bosnia and its new diplomatic forays into Gabon and Nigeria to press for no votes on sanctions. These activities are all of interest to NSA's Turkish communications interception personnel.

WMR has learned from State Department sources that the Obama administration is also pushing for secondary sanctions against nations that would continue to trade with Iran after the U.S. gets UN authorization for strong sanctions against Tehran. Such sanctions would be applied by the United States Treasury Department against companies in second countries that refuse to abide by sanctions with the primary targets being companies in Sweden, Austria, Cyprus, and Turkey.

The proposed UN Security Council text on sanctions being crafted by the United States, United Kingdom, and France is not being shared with the governments of Turkey and Brazil, the fear being that Ankara and Brasilia will share the text with Iranian officials. One Turkish official said, "the Americans are asking us to vote for a UN Security Council resolution we have not seen." Turkey and Brazil are not alone. Because of Uganda's and Lebanon's close ties with Iran, the UN delegations of both countries are not being shown the draft text of the Security Council sanctions resolution.

August 26, 2010 -- Gareth Williams murder story represents an old British intelligence modus operandi

The discovery of the body of 31-year old British Government Communications Headquarters (GCHQ) officer Gareth Williams in a posh flat in Pimlico, just a mile from the "Ziggurat" headquarters of the British MI-6 Secret Intelligence Service headquarters along the banks of the Thames in Vauxhall, bears all the markings of a British intelligence hit.

Williams, who had frequently traveled in the past to visit his counterparts at the National Security Agency (NSA) in Fort Meade, Maryland and was due to return home to Cheltenham, the headquarters of the signals intelligence (SIGINT) agency GCHQ, was found stuffed in a bag in the flat's bathroom. Police estimated Williams, whose body was decomposed and reportedly, dismembered, had been dead for some two weeks.

Several cell phone and SIM cards were found neatly arranged in the flat.

There was no sign of a break-in at the flat on Alderney Street, where two former British Home Ministers, Michael Howard and Lord Brittan, also reside, and police report that Williams may have known his murderer or murderers. The flat property is owned by a company called New Rodina [Rodina is Russian for "new motherland"], said to be a Russian company registered in the British Virgin Islands. However, the reported presence of retina scanners on the flat's lock suggests the flat was used by MI-6 as a safe house of some sort. There is little known about New Rodina because of British Virgin Islands company secrets laws. New Rodina bought the property in 2000 with a mortgage from the Royal Bank of Scotland and *The Guardian* has reported that the agent for the property was the law firm Park Nelson, which had offices off Fleet Street in London. "New Rodina" is a term used by British intelligence members to refer to being stationed in London. It is a term used by Russian exiles living abroad -- "new motherland."

British media are now reporting that Williams was a gay transvestite who, because of the reported "Russian" connection to the flat owners, was somehow involved in a Russian gay sex plot. However, this fits a long pattern with British intelligence. Past deaths of male British officials have seen post-mortem reports of women's underwear and clothing being discovered, as well as child pornography. The resulting embarrassment to the families of the deceased prevents them from seeking a wider investigation and the cases simply fade away from the public's attention. It is classic British intelligence trade craft to cover up murders carried out by British intelligence or other agents acting on their behalf.

The Sun of London is reporting that police discovered women's clothing of Williams's size in the Pimlico flat. *The Sun* is owned by neocon publisher Rupert Murdoch.

In March 1994, former British MI-agent James Rusbridger was found hanging in his home in Cornwall. Rusbridger's body was found suspended from two ropes and dressed in an NBC (nuclear-biological-chemical) protective suit and a rain coat. Rusbridger was wearing rubber gloves and a gas mask. Police reported they found sexual bondage photos and magazines scattered around Rusbridger's hanging corpse and they later concluded Rusbridger killed himself accidentally while engaged in a sexual strangulation act. Rusbridger was found with his legs bound at the ankles, knees, and upper thighs. Police also reported that Rusbridger was lonely, unhappy, and in financial distress.

Rusbridger was the cousin of retired MI-5 agent Peter Wright, whose book "Spycatcher" resulted in then-Prime Minister Margaret Thatcher seeking to ban its publication in Britain and abroad due to damaging revelations that British intelligence bugged Commonwealth conferences, tried to assassinate Egyptian President Gamal Abdel Nasser, and failed the investigate Sir Roger Hollis, director of MI-5 as a Soviet mole.

Rusbridger, who, like Wright, was an author of intelligence books, was investigating the death of Conservative Member of Parliament Stephen Milligan, whose body was found naked, except for wearing a pair of women's stockings, in his west London home just a month before Rusbridger was found hanging in Cornwall. Milligan, a former journalist and rising political star in the Conservative Party, was parliamentary private secretary to junior defense minister Jonathan Aitken in the Tory government of British Prime Minister John Major. There were reports that Millgan had been been found gagged and bound in addition to wearing a pair of women's stockings.

Aitken was sentenced to prison in 1999 after he was convicted of perjury for his testimony in an investigation of a British arms scandal involving Matrix Churchill, the Saudis, and arms sales to Saddam Hussein. While Chief Secretary to the Treasury, Aiken signed a "gag order" preventing evidence to be revealed in the 1992 trial of Matrix Churchill for weapons sales to Iraq. Aitken had been a director of BMARC, a subsidiary of the Swiss firm Oerlikon, which stood accused of indirectly supplying anti-aircraft systems to Saddam Hussein during the 1980s. BMARC was a subject of the Matrix Churchill investigation.

Aitken was also chairman of a secretive right-wing think tank known as Le Cercle, established after World War II and which was funded by the CIA, the Ford Foundation, and the Rothschilds.

In 2005, the commander of British forces in Gibraltar, Royal Navy Commander David White, was found dead and fully clothed in his swimming pool in The Rock section of Gibraltar. White had been ordered to return to Britain and go on mandatory leave by Britain's Ministry of Defense. After his death, police said White had been under investigation for possession of child pornography. White, whose job put him in command of a GCHQ SIGINT installation in the British colony, was determined to have committed suicide and that there was no sign of foul play.

2011

January 10, 2011 -- NSA "Q Group" protecting sex scandals while plugging potential leaks

WMR's intelligence sources report that the National Security Agency's "Q Group," the directorate responsible for overall security for NSA, is actively investigating and harassing NSA employees who have reported on senior officials at the sprawling intelligence agency, which now includes the new U.S. Cyber Command, of engaging in adulterous trysts with subordinates and possessing improper sexual material, including child pornography.

WMR has previously reported on the improper activities of the Q Group, which has become a virtual uncontrolled FBI within the NSA. Q continues to protect NSA senior officials who engage in and promote a culture of sexual exploitation of junior employees at the intelligence agency. Q Group has also misused NSA psychologists and psychiatrists to deem anyone who charges senior officials of the agency with sexual misconduct or harassment unfit to hold a security clearance for reasons of mental impairment.

Q Group has also gone outside of its legal authority to harass the families and friends of former agency employees who have brought charges against NSA for sexual harassment and misconduct. WMR has learned of NSA personnel illegally masquerading as phone company technicians who entered the property of the family of one such ex-employee. In another case, Q Group personnel poisoned two pet dogs of the family of an ex-employee under NSA surveillance. Q Group personnel have also been used to harass the ex-spouses of senior NSA officials involved in child custody cases. WMR has also been informed that Q Group has harassed NSA employees who have married the ex-wives of NSA senior officials who have ongoing legal battles with their ex-husbands.

Q Group is able to conduct its harassment of civilians in the Fort Meade area with a "wink and a nod" from local law enforcement and other officials. NSA senior managers have dipped into NSA's substantial slush fund to lavish money on community service projects and programs in cash-strapped local municipalities and counties. The concept of the "friendly NSA that provides funds and jobs" has bought loyalty and silence from local and state of Maryland officials. In addition, WMR has learned that NSA has placed agents within the congressional offices of local members of Congress in order to interdict and retaliate against NSA whistleblower congressional complaints. The NSA "embeds," who work in concert with NSA's Office of Legislative Affairs, are found within the offices of Maryland Senators Barbara Mikulski and Ben Cardin, and Maryland Representatives C.A. "Dutch" Ruppersberger, Steny Hoyer, Elijah Cummings, Chris Van Hollen, and Paul Sarbanes, and is currently inserting an agent into the office of freshman Representative Andy Harris.

January 18-19, 2011 -- Stuxnet: a violation of US computer security law

If a January 15 report in *The New York Times*, which has a dubious past in reporting on computer security and hacking issues, is true -- that the United States Department of Homeland Security, Department of Energy -- via the Idaho National Laboratory -- Siemens (which has a long-standing intelligence relationship with the National Security Agency), the CIA, Britain's intelligence services, Germany, and Israel's Mossad cooperated to develop the Stuxnet computer worm to disable Iranian nuclear program centrifuges, the U.S. government violated a number of federal computer security laws that prohibit the development of malicious computer programs that damage "federal interest" computers. The Stuxnet worm, which, according to the *Times*, was tested at Israel's Dimona nuclear weapons development facility in the Negev, not only infected Iranian nuclear program computers but spread to computers in other countries, including the United States. Stuxnet code was discovered through computer forensics to contain key words from the Jewish Old Testament Book of Esther, further establishing Israeli fingerprints on the malicious code. The malicious code's file name, Myrtus, is the Hebrew word for Esther. According to myth, Esther saved the Jews from a Persian plot to exterminate them.

The New York Times article by William Broad, John Markoff, and David Sanger states that when Stuxnet first appeared around the world in June last year, it did little harm and did not slow computer networks. However, this is merely an attempt to let the U.S. and Israeli governments off the hook by falsely claiming that the only damage done by Stuxnet was to the centrifuge systems used by Iran to enrich uranium. Although Stuxnet likely did disable Iran's centrifuges, causing a set-back to its nuclear program, the Stuxnet worm, contrary to *The New York Times* report, resulted in computer down time and disruption far beyond Iran. The disruption by a digital version of a U.S. and Israeli military first strike makes the United States government and Israel civilly liable for the damage and disruption caused by Stuxnet.

The involvement of the Homeland Security Department, which includes the U.S. government's National Cyber Security Division that is tasked to protect U.S. "federal interest" computer systems from attack, makes the department and Secretary Janet Napolitano criminally culpable in permitting the Development and launch of malicious software that affected U.S. computer systems. If President Obama authorized the Stuxnet deployment through a classified Presidential Finding, he, too, may have committed a crime, an impeachable offense.

As Stuxnet propagated around the world last year, the Homeland Security Department's Industrial Control System-Cyber Emergency Response Team (ICS-CERT) posted a series of alerts and bulletins about the worm. Either ICS-CERT was unaware of its own department's involvement in creating the worm it was warning people about or it was part of a clever disinformation program is unknown, however, some computer security specialists suspected that ICS-CERT was putting out stale information on Stuxnet. On October 3, 2010, the *Christian Science Monitor* reported that Dale Peterson, the CEO of Digital Bond, a SCADA control systems security company, stated on his blog on September 20, "It [ICS-CERT's warning alerts] seems to me to have been a delayed clipping service."

The possible involvement of computer security officials, like Sean McGurk, the DHS's director of the Control System Security Program, in covering up the true origin of Stuxnet, cannot be overlooked. As a founding board member of the International Information System Security Certification Consortium (ISC2), this editor warned against the infiltration of NSA and other intelligence operatives into the computer security profession. The warnings were backed by colleagues from other nations, including Finland and Australia. Placing intelligence operatives inside computer security management positions can always result in the use of computers for sabotage and intelligence. Stuxnet may be the culmination of such infiltration of the computer security profession. In 2000, this editor resigned from the ISC2 board over the acquiescence of the board and consortium to dictates from NSA and other problematic U.S. government agencies. This editor and a minority of board members also disagreed with offering professional certifications to employees of foreign intelligence agencies in countries with abominable human rights and civil liberties records.

Stuxnet was specifically designed to attack supervisory control and data acquisition (SCADA) computer systems. These systems control everything from electrical power grids and chemical processing plants to the computers that operate traffic light and rail systems. Stuxnet disabled SCADA systems not only in Iran but also in India (where India's satellite program may have been severely impacted), Pakistan, Indonesia, Germany, Canada, China, Malaysia, South Korea, Russia, Kazakhstan, United Kingdom, Finland, Saudi Arabia, United Arab Emirates, Qatar, Brazil, Australia, Brunei, Netherlands, Taiwan, Myanmar, Bangladesh, Thailand, Belarus, Denmark, Bahrain, Oman, Kuwait, and the United States. Stuxnet was found on 63 computers in Japan. New Zealand, Japan, and Hong Kong issued alerts about Stuxnet's impact on their SCADA systems. Britain's integrated national rail transport network was reported to be particularly vulnerable to Stuxnet. Turkey reacted to Stuxnet by mandating a "National Virtual Environment Security Policy."

By the end of September of last year, over 100,000 computers worldwide had been infected by Stuxnet. So much for *The New York Times'* specious report that the worm did little damage. Industrial control system security specialists from the chemical, oil, and gas industries expressed concern that the U.S. government was less-than-forthcoming about the effects of Stuxnet on their industries. The computer security firm Symantec appears to have been laundering information to private industry from the government.

China, which feared Stuxnet could infect its SCADA systems, issued a national security report about the worm, especially its impact on oil drilling systems. WMR has learned from its Beijing sources that China is growing tired of Israelis, in general, and international banks like Goldman Sachs having strong ties to Israel, in particular, over what it sees as an attempt by Israel and certain international banks to undermine China's new strong industrial and financial position in the world. Representatives of the People's Bank of China, China's central bank, are wary of their contacts with Israelis and bankers and WMR has learned that Japanese central bankers shared the concerns of their Chinese counterparts when it comes to Israel and firms like Goldman Sachs. Chinese authorities were particularly incensed over initial disinformation reports, distributed by the Pentagon-linked media, that China created Stuxnet.

U.S. government involvement in the creation and first strike deployment of a destructive cyber-weapon like Stuxnet and its "bounce back" to "protected" U.S. systems and networks, including SCADA systems, is a violation of the Computer Fraud and Abuse Act (CFAA), 18 U.S.C.§ 1030. The CFAA imposes criminal and civil penalties for anyone who disrupts a "protected computer." A protected computer is defines as one:

- "exclusively for the use of a financial institution or the United States Government, or, in the case of a computer not exclusively for such use, used by or for a financial institution or the United States Government and the conduct constituting the offense affects that use by or for the financial institution or the Government;" or
- "which is used in interstate or foreign commerce or communication."

Criminal activity under the law applies to anyone who "knowingly transmits a program, code or instruction, and as a result, intentionally causes damage, without authorization, to a protected computer." Thus, anyone in the U.S. government or acting as a government contractor, or a foreign national acting on behalf of a foreign government like Israel, who participated in the creation and deployment of the Stuxnet worm could be fined and sentenced to prison. In 2002, New Jersey programmer David L. Smith, the creator of the Melissa worm in 1999, which brought down computer systems across North America in 1999, was sentenced to 20 months in federal prison and a $5000 fine. The chief federal prosecutor of Smith was Chris Christie, now the governor of New Jersey. Under federal law Smith faced a maximum of five years in prison and a $250,000 fine but Christie argued for a lighter sentence because Smith cooperated with prosecutors.

The National Information Infrastructure Protection Act of 1996 further codified the CFAA to address new technologies and criminal activity.

On February 29, 2000, the Deputy Attorney General testified before the House Judiciary Committee subcommittee on crime about the danger posed by malicious computer programs. He said, "We are seeing more 'pure' computer crimes, that is, crimes where the computer is used as a weapon to attack other computers, as we saw in the distributed denial of service attacks I just spoke about, and in the spread of malicious code, like viruses. Our vulnerability to this type of crime is astonishingly high - it was only this past December that a defendant admitted, when he plead guilty in federal and state court to creating and releasing the Melissa virus, that he caused over 80 million dollars in damage . . . These crimes not only affect our financial well-being and our privacy; they also threaten our nation's critical infrastructure. Our banking system, the stock market, the electricity and water supply, telecommunications networks, and critical government services, such as emergency and national defense services, all rely on computer networks. For a real-world terrorist to blow up a dam, he would need tons of explosives, a delivery system, and a surreptitious means of evading armed security guards. For a cyberterrorist, the same devastating result could be achieved by hacking into the control network and commanding the computer to open the floodgates."

That Deputy Attorney General was Eric Holder, now President Obama's Attorney General. Holder has, either through ignorance or involvement, permitted the U.S. and Israeli governments to release a destructive malicious computer program, the very type Holder warned against in 2000.

March 22-23, 2011 -- NSA, DOJ, and courts conspire to cover-up NSA fraud, waste, abuse, and criminal conspiracy at trial

In the trial of former National Security Agency (NSA) executive Thomas Drake, federal prosecutors have convinced an agreeable federal judge, Richard D. Bennett, to place under court seal previously-released trial documents because they have been deemed "For Official Use Only" or FOUO. Drake is accused of leaking classified materials to the media and is only the fourth person in U.S. history to be charged with violating the 1917 Espionage Act.

FOUO is not a national security classification and it never has been one, although there were attempts by the Reagan, George H W Bush, and George W. Bush administrations to create a "restricted" or "sensitive but unclassified" (SBU) national security classification immediately below the current lowest national security classification, which is Confidential. Expansion of national security classification categories beyond the current three -- Top Secret, Secret, and Confidential, in addition to Sensitive Compartmented Information (SCI) special access categories -- but these have been unsuccessful. George W. Bush's creation of a Controlled Unclassified Information (CUI) category was rescinded by Executive Order 13556 on November 4, 2010.

Although President Obama rescinded Bush's CUI presidential memorandum, federal prosecutors are trying to argue that CUI continues to exist as a national security classification under the guise of FOUO. The argument demonstrates a complete lack of understanding of the classification scheme used by NSA. However, in past trials, notable that of NSA analyst Kenneth Ford, Jr., jailed after a political show trial waged by DOJ neocons in league with a "shopped" federal judge. In the Ford case, the NSA wanted to cover up the cooking of signals intelligence from Iraq in order to justify the attack on and occupation of Iraq

However, NSA and Justice Department prosecutors are continuing to insist that FOUO is a security classification in the trial of Drake, however, NSA and DOJ decided to go after Drake because the documents he stands accused of passing to *The Baltimore Sun* points to massive misuse of taxpayer's money and contract fraud under the NSA directorships of retired General Michael Hayden and current director General Keith Alexander. Alexander is also the commander of the U.S. Cyber Command. The fraud committed by Hayden, Alexander, and senior NSA officials amounted to hundreds of millions of dollars in wasteful expenditures. In some cases, the waste on certain contractor-supplied intelligence systems were life threatening, as far as troops on the ground were concerned. The fraudulent contract expenditures were part of NSA's massive TRAILBLAZER and GROUNDBREAKER outsourced modernization and restructuring programs.

On March 18, in response to a request from federal prosecutors, Bennett sealed two documents that were previously available on the court's own website. The documents sealed describe the classified contents of several documents seized at Drake's home, however, the documents appear to be unclassified working papers that the government, after the fact, is trying to argue are classified at the levels of Secret and Top Secret.

Drake's federal public defenders have argued in one of the sealed documents that the government's argument that the documents found in Drake's home in flawed due to the fact that the documents could not be construed as classified at Secret or Top Secret merely because they contain the words "FOUO" and "COMINT." COMINT is communications intelligence and by itself does not mean that the document is classified at "Handle Via COMINT Channels Only," a special handling caveat for SCI special access categories. In fact, the National Cryptologic Museum, which is adjacent to NSA headquarters and open to the public, freely uses "COMINT" in its displays. In addition, the commercial International Spy Museum in downtown Washington, DC has held public seminars on issues dealing with, among other tradecraft, "COMINT."

From the sealed DOJ letter arguing that the documents found in Drake's home are classified, it is clear that NSA, which has played fast and loose with the truth in previous trials and administrative actions against its whistleblowing employees, has tried to re-classify previous unclassified "working papers" as being Secret and Top Secret to bolster its case against Drake.

WMR has previously obtained NSA contractor documents that were deemed by the contractor and NSA, itself, as unclassified and the Drake documents appear to fall within the same category. The unclassified documents that were re-classified as Top Secret and Secret have titles such as "Trial and Testing," "Collections Sites," "Volume is Our Friend," "What a Success," "Regular Meetings," "Shoestring Budget," "BAG," "Buy vs. Make," "TT Notes," "Terrorism Threat," "Note Card 1", "Note Card 2," and more intriguing, "9/11 Commission." WMR previously reported that NSA's security directorate, the "Q Group," has engaged in massive surveillance of employees and journalists, including this editor, to plug any leaks on NSA information on the 9/11 attacks. Bennett, in his ruling on March 18, agreed to NSA's and lead federal prosecutor William Welch II's request that previously unclassified court filings be placed under seal.

While NSA and DOJ seek to convict Drake for having unclassified For Official use Only documents in which the terms "FOUO" and "COMINT" appear, WMR has obtained a similar Unclassified For Official Use Only (FOUO) document written by Computer Sciences Corporation (CSC), one of the major contractors for the fraud-ridden GROUNDBREAKER program. In the document, from which WMR is providing excerpts, there are clearly many more NSA-unique systems and terms described.

Cover terms for classified NSA systems such as HIGHCASTLE, LOOKINGGLASS, MILENIUM, FAST TRACK, ROTUNDPIPER, and BRASSCOIN are listed, along with "SIGINT" or "Signals Intelligence," an NSA mission term comparable to the "COMINT" acronym found in the working papers confiscated from Drake's home.

The CSC document, maintained by CSC contractors and sub-contractors in their cars, briefcases, and homes, were never indicted by the Justice Department on grounds they violated national security. On the other hand, many at NSA feel that companies like CSC, SAIC, Northrop Grumman, Lockheed Martin, and others, should have been indicted for the massive contract fraud carried out under the watches of Hayden and Alexander.

In post-9/11 America, the whistleblowers to fraud, waste, and abuse stand accused of being criminals while the criminals rake in billions of dollars in taxpayers' money and are lauded as critical components of the "intelligence team."

NSA's GROUNDBREAKER and TRAILBLAZER contractors were eager to compile as many NSA systems and sub-systems as possible to cash in on the billions of dollars they could make from the NSA outsourcing work. The database that contained all the NSA systems, projects, and components ripe for outsourcing work was code-named JACKPOT. For CSC, SAIC, and certain NSA officials who spun through the revolving door after retirement and landed high-paying jobs with the contractors, it certainly was a JACKPOT and one that NSA, Q Group, the FBI, Department of Justice, and the White House earnestly want to cover-up in the trial of Thomas Drake.

During Drake's trial, which begins next month in Baltimore, FBI agents are expected to use code words to describe different aspects of the case. One code-word that will most definitely not be heard is JACKPOT, the database of NSA contracts in which contractors and NSA retirees enriched themselves -- criminality that is only met with chirping crickets from the so-called "crime fighting" Department of Justice and FBI.

April 22-24, 2011 -- I-Phone, Android back doors are courtesy of the NSA.

News reports that Apple's I-Phone and I-Pads, as well as Google's Android operating system-enabled phones can track a user's location, as well as Internet activities, is nothing new, according to a well-placed intelligence source. In fact, the Apple and Google "spy ware" is courtesy of a deal struck with the U.S. National Security Agency (NSA), which is the ultimate recipient of the location and web data being collected by Apple and Google.

NSA's aggressive insistence that it have "back door" access to state-of-the-art commercial communications products was on display in the 1990s when Britain's Ministry of Defense discovered eight different back doors installed in Windows 98 and subsequent releases of the operating system. Microsoft is a long-time partner of the NSA in ensuring that its products are accessible by the American eavesdropping agency.

Although Britain's Government Communications Headquarters is a signals intelligence (SIGINT) partner of the NSA, a "rainbow team" representing computer security experts, drawn from multiple British government agencies discovered the NSA back doors while conducting a security evaluation of Britain's latest tank battlefield system. While back engineering the Microsoft source code at their research facility at Farnborough, the team discovered the eight NSA back doors.

Microsoft threatened legal action against the British government for what the firm considered to be the illegal examination of its source code. However, after the British government claimed Crown immunity and threatened to leak the information about the NSA back doors to the media, Microsoft backed down. Britain removed the eight back doors and was able to secure its tank and other battlefield systems from the NSA.

Apple and Google, like Microsoft, have remained quiet about the surveillance capabilities of their products. WMR's intelligence source stresses that the silence from Apple and Google is being directed by the actual developer of the surveillance back doors, the NSA.

July 1-4, 2011 -- NATO using geo-location technology to assassinate key Libyan officials

NATO's campaign in Libya goes far beyond trying to assassinate Libyan leader Muammar Qaddafi and members of his family, according to informed sources in Tripoli. NATO is using sophisticated geo-location intelligence provided by the U.S. National Security Agency (NSA) and National Geospatial Intelligence Agency (NGA) to pinpoint key figures in the Libyan government, as well as close friends of Qaddafi, for assassination by missiles fired from U.S. unmanned drones and NATO piloted aircraft.

State Department legal adviser Harold Koh recently testified before the U.S. Senate Foreign Relations Committee that the U.S. and its allies were not trying to target Qaddafi or members of the Libyan government. Koh stated, "We don't target individuals."

However, it is clear from the evidence of U.S. and NATO strikes on residential areas, particularly homes where key Libyan government officials live, as well as their vehicles, that Koh perjured himself during his Senate testimony.

NATO's attack on June 20 of a residential compound in Sorman, west of Tripoli, was a clear example of the strategy to assassinate key Qaddafi advisers and government officials. The compound struck by NATO in Sorman is owned by Khweildi Hmeidi, a senior adviser to Qaddafi. Fifteen civilians, including six members of Hmeidi's family, were killed in the attack. The compound was attacked because a surge in cell phone activity was detected by NSA signals intelligence (SIGINT) assets and the target coordinates were developed by NSA, working with NGA, and passed to NATO and U.S. forces. NSA has compiled the cell phone numbers of top Libyan officials and any time the cell phone numbers and active frequencies "light up" on sophisticated SIGINT eavesdropping and monitoring systems at NSA headquarters at Fort Meade, Maryland and the NSA field station at Menwith Hill in England, the geo-location coordinates are quickly passed to U.S. and NATO forces in order that they can calibrate their weapons systems for attacks on the Libyan officials.

Note: It was reported in July 2013 that NSA's team that conducted cell phone tracking and targeting in association with the Joint Special Operations Command was called the Geolocation Cell or "Geo Cell."

July 28--31, 2011 -- John Key's threat to U.S. national security

The waffling engaged in by New Zealand's conservative Prime Minister John Key over the uncovering by the New Zealand Security Intelligence Service (NZSIS) and the New Zealand police of a major Israeli Mossad intelligence operation in Christchurch that, among other things, attempted to access New Zealand government databases in Canterbury after last February's devastating earthquake, calls into question Key's suitability to have access to U.S., Australian, British, and Canadian signals intelligence (SIGINT) shared with New Zealand pursuant to the UK-USA SIGINT alliance.

Key has brushed off concerns that he has not been forthcoming about what he discussed with Israeli Prime Minister Binyamin Netanyahu during four phone calls on the day of the quake. Key maintains he spoke to Netanyahu only once. Key said Netanyahu was interested in locating Israelis who had died in the quake. One suspected Mossad agent, Ofer Mizrahi, was killed in a van damaged during the quake and police later discovered that he had in his possession five passports. Two Israeli accomplices of Mizrahi rapidly fled the country. Questions remain over Key's possible role in facilitating the quick departure of the Israelis before police could question them.

Key was asked a number of questions by the New Zealand media while he was in San Francisco, where he is suspected of having attended the annual super-secret and homo-erotic gathering of U.S. and foreign political and business elite at the Bohemian Grove, north of the city. Following his visit to San Francisco, Key paid a visit to Barack Obama at the White House.

A number of Mossad agents reportedly fled New Zealand after the quake and an unofficial Israeli rescue team sent for quake relief was found to be rifling through files at the central police department building in Christchurch. High-level Israeli government intervention was evident as the Mossad team and the Israeli rescue team were exfiltrated from the country. The question remains is what role Key played in the exfiltration and whether he interfered with an NZSIS and police investigation of the Israeli operations in New Zealand.

Key is currently privy to highly-classified intelligence shared by the U.S. National Security Agency (NSA) and its Canadian, Australian, British, and New Zealand partners. To illustrate the danger of an Israeli mole occupying the highest political office in New Zealand, the following is excerpted from a 1995 draft article by WMR's editor describing the SIGINT relationship between the U.S. and New Zealand as it existed at the time:

¶"NSA's New Zealand partner, the small and secretive Government Communications Security Bureau (GCSB), operates a modern $40 million eavesdropping station in a serene valley at Waihopai, near the town of Blenheim, in the northeast part of the South Island. The station, along with its 56-foot parabolic dish antenna, was completed in mid-1989. Waihopai, which was partially built with funding from the Puzzle Palace, has a crew of about thirty technicians, including some NSA personnel. An older listening station at Tangimoana on the North Island of New Zealand sends its data to Waihopai. Waihopai's main function is to listen in on satellite communications throughout the Pacific Ocean region. Tangimoana and its newly-installed HFDF equipment played an important part in monitoring Argentine naval communications during the 1982 Falklands War. GCSB intercepts of Argentine ships were passed immediately by the Kiwis to their British colleagues at GCHQ in Cheltenham.

¶Operation Deep Freeze, located in New Zealand's Antarctic territory, also may serve a SIGINT function. The base has been periodically put on military alert during times of crisis and, like the GCHQ base at Cheltenham, New Zealand employees of Deep Freeze are barred from joining labor unions. Deep Freeze's support base at Harewood near Christchurch has twice weekly serviced U.S. Air Force Starlifters transporting computer equipment to and from NSA's base at Pine Gap, Australia. To highlight New Zealand's electronic surveillance role in the region, a U.S. Pacific Fleet order, dated October 1988, assigns New Zealand responsibility for monitoring all shipping communications in an area extending halfway across the Tasman Sea to the west, north to the equator, and about 950 miles to the east beyond the Chatham Islands. A fleet of Royal New Zealand Air Force P3 Orions patrol a 3,000,000 square mile region of the Pacific and then ships its SIGINT "catch" off to Waihopai where it is then transmitted to Fort Meade.

¶The Waihopai base has been a focal point for New Zealand's vocal peace movement which has charged that the base is tasked with intercepting the private telephone calls of New Zealand citizens. In 1988, New Zealand's Prime Minister David Lange said the intercepts performed by the station were like "trying to get a cup of water from Niagara Falls." Defending the establishment of the base, he affirmed that the base was not targeted against New Zealanders' private communications. It was ironic that Lange, a vocal critic of American foreign policy, remained supportive of the construction of one of the NSA's southernmost ears. Lange announced the construction of the Waihopai station on December 2, 1987:

"To further enhance our own intelligence capabilities a defense satellite communication station will be constructed in the Waihopai Valley, near Blenheim.

A site in the Waihopai Valley of about 77 acres has been purchased. It was selected for technical reasons, including lack of radio interference, climate, and freedom from salt corrosion, and for the availability of support from RNZAF (Royal New Zealand Air Force) Woodburne nearby. A satellite dish will be erected there. There will be in addition an operations building and workshop and the usual security forces. Construction will begin in 1988 and the station is expected to be operational in 1989.

The station will be staffed an operated by the Government Communications Security Bureau. It will be wholly New Zealand owned and controlled . . . The station will mark a new level of sophistication in our independent intelligence capability."

¶In March 1988, New Zealand's Defense Minister Bob Tizard inadvertently disclosed the missions of both Waihopai and Australia's Geraldton facility. Tizard, appearing at a press conference while on a tour of Australia with Australia's Defense Minister Kim Beazley, stated that the two listening stations would be used to monitor the satellite communications of third countries. For example, three Mexican Ilhuicahua communications satellites were located within Waihopai's coverage area. Beazley was so upset over the gaffe that he canceled the rest of Tizard's Australian "walkabout" which would have eventually taken him to Pine Gap and Nurrungar. New Zealand had already been cut off from the UKUSA SIGINT data because of a dispute arising from New Zealand's ban on U.S. Navy ships carrying nuclear weapons. The NSA, CIA, NRO, and GCHQ were so concerned about U.S. intelligence inadvertently being provided to New Zealand, the Australians were forced to employ a large staff whose sole purpose was to filter out U.S. and British intelligence from Australian intelligence destined for New Zealand. Adding insult to injury, the Australians billed the New Zealanders for this unsolicited censorship service.

¶It appears that New Zealand and its SIGINT allies have long since made up. Tizard let the cat out of the bag early when he was asked if Waihopai would share intelligence with the Kojarena base in Australia. Tizard said, referring to satellite SIGINT, "when you've got it, you've got something to exchange if you want to." In February 1994, the New Zealand SIGINT relationship with the United States was fully restored when President Clinton signed a directive restoring high-level intelligence contacts between Washington and Wellington. President Bush had already restored some intelligence links with New Zealand during Operation Desert Storm.

2012

March 2-3, 2012 -- NSA continues to spy on U.S. citizens

The National Security Agency (NSA) continues to conduct warrantless wiretapping of U.S. citizens at a frenetic pace, according to informed NSA sources. Much of the surveillance of American citizens and legal residents, known as "U.S. persons" in the NSA eavesdropping lexicon, is now being conducted under the aegis of the U.S. Cyber Command. NSA director General Keith Alexander doubles as the commander of the Cyber Command. Both agencies' headquarters are located at Fort Meade, Maryland.

Warrantless wiretapping began during the George W. Bush administration in the wake of 9/11. The program was authorized by Vice President Dick Cheney's chief counsel David Addington and was never known as the so-called "Terrorist Surveillance Program," or "TSP." The Terrorist Surveillance Program moniker was a cover story developed by NSA, Justice Department, and White House officials to mask the true targets of the warrantless eavesdropping operation: U.S. citizens on U.S. soil. Primary targets include journalists, their government sources, and political office holders and other government officials. The latter includes members of Congress, state governors, senior military officers, U.S. diplomats, and Cabinet officers. Some of the intercepted communications of Americans was entered into an NSA database known as PINWALE.

WMR has learned that although NSA's acting general counsel Vito Potenza and NSA Inspector General Joel Brenner claimed they were not given access to "The Program's" key implementing documents, both individuals had worked with Addington and other members of the Bush White House, including chief of staff Andrew Card, to implement massive NSA spying on U.S. citizens. The two NSA lawyers worked closely with Justice Department's Office of Legal Counsel attorney John Yoo to craft the illegal program. Yoo's actions were approved by Attorney General Alberto Gonzales.

At NSA, the warrantless eavesdropping program is simply known as "The Program." The classified code word for "The Program" was STELLAR WIND before the code phrase was leaked to the media. The Bush administration used "The Program" to gain intelligence on its political enemies and friends, alike. The Obama administration maintains "The Program" to similarly engage in political surveillance within the United States.

"The Program" was largely the brainchild of then-NSA director Michael Hayden, who was later promoted to the first Deputy Director of National Intelligence and, subsequently, to Central Intelligence Agency director.

Warrantless wiretapping was also instituted to ensure that critical intelligence possessed by NSA about the planned 9/11 attacks was withheld from the Congress and the public after what became known as the "second Pearl Harbor." In the aftermath of 9/11, several NSA employees knew that the agency was in possession of actionable intelligence that could have prevented the attacks. As a result, many career and military NSA personnel suffered physical ailments and severe mental stress amid a climate of absolute enforced silence about what NSA knew beforehand. As a result, a number of NSA personnel were either prevented from testifying or not invited to testify before the 9/11 Commission.

However, NSA's director of signals intelligence, Maureen Baginski, termed 9/11 as a "gift" to NSA. Hayden ensured that NSA craftily hid behind the FBI and CIA to avoid any blame for the 9/11 attacks and stay "clean."

In an unprecedented manner, the Obama administration is using the 1917 Espionage Act, with its 1950 amendment, known as the McCarran Internal Security Act -- passed during the espionage scandal involving State Department official Alger Hiss and the "Pumpkin Papers" affair -- to indict government officials who leak information to the press. The Obama administration has also stepped up NSA and other surveillance of journalists in an effort to discover their sources.

The doctrine being followed by the Obama administration comes from a 2010 book, titled *Necessary Secrets: National Security, the Media, and the Rule of Law,* authored by the neo-con Hudson Institute's senior fellow Gabe Schoenfeld. In the book, Schoenfeld called for the government to prosecute reporters and editors, particularly those at *The New York Times*, for revealing details of the warrantless wiretapping program. Schoenfeld is a former senior editor of the Jewish Zionist publication *Commentary*. He has also written for the neo-con *Weekly Standard* and *New York Sun*. NSA sources have told WMR that the Obama administration has "taken a page from Schoenfeld's book" in continuing the NSA warrantless surveillance program.

Meanwhile, the Justice Department continues to use prosecutor William M. Welch II, the former chief of the Public Integrity Section at Main Justice, to investigate government whistleblowers and journalists. However, in a serendipitous development, WMR has learned of four run-ins with the law that Welch had in his native Massachusetts. Covered up by the Justice Department, these infractions of the law call into question Welch's suitability to hold down a job as a Justice Department prosecutor. WMR is pursuing leads in the Welch matter.

April 5-6, 2012 -- The background to the Israeli penetration of NSA

In June 2005, WMR's first report at itgs inception dealt with Israeli intelligence penetration of the National Security Agency. Jim Bamford has written about further details of this penetration in an April 3 article in *Wired* titled "Shady Companies with Ties to Israel Wiretap the U.S. for the

NSA." In the article, Bamford describes the penetration of NSA's ultra-secret surveillance technology research and development "skunk works," the Signals Intelligence Automation Research Center (SARC), located at NSA's headquarters on the third floor of Operations Building 2B, a few doors down from the center where NSA monitored sensitive government communications in Russia.

The SARC is where companies linked to Israel helped set up NSA's controversial and top secret warrantless eavesdropping program code-named STELLAR WIND. SARC's chief of staff, J. Kirk Wiebe, and the center's co-founded, Bill Binney, realized that a private company with links to Israel, Technology Development Corporation (TDC), a two-man operation with an Annapolis Junction post office box run by two brothers, Randall and Paul Jacobson of Clarksville, Maryland, was running the Stellar Wind operation using software and equipment provided by two Israeli firms, Narus, later bought by Boeing, and Verint, owned by Comverse Technology, formerly Comverse Infosys. Both companies were formed by ex-Unit 8200 personnel. Unit 8200 is the Israeli counterpart of NSA. The NSA program manager for Stellar Wind was Ben Gunn, a U.S. naturalized Scotsman who once worked for Britain's NSA equivalent, the Government Communications Headquarters (GCHQ) in Cheltenham, UK.

Rather than investigate the Jacobsons, Gunn and their Israeli interlocutors, FBI agents raided the homes of Wiebe and Binney and confiscated their computer equipment as part of the failed Justice Department investigation of former NSA official Thomas Drake, the whistle blower who exposed massive contract fraud and illegal surveillance by NSA.

Paul Jacobson had his security access pulled by NSA in 1992 and he later changed his name to "Jimmy Carter" and "Alfred Olympus von Ronsdorf." Randall Jacobson continued working for NSA and when Science Applications International Corporation (SAIC) was brought in to run the nascent Stellar Wind program, taking over from TDC, Randall Jacobson tipped Binney off to the illegal nature of the eavesdropping program, which included installing wiretapping rooms in some 20 telecommunications company switches around the United States, including the one exposed by former AT&T technician Mark Klein that was installed at the AT&T switch in downtown San Francisco.

Binney told Bamford that the NSA's advanced eavesdropping and data mining high-data analytical software may have been originally passed to Israel by a pro-Israeli technical director in NSA's Operations Directorate. The original software helped Narus and Comverse/Verint to improve on the work already performed by NSA and more advanced systems were then sold back to the NSA. The major compromise of NSA technology to the Israelis should have been made known to Binney, who was then the chairman of the NSA's Technology Advisory Panel, which monitored the signals intelligence capabilities of foreign nations. Rather than pass on to NSA the intelligence "take" of Unit 8200 using the NSA technology, Binney told Bamford that he believed that the Israeli government simply passed on the technology to Israeli start-up companies that used the NSA-developed know-how to spy on foreign countries, including the United States, and sell the technology back to countries like the United States.

The Israeli penetration of NSA was brought to WMR's attention by NSA personnel in June 2005. One of the firms mentioned as being involved in the compromise to Israel was CACI, part of an alliance of NSA contractors called the "Eagle Alliance."

May 17-18, 2012 -- Federal judge rejects Ken Ford's legal representation complaint regardless of conflict-of-interest

U.S. Federal Judge for the Southern District of Maryland Peter J. Messitte was the trial judge who sentenced former National Security Agency (NSA) analyst Kenneth W. Ford, Jr. to seven years in prison for violating the Espionage Act. Ford was the first conviction under the 1917 law for retaining classified information. Other indictments and convictions, including the unprecedented six brought by the Obama administration, were for transmittal of classified information to unauthorized parties.

WMR previously reported that Ford, who authored a signals intelligence report while working in the "Iraq shop" of NSA, was the subject of a political retaliation for reporting that intercepts of Iraqi government communications could not support the contention that Iraq possessed weapons of mass destruction.

On March 30, 2006, "US Judge Peter Messitte today sentenced former NSA 'Iraqi shop' signals intelligence analyst Ken Ford Jr., to six years in prison and no fine as a result of his politically-motivated conviction for allegedly removing two boxes of classified materials from NSA during broad daylight without detection. In fact, the documents were planted in Ford's home in retaliation for his SIGINT report casting doubt on the White House contention that Iraq possessed weapons of mass destruction. That report, which contained Ford's name as preparer, eventually ended up on the desk of Vice President Dick Cheney. As a result, Ford became a target of the neo-con cell operating from within Cheney's office and the White House Iraq Group (WHIG), the same cabal that compromised Valerie Plame Wilson's covert identity and mission.

Ford was given six years on the first count of unauthorized removal of classified information and three years (to be served concurrently) for making a false statement on a government security clearance form for a classified job with Lockheed Martin filled out nine months after his arrest. In fact, Ford stated on the form that his arrest was wrongful but that was construed by Assistant US Attorney David Salem as a false statement."

There is a strong reason to believe that a single classified document was planted inside Ford's Waldorf, Maryland home by an FBI confidential informant in order to manufacture evidence to convict Ford of illegally retaining classified material as punishment for his Iraqi signals intelligence analysis report.

Ford was released from the Lewisburg Pennsylvania federal correctional institution last year and is now subject to five years of probation that stipulates he remain within a fifty mile radius of Washington, DC unless he receives permission from his probation officer to travel beyond the area.

A grievance by Ford against his defense attorney for ethics violations was filed with the Attorney Grievance Commission. The Commission sent the complaint to Disciplinary and Admissions Committee for the U.S. Court for the Southern District of Maryland for consideration. In a May 8, 2012, letter to Ford, the chairman of the committee rejected Ford's complaint. In what appears to be a gross conflict-of-interests, the rejection was made by Messitte, the same judge who sentenced Ford and who, conveniently for NSA and the government, chairs the Disciplinary and Admissions Committee for the federal court.

Three judges on the U.S. Appeals Court for the Fourth Circuit in Richmond, Virginia rejected an appeal of Ford's conviction without ever having held a hearing. The same three judges will shortly begin hearing oral arguments in the attempt by the Obama administration to force *New York Times* reporter James Risen to testify ablout his sources in the case *U.S. v Sterling*. Former CIA officer Jeffrey Sterling has been indicted for passing classified information on the CIA's Operation Merlin, which covertly tampered with industrial equipment sold to Iran for its nuclear power program. The government believes that Sterling passed classified information on Merlin to Risen and has subpoenaed Risen to testify under oath about his source or sources on his story. U.S. Judge Leonie Brinkema of the U.S. Court for the Eastern District of Virginia in Alexandria quashed the subpoena but the Eric Holder Justice Department has appealed the decision to the appellate court in Richmond.

Based on the three appellate judges' decision in the Ford case, there is a fear that the decision on the Risen matter will be favorable to the U.S. national security state. The case would then go to the U.S. Supreme Court. If the Supreme Court fails to grant a Writ of Certiorari in the case or rules for the government and, upon which, Risen refuses to testify pursuant to the subpoena, he would be declared in contempt and would likely be jailed.

WMR previously reported on the "cabalism" that exists within the federal court system for Maryland, particularly with regard to the Ford case. On July 3, 2009, WMR reported: "Ford was convicted by a tainted jury and sentenced to seven years in federal prison. Ford, who is African-American, originally had an African-American federal trial judge. However, the judge was replaced by a pro-Iraq war U.S. judge, Peter Messitte, who set out to ensure a guilty conviction of Ford in cahoots with U.S. Attorney for Maryland Rod Rosenstein, and Assistant U.S. Attorney for Southern Maryland David Salem, both Bush appointees. Nothing was done by the judge or prosecutors to dismiss from the jury a contractor whose company had major contracts with NSA. The trio of Messitte, Rosenstein, and Salem have also 'rocket-docketed' a number of cases, resulting in slam dunk convictions, against Arab- and Iranian-Americans in the southern district of Maryland."

WMR's editor covered a number of hearings during the Ford case at the U.S. court house in Greenbelt, Maryland. During one hearing where the editor was not present, Messitte called Ford to the stand and placed him under oath to answer questions about where WMR had obtained information on Ford's Iraqi signals intelligence work at NSA. Ford testified that he was not the source for the information. Messitte then inquired, "Is Mr. Madsen present in the court room?" Those in attendance at the trial reported that Messitte wanted to call this editor to the bench and, under oath, provide the source or sources for the information about Iraq and the signals intelligence report.

Had I been present I would have refused to answer Messitte's question and would have likely been found in contempt and jailed until I agreed to answer Messitte's question. It would have been a very long prison stay because I would have refused to answer any questions from Messitte. It is, therefore, apparent that Messitte, a President Clinton nominee, is an ethically-conflicted federal judge who has little regard for the First Amendment.

WMR has learned from legal sources that a number of federal judges have shown an increased willingness to call individuals in attendance at trials to the witness stand or bench to answer questions under oath with the belief that a judge can do anything he or she desires within their court room. The judges include those on the U.S. Appeals Court in Richmond.

2013

<u>May 30-June 3, 2013 -- Woolwich and in-fighting between UK intelligence agencies</u>

WMR's sources in the UK are reporting significant infighting between top officials of the Secret Intelligence Service (MI6), which handles foreign intelligence matters, and the Security Service (MI5), which is mainly responsible for domestic law enforcement matters.

The row centers around the savage meat cleaver slaying of British soldier Drummer Lee Rigby near a British Army installation in Woolwich is southeast London by accused assailants Michael Adebowale and Michael Adebolajo, who were said to have attacked Rigby with meat cleavers and knives. However, before the two attacked Rigby, the soldier was reportedly struck by a car, described as a blue Vauxhall Tigra with British license plate N696 JWX. Rigby reportedly died from the cleaver and knife attack and not from the vehicle hitting him.

Adebolajo, a native of Nigeria with a British passport, converted to Islam under the tutelage of one-time London-based Islamist radical Omar Bakri, later expelled from from Britain. Bakri was the leader of the al-Muhajiroun group and Adebolajo is said to have taken the Muslim name Mujaahid after his conversion.

In 2010, Adebolajo traveled to Kenya where he made contact with "Al Qaeda"-linked Islamist guerrillas, some linked to Somali al-Shabaab militants. Adebolajo, whose British passport identified him as "Michael Olemindis Ndemolajo," was arrested by Kenyan police after having made contact with known Islamist militants on the Kenyan islands of Lamu and Pate, the latter only 40 miles from the Somali mainland. Kenyan police arrested Adebolajo on a stone jetty at Kizingitini on Pate. However, British law enforcement gave Kenyan authorities a "clean" notice on Adebolajo and he was freed. It later emerged that MI5 had attempted to recruit Adebolajo as an agent and that he was tortured while being detained in Kenya. Adebolajo was deported to the UK.

It is ironic that Adebolajo would have made contact with Al Qaeda-linked militants in a region that is heavily surveilled by Kenyan, British, and American intelligence agents. It is well known that Kenyan intelligence pays coastal fishermen and ferry captains for any information on suspected Islamist militants in the area and, as discussed in the editor's book *Jaded Tasks*, the region is brimming with intelligence bases: "The U.S. also had surveillance stations on the island of Burr Gaabo in Somali territorial waters and Ras Kambooni, the recent site of a U.S. bombing run that reportedly intended to kill Al-Qaida member Fazul Abdullah Mohammed, the prime suspect in the U.S. Embassy bombings in Nairobi and Dar es Saalam in 1998. The U.S. had several signals intelligence (SIGINT) stations in Kenya. One was located on the island of Lamu and a separate station was in Kilifi." In addition, U.S. Special Forces maintain a base, Camp

Simba, on the Kenyan mainland at Manda Bay from which it inserts its forces secretly into Somalia. The commando unit is known as Task Force 88. British Special Forces accompany their American colleagues on anti-terrorist "search, capture, or destroy" missions on Lamu, Pate, and Manda islands. Ocassionally, the Americans and Brits are accompanied on their missions by Kenyan, Ethiopian, Djiboutian, French, and, more clandestinely, Israeli troops.

Moments after Adebolajo's friend Abu Nusaybah was interveiwed by the BBC's *Newsnight* about the MI5 ties of Adebolajo, Nusaybah was arrested by the London Metropolitan Police Counter-Terrorism Command. It is believed that MI5 ordered Nusaybah's arrest lest he provide any more details of Adebolajo's links to MI5.

However, after Nusaybah's arrested, *The Telegraph*, known to have close links to MI6, published further details of Adebolajo's past ties to MI5. WMR has learned that there is a major turf battle between the two intelligence services over what MI6 believes is MI5's trespassing on MI6's jurisdiction over counter-terrorism operations not only in east Africa but around the world.

To assist her old outfit MI5, its retired director, Stella Rimington, decided to break her retirement silence to claim that everyone should spy on their neighbors, giving MI5 a free pass on such surveillance, regardless of location.

Nusaybah claimed that MI5 continued to harass Adebolajo, insisting that he spy for them on other Muslims. Adebolajo's brother-in-law confirmed Nusaybah's comments in stating that MI5 tried to recruit Adebolajo after his return to Britain from Kenya. Nusaybah's and Zubayr's comments are similar to those of the parents of Tamerlan Tsarnaev, who claimed the FBI continued to pressure the accused Boston Marathon bomber to spy for them after a tip-off by Russian security to the FBI over Tsaranev's ties to known terrorists in Dagestan in Russia. In fact, Zubayr told *The Independent* of the UK that he was harassed in London by phone calls from self-described FBI agents who were very interested in Adebolajo.

In the case of the Woolwich attack, Prime Minister David Cameron, who had been facing a significant Tory backbencher revolt within his parliamentary ranks, quickly left Paris, cutting short a summit meeting with the French president and returned to London to meet with the counter-terrorism COBRA committee. Rigby's murder was the first terrorism-related death in the UK since the July 7, 2005 London transit bombings.

Whether it is George W. Bush amid plummeting popularity and a perceived illegal presidency, Barack Obama during multiple scandals, or David Cameron during a Tory rebellion and a faltering coalition government, terrorist acts are always welcomed as the last refuge for beleaguered governments.

June 12-13, 2013 -- There is an NSA-CIA hybrid agency that may explain Snowden's involvement in SIGINT and HUMINT

The media is quoting a number of intelligence "insiders" who are questioning NSA whistleblower Edward Snowden's involvement in National Security Agency (NSA) signals intelligence and meta-data mining programs like PRISM and CIA human intelligence (HUMINT) operations.

However, the U.S. intelligence "insiders" may be trying their best to cover up the operations of a little-known hybrid NSA-CIA organizations known as the Special Collection Service (SCS), known internally at NSA as "F6," and which is headquartered in Beltsville, Maryland in what appears to be a normal office building with a sign bearing the letters "CSSG" at its front driveway off of Springfield Road. Adjacent to the CSSG building is the State Department's Beltsville Communications Annex, known internally at the State Department as SA-26 and part of the Diplomatic Telecommunications Service, which also handles encrypted communications to CIA stations around the world.

CSSG is listed in area phone directories as *Communications Systems Support Group,* 11600 Springfield Road, Laurel, Maryland, 20708-3528, with a phone number of (301) 210-1776. "1776," in this case, is the farthest thing from the ideals of founders like Thomas Jefferson, who developed his own encryption code, still known as the "Jefferson cipher," in order to encode messages sent between the covert revolutionary Committees of Correspondence.

The SCS uses the State Department's secure communications satellite channels to communicate with SCS covert electronic eavesdropping facilities embedded in U.S. diplomatic embassies and missions abroad. One of the SCS units is located at the U.S. Mission to the United Nations in Geneva, Switzerland. Snowden said he was responsible for maintaining network security at the mission.

According to the list of key foreign service officers at U.S. diplomatic posts, dated 2008, mission is located at 11 Rte de Pregny, 1292 Chambesy in Geneva. While Snowden worked at the mission, the ambassador was Warren Tichenor and the deputy chief of mission was Mark Storella. Other diplomats assigned to the mission when Snowden was assigned to it included: David Gilmour, Anne Coughlin (the Regional Security Officer), Mark G. Bandik (USAID), David Reimer, Lisa Myers, Louis Nelli, Nance Kyloh, Ritchie Miller, Kathy J. Beck (Internal Revenue Service), Don Greer, Doug Wells, Ann Chick, Jeffrey D. Kovar (FBI Legal Attaché), and Michael Klecheski (Political Officer).

Evidence is mounting that Snowden was working for the SCS in Geneva. The Swiss Foreign ministry has confirmed that Snowden was declared by the U.S. State Department as an "attaché" assigned to the mission from March 2007 to February 2009. Snowden's name would not necessarily appear on the State Department's diplomatic list because it only specifies "key" foreign service officers and not normally Diplomatic Telecommunications Service personnel, of which Snowden was likely one. In 2009, Snowden left the CIA to work for Dell Computers and thereafter went to work for Booz Allen Hamilton as a contractor for the NSA at "NSA Hawaii," the Regional security Operations Center located at Kunia on Oahu and which is responsible for eavesdropping on the Asia-Pacific region.

Snowden told *The Guardian* that he witnessed CIA agents routinely getting a Swiss banker drunk and then encouraging him to drive home. After the banker was arrested for drunk driving, the CIA offered to bail him out of trouble if he became a CIA source.

Snowden's involvement with the SCS would have also given him access to information on CIA stations, CIA official cover agents assigned to U.S. diplomatic posts like Geneva, and surveillance priorities for NSA, such as those depicted on a Top Secret map contained in a slide on NSA's BOUNDLESSINFORMANT global electronic surveillance program.

SCS permits NSA to conduct surveillance on targets that are normally denied due to high levels of physical security and encryption. Black bag CIA and NSA teams penetrate physical security and place listening devices in secure areas and embed Trojan horse programs in computer systems and networks that allow NSA to bypass encryption controls.

The SCS is also used to recruit foreign nationals who would be helpful in providing access to government and commercial networks and databases. Chief targets for such recruitment are database managers, systems administrators, and computer security technicians, in other words, people like Snowden. Even Swiss bankers with access to secret accounts would be targeted by the SCS to provide system passwords and remote access techniques to banking networks. The Swiss government has sent a diplomatic note to the U.S. government demanding an explanation of Snowden's allegations about the recruitment of the Swiss banker. Swiss counter-intelligence is rated among the best in the world.

Communications Security establishment Canada (CSEC) officer Mike Frost was the first to reveal details about SCS in his 1994 book *Spyworld: Inside the Canadian and American Intelligence Establishments.* Frost was trained to conduct covert communications surveillance in foreign capitals at SCS, which, before moving to the Beltsville facility, was located in a strip shopping center in College Park, Maryland behind a false retail operation. CSEC's operation was code named PILGRIM and it used an NSA system code named ORATORY to conduct surveillance from Canadian embassies in countries around the world.

NSA, like CSEC, Britain's Government Communications Headquarters (GCHQ), Australia's Defense Signals Directorate (DSD), and New Zealand's Government Communications Security Board (GCSB)-- known as the UK-USA or "Five Eyes" countries -- conduct covert electronic surveillance from the nation's embassies and consulates abroad. The operations are supported by SCS. Not only does the NSA and CIA maintain special collections units at the U.S. mission in Geneva but most U.S. diplomatic missions, including the ill-fated diplomatic mission in Benghazi, housed SCS surveillance units.

Snowden, in his televised interview with *The Guardian*, referred to NSA's "partners," which are the Five Eyes English-speaking nations. He also spoke of "third parties," which are non-English speaking nations that are part of the signals intelligence "club," countries like Japan, South Korea, Thailand, Germany, Denmark, Spain, Italy, Norway, Sweden, the Netherlands, and Belgium. NSA also maintain agreements with Third Parties, which, in what could be an unfortunate for Snowden, the People's Republic of China. Two NSA listening stations in Xinjiang in western China, located at Qitai and Korla, were code named SAUGUS and SAUCEPAN, respectively. In addition, GCHQ maintains an SCS surveillance station at its Hong Kong consulate, which is nicknamed "the Alamo."

The NSA's eavesdropping system ran out of the U.S. embassy in Moscow was once code named BROADSIDE. CSEC PILGRIM surveillance units, operated under Canadian embassy and high commission diplomatic cover and supported by SCS, were present in Caracas (ARTICHOKE), Beijing (BADGER), Mexico City (CORNFLOWER), New Delhi (DAISY), Kingston, Jamaica (EGRET), Rabat (IRIS), Abidjan (JASMINE), Bucharest (HOLLYHOCK), and Moscow (SPHINX). Other PILGRIM units operated in Canadian embassies in Rome; San Jose, Costa Rica; Tokyo; and Warsaw.

Among the most storied SCS operations was the planting in 2001 of 27 bugging devices on the Boeing-767 delivered to China for use by Chinese President Jiang Zemin as his official plane. Chinese counter-intelligence discovered the bugs before they were activated. SCS also reportedly set up a surveillance unit a mile from Osama Bin Laden's alleged compound in Abbottabad, Pakistan. SCS units were also deployed to Chechnya during the first Russo-Chechen war to assist Chechen leader Dzhokhar Dudayev in evading Russian signals intelligence direction finding operations targeting his personal satellite phone. In 1996, Dudayev ran out of luck after visiting President Bill Clinton helped embattled President Boris Yeltsin's re-election chances by providing the Russian President with Dudayev's NSA-triangulated fix. Dudayev was killed, while talking on his phone, by a Russian air-to ground missile.

June 17-18, 2013 -- NSA employs huge surveillance web with numerous cover terms and code names

WMR can exclusively report that the National Security Agency's program to conduct widespread surveillance of the American people began with a pet multi-billion dollar project of former NSA director General Michael Hayden in 2002. The project known as TRAILBLAZER was rushed through so rapidly, an internal unclassified, For Official Use Only report obtained by WMR contains numerous references to failed performance testing of signals intelligence systems.

The document also provides some insight into NSA's worldwide reach. For example, one NSA system cited in the documents obtained by WMR, named ENRICHMENT, is described as a

"Balkans Portal," while a system called ASPEN deals with "weapons and space."

The Pentagon maintains a large military base in southern Kosovo at Camp Bondsteel. There is no confirmation whether Bondsteel is the location of the NSA Balkans portal but NSA does maintain a presence at the large U.S. base.

While controversy rages about the possible illegality of NSA's PRISM meta-data vacuuming system and collection of the telephone number records of U.S. citizens, the NSA documents show that NSA has a system called LEGAL REPTILE.

WMR has also learned that Hayden opted for a TRAILBLAZER system called WEALTHYCLUSTER over THINTHREAD. THINTHREAD was less invasive of the privacy of American citizens than the more expensive WEALTHYCLUSTER.

Privacy issues were raised within NSA concerning TRAILBLAZER and WEALTHYCLUSTER but to no avail. It turns out that NSA had an ombudsman and Hotline Manager to handle internal complaints about fraud, waste, and abuse, including violations of United States Signals Intelligence Directive 18 (USSID), which governs the application of the privacy provisions of the Foreign Intelligence Surveillance Act regarding intercepts of U.S. persons. In such cases, intercepts of U.S. persons are to be masked or destroyed. However, in training exercises, prohibitions on intercepts of U.S. persons, a process known as "minimization," were often bypassed. WMR has in its possession a number of e-mails from the years following 9/11 that were sent from the NSA ombudsman and Hotline Manager William (Bill) Shea. Often, Shea swept complaints under the carpet. Shea's immediate supervisor was Nancy Sondervan.

According to one NSA document authored by Hayden and obtained by WMR, in February 2002, President George W. Bush sent a short note to Director of Central Intelligence George Tenet that that "swept away all the theological fine points about 'data at rest.'" "Data at rest" was static data held in databases and phone call records held by telecommunications companies. From Bush's dictate to Tenet, systems like PRISM were born. Hayden also declared that it was his intention to improve cooperation with NSA's foreign partners in the collection of signals intelligence, "I also believe that we have not yet fully realized all that we can from our many foreign partnerships." Hayden also addressed the problem of U.S. law standing in the way of meta-data collection: "US law and policy present more serious issues . . . Can we use the kind of technology we're developing to deal with information overload for our analysts to suppress (to a standard of reasonableness) information with too high a US person content or strip out that which is unlikely to have intelligence value. We'll have to do that (or address the policy limits themselves) if we want to allow "customers" to swim up the SIGINT production stream to become far more active participants in the creation of SIGINT products and services."

Hayden said that one of his predecessors, Admiral William Studeman, came up with an idea on how to bypass controls that limited NSA access to databases containing personal data on U.S. persons: "Bill Studeman has suggested that we need to designate 'roving patrols' to move between data pools and match related bits of information across the INTs, producing intelligence of value to national security." Note that INTS are the various forms of intelligence collection: signals intelligence, human intelligence, imagery intelligence, communications intelligence, etc.

WMR is receptive to any further information on the role that these and other systems play in the widespread illegal surveillance of the American people and the numerous "problems" cited by the NSA in the testing and fielding of these surveillance systems. And, as always, confidentiality of sources is always maintained at our end.

SID Systems Integration
Planning Program
Windows 2000 Migration Plan
26 November 2002
MDA904-01-G-0059/0001

Prepared by:
Computer Sciences Corporation
7471 Candlewood Road
Hanover, Maryland 21076

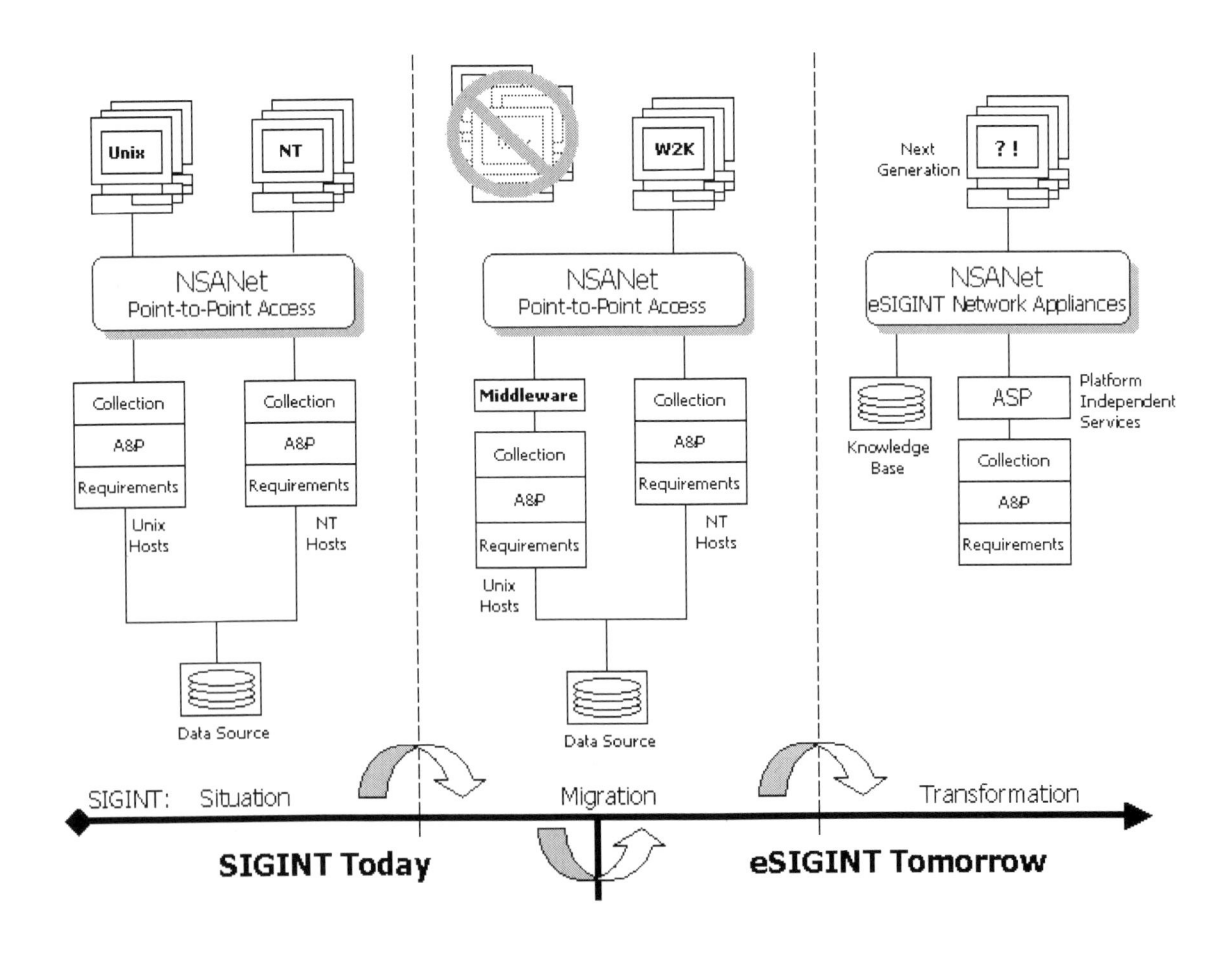

Figure 1 (U) Windows 2000 Migration & Transformation

(U//FOUO) Nearly 5,000 Unix and 4,000 NT workstations support the current SIGINT situation on NSANet. Over the years, the SID, like other NSA organizations, has tolerated the creation of stovepipe development in order to accomplish the mission. Previous attempts to force change to a common, Windows-based platform, has been met with resistance—much of it due to preference versus technical capabilities. With the core competencies, such as acquisition, analysis, processing, and reporting, mixed between Unix and NT systems, sharing of intelligence within the enterprise is burdened with extra automated and manual processing. Migrating the users to a Wintel environment will standardize these competencies as well as corporate-support functions.

3.3 (U) TRANSFORMING THE SIGINT MISSION

(U//FOUO) The desired strategic transformation is purposefully directed away from dependence on specific hardware and/or operating system software. Webbased (eSIGINT), platform independent network appliances will be utilized, without restrictions, based upon independent services. Control will be provided by the Application Service Provider (ASP) function within the SIGINT Directorate—key to transformation success. Data sources will be directly available to all users via platform independent services. The increased ability to competitively procure new technologies from commodity-based offerings will be the most cost effective derivative. More importantly, the data and information sharing capability within the enterprise and the entire intelligence community will be attainable.

SECTION II

4 (U) MIGRATION GOALS, OBJECTIVES, AND PRINCIPLES

(U) Application migration, as defined in this plan, aims to reduce dependencies on native GOTS applications and integrate COTS applications at the enterpriselevel. The plan moves towards the strategic goal of true platform independence by means of a tactical, Windows 2000 Migration, effectively expanding linkage throughout the intelligence community.

4.1 (U) VISION

(U//FOUO) In concert with the goals of the NSA/CSS Strategic Plan, the top-level action item for the SID is the "Transformation of the SIGINT Mission," wherein transformation is the perpetual state of modernization for SIGINT legacy components. Current technology dictates that transformation take the form of a web-based, or eSIGINT, enterprise where analysts can expect near 100% availability due to a robust, yet flexible, service-based infrastructure integrating Commercial-Off-The-Shelf (COTS) products. For client environments, this also requires divesting the desktop of its resident Government-Off-The-Shelf (GOTS) applications not currently under the control of a centralized distribution domain or Application Service Provider (ASP). As indicated within figure 2, ASP scope can be expected to increase as achievements are made in platform-dependency reductions.

(U//FOUO) This "industrial-strength" SIGINT is fortified by the Unified Cryptologic Architecture (UCA) whose fundamental objective is to break down existing "stove pipes" and foster greater collaboration across the community, i.e., modernize, interoperate, and interconnect. Enabling future transformation and its eSIGINT theme should be considered tantamount, if not paramount, to any other stated migration goal.

Windows 2000 Migration Plan

5.3 (U) APPLICABLE HARDWARE INVENTORY PERSPECTIVES

(U//FOUO) An initial desktop hardware inventory was collected in an effort to relate users to applications, users to equipment, and equipment to geographical locations. Using the hardware inventory, the migration implementation team will be able to identify potential workstation replacement schedules based upon hardware attributes and application readiness. Other rudimentary surveys (non-NSAW desktops) were made as a byproduct of collecting user account data on systems serving SIGINT applications.

5.3.1 (U//FOUO) NTSS SERVERS

(U//FOUO) One of many collection points for SID-owned servers, the National Time Sensitive System (NTSS) server inventory is included as a representative list of assets that should be evaluated for underutilization. The prevailing belief is that too many of these servers are functioning as direct-access storage devices (DASD). Further evaluation would determine if computational requirements could be reapportioned among NSA server farm components if divested of their DASD through widespread addition of networked appliances specifically designed for high-speed storage and retrieval. Successful modernization and reapportionment of these assets would be consistent with both tactical and strategic goals mentioned throughout this plan.

Table 8 (U//FOUO) National Time Sensitive System Server Inventory

LOCATION	SYSTEM	OS	MODEL	CPUs	MEMORY	MB	DASD
OPS 1 OP270-2	Canucks	5.5.1	SC2000	4	1024MB	2	2.1GB(6)
OPS 1 OP270-2	Dollar	5.6	SC2000	4	1024MB	2	2.9GB(6)
OPS 1 OP270-2	Eastcake	5.8	U4500	2	1024MB	1	9GB(x)
OPS 1 OP270-2	Healycuff	5.8	Sparc20	2	96MB	1	2.1GB(2)
OPS 1 OP270-2	Muddyswelt	5.8	U4500	4	2048MB	2cpu/2io	18GB(2)
OPS 1 OP270-2	Needywhat	5.8	E220R	2	1024MB	1	18GB(2)
OPS 1 OP270-2	Rimtitle	5.8	U5500	4	1024MB	2cpu/2io	18GB(2)
OPS 1 OP270-2	Riskdime	5.8	E220R	2	512MB	1	18GB(2)
OPS 1 OP270-2	Rowload	5.8	18GB(2)	2	18GB(2)	1	18GB(2)
OPS 1 OP270-2	Seawater	5.8	E420R	2	2048MB	1	18GB(2)
OPS 1 OP270-3	Curacao	5.8	SC2000	4	1024MB	2	2.9GB(6)
OPS 1 OP270-3	Half	5.6	SC2000	4	1024MB	2	2.9GB(6)
OPS 1 OP270-3	Healymink	5.8	Sparc20	2	96MB	1	2.1GB(2)
OPS 1 OP270-3	Learngilt	5.8	E220R	2	512MB	1	18GB(2)
OPS 1 OP270-3	Linefurl	5.8	U5500	4	1024MB	2cpu/2io	18GB(2)
OPS 1 OP270-3	Mobloose	5.8	U4500	4	2048MB	2cpu/2io	18GB(2)
OPS 1 OP270-3	Spellbeak	5.8	E220R	2	512MB	1	18GB(2)
OPS 1 OP270-3	Thosehot	5.8	U4500	2	1024MB	1	9GB(x)
OPS 1 OP270-5	Seawater	5.8	E420R	2	2048MB	1	18GB(2)

(U//FOUO)

5.2 (U//FOUO) SIGINT MISSION BASELINE

(U//FOUO) The SIGINT Mission Baseline consists of SID-controlled, mission related desktop components, that is, applications, utilities, and remote access to systems and/or databases. The baseline, however, is fluid by its nature due to changing mission requirements (and small pockets of enthusiastic programmer analysts) introducing new and modified components to the baseline. Therefore, the plan addresses the SIGINT Mission Baseline as a living document consisting of identified, migration groups of software components captured in the Migration Component List, a database developed specifically for this effort. The following paragraphs describe how the initial baseline was established and the perpetual reevaluation required to maintain accuracy and completeness.

5.2.1 (U) COLLECTION AND ASSEMBLY

(U//FOUO) Baseline candidates were initially derived from both ITIS and SID resources. Two significant events at the beginning of the decade established the groundwork for an adequate preliminary inventory and general assessment; the requirement to assess all software products in response to the impending Year 2000 (Y2K) problem and the requirement to assess all projects in response to a Congressionally Directed Action (CDA) for retirement of those no longer needed. Capitalizing upon work performed in response to these events under the MILLENIUM and FAST TRACK projects, an inventory that focused upon migration components rather than projects or systems was derived by means of cross-correlating all SID items within the Information Technology Inventory (ITIDB) and JACKPOT databases.[2]

(U//FOUO) Potential sources from which to assemble the SIGINT mission applications baseline list were identified by the SID. The SID/SEO task manager initially directed the migration planning team to various lists produced to support internal tasks, on-line (NSA Web) published documentation, and to each Office of Primary Responsibility (OPR). Additional data was 'discovered'; either by searching the web on key words or discovering links from pages that were being reviewed for content. The value of each list to the migration plan had to be considered and the data contained in the lists was incorporated into a master baseline of SIGINT mission applications based upon that assessed value.

Sources of data include:
—————————————————HIGHCASTLE/LOOKINGGLASS. Contained applications considered primary candidates for migration to an NT desktop.
NSOC list. Contained COTS and other miscellaneous items that were not 'applications' per se.
—————————————Mission App NT Compatibility Matrix. Contained essentially LOOKING GLASS/HIGHCASTLE applications, as published by ITIS.
—————————————S2 Data Call from the "Catch-up Task." Provided a reasonably exhaustive list of current S2 applications despite being almost a year old.
—————————————SCE Projects (S3). This list of projects was discovered from another link. While extensive, it does not represent a complete list of S3 projects, systems, or applications.
ROTUNDPIPER (Verified List). Suggested as the 'master' list. However, it is a new database designed to support budgeting and financial plan objectives; so most data available represents

---

[13](U//FOUO) ITIDB was superseded by BRASSCOIN for NSA project information; JACKPOT was superseded by ROTUNDPIPER for SID system information.

project-level information, not component-level.
———————————————BRASSCOIN. Another financial planning-based repository used as a cross reference for obtaining project descriptions.
———————————————JACKPOT. Used as the primary cross-reference. JACKPOT has been under development and gathering data on NSA projects, systems, and components for more than two years. It is the most comprehensive data repository of its kind available, and using it to initially verify the
components and status of projects saved countless hours of effort.
———————————————Miscellaneous. Lists from individuals or offices that appeared to add information to the aggregate component listing were used as they were discovered.

5.3.2 (U) BEANSTALK REVIEW (LOCAL DESKTOPS)

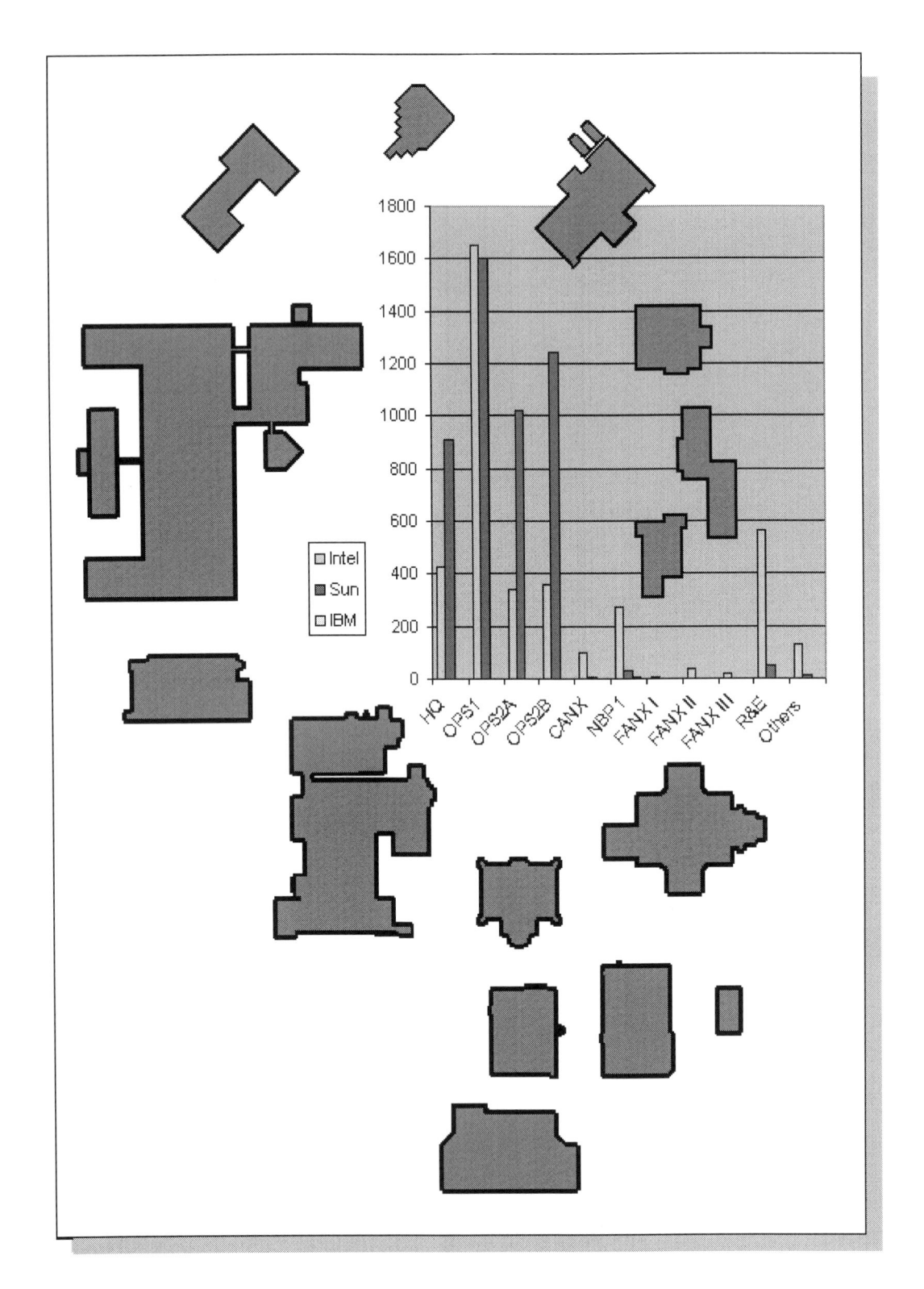

Figure 6 (U//FOUO) BEANSTALK Overview of Local SID Desktops

DEVELOPMENT, TEST AND EVALUATION (DT&E):

(U//FOUO) The third test was a functionality test. This DT&E test was conducted using

Tarantella Enterprise 3. Testing was conducted on each of the applications to determine if they could functionally complete the task they were meant to perform while remotely displayed via Tarantella. Testing was conducted using both predetermined test data and live data information. Each tool was launched and tested as if being used in an operational environment. While only one person performed testing, many applications were launched and used simultaneously.

(U//FOUO) In addition to the application tools, Solaris CDE was also included in the DT&E testing. Solaris CDE provides the user with virtual windowing, customizable settings and also allows the user to implement a pull down window schema. The Solaris CDE pull-down menus proved to be an ideal method of launching all subsequent applications. All applications were launched via Tarantella through the CDE application.

(U//FOUO) A marked improvement in the performance of Tarantella was noted with the Enterprise 3 version. This improvement may be with Tarantella itself or with the integration, but a noticeable difference was apparent. Launch times for the DT&E testing will not be included as all applications responded within 1 or 2 seconds of the request. This launch time performance was well within expected perimeters and was not an issue during testing.

(U//FOUO) The same applications listed above were tested during DT&E. Since most of the applications tested resulted in a favorable performance only those applications that produced a discrepancy will be noted in these results.

(U//FOUO) Six applications failed to even launch during DT&E testing. While there may be a simple solution to correct this situation, no troubleshooting has yet been conducted. No error message could be provided as all applications were launched via Solaris CDE. The following applications failed to launch during DT&E testing: BRIO QUERY, INFOCOMPASS, PATHFINDER, CVW, MOTIF ART, and RCMM.

(U//FOUO) Although the COASTLINE application GUI launched properly, KLASHES was not configured during the DT&E test period and therefore was not tested.

(U//FOUO) While most of the applications performed favorable a few did experience some problems. The following break down explains observations made during single user DT&E:
———————————————MAGNIFORM: While the tool performed well an issue was noted when trying to exit/close MAGNIFORM. The exit button for MAGNIFORM is located at the bottom of a tall menu which was larger than the viewable space on the monitor. This menu is not resizable and could not be moved vertical any more so reaching the exit button proved impossible. ——————————————— PLUS: Results from a PLUS pull cannot be displayed in a graph format. While the pull executed as expected, the results could not be displayed in a graph format. Displaying the results in the table format worked fine.

SANDTERM: There is a definite keyboard mapping issue. Standard keyboard strokes do not work on SANDTERM.

—————————————COALESCE: Audio cuts can be retrieved; however, the ROSECROSS GUI cannot play them. The play button will not activate.
—————————————ZIRCON: this tool works fully; however, the font style appears a little odd within ZIRCON.
—————————————COLORS: Certain applications rely heavily on system resources and video color issues did arise. As an example, when GALE LITE is launched, most of the system colors are taken and become unavailable for use by other applications. When subsequent applications are launched they default to only available colors which are often difficult to work with (hot pink and bright green).

6.1.2 (U) TRAILBLAZER FINDINGS

(U//FOUO) The TRAILBLAZER Test Training and Operational Facility (TTOF) was outfitted with Windows NT workstations in order to have analysts stress-test the current set of analytic applications used by the SID in conjunction with Tarantella. This effort was (and continues as) a laboratory for tool exercise and not an operational test of a cadenced migration strategy. The bottom line is that after identified issues were handled, only minor usage problems occurred and the test was a success. However, several lessons should be learned from the experience in order to ensure that future efforts are well embraced. The following are summary highlights extracted from the "TOP After Action Review" published on September 11, 2002 by the TRAILBLAZER Target Operational Pilot team working on the NT Migration problem:

(U//FOUO) Administrative Problems:
—————————————— Analysts were unclear about the migration goal.
——————————————Incomplete set-up prior to declaring desktops ready for use.
——————————————No "corporate game plan" for coordinating ISP/ESP/ASP efforts.
——————————————No training on the MS-COTS toolset.

(U//FOUO) Technical Problems:
——————————————System memory requirements appear to be 512MB (minimum).
——————————————Analysts complained that they were unable to use Java and Tarantella at the same time.
——————————————Analysts complained that the cut/paste function between environments did not work.

(U//FOUO) ESP Problems:
——————————————"Analysts had to go through multiple requests to get things done. The users tried submitting group tickets, but EA [Eagle Alliance] suggested that individual tickets be submitted so that the problems could be tracked better. Many users never heard back from Eagle on group tickets."

——————————————"The quality of EA support seems to be very personality driven. Some know what to do and some do not. Sometimes you have to spoon-feed them what to do step to step. You have to know the level of the EA support person."

(U//FOUO) Recommendations:
———————————————A migration plan, which delineates both user and service provider responsibilities, needs to be issued ahead of time in order to ensure that all files and accounts are transferred prior to declaring desktops ready for use.
———————————————Analysts should be trained on environmental differences.

6.7.3 (U) NSA CORPORATE AUTHORIZATION SERVICES (CAS)

(U//FOUO) NSA has built Corporate Authorization Services (CAS) to implement enhanced security in granting access to sensitive resources available through NSAnet. The CAS is built upon commercial, off-the-shelf, software that performs the function of determining access and authorization rights to resources based upon constraints provided by information resource owners. The CAS provides a rules-based solution that centrally controls and manages user access privileges to resources; based on definable user attributes, business rules and security policies as established by the data owners in concert with the NSA CAS team.

(U//FOUO) Whenever new resources must be put in place that may require credentials for authentication and access control, said control should be managed through the NSA CAS office. This will ensure that authentication is strong enough to prevent even the casual observer from accessing unauthorized data or systems, as well as full compliance with security policies as set forth by the NSA/CSS CIO office.

7.4 (U) APPLICATION REDEPLOYMENT PRIORITY AND SCHEDULE

(U//FOUO) With roles and responsibilities delineated, a timely, orchestrated migration is achievable. As identified in the Time Sensitive and Field Support Division inspection findings (IN-00-0013) and follow-up inspection (IN-02-0006), no organization had yet taken responsibility for ensuring that Unix-based analysis and reporting tools and applications could be run from a workstation running the NT operating system. This oversight prompted the HIGHCASTLE team to request a waiver to use Sun workstations instead of Wintel desktops for modernizing sites scheduled through 2003. In June 2002, the SID/SEO accepted responsibility for managing the overall migration program. A SIGINT directorate migration effort has been sized, the applications prioritized, and a schedule developed. Below are the migration and transformation activities necessary to
make that happen.

7.4.1 (U) MIGRATION ACTIVITIES

(U//FOUO) The rewrite of voice and other applications, and the TTOF efforts to migrate HIGHCASTLE applications, were the starting points for migration activity. These efforts have proven useful in that the voice applications are ready for fielding and the HIGHCASTLE applications—with a few exceptions—have been tested and proven to work using Tarantella as the display-back middleware. Exceptions (such as MOTIF ART) were identified and placed under development.

(U//FOUO) The SID/SEO recognized that the HIGHCASTLE applications represented only a subset of applications that needed to be migrated, in order to complete modernization in accordance with CIO direction, and initiated the task to write a Windows 2000 Migration Plan. The Migration Component List and the plan have captured the results of that effort. Implementation of the plan, in full coordination and cooperation with other migration and modernization efforts, will pave a path to successful migration of applications and replacement of desktops that will satisfy near-term CIO requirements while ensuring that mission success is not adversely affected. The following figure depicts a high-level migration activity process that leads to a near-term W2K solution, and eventual transformation to platform independence.

7.4.1.1 (U) NEAR-TERM MIGRATION DECISIONS

(U//FOUO) The Application Migration Decision Flow depicts the decision points for each application in order to reach an appropriate migration methodology. A decision flow diagram will be used to evaluate every application from the Migration Component List. As migration tools are selected and applications are migrated, mission requirements need to be addressed in addition to the technical aspects of the application migration.

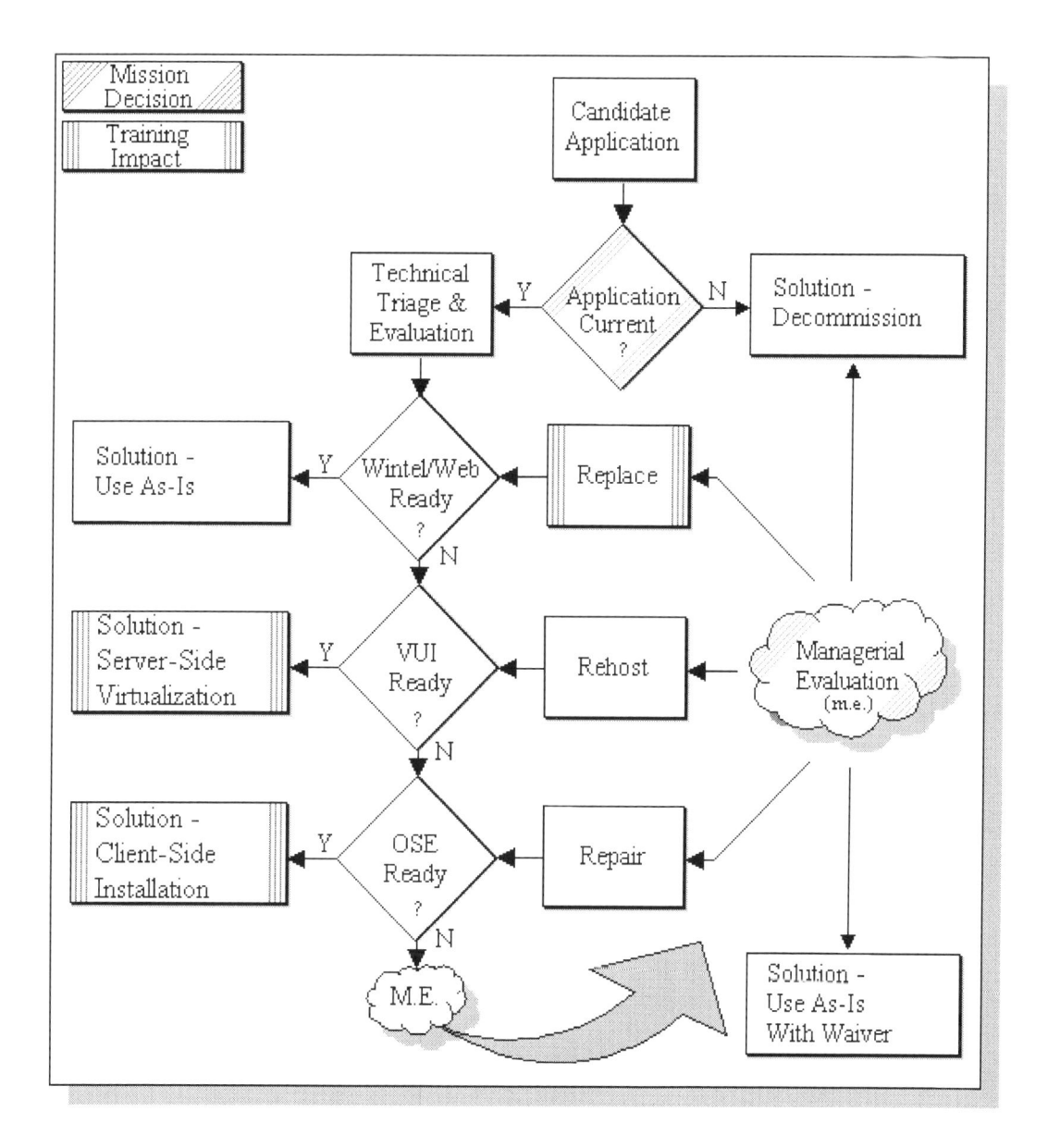

Figure 10 (U) Application Migration Decision Flow

7.4.1.1.4 (U) Client-side Emulation

(U//FOUO) If the application will not execute properly using Tarantella, or if there is some other concern such as a requirement for stand-alone workstations, then the application has to be considered for client-side emulation. These applications also may have been identified as incapable, or justifiably undesirable, for execution on a Wintel platform without some form of source-code modification. First, source code and associated software libraries must be available in order to use one of the primary porting tools, NuTCracker or Interix. If not available, then the only course of action, short of maintaining a legacy software/hardware base, is to redevelop the application using existing functionality as requirements. It is important to note that some applications were found to be already undergoing independent porting efforts. In such cases, information about the effort was captured in the Migration Component List but the application was not evaluated. There are several factors to consider when deciding between NuTCracker and Interix. Ease of compilation, supported functionality, and even personal preference may be considered, but principal to the decision is the availability of vendor software libraries (e.g., Sybase, Oracle), with consideration for future development to platform independence.

7.4.1.2 (U) ADDITIONAL FACTORS AFFECTING MIGRATION DECISIONS

(U//FOUO) Application Test and Certification. While every application that is in some way migrated must go through a thorough OAT&E, porting and rewrite come with additional burdens. Both Interix and NuTCracker require alterations to the source code, which points to a disadvantage to porting an application. When source code is modified, there is a requirement to completely test, and possibly re-certify, the modified application. Software testing requires two types:

——————————————————Regression testing, to demonstrate that the system functions the same as it did prior to modification; and,
——————————————————Validation, to demonstrate that any changes made to the system work correctly. To minimize this effort, new requirements should not be introduced into the porting effort. Documentation related to each application, especially existing test plans and procedures from the original development will be of great benefit. All of this data will need to be collected in the Transformation Database to support future transformation efforts.

(U//FOUO) Information Systems (IS) must be re-accredited whenever security relevant changes occur in the IS itself or its operational environment. Activities that result in the identification of an NSA/CSS information system for certification and accreditation starts with notification from a Project Manager, etc., that development of or modification to an NSA/CSS IS has been identified to support mission needs.

straightforward to identify those applications that must be merged and improved to remove parallel maintenance responsibilities.

(U//FOUO) The Transformation Database should not be a separate entity from other project databases such as ROTUNDPIPER. Instead, tables should be built within an existing project database and components related to master project records.

7.4.2 (U) TRANSFORMATION ACTIVITIES

(U//FOUO) An integrated set of projects is under development to modernize SIGINT systems and make them more responsive to customer needs. The findings from these efforts will be directly applicable to modernizing SID applications. For example, the following table extracted from the Production Migration Plan lists projects that are exploring presentation technologies and services for a future Analyst Cockpit.

Table 11 (U//FOUO) Projects Exploring Services for the Analyst Cockpit

Name	Org	Status	Future
Analyst Cockpit (RebA)	Rebuilding Analysis	Under Development	Corporate Solution
Analyst Assistant	Rebuilding Analysis		Migration to Analyst Cockpit (RebA)
Interim Transformational Activity – Data Center	Trailblazer	Under Development	Migration to corporate solution
TDP Integrated Analytic Environment	Trailblazer	Under Development	Migration to corporate solution
ASPEN	Weapon & Space	Under Development	Migration to corporate solution
ENRICHMENT (Balkans Portal)	Production Lines (Regional Target)	Operational	Migration to corporate solution

(U//FOUO)

(U//FOUO) In addition, the Customer Relations and Data Acquisition Directorates have ongoing efforts to reduce cost the hosting of applications on modernized workstations using tools that can support transformation goals. These efforts need to be captured in the Transformation Database, and the SID migration implementation team needs to work closely with them in order to reduce costs and avoid duplication of effort.

7.4.2.1 (U) APPLICATION IDENTIFICATION AND REUSE

(U//FOUO) An essential element of the near-term migration process is to capture data in the Transformation Database about applications that will support the long-term transformation activities. Part of the transformation process is identifying where different applications essentially process the same information. Those applications must be merged and improved to remove parallel maintenance responsibilities and provide a more common, uncomplicated operation. The Agency has ongoing efforts aimed at reducing duplication of effort in software,

(U//FOUO) As the modernization turns toward potentially problematic desktop replacements, just-in-time requirements can be easily solicited, obtained, and digested over a 72-hour period to produce application-sensitive modernization steerage. It is anticipated that, by the time this information becomes critical, the number of applications that are not, at the least, Wintel-tolerant will have diminished significantly. For this reason, responses to an application survey, as depicted below, should be requested no earlier than just before schedule dictates.

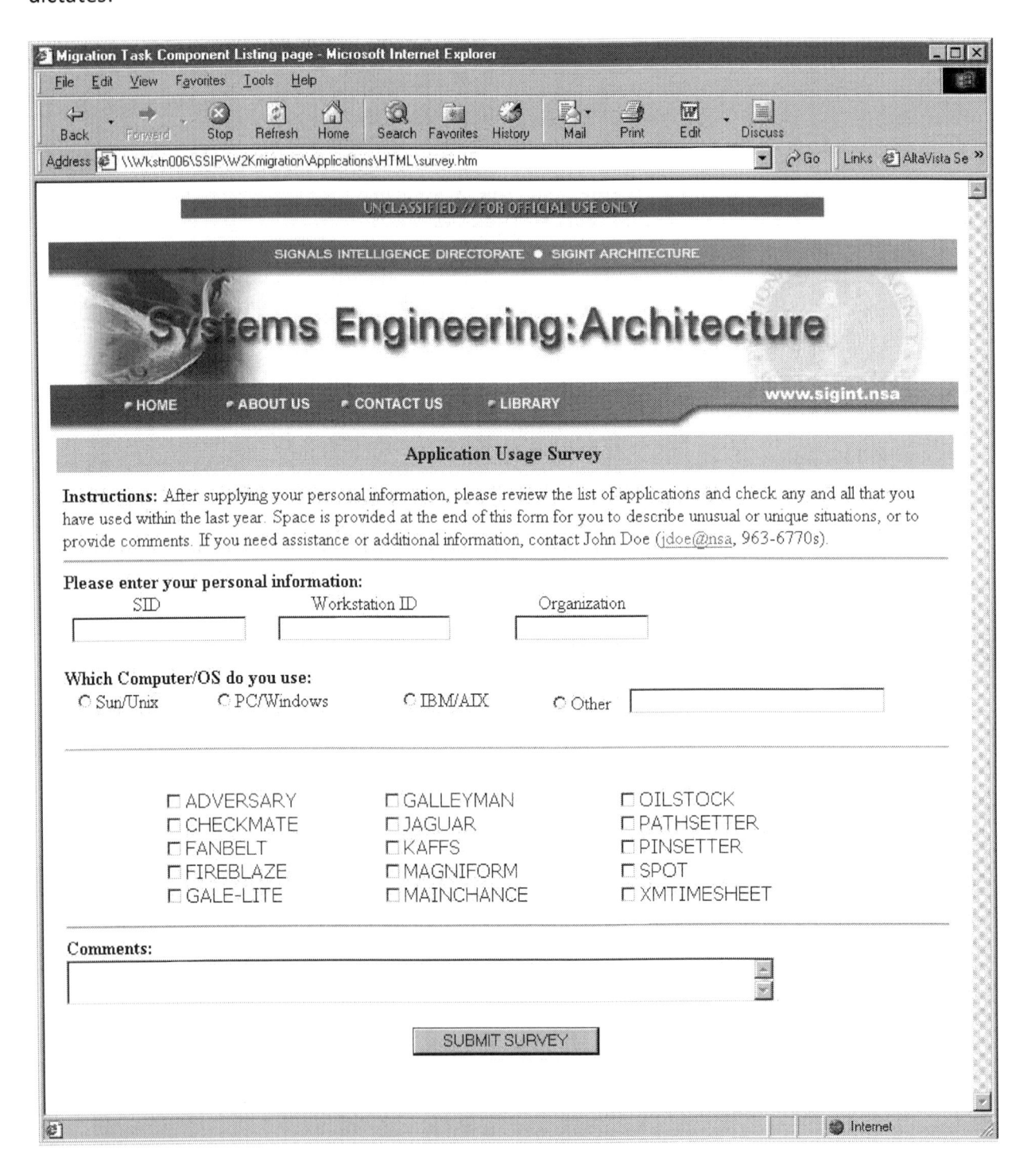

June 30-July 1, 2013 -- NSA's joint operations with European nations

The Observer of the UK interviewed the editor on the National Security Agency's Second, Third, and Fourth Party agreements with other intelligence services that pointed out that German and French protestations about the NSA and British Government Communications Headquarters (GCHQ) jointly tapping the transatlantic cable in Cornwall not withstanding, the NSA also cooperates with Berlin and Paris in collecting private information on European citizens.

On June 29, after *The Guardian* ran the story prior to *The Observer* running it on its web site and featuring it as a splash in its June 30 print edition, the story was pulled by *The Guardian* and *The Observer*. The second print edition of *The Observer* also deleted the story but not before the first print run reached London area news agents, as well as those in other British and European cities.

The decision appears to have been made after a well-coordinated campaign was launched by a number of web activists, including a Professor John Schindler who identifies himself as a professor with the U.S. Naval War College in Newport, Rhode Island. Schindler has been particularly critical of NSA whistleblower Edward Snowden and *The Guardian* journalist Glenn Greenwald who broke most of Snowden's revelations on NSA surveillance.

Schindler immediately began sending out Twitter messages, soliciting further responses and messages from dubious right-wing sites like LittleGreenFootballs and BusinessInsider.com. The tactic is a familiar one. It was used in the campaign to bring down CBS News anchor Dan Rather on a story about President George W. Bush's AWOL status during his service with the Texas Air National Guard.

The Guardian is the sister paper of *The Observer*. *The Guardian* ran the *Observer's* story on Third Parties late afternoon on June 29. In a few hours, as the right-wing web campaign went into full throttle, the story was pulled from *The Guardian*.

theguardian | The Observer

Revealed: secret European deals to hand over private data to America

Germany 'among countries offering intelligence' according to new claims by former US defence analyst

Jamie Doward
The Observer, Saturday 29 June 2013 21.02 BST

Wayne Madsen, an NSA worker for 12 years, has revealed that six EU countries, in addition to the UK, colluded in data harvesting.

At least six European Union countries in addition to Britain have been colluding with the US over the mass harvesting of personal communications data, according to a former contractor to America's National Security Agency, who said the public should

After a few hours, *The Guardian* page showed the following:

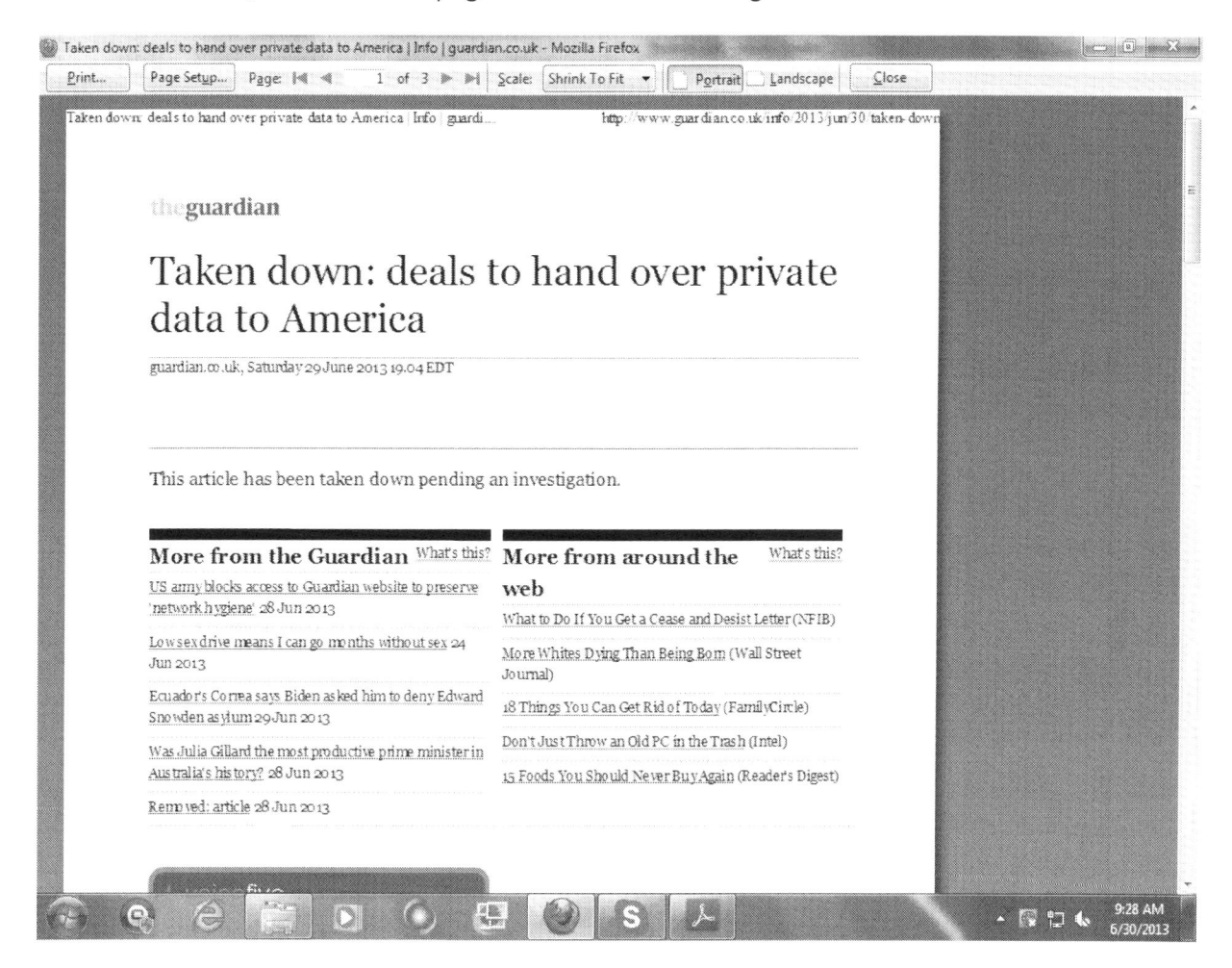

This is how BusinessInsider covered the article's take down with Schindler's quote:

Some of Madsen's controversial views include the belief that President Obama is secretly a homosexual and that the Boston bombing suspects were government agents. He's also reported on a "former CIA agent" alleging the 2000 USS Cole bombing was perpetrated not by al Qaeda terrorists, but by a missile fired from an Israeli submarine.

John Schindler, a professor at the Naval War College and intelligence expert, called Madsen "batsh-- crazy, to use the technical term."

This editor has been in touch with the Naval War College and a public statement by the college that Schindler's views are personal and do not reflect the opinion of the Naval War College has been demanded. I hold a graduate studies completion certificate in International Relations from the Naval War College and it is my contention that Schindler has no right to use his academic affiliation in a defamatory screed, especially toward an alum of the War College. And as a taxpayer, it is beyond reprehensible to have a seeming spokesman for a government institution launch personal insults against a journalist. Schindler's personal attacks on Greenwald have been just as defamatory.

On June 30, *The Guardian* published an additional story referring to the declassified NSA and other intelligence documents I sent them about Third Parties and the code names used to exchange signals intelligence with Third and Fourth Parties.

The declassified formerly Top Secret-S-CCO document is titled "Third Party Nations: Partners and Targets." In the case of Germany, France, and others, they are both partners and targets and leaders like German Chancellor Angela Merkel is well aware that the German intelligence agencies assist NSA in spying on Germans and others in the same manner as the UK, Canada, Australia, and New Zealand, the so-called "Five Eyes [FVEY]" English-speaking club of signals intelligence partners.

DOCID: 411668

TOP SECRET

Third Party Nations: Partners and Targets (S-CCO)

The second declassified document, a formerly Top Secret National Reconnaissance Office declassification guideline, refers to Signals Intelligence (SIGINT) Exchange descriptors. I explained to *The Observer* that code words found on Page 9 of the document like DIKTER and SETTEE, stood for Third Party SIGINT exchanges with Norway and the Republic of Korea, respectively. I also impressed on The Observer that these agreements, like the Second Party arrangements, are truly one-way streets, whereby NSA grabs all of the SIGINT from partner countries with the partners, especially the Third and Fourth Parties -- the latter include China, Sweden, Finland, Austria, and Switzerland -- receiving relatively little in return.

f. (U) The satellite imagery product code word "RUFF."[8]

g. (U) The satellite imagery product code word "DAFF."[27]

h. (U) The satellite SIGINT product code word "ZARF."[54]

i. (U) References to "continued control" control markings.[8]

j. (U) References to the term, "Sensitive Compartmented Information" and its abbreviation "SCI."[5, 25]

k. (U) The following SIGINT product code words:[25]

ACORN	CREAM	FLARE	KIMBO	PIXIE	THUMB
AMBLE	CRONE	FROTH	LARUM	SABRE	TRINE
BASTE	DAUNT	GAVEL	MAGIC	SAPPY	TWEED
CANOE	DENIM	GLINT	MORAY	SAVIN	ULTRA
CHEER	DINAR	HERON	PEARL	SPOKE	UMBRA
CHUTE	EIDER	HYSON	PINUP	SPRIG	USHER
COPSE		IVORY	PIVOT	SUEDE	WITCH

l. (U) The following SIGINT Exchange Designators:[25]

ARCA	FRONTO	NECTAR	SARDINE
DIKTER	KAMPUS	PROTEIN	SEABOOT
DIVERSITY	KEYRUT	PYLON	SETTEE
DRUID	MUSKET	RORIPA	THESPIS

m. (U) The following COMINT flags:[25, 77]

DELTA (Effective 9/7/01)
ECI
GAMMA
Handle via COMINT Channels Only
Special Intelligence (SI)
Very Restricted Knowledge (VRK)

n. (U) The following SIGINT-related paragraph portion-marking conventions:[25]

In its later article, *The Guardian* put it in the following way, this time without naming the source:

"Meanwhile, it has emerged that at least six European member states have shared personal communications data with the NSA, according to declassified US intelligence reports and EU parliamentary documents.

The documents, seen by the *Observer*, show that – in addition to the UK – Denmark, the Netherlands, France, Germany, Spain, and Italy have all had formal agreements to provide communications data to the US. They state that the EU countries have had "second and third party status" under decades-old signal intelligence (SIGINT) agreements that compel them to hand over data which, in later years, experts believe, has come to include mobile phone and internet data.

Under the international intelligence agreements, nations are categorised by the US according to their trust level. The US is defined as 'first party' while the UK, Canada, Australia and New Zealand enjoy 'second party' trusted relationships. Countries such as Germany and France have 'third party', or less trusted, relationships."

None of the campaign at character assassination comes as a surprise. Ever since Snowden's revelations to Greenwald, both have come under incessant attack from the "sock puppet" army crafted by President Obama's former "information policy czar" Cass Sunstein, whose wife, Samantha Power, is due to replace Susan Rice as UN ambassador.

Sunstein's machinations are nothing new. They merely build upon the methods of Nazi propaganda chief Joseph Goebbels to adapt to new media technology.

One thing that is certain after four and a half years of the Obama administration. The president's team of propagandists, is, indeed, the gang that can't shoot straight.

The pressure exerted on *The Observer* and *The Guardian* to pull its stories quoting me backfired badly. *The Observer's* first print edition hit the newsstands and for some, it became an instant collector's item.

The Observer

Sunday 30 June 2013 | www.observer.co.uk | £2.50

PLUS: JESSIE WARE — The singing sensation on playing Glastonbury, writing sad songs and sharing a stage with Beyoncé. *In the Magazine*

EXCLUSIVE INTERVIEW: MARK RYLANCE — One of our great stage actors on his latest theatrical challenge. *The New Review*

Revealed: secret European deals to hand over private data to America

- Germany 'among countries offering intelligence'
- New claims made by former US defence analyst

by Jamie Doward

At least six European Union countries in addition to Britain have been colluding with the US over the mass harvesting of personal communications data, according to a former contractor to America's National Security Agency, who said the public should not be "kept in the dark".

Wayne Madsen, a former US navy lieutenant who first worked for the NSA in 1985 and over the next 12 years held several sensitive positions within the agency, names Denmark, the Netherlands, France, Germany, Spain and Italy as having secret deals with the US.

Madsen said the countries had "formal second and third party status" under signal intelligence (Sigint) agreements that compels them to hand over data, including mobile phone and internet information to the NSA if requested.

Under international intelligence agreements, confirmed by declassified documents, nations are categorised by the US according to their trust level. The US is first party while the UK, Canada, Australia and New Zealand enjoy second party relationships. Germany and France have third party relationships.

In an interview published last night on the PrivacySurgeon.org blog, Madsen, who has been attacked for holding controversial views on espionage issues, said he had decided to speak out after becoming concerned about the "sanctimony" told by EU politicians regarding the extent of the NSA's activities in Europe.

He said that under the agreements, which were drawn up after the second world war, the "NSA gets the lion's share" of the Sigint "take". In return, the third parties to the NSA agreements received "highly sanitised intelligence".

Madsen said he was alarmed at the "sanctimonious outcry" of political leaders who were "feigning shock" about the spying operations while staying silent about their own arrangements with the US, and was particularly concerned that senior German politicians had accused the UK of spying when their country had a similar third party deal with the NSA.

Although the level of co-operation provided by other European countries to the NSA is not on the same scale as that provided by the UK, the allegations are potentially embarrassing.

"I can't understand how Angela Merkel can keep a straight face, demanding assurances from Obama and the UK

Continued on page 8

Wayne Madsen, an NSA worker for 12 years, has revealed that six EU countries, in addition to the UK, colluded in data harvesting.

GPs told to charge non-Britons

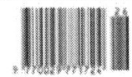

by Daniel Boffey, Policy Editor

Health secretary Jeremy Hunt will ask GPs to crack down on the use of free NHS services by non-Britons, under controversial plans to be unveiled this week. A registration and tracking system, possibly linked to NHS numbers, will allow practices to spot people who do not qualify for free healthcare.

It is one of several measures to be announced by Hunt that are designed to close so-called "NHS tourism" loopholes that allow some non-eligible immigrants access to care without being identified or charged. These will not restrict access to emergency treatment, but some people will be required to

Continued on page 4

Jeremy Hunt: 'We want a system that is fair for the British taxpayer.'

THE COMEBACK GIRL — Britain's Laura Robson celebrates yesterday after beating New Zealand's Marina Erakovic in her third-round women's singles match at Wimbledon. The 19-year-old battled back after losing the first set to take the match 1-6, 7-5, 6-3 and will face Estonia's Kaia Kanepi in the fourth round of the tournament. *Sport, pages 12-16* Photograph by Adrian Dennis/AFP

INSIDE ▶ WEATHER THIS SECTION PAGE 48 | CROSSWORDS SPEEDY, THIS SECTION PAGE 48 EVERYMAN, PAGE 46 • AZED, PAGE 47 IN THE NEW REVIEW

Above image: Before and after (The Observer before spiking and after)

But lo and behold, there is yet a third edition of The Observer, with Mick Jagger and the NSA spying story both on the front page!

Die Welt of Germany also took down their own story but after a few days restored it in its original:

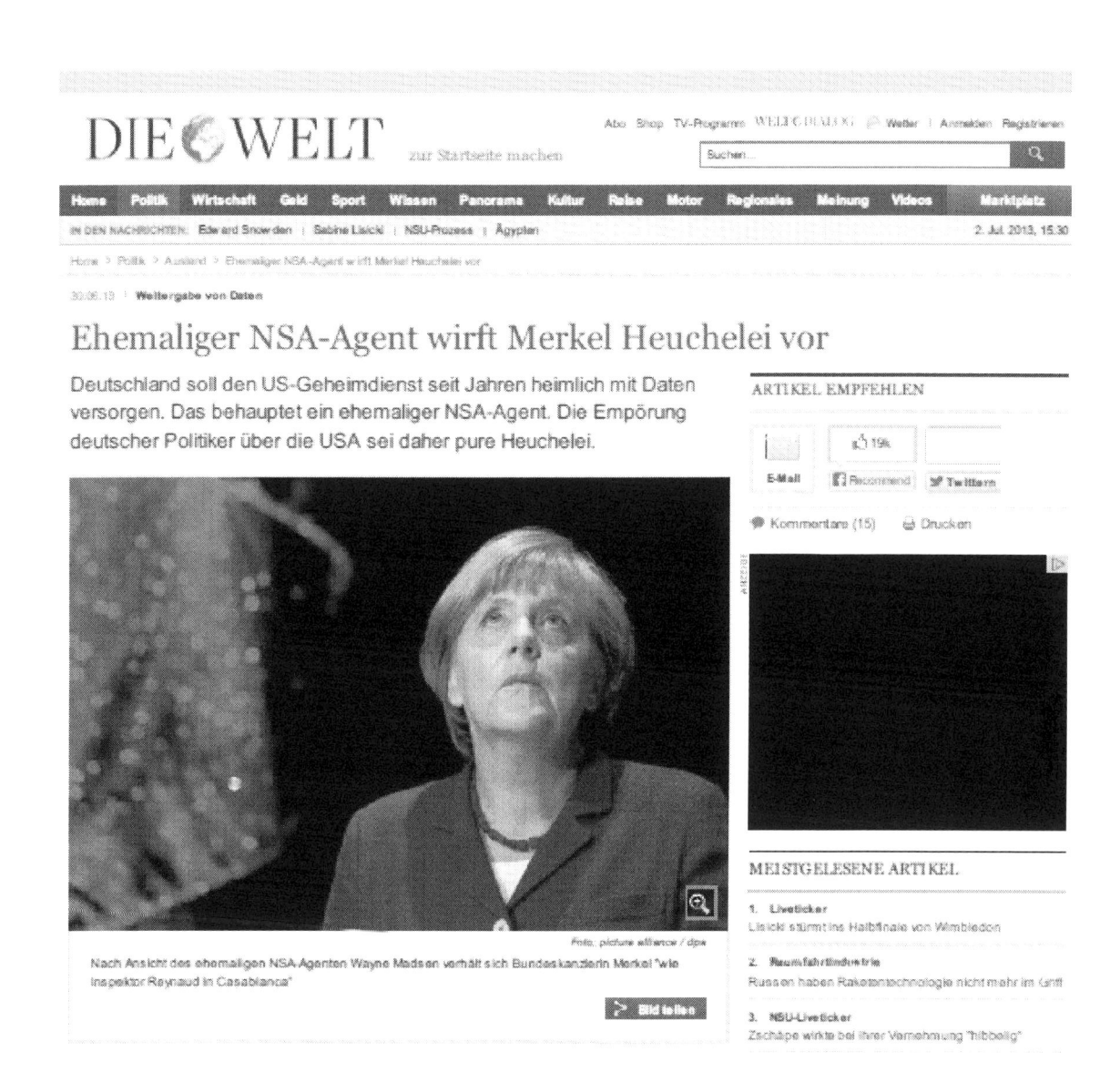

Ehemaliger NSA-Agent wirft Merkel Heuchelei vor

Deutschland soll den US-Geheimdienst seit Jahren heimlich mit Daten versorgen. Das behauptet ein ehemaliger NSA-Agent. Die Empörung deutscher Politiker über die USA sei daher pure Heuchelei.

Nach Ansicht des ehemaligen NSA-Agenten Wayne Madsen verhält sich Bundeskanzlerin Merkel "wie Inspektor Reynaud in Casablanca"

And *Salon*, McClatchy, and several European media outlets reported the original *Guardian/Observer* story without pulling it down or adding snarky comments. This is true journalism -- editors and reporters who refuse to be intimidated.

De Telegraaf (Netherlands)

Today (Italy)

Repubblica (Italy) TV

La Repubblica (Print and web)

El Sol (Spain)

Na Temat (Poland)

Ilta-Sanomat (Finland)

Kaleva (Finland)

ANSA (Italian news agency)

Gercek Gundem (Turkey)

Nova (Czech Republic)

Adevarul (Romania)

Gazeteport (Turkey)

Haberler (Turkey)

Tagesanzeiger (Switzerland)

Der Westen (Germany)

Obozrevatel (Russia)

Deutsche Wirtschafts Nacrichten (Germany)

L'Humanite (France)

Radio Vaticana (Vatican City)

Network World (USA)

The Sacramento Bee (USA)

InSerbia News (Serbia)

Press TV (Iran)

South China Morning Post (Hong Kong)

MINA (Macedonia)

DPA news agency (Germany)

Ulusal Kanal (Turkey)

Nanopress (Italy)

Cameroon Voice (Cameroon)

Basler Zeitung (Switzerland)

Kolnische Rundschau (Germany)

And these outlets reported on *The Guardian/Observer* story but also on Obama being gay and/or the CIA links to the Boston Marathon bombing:

Neues Deutschland (Germany)

OmediaMania (Czech Republic)

L'Unita (Italy)

der Standard (Austria)

Corriere della sera (Italy)

Voice of Russia (with interview with Wayne Madsen)

Hindu Business Line (India)

The Examiner reported that the entire episode was a case of censorship.

Had the neocon sock puppets not launched their campaign of defamation, the story about EU nations helping NSA spy would have added to the NSA news peg and in a few days died out. However, by attacking this editor, people all over the world are talking about Obama's homosexuality, CIA links, the Tsarnaev false flag, and the list goes on. Neocons are radical fascists and they seldom think before they leap. That is why there is still some hope that these creatures will one day shout themselves into oblivion.

And as can be seen above, the legitimate media outlets, not obscure blogs funded by Soros and the neocons, outnumbered those that believed the NSA story was more important than attacking Wayne Madsen. In two words, the neocon attack machine's results: EPIC FAIL.

UPDATE 1X. NSA job networking websites currently reference some of these systems:

Tools Used: CADENCE/UTT, BLAZING SADDLES, XKEYSCORE, MARINA, MAUI/ANCHORY,

SHARKFINN, AGILITY, AGILEVIEW, MASTERSHAKE, PINWALE, UIS, TKB, Target Profiler, Agent Logic, NKB/Foxtrail, Banyan, BELLVIEW, OCTSKYWARD, CINEPLEX, ARCMAP, Analyst Notebook/RENOIR, NSLOOKUP, TRACEROUTES, TREASUREMAP, GOLDPOINT, NUCLEON, GOLDMINER, ROADBED, RT-RG Tool Suite, PATHFINDER, CLOUD-ABR, AIRGAP/COZEN, AIGHANDLER, ARCANAPUP, ARTEMIS, ASSOCIATION, AUTOSOURCE, BEAMER, BLACKPEARL, CADENCE/GAMUT, CHALKFUN, CLOUD, COASTLINE, COMMONVIEW, CONTRAOCTAVE,CONVERGENCE, COURIERSKILL, CREEK, CREST, CROSSBONES, CULTWEAVE, CYBERTRANS, DOUBLEARROW, DRAGONFLY, ENHANCED WEALTHYCLUSTER (EWC), ETHEREAL, FASTSCOPE, FOREMAN, GISTQUEUE, GJALLER, GLAVE, GLOBALREACH, GOSSAMER, GROWLER, HIGHTIDE/SKYWRITER, HOMEBASE, INFOSHARE, JOLLYROGER, KINGFISH, LIQUIDFIRE, MAINWAY, MASTERLINK, MASTERSHAKE, MESSIAH, METTLESOME, NAVIGATOR, NEWHORIZONS, NIGHTSURF, NORMALRUN/CHEWSTICK/FALLENORACLE, OCTAVE, PATHMASTER/MAILORDER, PANOPTICON, PRESENTER, PROTON, RAVENWING, SCORPIONFORE/CPE, SKIDROWE, SKOPE, SNAPE, SPOTBEAM, STINGRAY, SURREY, TAPERLAY, TAROTCARD, TEMPTRESS, TRACFIN, TRAILMAPPER, TRICKLER, TUNINGFORK/SEEKER, TURMOIL, TUSKATTIRE, TWISTEDPATH, WIRESHARK, WITCHHUNT, YELLOWSTONE/SPLITGLASS.

July 16-17, 2013 -- Seized North Korean vessel an attempt to boost NSA's image in Latin America

The Obama administration and the National Security Agency (NSA) are conveniently using the Panamanian seizure in the Caribbean of the North Korean merchant vessel *Chong Chon Gang* after a routine search for drugs yielded two green containers under a shipment of sugar. The ship was due to transit the Panama Canal.

In a bizarre move, Panama's President Richardo Martinelli, a right-wing billionaire supermarket chain owner, sent out a Twitter message claiming that the green containers were "undeclared weapons." Martinelli's message stated: "Panama has captured a ship with a North Korean flag that was coming from Cuba with an undeclared weapons shipment."

Martinelli also provided a photograph of the two containers before they could be properly analyzed by intelligence experts. Martinelli later increased the hype over the ship seizure by claiming that the green cylinders were "suspected sophisticated missile equipment." Martinelli also claimed the captain of the 35-member crew tried to commit suicide during the search.

The North Korean vessel and crew have been detained at the port of Manzanillo on the Caribbean coast. UN sanctions only permit the importation of small arms into North Korea.

The Obama administration and the NSA have come in for heavy criticism by individual Latin American nations and regional bodies such as the Organization of American States, Mercosur,

Union of South American Nations (UNASUR), and the Community of Latin American and Caribbean States (CELAC). Revelations by NSA whistleblower Edward Snowden that the NSA conducts massive eavesdropping on Latin American communications has resulted in a Brazilian legislative inquiry on the matter and offers of asylum for Snowden from Venezuela, Bolivia, and Nicaragua.

The involvement of the U.S. State Department in convincing France, Italy, Spain, and Portugal to deny overflight privileges to Bolivian President Evo Morales, forcing his plane to land in Austria for an attempted search by the Spanish ambassador to Vienna, has heightened hostility toward the United States in Latin America.

Martinelli is one of Washington's few allies in the region and it comes as no surprise that he would shift attention to North Korea and Cuba. The commander of the U.S. Southern Command (SOUTHCOM), Marine Corps General John Kelly, was in Panama in February to met with Martinelli and the two officials who were in charge of the operation against the North Korean ship, Public Security Minister Jose Raul Mulina and Javier Caraballo, the counter-narcotics chief.

Martinelli has reportedly had close ties to the CIA ever since his time attending the U.S. Agency for International Development (USAID)-funded Central American Institute of Business Administration (INCAE) in San José, Costa Rica following his graduation from the University of Arkansas. Martinelli increased his links to the CIA while at Citibank and later as the owner of the Super 99 supermarket chain.

Martinelli's participation in NSA's program to polish its image in Latin America comes as no surprise. After financing the construction of a number of naval and air bases, the U.S. has been increasing its military and intelligence presence in Panama. The seizure of the North Korean ship by U.S.-trained Panamanian security forces and Martinelli's Twitter photographs of the "suspicious" cargo are intended to show Latin America that NSA's surveillance of the region is aimed at "rogue states" like North Korea and Cuba, not at Brazil, Chile, Peru, Mexico, and other friendlier Latin American nations where the U.S. has been stung by criticism of the NSA eavesdropping using systems code named FAIRVIEW, SILVERZEPHYR, and XKEYSCORE.

June 17-19, 2013 -- Swiss President doubts U.S. spying on banks in Switzerland

Swiss President Ueli Maurer has said he doubts Edward Snowden's story of the CIA setting up a Swiss banker in a drunk driving blackmail operation because Snowden was merely 23 at the time that the event is said to have taken place. Maurer is likely unaware that a number of U.S. military personnel younger than Snowden was at the time, including Special Forces troops, are involved in sensitive and dangerous covert operations.

The Swiss Foreign Ministry has confirmed that Snowden was attached to the US Mission to the UN in Geneva between 2007 and 2009. The Swiss Foreign Ministry has sent a note to the U.S.

government asking for an explanation about the charge of blackmail espionage by the CIA in Geneva.

Snowden was declared by the U.S. State Department to be a telecommunications specialist, which was "official cover" for his work for what is known as the NSA Special Collection Element (SCE), which reports via the joint NSA/CIA Special Collection Service (F6) in Beltsville, Maryland to the NSA and CIA.

In October 2000, the U.S. firm Verestar, based in Fairfax, Virginia, bought the satellite ground stations of SWISSCOM in Loèche, Geneva, Basel, and Zurich. Shortly thereafter, NSA's ability to eavesdrop on Swiss phone calls and email increased dramatically and among the chief NSA targets were the Swiss banks. The SCE at the US Mission in Geneva, which is also accredited to the Conference on Disarmament and the World Trade Organization, in addition to the UN specialized agencies, likely targeted the Geneva offices of Credit Suisse, Julius Baer, Pictet, and HSBC.

NSA's aggressive collection of economic intelligence, some of which is filtered through the U.S. Commerce Department to benefit U.S. companies, has also been exposed with the release of TOP SECRET STRAP documents by Snowden to *The Guardian* showing that NSA's British counterpart, Government Communications Headquarters (GCHQ), conducted surveillance on the phones and e-mails of participants of the G20 conference in Britain in 2009. Among those targeted were Russian President Dmitri Medvedev, Turkish Finance Minister Mehmet Simsek, and South African government officials.

July 18-19, 2013 -- WMR Exclusive. Inside Menwith Hill: Largest NSA base outside the United States

In the middle of the Yorkshire moors near Harrogate, England sits the largest National Security Agency facility outside the United States. Known officially as Royal Air Force Station Menwith Hill, the eavesdropping station employs more Americans than British nationals. Menwith Hill's official mission is to provide "intelligence support for UK, US and allied interests." In other words, Menwith Hill spies on foreign satellite and terrestrial communications in the United Kingdom and abroad and the intelligence "take" is swept up into NSA's massive databases in the United States.

Menwith Hill is dominated by white radomes, 33 at last count. Spread over 560 acres, these white "golf balls," as they are called, are actually operational security and weather covers for satellite dishes that point to satellites positioned over the Atlantic and Indian Oceans in order to intercept their transmissions. The last major upgrade to Menwith Hill was code named PHOENIX. However, Menwith Hill, like NSA headquarters, hosts a number of classified surveillance and support subsystems that have been assigned the usual but oddly-named NSA cover terms.

In addition to the 1400 American NSA military, government civilian, and contractor personnel who work at Menwith Hill, 400 British military and civilian personnel, attached to the Government Communications Headquarters (GCHQ), work at the base. The number of personnel is expected to increase to over 2500 in 2015

WMR is, for the first time, publishing a list of Menwith Hill systems and subsystems, which although somewhat dated, provides an insight into the amount of surveillance that takes place at NSA's largest overseas facility:

ABERFORD
ACTUATOR
ADVANCED RUTLEY
AFLAME
AFTERIMAGE
ALPENSTOCK
ANF
ANISETTE
AUBURN
BAYA
BAYRUM
BEACHMAN II
BEAMHOUSE
BFTAETTE
BROWNPRINT
BROWNWARE
BOOKSHELF
BONANZA
BULLWHIP
CAPLOCK
CAROUSEL II
CASTLEMAINE
CLOUDFUNNEL
COASTLINE
COMFY HARVEST
COMFY RIDGE II
CORAL BOY
DATOLITE
DATOPORT
DAYSHINE
DEAL
DECEPTION
DISPATCHER

DRIBBLER
DROOPY
DUSTPAN
ELOQUENCE
ENAMELWARE
ENSCORE
EQUALISER I
FASTFOOD
FATBIRD
FATCAT
FIRETHORN
FOOTWAY
GIGSTER
GRAPNEL
GRAYWHALE
GREENGLASS
HAMSTRUNG
HARDLINE
HAYSTACK
HERCULES
INCEPTION
JAILHOUSE
KAISER
KNIGHTHAWK
LANDFORCE
LATTICE
LIFEMAN
LONGSHOREMAN
MAGISTRAND
MARBURG
MESSALINE
MICROBIC
MILLPOOL
MOONPENNY [foreign satellite interception]
MOOR
NEWSDEALER
NIGHTFIRE
OILSTOCK
OMELET
OMELET II
OUTCURVE
OUTWARD
PAILETTE
PAINTPOT

PALANKA
PARADIGM
PELKEY II
PLATINIZE LAN
POOLFISH
PUSHER
QUADARITE
RAGDOLL
RECEPTION
REGULATOR
RESCUER
ROWBOAT
RUNWAY
RUTLEY
SADDLEMAKER
SAEDAC
SAILBIRD
SANDBANK
SAYA
SCRATCHPAD
SENSATION
SHARPSHOOTER
SHAWNEE II
SHUFFLEBOARD
SILKWORTH
SILVERSTREAK
SILVERWEED
SINKBOX
SKYSWEEPER
SLAGSTONE
SLEEVEBOARD
SLYGOOSE
SPARKPROOF
SPRINGTIME
SPRINKLER
STARSTONE
STEEPLETOP
STOREROOM
STROKE
SUNDANCE
TABLETOP
TARN
TARSIS

TENORMAN
TENORMAN II
THISTLE
TOGA
TRACKSHOE
TRACKWALKER
TRANSCRIBER
TROJAN
TROUTMAN
ULTRAPURE
VARIATION
VELODROME
VOICECAST
WAITRESS
WALKOUT
WAKE
WATCHOUT
WATERWALL
WICKETKEEPER
WITHROW
YELLOWCROWN
YELLOWHAMMER
ZORILLO

Documents retrieved by WMR show that Menwith Hill receives a number of visitors from the UK Government Communications Headquarters (GCHQ) in Cheltenham, England; NSA Headquarters in Fort Meade, Maryland; NSA units in Germany; Cheadle, outside of Manchester, where the only military presence are some RAF storage units at the former and largely abandoned RAF Handforth; RAF Mildenhall; RAF Base Molesworth, England; NSA-CSS Representatives in Wiesbaden and Frankfurt, Germany; Buckholz Army Airfield, Kwajalein Atoll, Marshall Islands; the Pentagon; Misawa Airbase, Japan; and Bude, Cornwall.

In the early 1990s, the Menwith Hill chief of station was Dr. Addison Ball. His deputy chief of station was a U.S. Navy Captain, Terrence Lapierre, who had previously been the commanding officer of the U.S. Naval Security Group Activity in Edzell, Scotland. The Scotland unit, part of the NSA network, was closed down in 1997. The Senior U.S. Air Force officer was Col. Louis N. Hurtado. The chief of operations was Robert C. (Bob) Taylor. The Senior UK Officer was Gordon White. Each satellite interception operation had its own director. For SILKWORTH and RUNWAY it was John T. Sandell; for MOONPENNY and SPRINKLER is was Thomas L. Peters. For THISTLE transcription, analysis, and reporting (which included intercepts of Farsi, Arabic, Hebrew, Russian, Serbo-Croatian, and Albanian), the director was Barbara J. Lovett; the Technology director was John W. (Bill) Milne.

WMR has obtained a CONFIDENTIAL Menwith Hill memo announcing a training course on SILKWORTH operations. It includes training on targeting communications systems, including microwave. While, Mr. Alan Pitchfork, the training coordinator at the time for Menwith Hill may have been a very nice chap, the idea of a person named "Pitchfork" offering training on the surveillance, legal or illegal, of private communications is just a wee bit Faustian for our tastes.

July 22-24, 2013 -- NSA chief Hayden saw warrantless wiretapping as driving to DC on highway shoulder

General Michael Hayden, the director of the National Security Agency under Bill Clinton and George W. Bush, saw requirements for warrants for the collection of the personal communications of Americans as akin to traffic on the highway that could be bypassed by driving with an emergency light on the shoulder of the road. That interpretation comes from a "For Official use Only" memorandum written by Hayden in the months after the 9/11 attack. WMR has obtained a copy of the undated memorandum.

The memo, titled "Transformation 2.0: Cryptology as a Team Sport," refers to external pressures that wanted the agency to provide access to NSA's "raw SIGINT," or signals intelligence. Hayden wrote, ". . . there are forces both within and beyond our discipline of cryptology that are demanding a different kind of relationship between us and those we have traditionally called customers and consumers. Each instance seems to call for a candid re-examination of how we view sharing." The "raw SIGINT" most requested by "those who have been clamoring for more extensive access to our databases and other SIGINT derived information," Hayden's words, was "English language transcripts of intercepted communications."

Hayden also saw the collection of global communications by NSA as taking the "knowledge and intentions" away from a "species," in this case "mankind." The following are Hayden's words: "Never before has mankind put so much of his knowledge (and intentions) into the electromagnetic spectrum. In 2001 our species spent some 187 billion minutes on the phone— in international calls alone."

Hayden believed that NSA had an inherent right to eavesdrop on every minute the human species spent of the phone. Such dystopian commentary is usually the staple of Hollywood futuristic thriller screenwriters.

The memo provides a rare look inside the decision-making processes of the Bush administration that led to the warrantless wiretapping program first code-named STELLAR WIND and now code-named PRISM. Hayden's memo reveals that it was a 2002 directive from President Bush to Director of Central Intelligence George Tenet that authorized NSA to begin amassing "stored data" in addition to real-time communications traffic.

Hayden wrote: "In a short note to the DCI, the President in February 2002 swept away all the theological fine points about "data at rest". He empowered NSA to be hunters of electronic information in all of its forms and states."

It is now known that those "theological fine points" were Fourth Amendment and legal protections against the wholesale warrantless interception of Americans' real-time communications and stored electronic records, including e-mails. Hayden's push to violate Fourth Amendment were revealed thanks to the actions of NSA whistleblowers Thomas Drake, William Binney, Kirk Wiebe, Ed Loomis, Russell Tice, and Edward Snowden, as well as Justice Department whistleblower Thomas Tamm, AT&T engineer Mark Klein, and U.S. House Intelligence Committee staffer Diane Roark. In the 1990s, NSA was working on a program code-named THINTHREAD, which would have provided Fourth Amendment privacy protections for the communications of U.S. persons. However, in the weeks after 9/11, Hayden's zeal to collect everything conceivable type of communication resulted in the award of project TRAILBLAZER to his friends at Science Applications International Corporation (SAIC).

Hayden even pulled William Black, a senior SAIC official, out of retirement to become NSA's deputy director.

The NSA director also engaged in some internal intelligence-community chest-beating by claiming that modern technology permitted new "opportunities" for NSA to gather intelligence: "Modern technology presents challenges—we're fond of stressing the volume, variety and velocity of modern communications—but more than anything else, today's world presents opportunities. We're reluctant to say it (at least publicly, for fear of being thought arrogant or 'non-communal'), but our discipline has become dominant. So much can be gleaned from the electromagnetic spectrum that SIGINT and IA have become war winners."

The memo also shows that it was under Hayden's direction that the compartmentalization that would have prevented Snowden from accessing a wealth of "national" SIGINT information was weakened to allow more sharing among NSA, military services, and other intelligence agencies. Hayden refers to such access as "unprecedented" as seen in this following statement: "During OIF [Operation Iraqi Freedom], we allowed Marine, Army, Navy and Air Force forces well forward to have **unprecedented** access to NSA databases."

Hayden also revealed that NSA concluded, under his watch, an intelligence-sharing agreement with the National Geospatial-Intelligence Agency (NGA) that also permitted sharing of intelligence from both agencies with NSA's "second parties," what are officially known as the "Five Eyes" alliance partners of NSA, i.e., UK, Canada, Australia, and New Zealand.

"Our recent agreements with NGA on how we intend to connect our networks represent a true breakthrough. NSA and NGA analysts will be able to work in a **common collaborative space, with second parties**, and will **have access to key portions of each other's databases**."

Hayden states that governing U.S. law and the U.S. Constitution prevented NSA from wholesale monitoring without a legal predicate: "E.O. [Executive Order] 12333 tells us that information derived from electronic surveillance is not to be shared unless two criteria are met: US person information has been minimized so as to uphold 4th Amendment protections from unreasonable search and the information provided is of inherent intelligence value."

However, on January 23, 2006, Hayden, who was Deputy Director of National Intelligence, told a National Press Club news conference that "probable cause" is not in the 4th Amendment. In fact, the Fourth Amendment specifically states that search warrants cannot be issued without probable cause and that blanket warrants are unconstitutional.

Although the Arabic word for "wedding" was used as a code word in communications referring to the planned 9/11 attack, Hayden appears to indicate that use of the term "wedding" in communications obtained by external users of raw NSA SIGINT may have been used to erroneously attack innocent wedding parties with the loss of innocent civilian lives. In late summer 2001, the Jordanian General Intelligence Department (GID) informed the CIA that a major attack inside the United States and using aircraft was being planned and that the operation was code named "the big wedding." Hayden stated: "'Wedding' is sometimes a barely veiled reference to an upcoming terrorist attack but it is also true that even very bad people occasionally get married." The "wedding" reference may be engrained in decision-support systems used to this day to target wedding parties.

In June 2012, 18 people, including women and children, were killed in a NATO strike on a wedding party in Sajawand village, Afghanistan. In June 2010, residents of Kandahar claimed that a NATO airstrike killed 40 people at a wedding party. In July 2008, a U.S. military air strike on a wedding party in Dih Bala in Nangarhar province, Afghanistan, killed 47 civilians, including women and children. In November 2008, 37 civilians, including 23 children and 10 women, were killed in a U.S, airstrike on the Shah Wali Kot district in Kandahar province. In September 2012, innocent civilian members of a wedding party in Paktia province were killed in a U.S. airstrike. In May 2002, ten civilians were killed in a U.S. airstrike on a wedding party in Bal Khel village in Khost Province.

In May 2004, a U.S. attack on a wedding party in Makr al-Deeb village, Iraq, near the Syrian border, killed over 45 people, including some 10 children. In October 2004, a U.S. attack on a wedding party in Fallujah, Iraq killed some 14 people, including the groom. In August 2005, a U.S. attack on a wedding party in Hit, Iraq, killed one civilian and wounded 15.

There have been so many U.S. air and drone attacks on weddings in Afghanistan, Pakistan, and Yemen people are afraid to attend them out of fear of being killed.

Hayden's memo also discusses the "scraps" of non-responsive intelligence that is often collected but not used in intelligence reports. He clearly indicates a desire to save such data for future use, i.e., to match up data points that don't reach reporting thresholds. Such data might, of course, include "minimized" data on U.S. persons that was to be discarded, according to U.S. Signals Intelligence Directive 18. Hayden wrote about placing such "scraps" of data in "data pools." It is apparent now that the NSA Utah Data Center, with its yottabyte (one septillion or 1000000000000000000000000bytes) of computing power, was intended to store many "scraps" of NSA data.

"After processing the data it collects, each INT-producing agency reports information to fulfill customer requirements in accordance with established priorities and thresholds. Each agency is **left with unreported data and information on the proverbial editing room floor.** These scraps are data points that don't self-associate and that are **well below** anyone's reporting thresholds. **Those scraps that aren't ignored or disposed of are maintained in data pools in each agency and are largely never touched again. But if, say, the SIGINT data points were married up with the data points from HUMINT or IMINT, might we end up with information that does self-associate and is of value to national security.**"

So how did Hayden address the problem of legal impediments to storing such data, itself prohibited by the U.S. Constitution, federal statutes, and NSA's own internal directives? He likened the solution to his bypassing traffic on the highway from NSA headquarters in Fort Meade, Maryland to the U.S. Capitol:

"I've taken to referring to this problem as one of traffic—not in the communications sense, but in the sense of vehicles on roads. It usually takes an hour to get from NSA to the Capitol. If I chose to, I could tell the EPU to put on the red and blue lights, turn on the siren, **drive on the shoulder, and disregard all traffic rules and laws.** I could get there in under half an hour that way."

How would Hayden justify bypassing the rules of the road? By using an "emergency vehicle": "Even during rush hour, the police and fire vehicles bypass the rules of the road when the circumstances justify it." It now appears that STELLAR WIND, PRISM, and other NSA mass surveillance systems in operation or on the drawing board were viewed by Hayden and his successor, General Keith Alexander, as "emergency vehicles" with an uncontested right-of-way.

July 25-26, 2013 -- NSA's first major public enemy number one -- long before Ed Snowden

In the late 1960s, the National Security Agency was still reeling from Israel's willful June 8, 1967, attack on the NSA intelligence collection ship, the *USS Liberty*. The attack saw Israeli war planes and gun boats strafe surviving Navy and NSA personnel clinging to life rafts with machine gun fire. There was little sympathy for Israel, which killed 34 Navy and NSA personnel on the *Liberty*, within the NSA's walls at Fort Meade, especially from deputy director Louis Tordella, who ensured that NSA's Third Party signals intelligence sharing agreements that he was charged with negotiating with other countries would never include Israel.

Israel's supporters became alarmed that one U.S. intelligence agency not only harbored resentment against Israel but would not alter intelligence to please Israel's supporters in the U.S. government.

When the pro-Israel Henry Kissinger became Richard Nixon's national security adviser in 1969, at the urging of the Rockefeller family, NSA began to feel the pressure to change. Eventually, NSA Hebrew linguists who listened in on Israeli communications, were ordered to say they were "Special Arabic" linguists, so they would not offend an increasing number of visiting Jewish congressmen and their senior staffers to Fort Meade. NSA would also soon have among its senior ranks officials who would falsely claim that the Israeli attack on the Liberty was a tragic "mistake" for which Israel fully paid compensation.

In 1972, NSA discovered that it had a major public enemy "down under." The Australia Labor Party swept into power and Gough Whitlam, who wanted the United States to fully explain to him the purpose of intelligence collection facilities located at Pine Gap, near Alice Springs, and in Nurunga, South Australia, became Prime Minister. In many ways, Whitlam in 1974 was more of a danger to NSA's operations than whistleblower Edward Snowden is today. NSA and the CIA and National Reconnaissance Office (NRO) were engaged in major intelligence operations in Australia and exposure of Pine Gap and Nurunga would threaten the intelligence bases since Australians would realize that their presence on Australian soil made the country a prime target for a Soviet nuclear strike in the event of World War III.

By 1974 and 1975, NSA was firmly under the grasp of Kissinger, who had become Secretary of State as well as national security adviser in 1973 after it became apparent that Secretary of State William Rogers was not sufficiently "pro-Israel."

It did not take long for NSA and its friends in Australia to start a campaign to ruin Whitlam and force his government from office. Members of NSA's partner down under, the Defense Signals Directorate, began leaking information to News Ltd. newspapers that the Whitlam government had "leaked" a top secret code word document. News Ltd. was owned by Rupert Murdoch, a major supporter of Israel. The U.S. embassy was headed by America's ambassador in Canberra, James Hargrove, a Houston venture capitalist who was also a lifelong friend of George H. W. Bush, the man who President Gerald Ford would place in charge of the CIA in 1976. The embassy was at the center of the plot to bring down Whitlam.

MEMORANDUM

THE WHITE HOUSE
WASHINGTON

~~SECRET~~/NODIS/XGDS

MEMORANDUM OF CONVERSATION

PARTICIPANTS: President Ford
Amb. James W. Hargrove, Ambassador to Australia
Lt. General Brent Scowcroft, Assistant to the President for National Security Affairs

DATE AND TIME: Friday, February 6, 1976
10:15 - 10:25 a.m.

PLACE: The Oval Office

President: I am delighted to have you going to Australia. When are you leaving?

Hargrove: I am going to Houston tonight, and to Australia a week from today.

[There followed a discussion of glasses.]

President: You are going to a government we approve of more than when Whitlam was there. Fraser has already taken some steps in our favor, and his economic plan is compatible with ours. You can tell him we support him with enthusiasm. I don't think I ever met him, did I?

Scowcroft: [The story about Fraser visit plans].

Hargrove: He wants to come but we both think this year is not the one. Incidentally, I hope you win.

The Australian Security Intelligence Organization (ASIO), the CIA's Australian counterpart, investigated the leak and blamed it on the "open government" policies of Whitlam's government.

Thanks to the efforts of Murdoch and Hargrove, Whitlam was also painted in the press as "anti-Semitic" because his campaign never accepted campaign money from Zionist and pro-Israeli lobby groups in Australia. The CIA and Hargrove, who was rumored himself as being a CIA asset, began conspiring with another Australian Labor Party leader named Bob Hawke, who told Hargrove and the CIA that Whitlam's even-handed Middle East policy was "beyond belief." Hawke also said that Whitlam was "politically crazy." Hawke's enmity toward Whitlam grew. He accused the prime minister of being "immoral, unethical and ungrateful" toward Israel and referred to Whitlam's Middle East policy as "Whitlam's fucking even-handed fucking Arab policy."

In 1974, while Whitlam was campaigning in Melbourne and answering questions posed by some haranguing Jewish breakfast attendees, he said, "You people are hard to please."

The U.S. embassy also conspired with New South Wales Labor Party leader John Ducker and an Australian Young Labor President named Bob Carr. Carr would become Foreign Minister in the strongly pro-Israel government of Prime Minister Julia Gillard, recently ousted by Kevin Rudd in a replay of what she did to Rudd while he was serving his first term as prime minister.

The U.S. sought to have Hawke replace Whitlam as prime minister of a Labor Party government but the CIA instituted, with the approval of Kissinger, another plan.

A longtime CIA asset, Governor General Sir John Kerr, who represented Queen Elizabeth II in Australia as head of state, simply dismissed Whitlam and his government in November 1975. It was viewed by many Australians as a constitutional coup d'etat. Whitlam was replaced by Liberal-Country coalition opposition leader Malcolm Fraser. Just a few months later, Hargrove was in the Oval Office being complemented by President Ford and national security adviser Brent Scowcroft, who succeeded Kissinger in the White House post on November 3, 1975, just eight days before Kerr dismissed Whitlam on November 11.

After Whitlam was dismissed, Hargrove began sending cables to the State Department claiming that Whitlam had admitted to knowing about a plan by the Labor Party, which he still led, to obtain a $500,000 donation from Iraq, then led by President Ahmed Hassan al Bakr and Vice President Saddam Hussein. The anti-Whitlam information had been leaked again to Murdoch's papers. In a selective release of State Department cables from that era, Hargrove wrote that three months after Whitlam's dismissal -- and just after Hargrove returned from Washington where he met Ford and Scowcroft in the Oval Office and Kissinger at State -- the ex-prime minister sat in his Canberra office and "admitted" that he knew about plans by his party to accept a donation of $500,000 from Iraq and that the whole thing was the brainchild of Labor's left-wing Victoria leader Bill Hartley and party federal secretary David Combe.

Whitlam also allegedly told Hargrove that Hawke was a "pro-Israel fanatic" and that he wanted the Treasurer in his government, Bill Hayden, to replace him as leader. The statement about Hawke being fanatically pro-Israel appears to be the only truthful one made in Hargrove's cable to Kissinger. The rest constitutes typical CIA disinformation. What is true is that Whitlam often complained that Australian Jewish leaders were trying to blackmail him into supporting Israel at all costs.

In December 1975, a French-Australian businessman named Henri Fischer, aka Henry John Fischer, arranged for two Iraqis -- Farouk Al Jezirah Yeeyah, a Mukhabarat intelligence officer, and Ghafil Jassem Al-Tikriti, Saddam Hussein's nephew, to visit Australia. Fischer claims that he and the Iraqis met on December 10 in his Sydney apartment with Whitlam and Combe to offer a $500,000 donation to the Labor coffers. Fischer claimed an earlier November 16 meeting with Whitlam and Combe, as well as a meeting in Baghdad with Saddam Hussein.

According to Fischer, no money ever changed hands between the Iraqis and the Labor officials and the meeting, even if it occurred, was likely a ruse by Mossad, the CIA, and ASIO to embarrass Whitlam.

Instead, Fischer stole the Iraqi money and invested it in California real estate. Fischer accompanied the Iraqis from Australia to Hong Kong. In all likelihood, Fischer deposited the Iraqi $500,000 in a Hong Kong bank account and then transferred it to the United States.

In February 1976, while Hargrove was briefing Ford, Kissinger, and Scowcroft on the operation that unseated Whitlam and assuring them of the loyalty of the new prime minister, Fischer, who was in New York, phoned Murdoch, who was in Switzerland. Fischer told Murdoch about the meeting that took place in his apartment in Sydney. Murdoch, in turn, relayed the information directly to Prime Minister Fraser in Canberra.

There was clearly an attempt by Hargrove, acting on behalf of Kissinger, Ford, Scowcroft, and Murdoch, to convince Whitlam to step down as Labor Party leader in favor of Hawke. However, Labor Party progressives stuck by Whitlam's side and he remained as party leader until the party's defeat in the 1977 election. Hawke became Labor Party leader in 1983 and went on to become Prime Minister. There are various reports about what happened to Fischer. One is that Fischer later re-surfaced in California where he had shed his leftist and pro-Palestinian credentials and became a far-right wing Zionist operative. Another is that his body was found floating in Hong Kong harbor in the 1980s. Those Australians who have covered the "Iraqi Loans Scandal" in detail doubt either story about Fischer is true. The truth is more likely that Fischer was working for Israeli intelligence and his services to take down Whitlam and his allies also became beneficial to the CIA, NSA, and ASIO.

In any event, it now appears that Fischer was an operative for the Israelis and Murdoch who had penetrated the organization of a wealthy Australian-Lebanese businessman and was tasked with humiliating and destroying the career of Whitlam and other progressive members of the Australian Labor Party who were opposed to Israeli policies in the Middle East.

Fischer claimed to be pro-Palestinian when dealing with his Iraqi interlocutors. The record now shows that the two Iraqis were more interested in information on Kissinger's meetings with Yitzhak Rabin and Hafez al Assad than in Australian internal politics. Fischer was also the managing director of the Reuben Scarf Foundation in Australia, named for a wealthy Australian-Lebanese men's clothing store owner. Fischer later told Murdoch in London that he had witnessed the two Iraqis hand an envelope to Whitlam and Combe, although he said he never actually saw any money changing hands.

There is no evidence, other than the dubious reports put out by Murdoch's newspapers, that Whitlam ever met with Fischer or any Iraqis in Sydney or anywhere else. As far as Fischer is concerned, he bore all the markings of a Mossad agent or asset who had penetrated a pro-Palestinian network in Australia. The U.S. ambassador, Hargrove, was a Bush family friend and likely old CIA asset who knew Bush going back to the Zapata Oil days in Houston. Nothing he wrote in his cables to Kissinger should be taken as proof of anything.

In any event, the ouster of Whitlam was great news for NSA. It would not have another problem with a Second Party partner until Labor Party leader David Lange became prime minister of New Zealand in 1984. Lange, like Whitlam, wanted more accountability and transparency for the New Zealand's Government Communications Security Bureau (GCSB), the Kiwi partner of NSA. NSA and its intelligence partners immediately went to work in organizing a back-bench Labor rebellion against Lange. Lange was forced to step down as prime minister in 1989, the year former CIA director George H. W. Bush became president of the United States.

Today, another former CIA asset, Barack Obama, is president. And he, NSA, and the Israel Lobby have launched the same concerted effort to destroy Edward Snowden as Ford, Kissinger, Scowcroft, and Hargrove and their Israeli friends used against Whitlam over three decades ago.

APPENDIX

<u>July 17-18, 2013 -- Analyzing and understanding Snowden's **slides**</u>

One of the National Security Agency (NSA) slides released by whistleblower Edward Snowden and published by Brazil's *O Globo* newspaper has received very little media attention. It is also significant that no British newspaper, including *The Guardian*, has published any more significant revelations or NSA slides since the British Ministry of Defense slapped a cautionary Defense Advisory notice on the British media warning it to refrain from revealing any more classified information pertaining to British secret communications and codes.

One slide titled "Foreign Satellite Collection Operations" shows all the NSA ground stations dedicated to intercepting global and regional telecommunication satellite signals.

The locations of NSA outstations and their code names are provided:

US Sites:

Sugar Grove, West Virginia - TIMBERLINE
Yakima, Washington -- JACKKNIFE
Harrogate, UK -- MOONPENNY
Sabana Seca, Puerto Rico -- CORALINE
Bad Aibling, Germany -- GARLICK
Misawa, Japan -- LADYLOVE
New Delhi, India -- SCS (Special Collection Service)
Brasilia, Brazil -- SCS (Special Collection Service)
Thailand -- LEMONWOOD

2nd Party:

Bude, Cornwall, UK -- CARBOY
Nairobi, Kenya -- SCAPEL
Cyprus [Ayios Nikolaos] -- SOUNDER
New Zealand -- MOWLAND
Oman -- YMCA

Geraldton, Australia - STELLAR
Darwin, Australia -- SHOAL BAY

However, one slide in particular has received little or no attention from the media. It is the one below titled "Where is X-Keyscore?"

On this slide, which is TOP SECRET//COMINT// REL TO USA, AUS, CAN, GBR, NZL (Releasable to US, Australia, Canada, Britain, and New Zealand), are locations of X-KEYSCORE units that collect phone call and e-mail data from telecommunications nodes in cities around the world using "US and allied military and other facilities as well as US embassies and consulates."

WMR previously reported on the use of Special Collection Elements consisting of civilian and military personnel from the joint NSA/CIA Special Collection Service in Beltsville, Maryland to conduct signals intelligence operations from U.S. diplomatic missions abroad. The X-KEYSCORE slide also denotes the use of foreign missions to conduct such surveillance.

X-KEYSCORE concentrates on Digital Network Intelligence (DNI) Analysis and Dialed Number Recognition (DNR) analysis. X-KEYSCORE operators typically have access to such databases as Anchory/MAUI, OCTAVE, and PINWALE.

One U.S. Consulate General where X-KEYSCORE is located is of extreme importance to NSA. It is the compound in Chengdu, central China. In 1985, the consulate consisted of only one U.S. foreign service officer. It has now quadrupled in size with most assigned U.S. personnel fluent in Chinese. It was in 2011 that Wang Lijun, the former police chief of nearby Chongqing, entered the consulate to seek asylum after he blew the whistle on Chongqing Communist Party boss Bo Xilai, who subsequently fell from power after his wife was charged and subsequently convicted of murdering suspected British intelligence agent and Bo confidante Neil Heywood. The U.S. obviously concerned about Chinese security ringing the compound, convinced Wang to leave the consulate. He was then grabbed by Chinese security personnel and quickly whisked off to Beijing.

Other X-KEYSCORE units are located at the U.S. embassies in Tashkent, Uzbekistan; Islamabad, Pakistan; and New Delhi, India; the U.S. Consulate in Karachi, Pakistan; the U.S. embassies in Abu Dhabi, United Arab Emirates and Kuwait, the U.S. Central Command compound at Al Udeid Airbase in Qatar, the U.S. Naval Support Activity in Bahrain; the U.S. embassy in Baghdad; U.S. Consulate General in Erbil, Kurdistan Regional Government; NATO base Erzurum, Turkey; U.S. embassy in Tbilisi, Georgia; U.S. Consulate General in Jidda, Saudi Arabia; U.S. embassies in Cairo and Khartoum, Sudan; in Hargeisa, Somaliland in what may be the embryonic British consulate; the U.S. Consulate General in Lagos, Nigeria; and U.S. embassies in Lusaka, Zambia;

Luanda, Angola; Tripoli, Libya; and Algiers, Algeria.

Other X-KEYSCORE operations are based at the joint NSA-Defense Signals Directorate stations at Geraldton, Western Australia; Shoal Bay, Darwin; Pine Gap near Alice Springs, and HMAS Harman, outside of Canberra. Another in maintained at the joint NSA-Government Communications Security Board ground station at Waihopai, New Zealand. In East Asia, there are X-KEYSCORE operations in Misawa, Japan, at the U.S. embassies in Manila; Kuala Lumpur, Phnom Penh, Bangkok, Jakarta, and Rangoon.

In Europe, X-KEYSCORE units are at the U.S. embassies in Moscow, Kiev, Madrid, Paris, Rome, Warsaw, Prague, Bratislava, Vienna, Budapest, Athens, Belgrade, Sarajevo, and Sofia; U.S. military bases in Darmstadt, Frankfurt, and Camp Bondsteel, Kosovo; the US Mission to the UN in Geneva, the U.S. Consulate General in Istanbul, the joint NSA-Government Communications Headquarters site at Bude, Cornwall; GCHQ Headquarters Cheltenham, NSA base Menwith Hill, Harrogate; and the U.S. Consulate General Edinburgh, Scotland. A previous Snowden release stated that on September 21, 2012, a program called TRANSIENT THURIBLE, described as "a new GCHQ-managed X-KEYSCORE (XKS) *Deep Dive"*, was declared operational.

In the Western Hemisphere, X-KEYSCORE units operate from NSA headquarters at Fort Meade, Maryland; Sugar Grove, West Virginia; Yakima, Washington; the NSA Texas site in San Antonio; and U.S. embassies in Mexico City, Bogota, Quito, Brasilia, Caracas, Panama City, Managua, San Salvador, and Tegucigalpa.

<u>Other systems disclosed by Snowden:</u>

- X-KEYSCORE processes signals for:
- NUCLEON (Voice)
- PINWALE (video)
- MAINWAY (phone call records)
- MARINA (Internet records)
- Fornsat Primary Collection Operations
- X-KEYSCORE collects data with the help of over 700 servers based in "US and allied military and other facilities as well as US embassies and consulates" in several dozen countries.
- Direct collection of computer /network data from installed software:

- Highlands: collects internal digital signals

- Vagrant: provides copies of computer screens

- Lifesaver: copies contents of hard disks

- Special Collection Service teams in Brasilia and New Delhi

- DISHFIRE used to query for words "Ericsson" and "radio" or "radar." One query targeted against Pakistan, but DISHFIRE also produced content on U.S. persons.

- SILVERZEPHYR

    63 SCS units monitoring foreign satellites, including five in Latin America, from US embassies:

    Bogota

    Caracas

    Panama City

    Mexico City

    Brasilia

- STEELKNIGHT partners

- DROPMIRE taps

    EU Mission to UN (PERDIDO)   **Italian embassy DC (BRUNEAU/HEMLOCK)**

    French Mission to UN (BLACKFOOT) **Greek mission UN (POWELL)**

    French embassy DC (WABASH)   **Greek embassy DC (KLONDYKE)**

TAILORED ACCESS OPERATIONS (TAO)

- GENIE – Program to control 85,000 computer "implants" to allow covert computer access by NSA.
- TURBINE – GENIE follow on that controls millions of computer implants for intelligence-gathering an active cyber-attacks.
ROYALNET: Breaks encryption of private networks, including those of Petrobras, SWIFT, and French Foreign Ministry using FLYINGPIG and HUSHPUPPY.

GCHQ

MASTERING THE INTERNET (MTI)

TOP SECRET//COMINT//REL TO USA, FVEY

"Collect-it-all"

"Why Can't We Collect All The Signals, All The Time? Sounds like a good summer homework project for Menwith!" -LTG Keith Alexander talking about FORNSAT during a 16 June 2008 visit to MHS

GCHQ/NSA undersea cable tap partners and code names:

BT (REMEDY)

Verizon Business (DACRON)

Vodafone Cable (GERONTIC)

Global Crossing (PINNAGE)

Level 3 (LITTLE)

Viatel (VITREOUS)

Interoute (STREETCAR)

TOP SECRET STRAP1

Conclusion

- You are in a privileged position — repay that trust.
  - You have ready access to *a lot* of sensitive data.
  - Understand your legal obligations — don't become a case study in a future legalities training presentation.
  - If you have legal or ethical concerns, speak to someone: they will be taken seriously.
- You are in an enviable position — have fun and make the most of it.

TOP SECRET//SI//ORCON//NOFORN

PRISM/US-984XN
Overview

OR

*The SIGAD Used **Most** in NSA Reporting*
Overview

April 2013

Derived From: NSA/CSSM 1-52
Dated: 20070108
Declassify On: 20360901

TOP SECRET//SI//ORCON//NOFORN

TOP SECRET//SI//ORCON//NOFORN

(TS//SI//NF) PRISM Collection Details

Current Providers

- Microsoft (Hotmail, etc.)
- Google
- Yahoo!
- Facebook
- PalTalk
- YouTube
- Skype
- AOL
- Apple

What Will You Receive in Collection (Surveillance and Stored Comms)?
It varies by provider. In general:

- E-mail
- Chat – video, voice
- Videos
- Photos
- Stored data
- VoIP
- File transfers
- Video Conferencing
- Notifications of target activity – logins, etc.
- Online Social Networking details
- **Special Requests**

Complete list and details on PRISM web page:
Go PRISMFAA

TOP SECRET//SI//ORCON//NOFORN

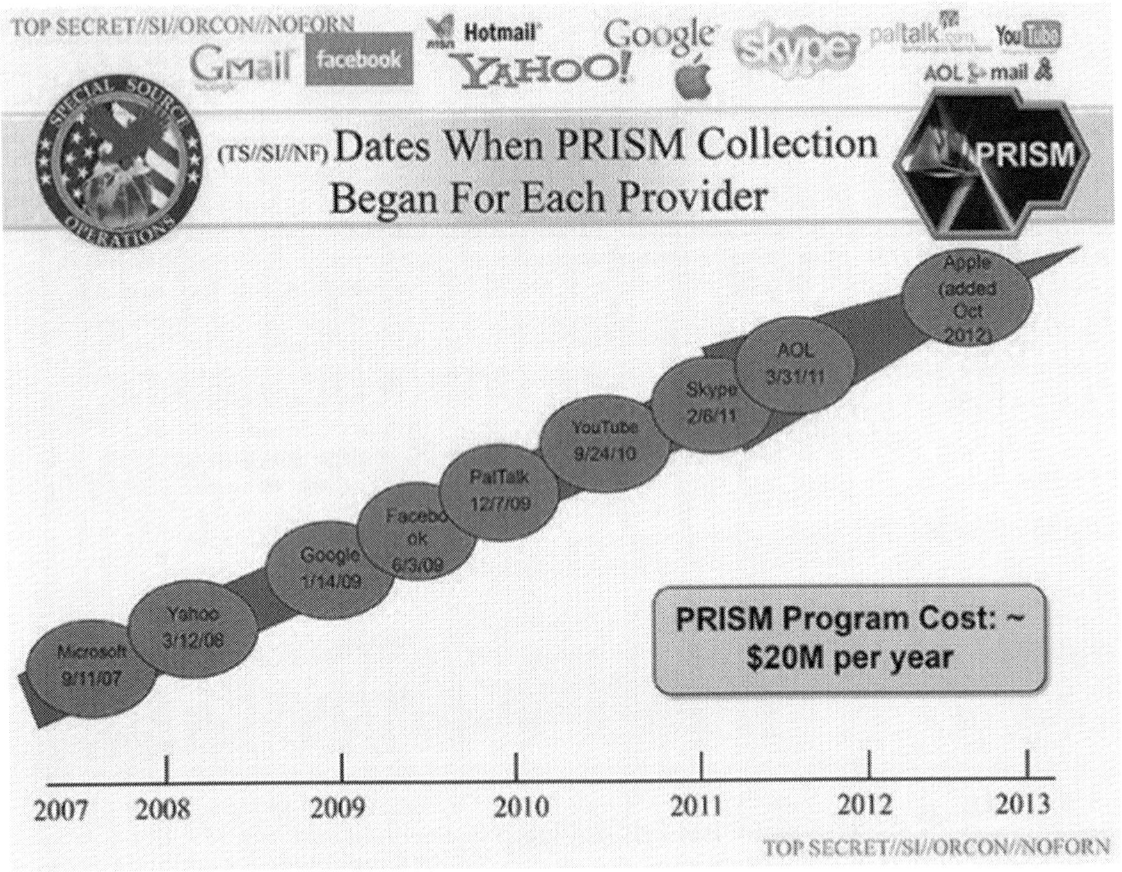
TOP SECRET//SI//ORCON//NOFORN
Hotmail
Google
Gmail
facebook
YAHOO!
paltalk.com
YouTube
AOL mail
(TS//SI//NF) Dates When PRISM Collection Began For Each Provider
PRISM
Microsoft 9/11/07
Yahoo 3/12/08
Google 1/14/09
Facebook 6/3/09
PalTalk 12/7/09
YouTube 9/24/10
Skype 2/6/11
AOL 3/31/11
Apple (added Oct 2012)
PRISM Program Cost: ~ $20M per year
2007
2008
2009
2010
2011
2012
2013
TOP SECRET//SI//ORCON//NOFORN

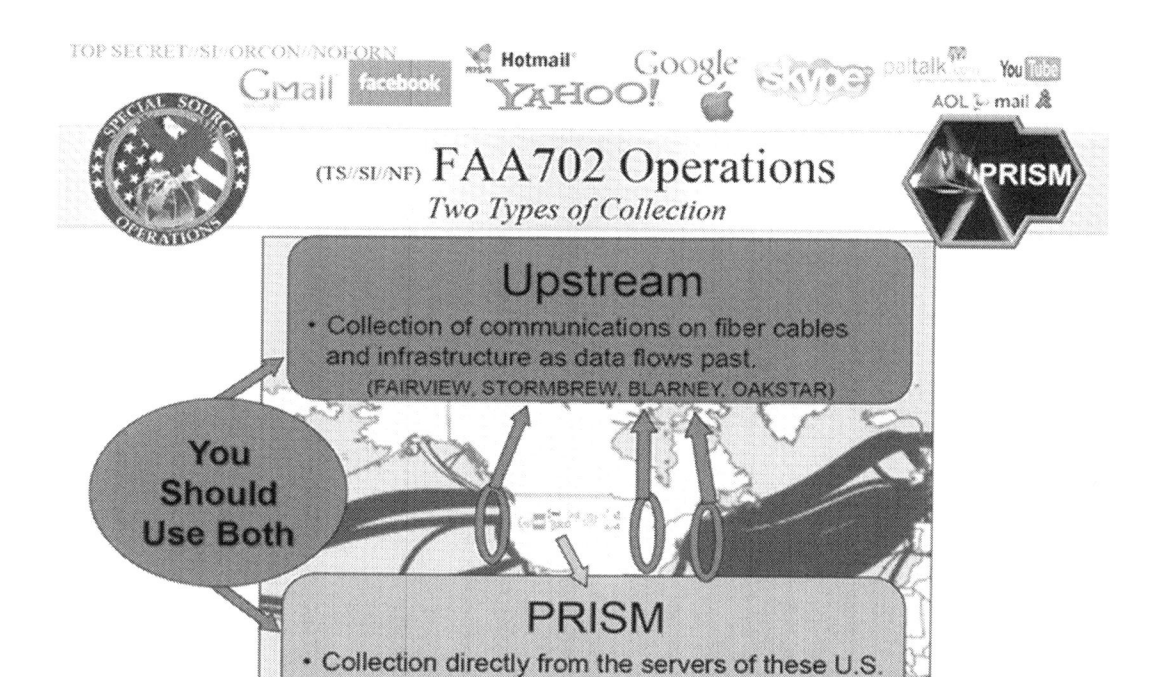

(TS//SI//NF) FAA702 Operations
Two Types of Collection

Upstream
- Collection of communications on fiber cables and infrastructure as data flows past.
  (FAIRVIEW, STORMBREW, BLARNEY, OAKSTAR)

You Should Use Both

PRISM
- Collection directly from the servers of these U.S. Service Providers: Microsoft, Yahoo, Google, Facebook, PalTalk, AOL, Skype, YouTube, Apple.

(TS//SI//NF) PRISM Tasking Process

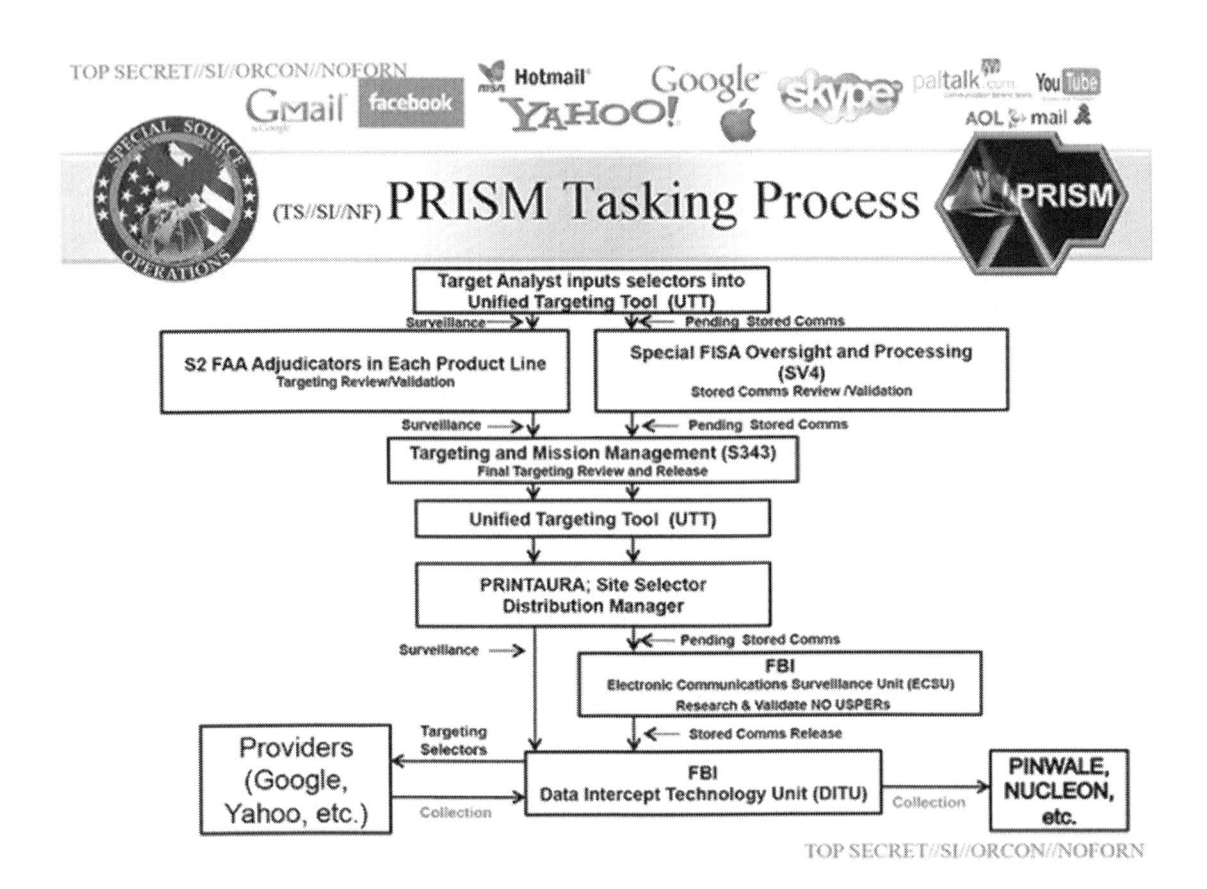

- Target Analyst inputs selectors into Unified Targeting Tool (UTT)
  - Surveillance → S2 FAA Adjudicators in Each Product Line — Targeting Review/Validation
  - Pending Stored Comms → Special FISA Oversight and Processing (SV4) — Stored Comms Review/Validation
- Surveillance / Pending Stored Comms → Targeting and Mission Management (S343) — Final Targeting Review and Release
- → Unified Targeting Tool (UTT)
- → PRINTAURA; Site Selector Distribution Manager
  - Surveillance →
  - Pending Stored Comms → FBI Electronic Communications Surveillance Unit (ECSU) — Research & Validate NO USPERs
- Stored Comms Release → FBI Data Intercept Technology Unit (DITU)
  - Targeting Selectors → Providers (Google, Yahoo, etc.)
  - Collection ← Providers
  - Collection → PINWALE, NUCLEON, etc.

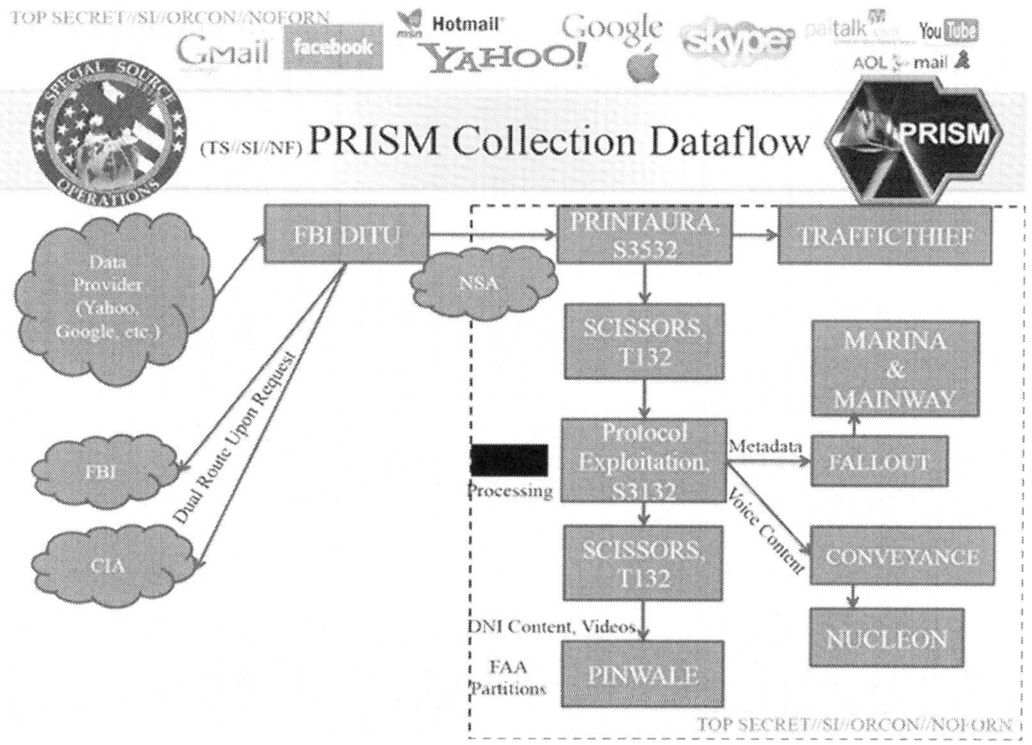

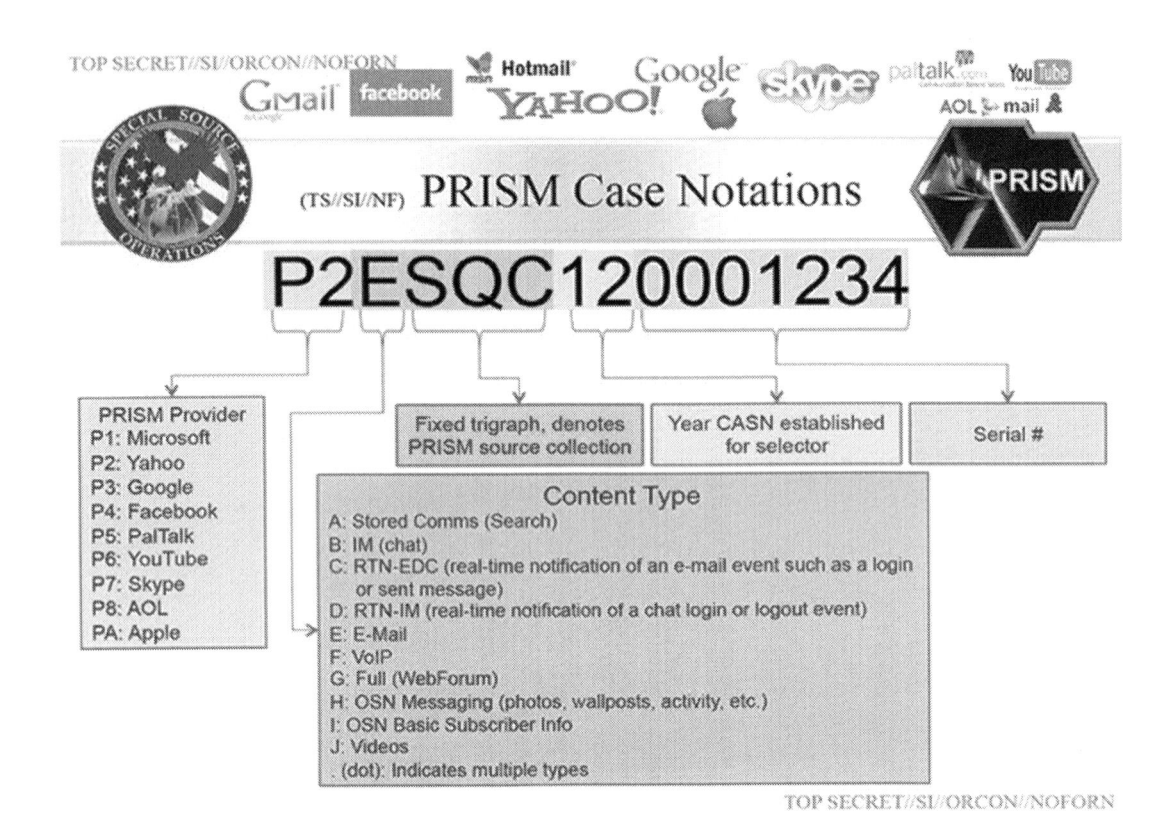

TOP SECRET//SI//ORCON//NOFORN

(TS//SI//NF) **PRISM Case Notations**

P2ESQC120001234

PRISM Provider
P1: Microsoft
P2: Yahoo
P3: Google
P4: Facebook
P5: PalTalk
P6: YouTube
P7: Skype
P8: AOL
PA: Apple

Fixed trigraph, denotes PRISM source collection

Year CASN established for selector

Serial #

Content Type
A: Stored Comms (Search)
B: IM (chat)
C: RTN-EDC (real-time notification of an e-mail event such as a login or sent message)
D: RTN-IM (real-time notification of a chat login or logout event)
E: E-Mail
F: VoIP
G: Full (WebForum)
H: OSN Messaging (photos, wallposts, activity, etc.)
I: OSN Basic Subscriber Info
J: Videos
. (dot): Indicates multiple types

TOP SECRET//SI//ORCON//NOFORN

TOP SECRET//SI//ORCON//NOFORN

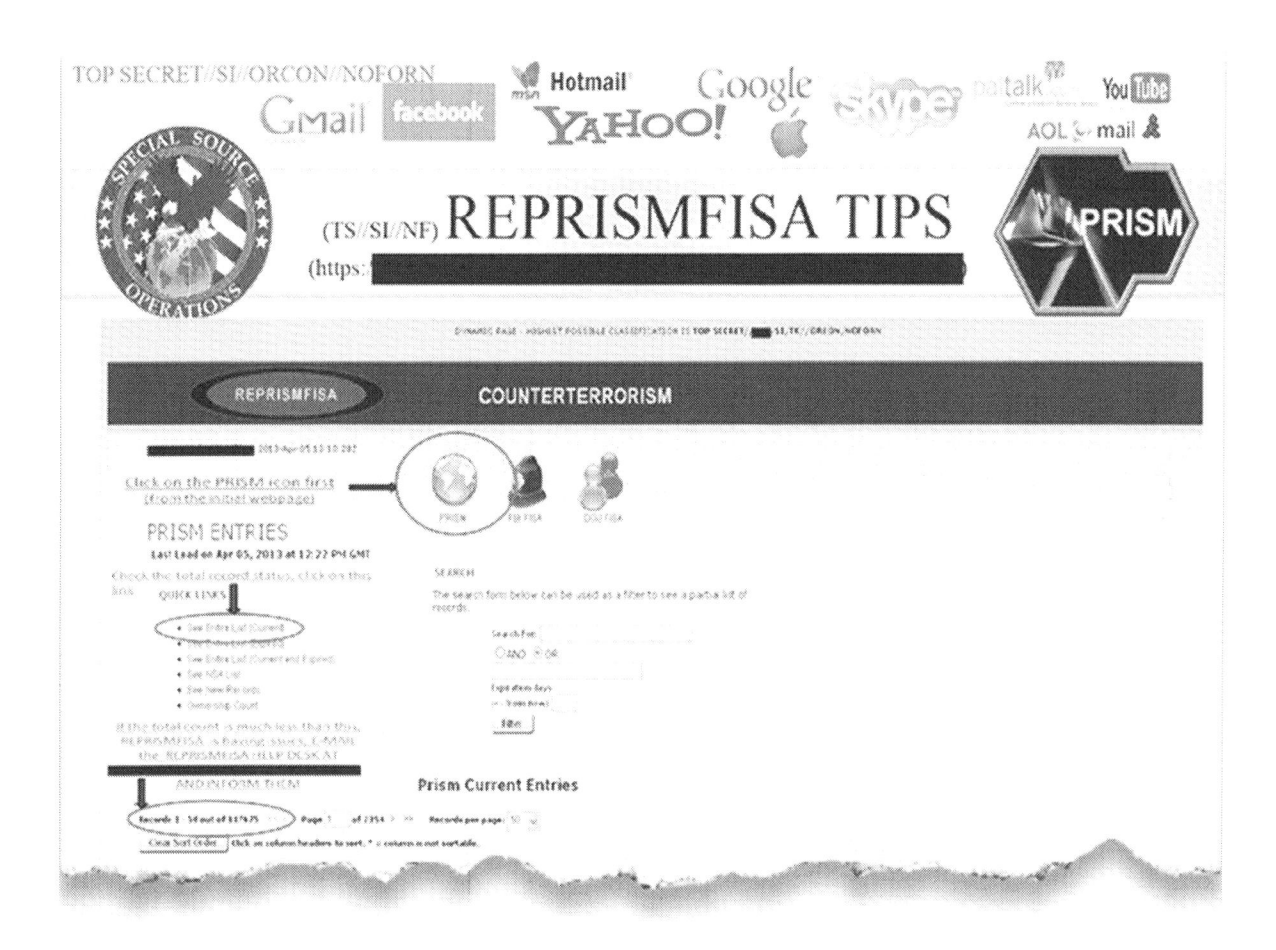

(TS//SI/NF) REPRISMFISA TIPS

(https:)

REPRISMFISA — COUNTERTERRORISM

Click on the PRISM icon first (from the initial webpage)

PRISM ENTRIES
Last Load on Apr 05, 2013 at 12:22 PM GMT

Check the total record status, click on this link.

QUICK LINKS
- See Entire List (Current)
- See Entire List (Current and Expired)
- See NSA List
- See New Records
- See Hg Count

If the total count is much less than this, REPRISMFISA is having issues. E-MAIL the REPRISMFISA HELP DESK AT _____ AND INFORM THEM

SEARCH
The search form below can be used as a filter to see a partial list of records.

Search For:
○ AND ○ OR

Expiration days

Prism Current Entries

Records 1-50 out of 117425   Page 1 of 2354 >   Records per page: 50

Clear Sort Order. Click on column headers to sort. * = column is not sortable.

BOUNDLESSINFORMANT

Global Access Operations
The mission never sleeps...

Describing Mission Capabilities from Metadata Records

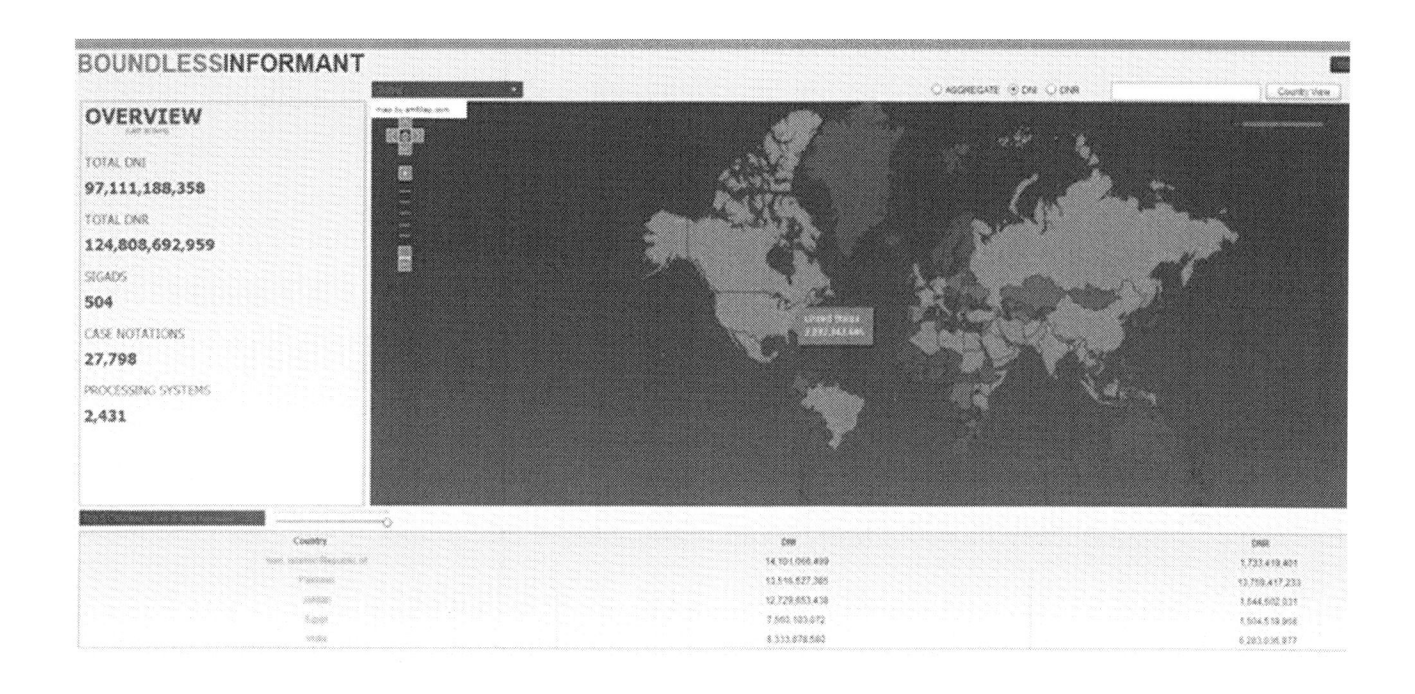

BOUNDLESSINFORMANT

OVERVIEW

TOTAL DNI
97,111,188,358

TOTAL DNR
124,808,692,959

SIGADS
504

CASE NOTATIONS
27,798

PROCESSING SYSTEMS
2,431

THE NEW WAY — BOUNDLESSINFORMANT

(U//FOUO) Use Big Data technology to query SIGINT collection in the cloud to produce near real-time business intelligence describing the agency's available SIGINT infrastructure and coverage.

(U//FOUO) Key Questions

1. How many records are collected for an organizational unit (e.g. FORNSAT) or country?
2. Are there any visible trends?
3. What assets collect against a specific country? What type of collection?
4. What is the field of view for a specific site? What type of collection?

(U//FOUO) Potential Users

1. Strategic decision makers (leadership team)
2. Tactical users (mission and collection managers)

DETAILS

1) (U//FOUO) Current focus is on SIGINT/COMINT

2) (U//FOUO) Review every valid DNI and DNR metadata record passing through the NSA SIGINT infrastructure
    a) (U//FOUO) For the Map View, only display aggregated counts of records with a normalized number or an administrative region populated.
    b) (U//FOUO) For the Org View, display aggregated counts of every valid record.

3) (U//FOUO) Raw data, analytics, and back-end database are all conducted in the cloud (HDFS, MapReduce, Cloudbase).

(U//FOUO) BOUNDLESSINFORMANT is hosted entirely on corporate services and leverages FOSS technology (i.e. available to all NSA developers).

THE OLD WAY

(U//FOUO) Typical SIGINT Data Calls/Questions

1. How many sites do we have in the region? How many records are they producing?
2. What type of coverage do we have on country X?
3. What type of collection and volume do we get out of site A? How do these types/volumes compare against site B? Against site C?

(U//FOUO) Ways to Get Answers

1. Map out the physical location of SIGINT assets
2. Send out a data call based on best guesses for who can answer the question
3. Review static reports/spreadsheets from previous data calls
4. Ask a 30-year SIGINTer

DROPMIRE

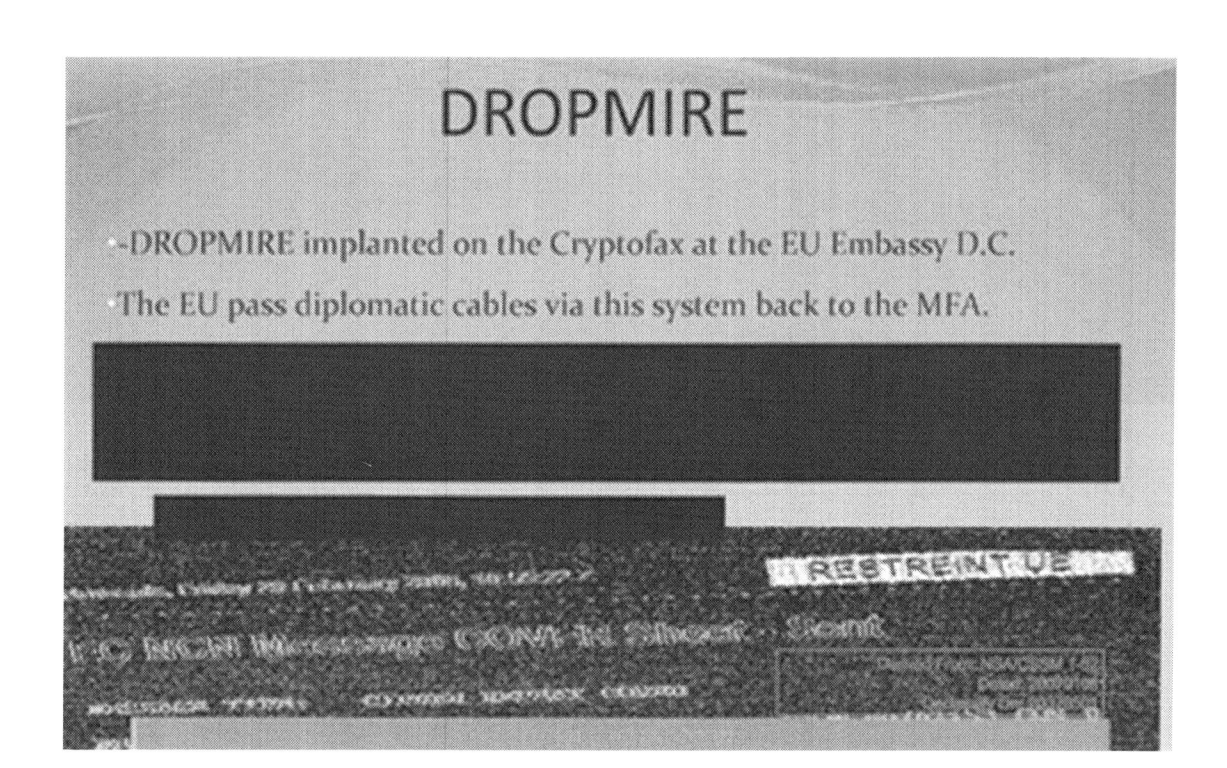

- DROPMIRE implanted on the Cryptofax at the EU Embassy D.C.
- The EU pass diplomatic cables via this system back to the MFA.

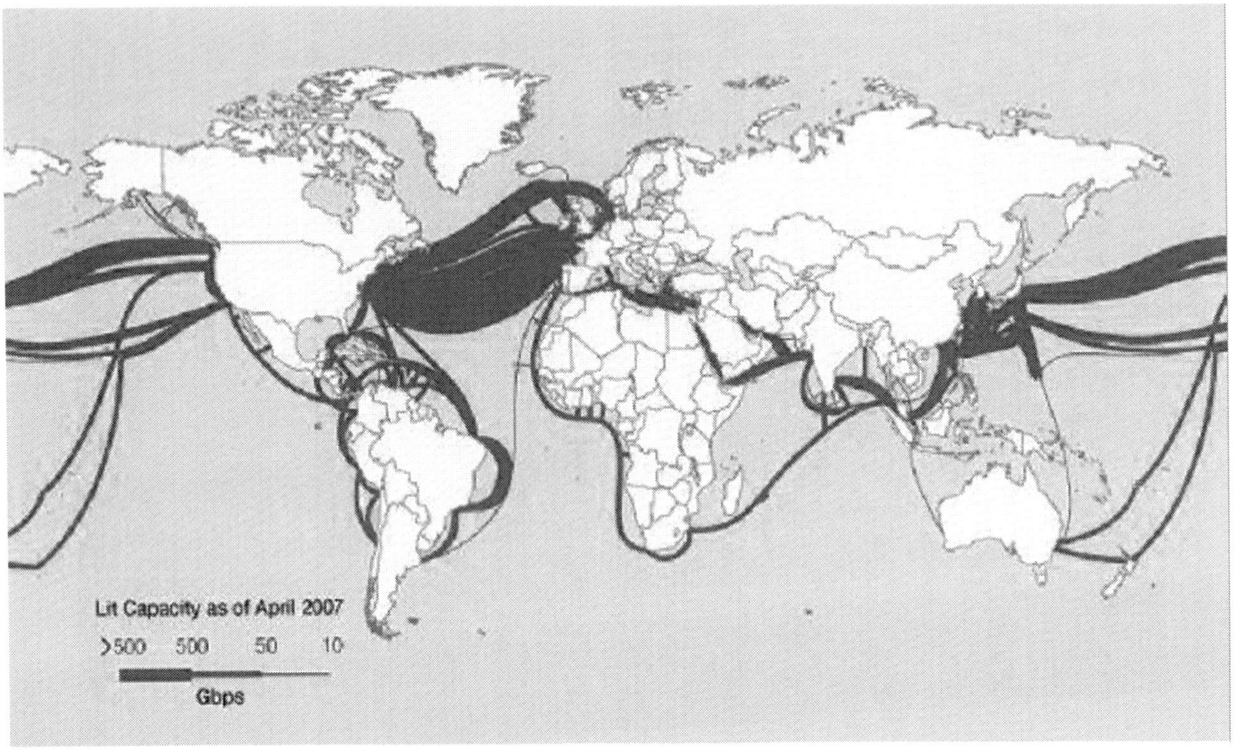

Lit Capacity as of April 2007
>500 500 50 10
Gbps

Foreign Language Proficiency Payments: Total NIP*

Top Foreign Languages	Civilian	Special Interest Languages	Civilian
Spanish	2,725	Tagalog	62
French	827	Indonesian	48
Chinese (All Dialects)	903	Hindi	73
Arabic (All Dialects)	1,191	Somali	5
Russian	736	Pashto	88
German	521	Persian - Afghan (Dari)	96
Korean	490	Urdu	89
Persian (Farsi) - Iranian	357	Punjabi	45
Portuguese	295	Hausa	3
Other Languages **	1,639		
Total	**10,193**	Total Special Interest	509

*Includes payments to 7,507 U.S. Government civilian personnel in CIA, DIA, FBI, NGA, NSA, and others included in the program volumes.

**There are up to 71 "Other" Languages for which proficiency payments are made. The complete list is available upon request.

Figure 5.

This Figure is SECRET//NOFORN

110030_vol01_005.ai

1 PRISM

(TS//SI) A Week in the Life of PRISM Reporting
Sampling of Reporting Topics from Jun 2-8

- Venezuela
- Military procurement
- Oil

- Mexico
- Narcotics
- Energy
- Internal security
- Political Affairs

- Colombia
- Trafficking

2 SILVERZEPHYR

TOP SECRET//

US-3273 SILVERZEPHYR

(TS//SI) US-3273 (PDDG: SK) Network access point through STEELKNIGHT partner. Operates under Transit Authority.

(TS//SI) Key Targets: South, Central, and Latin America.

(S//SI) DNR (Transit Authority) – Metadata, Voice, Fax

(S//SI) DNI (FAA Collection) – Content and Metadata

Closed access SIGINT Activity Designator (SIGAD) programs:

VAGRANT: Collects data from open computer screens

HIGHLANDS: Collects data from computer implant technology

MAGNETIC: Collection of digital signals

LIFESAVER: Images the hard drives of computers

What XKS does with the Sessions

Plug-ins extract and index metadata into tables

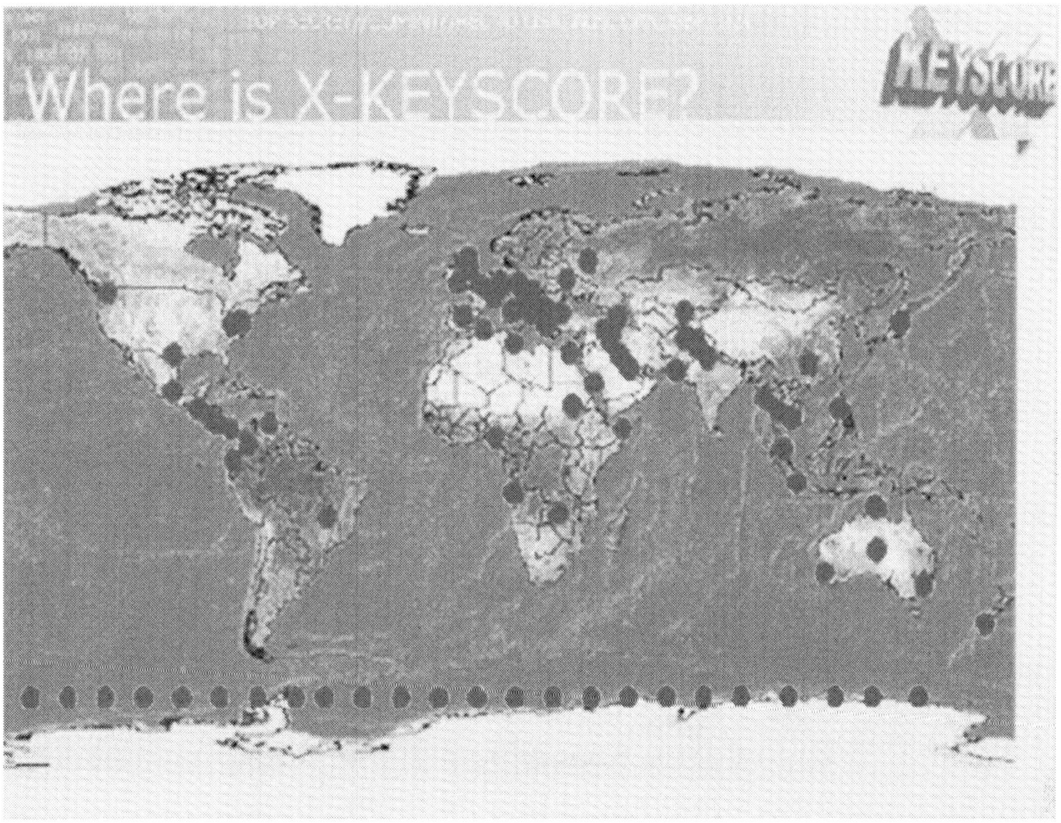
Where is X-KEYSCORE?
KEYSCORE

Google Maps

- My target uses Google Maps to scope target locations – can I use this information to determine his email address? What about the web-searches – do any stand out and look suspicious?

  - XKEYSCORE extracts and databases these events including all web-based searches which can be retrospectively queried
  - No strong-selector
  - Data volume too high to forward

TOP SECRET//SI//REL TO USA, FVEY

CLASSIFICATION GUIDE TITLE/NUMBER: (U//FOUO) PROJECT BULLRUN/2-16

PUBLICATION DATE: 16 June 2010

OFFICE OF ORIGIN: (U) Cryptanalysis and Exploitation Services

POC: (U) Cryptanalysis and Exploitation Services (CES) Classification Advisory Officer

PHONE:

ORIGINAL CLASSIFICATION AUTHORITY:

1. (TS//SI//REL) Project BULLRUN deals with NSA's abilities to defeat the encryption used in specific network communication technologies. BULLRUN involves multiple sources, all of which are extremely sensitive. They include CNE, interdiction, industry relationships, collaboration with other IC entities, and advanced mathematical techniques. Several ECIs apply to the specific sources, methods, and techniques involved. Because of the multiple sources involved in BULLRUN activities, "capabilities against a technology" does not necessarily equate to decryption.

2. (U//FOUO) The BULLRUN data label (for use in databases) and marking (for use in hard- or softcopy documents) are for internal NSA/CSS use only. It will appear in the classification line and corresponding portion markings after all applicable ODNI-approved markings are in place. The format is:
Classification//SCI Control System Markings//CAPCO-approved Dissemination Control Markings/BULLRUN. Examples include:
- TOP SECRET//SI//REL TO USA, FVEY/BULLRUN
- TOP SECRET//SI-ECI PIQ//ORCON/NOFORN/BULLRUN

3. (U//FOUO) Appendix A lists specific BULLRUN capabilities. Details may be protected by one or more ECI. Contact CES CAO for access to the appendix or further guidance.

Description of Information	Classification/Markings	Reason	Declass	Remarks
A. (U) General				
A.1. (U) The coverterm BULLRUN standing alone	UNCLASSIFIED	N/A	N/A	
A.2. (U//FOUO) The coverterm BULLRUN in association with	UNCLASSIFIED// FOR OFFICIAL USE ONLY	N/A	N/A	(U//FOUO) Related ECIs include, but are not limited to:

TOP SECRET//SI//REL TO USA, FVEY

BULLRUN: Encryption exploitation program. Related programs: APERIODIC, AMBULANT, AUNTIE, PAINTEDEAGLE, PAWLEYS, PITCHFORD, PENDLETON, PICARESQUE, PIEDMONT.

TOP SECRET//SI//REL TO USA, FVEY

Description of Information	Classification/Markings	Reason	Declass	Remarks
NSA/CSS, SIGINT, IC, or any of the related ECIs				APERIODIC, AMBULANT, AUNTIE, PAINTEDEAGLE, PAWLEYS, PITCHFORD, PENDLETON, PICARESQUE, PIEDMONT
B. (U) Partnering/Collaboration				
B.1. (U) The fact that Cryptanalysis and Exploitation Services (CES) works with: • NSA/CSS Commercial Solutions Center (NCSC) • Tailored Access Operations (TAO) • Second Party partners	UNCLASSIFIED	N/A	N/A	
B.2. (U//FOUO) The fact that Cryptanalysis and Exploitation Services (CES) works with: • NSA/CSS Commercial Solutions Center (NCSC) to leverage sensitive, cooperative relationships with specific industry partners • Tailored Access Operations (TAO) to leverage specific computer network exploitation activities • specific U.S. Government/IC entities to further NSA/CSS capabilities against encryption used in network communication technologies	TOP SECRET//SI// REL TO USA, FVEY See Remarks.	1.4 (c)	25 years*	(U//FOUO) Details may be protected by one or more ECIs and/or the secure BULLRUN COI. In addition, details may need to be marked with the BULLRUN data label. (U//FOUO) See paragraph #2 at the beginning of this guide for details on how to mark BULLRUN information. (U//FOUO) Appendix A lists specific BULLRUN capabilities. (U) Contact CES CAO for further information.
B.3. (TS//SI//REL) Details of the CES collaboration with: • NSA/CSS Commercial Solutions Center (NCSC) to leverage sensitive, cooperative relationships with industry partners • Tailored Access Operations (TAO) to leverage computer network exploitation activities • Second Party partners • specific U.S. Government/IC entities to further NSA/CSS capabilities against encryption used in network communication technologies	TOP SECRET//SI// REL TO USA, FVEY at a minimum See Remarks.	1.4 (c)	25 years*	(U//FOUO) Details may be protected by one or more ECIs and/or the secure BULLRUN COI. In addition, details may need to be marked with the BULLRUN data label. (U//FOUO) See paragraph #2 at the beginning of this guide for details on how to mark BULLRUN information. (U//FOUO) Appendix A lists specific BULLRUN capabilities. (U) Contact CES CAO for further information.

TOP SECRET//SI//REL TO USA, FVEY

(TS//SI//REL) MEMORANDUM OF UNDERSTANDING (MOU)
BETWEEN THE
NATIONAL SECURITY AGENCY/CENTRAL SECURITY SERVICE (NSA/CSS)
AND
THE ISRAELI SIGINT NATIONAL UNIT (ISNU)
PERTAINING TO THE PROTECTION OF U.S. PERSONS

I. (U) PURPOSE

a. (TS//SI//REL) This agreement between NSA and The Israeli SIGINT National Unit (ISNU) prescribes procedures and responsibilities for ensuring that ISNU handling of materials provided by NSA – including, but not limited to, Signals Intelligence (SIGINT) technology and equipment and raw SIGINT data (i.e., signals intelligence information that has not been reviewed for foreign intelligence purposes or minimized) – is consistent with the requirements placed upon NSA by U.S. law and Executive Order to establish safeguards protecting the rights of U.S. persons under the Fourth Amendment to the United States Constitution.

b. (TS//SI//REL) This agreement will apply to any SIGINT raw traffic, technology, or enabling that NSA may provide to ISNU. This agreement applies only to materials provided by NSA and shall not be construed to apply to materials collected independently by ISNU.

c. (TS//SI//REL) ISNU also recognizes that NSA has agreements with Australia, Canada, New Zealand, and the United Kingdom that require it to protect information associated with U.K. persons, Australian persons, Canadian persons and New Zealand persons using procedures and safeguards similar to those applied for U.S. persons. For this reason, in all uses of raw material provided by NSA, ISNU agrees to apply the procedures outlined in this agreement to persons of these countries.

d. (U) This agreement is not intended to create any legally enforceable rights and shall not be construed to be either an international agreement or a legally binding instrument according to international law.

II. (U) DEFINITIONS

a. (C//SI//REL) **Raw SIGINT** is any SIGINT acquired either as a result of search and development, or targeted collection operations against a particular foreign intelligence target before the information has been evaluated for foreign intelligence and minimized. Raw SIGINT includes, but is not limited to, unevaluated and unminimized transcripts, gists, facsimiles, telex, voice and Digital Network Intelligence (DNI) metadata and content.

b. (U//FOUO) **Minimization** is the process used to determine whether U.S. person information encountered in raw SIGINT is essential to assess or understand the significance of the foreign intelligence. The NSA Special US Liaison Advisor Israel (SUSLAIS) should be consulted any time U.S. person information is found in raw SIGINT data supplied by NSA.

c. (U) A **U.S. Person** is:

   1) (U) a citizen of the United States;

   2) (U) an alien lawfully admitted for permanent residence in the United States (informally referred to as a "green card" holder);

3) (U) an unincorporated group or association, a substantial number of the members of which constitute (1) or (2) above, or

4) (U) a company incorporated within the United States, including U.S.-flagged non-governmental aircraft or vessels, but not including those entities which are openly acknowledged by a foreign government or governments to be directed and controlled by them.

5) (U) Additionally, a person known to be currently in the United States will be treated as a "U.S. person" unless that person is reasonably identified as an alien who has not been admitted for permanent residence, or if the nature of the person's communications or other information in the contents or circumstances of such communications give rise to a reasonable belief that such person is not a U.S. person. Any person located outside the United States will be treated as a non-U.S. person unless there is a reasonable belief that such person is a U.S. person.

III. (U) BACKGROUND

a. (TS//SI//REL) NSA routinely sends ISNU minimized and unminimized raw collection associated with selectors from multiple Target Office Primary Interest (TOPI) offices in Analysis and Production, S2 as part of the SIGINT relationship between the two organizations. This mutually agreed upon exchange has been beneficial to both NSA's and ISNU's mission and intelligence requirements.

b. (TS//SI//REL) NSA and ISNU have previously discussed the protection of U.S. Person information, in relation to tasking joint collection operations, and agreed in principle to not task communications of U.S. citizens. The proposal to share unminimized raw collection requires additional procedures to meet formal requirements. In March 2009, ISNU was given an overview briefing during the Raw Material conference and agreed, in principal to protect U.S. Person information. It was determined that more formalized training is needed. The date of this training is TBD.

IV. (U) RESPONSIBILITIES

a. (U) NSA shall:

   1) (TS//SI//REL) Provide an annual review and training of these procedures with ISNU.

   2) (TS//SI//REL) Regularly review a sample of files transferred to ISNU to validate the absence of U.S. Persons identities.

b. (U) ISNU shall:

   1) (TS//SI//REL) Not use any technology or equipment that is furnished under the accommodation procurement process to (a) intentionally target communications to, from, or about U.S. Persons anywhere in the world or (b) intentionally target any person meeting the definition of a U.S. Person provided in Section II above.

   2) (TS//SI//REL) Not use any information provided by NSA, as raw material or otherwise, to intentionally intercept the communications to, from or about a U.S. person. "Intercept" means the use of words or phrases, such as a name, telex number or answerback, address, telephone number, email address or any

combination of such terms, to acquire non-public communications. It applies to both electronic and manual acquisition, including follow-on queries of stored communications.

3) (TS//SI//REL) Strictly limit access to storage systems containing raw SIGINT provided by NSA exclusively to properly cleared ISNU personnel and to properly cleared members of Israeli Intelligence services who ISNU has determined have a strict need to know. Access will be limited to those individuals who have been trained in the aforementioned procedures.

4) (TS//SI//REL) Disseminate foreign intelligence information concerning U.S. persons derived from raw SIGINT provided by NSA – to include any release outside ISNU in the form of reports, transcripts, gists, memoranda, or any other form of written or oral document or transmission -- only in a manner that does not identify the U.S. person. ISNU agrees that it will shield the identities of U.S. persons both by name and by context, i.e. its disseminations shall be in such a way that a reasonably well-informed person cannot identify the U.S. person from the other contents of the dissemination.

5) (U//FOUO) Ensure that any files containing the identities of U.S. persons withheld from dissemination are retained for no more than one year.

6) (TS//SI//REL) Ensure that any requests from outside parties, including all ISNU customers, for release of such identities are referred to NSA, and that same is not released without written permission from NSA.

7) (U//FOUO) Destroy upon recognition any communication contained in raw SIGINT provided by NSA that is either to or from an official of the U.S. Government. "U.S. Government officials" include officials of the Executive Branch (including the White House, Cabinet Departments, and independent agencies); the U.S. House of Representatives and Senate (members and staff); and the U.S. Federal Court system (including, but not limited to, the Supreme Court). "Officials" include civilian and military members and employees performing the official business of these branches of government, and is independent of seniority or position.

8) (U//FOUO) Process only for purposes unrelated to intelligence against the U.S any communications contained in raw SIGINT provided by NSA that include references to activities, policies, and views of U.S. officials.

V. (U) PROCEDURES

a. (TS//SI//REL) ISNU must inform NSA immediately upon detection, via the SUSLAIS, when the identity of a U.S. person is found in the raw SIGINT provided to ISNU. Additionally, ISNU must provide a written report, via the SUSLAIS and CHIPPEWA on a quarterly basis, detailing the circumstances of those instances.

b. (TS//SI//REL) ISNU must inform NSA immediately upon discovery, via the SUSLAIS, of inadvertent intercept of U.S. person communications where a selector that is believed to belong to a valid foreign target is subsequently found to belong to a U.S. person. ISNU further agrees to detask any and all such selectors, and to destroy any intercept collected as a result of such selectors, whether processed or not.

VI. (U) OVERSIGHT

a. (TS//SI//REL) ISNU agrees to put in place appropriate management controls to ensure adherence to the above policies, and to provide NSA with an annual report describing these controls and enumerating any and all violations of the above policies regarding access, collection, and dissemination. This report will be filed with the SUSLAIS, who will send it to NSA HQS Office of Inspector General and ISNU Oversight and Compliance.

b. (TS//SI/REL) NSA agrees to assist ISNU with the implementation of appropriate management controls. NSA will also provide an annual review and training of these procedures to ISNU.

VII. (U) REVIEW AND AMENDMENTS

a. (U) This MOU is effective immediately upon execution and shall remain valid until modified or rescinded by mutual agreement. It may be terminated unilaterally upon written notice by either party to the other.

b. (U) The terms and conditions of this MOU shall be reviewed at least every two years or upon request by any of the parties.

c. (TS//SI/REL) Amendments to this MOU will be in writing, mutually agreed to by both Parties, and executed by authorized delegates for the Israeli and U.S. Government. A copy of all amendments will be appended to each copy of this document, dated, and consecutively numbered.

d. (U) Any disputes or disagreements with regard to the interpretation of this MOU will be resolved through discussion by all parties. The parties agree that they will not attempt to enforce the terms of the MOU in any domestic, third party, or international court or tribunal.

VIII. (U) LANGUAGE

(U//FOUO) This agreement is executed in the English language.

IX. (U) FUNDING

a. (U) Except as provided herein, this agreement does not sanction the transfer or exchange of appropriated funds or authorized manpower between the parties.

b. (U) No appropriated funds are obligated by this agreement. Funding is subject to availability of appropriated funds, and must comply with the Anti-Deficiency Act, 21 U.S.C. § 1341 and § 1517.

X. (U) POINTS OF CONTACT

a. (TS//SI/REL) The NSA HQS point of contact for this MOU is the Country Desk Officer (CDO) for Israel, Foreign Affairs Directorate.

b. (TS//SI/REL) The NSA representative to Israel is the Special U.S. Special Liaison Advisor Israel (SUSLAIS).

c. (U//FOUO) The ISNU point of contact is the Head of ISNU Foreign Relations.

XI. (U) SIGNATURES

For the Israeli SIGINT National Unit (ISNU)

Signature: ███████████

Title: Commander, Israeli SIGINT National Unit

Date of Signature: _____

For the Government of the United States of America
National Security Agency/Central Security Service (NSA/CSS)

Signature: _____

Title: Director, National Security Agency

Date of Signature: _____

INDEX

ABERFORD, 273
ABEYANCE, 35
ACROPOLIS, 35
ACTUATOR, 273
ADROIT, 35
ADVANCED RUTLEY, 273
ADVANTAGE, 35
ADVERSARY, 35
ADVERSARY GOLD, 35
AFLAME, 273
Aflandshage, 118, 190
AFTERIMAGE, 273
AGILEVIEW, 269
AGILITY, 35, 269
AIGHANDLER, 269
Air Intelligence Agency, 10, 45, 58
AIRGAP, 269
AIRLINE, 35
AIRMAIL, 35
ALCHEMIST, 35
ALERT, 35
Alexander, Gen. Keith, 62, 63, 101, 124, 125, 139, 142, 146, 152, 173, 180, 182, 184, 190, 208, 220, 222, 228, 281
ALPENSTOCK, 273
AMBULANT, 316
American Israel Public Affairs Committee (AIPAC), 32, 122, 123, 158, 182
ANF, 273
ANISETTE, 273
ANTARES, 35
APERIODIC, 316
Apple, 223
APPLEWOOD II, 35
ARCANAPUP, 269
ARCHIVER, 35
ARCVIEW GIS, 35
Argentina, 56, 62, 168
ARROWGATE, 35
ARROWWOOD, 35

ARTEMIS, 269
ARTFUL, 35
ARTICHOKE, 239
Ashcroft, John, 124, 172
ASPEN, 35, 240
ASSOCIATION, 35
AT&T, 53, 56, 107, 109, 111, 113, 125, 166, 193, 231, 278
ATOMICRAFT, 35
ATTRACTION, 35
AUBURN, 273
AUNTIE, 316
AUTOPILOT, 35
AUTOSOURCE, 269
AUTOSTAR, 35
AXIOMATIC, 35
AZTEC ARCHER, 176
BABBLEQUEST, 35
BACKSAW, 35
Bad Aibling, 27, 287
BADGER, 239
Baginski, Maureen, 23, 42, 43, 79, 229
Balkans Portal, 240
Bamford, James, 16, 92, 94, 186, 192, 210, 230, 231
Banyan, 269
BANYAN, 35
BARAD, 35
BASERUNNER, 35
BAYA, 273
BAYRUM, 273
BEACHMAN II, 273
BEAMER, 35, 269
BEAMHOUSE, 273
BEANSTALK, 33, 246
BEARTRAP, 13
BEIKAO, 13, 25, 35
BELLVIEW, 35, 269
BETAETTE, 273
BIRD BATH, 168

BIRDHOUSE 1 & 2, 13
BIRDSNEST, 35
BISON, 35
BLACKBIRD, 35
BLACKBOOK, 35
BLACKFIN, 35
BLACKFOOT, 291
BLACKHAWK, 35
BLACKMAGIC, 35
BLACKNIGHT/SHIPMASTER, 35
BLACKONYX, 35
BLACKOPAL, 35
BLACKPEARL, 269
BLACKSEA, 35
BLACKSHACK, 35
BLACKSHIRT, 35
BLACKSMYTH, 35
BLACKSNAKE, 35
BLACKSPIDER, 36
BLACKSTAR, 36
BLACKSTONE, 167
BLACKSTORM, 36
BLACKSTRIKE, 36
BLACKSWORD, 36
BLACKWATCH PULL, 36
BLARNEY, 6
BLAZING SADDLES, 269
BLOODHUNTER, 36
BLOSSOM, 36
BLUEBERRY, 36
BLUESKY, 36
BLUESTREAM, 36
BND
    Bundesnachrichtendienst, 45, 46, 48, 49, 51, 53, 55, 57
Boeing, 26, 30, 31, 45, 80, 137, 167, 192, 230, 239
Bolton, John, 18, 42, 87, 90, 93, 123, 124
BONANZA, 273
BOOKSHELF, 273
BOOMVANG, 13, 25
Booz Allen, 15, 26, 30, 31, 94, 146, 167, 175, 238
BOTTOM, 36
BOTTOMLINE, 36
BOUNDLESSINFORMANT, 6, 238
BOWHUNT, 36
BRAILLEWRITER, 36

BRASSCOIN, 25, 222, 245, 246
BRICKLOCK, 36
BRIGHTENER, 36
BRIO INSIGHT, 36
BRIO QUERY, 248
BROADSIDE, 239
BROADWAY, 36
BROWNPRINT, 273
BROWNWARE, 273
BRUNEAU/HEMLOCK, 291
BUCKFEVER, 36
Buckley Air Force Base, 13, 29
BUILDINGCODE, 36
BULK, 36
BULLRUN, 316
BULLWHIP, 273
BUMPER, 36
Bureau of Intelligence and Research, 19
BYEMAN, 75
CACI, 23, 30, 31, 231
CADENCE, 36, 269
CADENCE/GAMUT, 269
CAINOTOPHOBIA, 36
Calipari, Maj. Gen. Nicola, 16, 17
CALLIOPE, 36
CALVIN, 36
CANDELIGHTER, 36
CANDID, 36
CANDLESTICK, 36, 167
CANUCKS, 34
CANYONDUST, 13, 25
CAPE LOOKOUT, 13, 25
CAPLOCK, 273
CAPRICORN, 36
CARBOY, 288
CARIBOU, 13
Carlyle Group, 69, 162
CARNIVAL, 36
CAROUSEL II, 273
CARRAGEEN, 36
CARTOGRAPHER, 36
CAT, 36
CATCOVE, 36
CELLBLOCK, 36
CELOTEX II, 131
CELTIC CROSS, 36
CELTIC II, 36
CENTERBOARD, 36

CENTERCOIL, 13, 36
CENTERPOINT, 36
Central Intelligence Agency (CIA), 110, 174
CENTRALIST, 36
CERCIS, 36
CHAGRIN, 36
CHALKFUN, 269
CHAMELEON, 36
CHAMITE, 36
CHAPELVIEW, 36
CHARIOT, 36
CHARMANDER, 36
CHARTS, 36
CHARTVEIN, 13, 25
CHATEAU, 36
CHECKMATE, 35, 36
CHECKWEAVE, 36
Cheney, Dick, 18, 19, 28, 70, 74, 86, 88, 90, 93, 97, 98, 99, 104, 105, 114, 119, 122, 123, 124, 135, 138, 142, 147, 156, 160, 173, 185, 186, 187, 195, 209, 228, 232
CHERRYLAMBIC, 36
CHEWSTICK, 36
CHICKENOFF, 36
CHILLFLAME, 13, 36
CHIMERA, 36
CHIPBOARD, 36
CHUCKLE, 36
CHUJING, 36
CINEPLEX, 269
CIVORG, 36
CLEANSLATE, 36
CLIENT, 36
CLIPS, 36
CLOSEREEF, 36
CLOUDBURST, 36
CLOUDCOVER, 36
CLOUDCOVER II, 36
CLOUDFUNNEL, 273
CLUBMAN, 36
COALESCE, 249
COASTLINE, 36, 248, 273
COASTLINE COMPASSPOINT, 36
CODEFINDER, 36
Collection Group, K2 division -- Global Network Programs, 109
COMFY HARVEST, 273
COMFY RIDGE II, 273

COMINT
    Communications intelligence, 24, 50, 52, 60, 74, 75, 80, 82, 126, 161, 179, 221, 222, 288
Common Remoted Systems, 34
COMMONVIEW, 36, 269
Communications Systems Support Group, 237
Computer Sciences Corporation (CSC), 23, 29, 222
CONCERTO, 36
CONDENSOR, 36
CONESTOGA, 36
CONFRONT, 36
CONTRAOCTAVE, 269
CONTRIVER, 36
CONUNDRUM, 36
CONVEYANCE, 36
COPPERHEAD, 36
CORAL BOY, 273
CORALINE, 287
CORESPACE, 36
CORNFLOWER, 239
CORTEZ, 36
COUNTERSINK, 36
COUNTERSPY, 36
COURIERSKILL, 269
CRAZYTRAIN, 36
CREEK, 176, 269
CREEK SAND, 176
CREST, 269
CRISSCROSS, 36
CRITIC, 34, 137, 138, 151, 155
CRITIC Alert, 34
CRUISESHIP, 36
Crypto A.G., 44, 45, 46, 47, 48, 49, 50, 51, 52, 53, 54, 55, 56, 57, 58, 59, 61, 62
CRYSTALLIZE, 36
CURACAO, 34
CVW, 248
CYBERENGINE, 36
CYGNUS, 36
DACRON, 292
DAFIF, 36
DAISY, 239
DANCEHALL, 36
DARKSHROUD, 36
DATATANK, 36
DATOLITE, 273
DATOPORT, 273

DAYPUL, 36
DAYSHINE, 273
DAZZLER, 36
DEAL, 273
DEATHRAY, 36
DECEPTION, 273
DECKPIN, 13
DECOMA, 36
Deep Dive, 289
Defense Advanced Research Projects Agency, 176
Defense Intelligence Agency (DIA), 16, 22, 32, 67, 70, 94, 136
DELTAWING, 36
Department of Energy, 176, 216
Department of Homeland Security, 216
DEPTHGAUGE, 36
DESERTFOX, 36
DESOTO, 36
DESPERADO, 36
DIALOG, 36
DIAMONDCHIP, 36
DIFFRACTION, 36
DIKTER, 260
DINDI, 32, 43, 44, 82
DISHFIRE, 290
DISPATCHER, 273
DISPLAYLINE, 36
DITCHDIGGER, 36
DITTO/UNDITTO, 36
DIVINATION, 36
DOITREE, 36
DOLLAR, 34
DOLLARFISH, 37
DOUBLEVISION, 37
DRAGONMAKER, 37
Drake, Thomas, 6, 193, 194, 195, 208, 209, 220, 221, 222, 223, 230, 278
DRIBBLER, 273
DROOPY, 273
DROPMIRE, 291
DUALIST, 37
DUSTPAN, 273
EAGERNESS, 37
Eagle, 23, 30, 31, 33, 173, 231, 249
Eagle Alliance, 24, 30, 33
EAGLE REACH, 13, 25
EAGLESTONE, 37

EASTCAKE, 34
EASYRIDER, 37
ECHELON, 15, 94
ECTOPLASM, 37
EGRET, 239
ELATION, 37
ELECTRIFY, 37
ELEVATOR, 37
ELINT
    Electronic intelligence, 13, 17, 24, 25, 28, 29, 33, 34, 63, 109, 146, 154
ELOQUENCE, 273
ELTON, 37
EMPERORFISH, 37
ENAMELWARE, 273
ENCAPSULATE, 37
ENDURING FREEDOM, 125
ENGRAFT, 37
ENRICHMENT, 240
ENSCORE, 273
Ensor III, Kemp, 14, 67, 185, 188
EQUALISER, 273
ETCHINGNEEDLE, 37
ETHEREAL, 269
EUREKA, 37
EXDIS, 128
EXPATRIATE, 37
EXPERTPLAYER, 37
EXTENDER, 37
EXTRACTOR, 37
ExxonMobil, 11
EYELET, 37
F6
    Special Collection Service, 14, 121, 237, 271
FAIRHILL, 37
FAIRVIEW, 37, 271
FALCONRY, 37
FALLENORACLE, 269
FALLOUT, 6
FALLOWHAUNT, 37
FANATIC, 37
FANBELT, 35
FANBELT II, 35
FANCINESS, 37
FARMHOUSE, 37
FASCIA II, 37
FAST TRACK, 222, 245
FASTFOOD, 273

FASTSCOPE, 269
FATBIRD, 273
FATCAT, 274
FATFREE, 37
FBI
   Federal Bureau of Investigation, 20, 23, 31, 32, 42, 52, 56, 68, 70, 71, 72, 73, 74, 75, 76, 77, 79, 84, 86, 92, 99, 100, 101, 102, 103, 108, 110, 112, 114, 116, 121, 122, 123, 124, 126, 127, 128, 130, 133, 135, 148, 149, 156, 157, 158, 163, 172, 181, 185, 193, 194, 195, 196, 208, 211, 215, 222, 223, 229, 230, 232, 236, 237
FENESTRA, 37
FIESTA, 37
FINECOMB, 37
FINETUNE, 37
FIREBLAZE, 35
FIREBOLT, 37
FIREBRAND II, 37
FIRELAKE, 37
FIRERUNG, 37
FIRETHORN, 274
FIRETOWER, 37
FIRSTFRUITS, 15, 91, 92, 93, 94, 97, 111, 161, 162, 163, 172, 186
FIRSTPOINT, 37
FIRSTVIEW, 37
FISHERMAN, 37
FISHINGBOAT, 37
FISHWAY, 37
Five Eyes, 239, 259, 279
FLAGHOIST (OCS), 37
FLASHFORWARD, 37
FLEXAGON, 37
FLEXMUX, 37
FLEXSTART, 37
FLIP, 37
FLODAR, 37
FLOTSAM, 37
FLOVIEW, 37
FLYINGPIG, 291
FOLKART, 37
FOOTWAY, 274
Ford, Jr., Ken, 6, 49, 68, 70, 71, 72, 73, 74, 75, 76, 77, 84, 85, 86, 98, 99, 100, 101, 102, 103, 104, 105, 106, 107, 110, 114, 121, 122, 123, 147, 148, 149, 155, 156, 157, 158, 159, 160, 162, 185, 187, 195, 196, 215, 220, 231, 232, 233, 234, 281, 285, 286
Foreign Denial and Deception Committee, 91, 93
FOREMAN, 269
FORESITE, 37
Fornsat, 290
FORTITUDE, 37
FOSSIK, 37
FOURSCORE, 37
FOXFUR, 37
FPGA, 37
FREESTONE, 37
FRENZY/GRANULE, 37
FROZENTUNDRA, 37
FUSEDPULL, 37
GALAXYDUST, 13, 25, 37
GALE LITE, 249
GALE-LITE, 35
GALLEYMAN, 35
GALLEYPROOF, 35
GAMMA, 75
GARDENVIEW, 37
GARLICK, 287
GATCHWORK, 37
GATOR, 37
GAUNTLET, 37
GAYFEATHER, 37
GAZELLE, 37
GEMTRAIL, 37
GENED, 37
General Dynamics, 23, 30, 31
GENIE, 291
GEOINT, 176
GERONTIC, 292
GHOSTVIEW, 37
GHOSTWIRE, 37
GIGASCOPE, 37
GIGASCOPE B, 37
GIGSTER, 274
GISTER, 37
GISTQUEUE, 269
GIVE, 37
GJALLER, 269
GLAVE, 269
GLIDEPLANE, 37
GLOBALREACH, 269
GNATCATCHER, 37

GOKART, 37
GOLDENEYE, 37
GOLDENFLAX, 37
GOLDENPERCH, 37
GOLDMINE, 37
GOLDMINER, 269
GOLDPOINT, 37, 269
GOLDVEIN, 37
GOMBROON, 37
Gonzales, Alberto, 124, 131, 172, 228
Google, 75, 176, 209, 223
GOSSAMER, 269
GOTHAM, 37
Government Communications Headquarters
   GCHQ, 230
   GCHQ, 15, 45, 46, 47, 49, 50, 51, 56, 57, 60, 94, 112, 118, 140, 161, 165, 189, 190, 213, 215, 226, 227
   GCHQ, 238
   GCHQ, 239
   GCHQ, 256
   GCHQ, 272
   GCHQ, 272
   GCHQ, 276
   GCHQ, 289
   GCHQ, 289
Government Communications Security Bureau (GCSB), 169, 190, 225, 286
GRADIENT, 37
GRADUS, 37
GRANDMASTER, 37
GRAPEANGLE, 37
GRAPEVINE, 37
GRAPHWORK, 37
GRAPNEL, 274
GRAYWHALE, 274
GREATHALL, 37
GREENGLASS, 274
GREENHOUSE, 37
GREMLIN, 37
Grevil, Frank, 116, 117, 118, 119
GROUNDBREAKER, 23, 25, 29, 30, 31, 33, 221, 222
GROWLER, 269
GSM ATTACK, 37
GUARDDOG, 37
GUIDETOWER, 37
HABANERO, 37

HACKER, 37
HALF, 34
HAMBURGER, 37
HAMMER, 37
HAMSTRUNG, 274
HARDLINE, 274
HARPSTRING, 13, 25, 37
HARVESTER, 37
HARVESTTIME, 38
Hayden, Gen. Michael, 12, 13, 14, 15, 16, 17, 20, 21, 22, 23, 24, 25, 26, 27, 28, 29, 30, 31, 33, 42, 62, 63, 65, 72, 73, 78, 79, 80, 81, 86, 91, 94, 99, 109, 110, 111, 115, 124, 125, 146, 152, 154, 162, 173, 174, 175, 180, 208, 220, 222, 228, 229, 240, 241, 277, 278, 279, 280, 281
HAYSTACK, 274
HEALYCUFF, 34
HEALYMINK, 34
HEARTLAND II, 38
HEARTLAND III, 38
HEDGEHOG, 38
HELMET II, 38
HELMET III, 38
Hensel Phelps, 174, 175
HERCULES, 274
HERONPOND, 38
Hersh, Seymour, 16, 52, 60, 92, 94, 129, 131, 160, 187, 210
HIGHCASTLE, 222, 245, 251
HIGHLANDS, 311
HIGHPOWER, 13, 38
HIGHTIDE, 38, 269
HILLTOP, 131
HIPPIE, 38
HOBBIN, 38
HOKUSAI, 13, 25, 38
HOLLYHOCK, 239
HOMBRE, 38
HOMEBASE, 38, 269
HOODEDVIPER, 38
HOODQUERY, 38
HOPPER, 38
HORIZON, 38
HOST, 38
HOTSPOT, 38
HOTZONE, 38
HOUSELEEK/SPAREROOF, 38

HTLINGUAL, 126
HUSHPUPPY, 291
HYPERLITE, 38
HYPERWIDE, 38
ICARUS, 38
ICICLE, 38
IMAGERY, 38
IMINT
    Imagery intelligence, 69, 109, 175, 281
INCEPTION, 274
INCOMING, 38
INFOCOMPASS, 38, 248
Information Assurance Directorate
    IAD, 14, 72
INFOSHARE, 269
INNOVATOR, 38
INQUISITOR, 38
INROAD, 38
INSPIRATION, 38
INTEGRA, 38
INTELINK, 34, 70, 136
INTERIM, 38
INTERNIST, 38
INTERSTATE, 38
INTRAHELP, 38
IOWA, 38
IRIS, 239
IRISH DEN, 13, 25
ISLANDER, 38
IVORY ROSE, 38
IVORY SNOW, 38
JABSUM, 38
JACAMAR, 13, 38
JACKKNIFE, 287
JACKPOT, 222, 223, 245
JADEFALCON, 38
JAGUAR, 35
JAILHOUSE, 274
JARGON, 38
JARKMAN, 38
JASMINE, 239
JASPERRED, 38
JAZZ,, 38
JEALOUSFLASH, 38
JETAVATOR, 13, 25
JEWELHEIST, 38
JOBBER, 38
JOBMASTER, 13

JOLLYROGER, 269
JOSY, 38
JOVIAL, 38
JUMBLEDPET, 38
JUPITER, 38
KAFFS, 35
KAHALA, 38
KAINITE, 38
KAISER, 274
KEBBIE, 38
KEELSON, 38
KEEPTOWER, 13, 38
KEYCARD, 38
KEYMASTER, 38
KEYS, 38
KEYSTONE WEB, 38
KINGCRAFT, 38
KINGFISH, 269
KINGLESS, 38
KINSFOLK, 13, 38
Kissinger, Henry, 133, 281, 285, 286
KLASHES, 38, 248
KLONDYKE, 291
KLOPPER, 38
KNIGHTHAWK, 274
KNOSSOS, 38
Koza, Frank, 189
KRYPTONITE, 38
LADYLOVE, 287
LADYSHIP, 38
LAKESIDE, 38
LAKEVIEW, 38
Lamberth, Royce C., 92
LAMPSHADE, 38
LAMPWICK, 38
LANDFORCE, 274
LARGO, 38
LASERDOME, 38
LASERSHIP, 38
LASTEFFORT, 38
LATENTHEART, 38
LATENTHEAT, 38
LATTICE, 274
LEARNGILT, 34
LEGAL REPTILE, 38, 240
LEMONWOOD, 287
LETHALPAN, 38
LIBERTY WALK, 38

LIFEMAN, 274
LIFESAVER, 311
LIGHTNING, 38
LIGHTSWITCH, 38
LINEFURL, 34
LINKAGE, 38
LIONFEED, 38
LIONFUSION, 181
LIONHEART, 38, 181
LIONROAR, 38, 181
LIONWATCH, 38
LIQUIDFIRE, 269
LITTLE, 292
LOAD, 38
LOCKSTOCK, 38
LOGBOOK, 38
Logistics Directorate, 14
LONG SHAFT, 126
LONGROOT, 38
LONGSHOREMAN, 274
LOOKINGGLASS, 222, 245
LUMINARY, 38
MACEMAN, 38
MACHISMO, 38
MADONNA, 38
MAESTRO, 38
MAGENTA II, 38
MAGIC BELT, 38
MAGICSKY, 39
MAGISTRAND, 39, 274
MAGNETIC, 311
MAGNIFORM, 35, 248
MAGYK, 39
MAILORDER, 269
MAINCHANCE, 35
MAINWAY, 39, 269, 290
MAKAH, 39
MARBURG, 274
MARINA, 269, 290
MARINER II, 13, 39
MARKETSQUARE, 39
MARLIN, 39
MAROON ARCHER, 32
MAROON SHIELD, 32
MARSUPIAL, 39
MARTES, 39
MASTERCLASS, 39
MASTERLINK, 269

MASTERSHAKE, 269
MASTERSHIP, 39
MASTERSHIP II, 39
MASTING, 39
MATCHLITE, 39
MAUI, 39, 269, 288
MAVERICK, 39
McConnell, Mike, 31, 168, 175
MECA, 39
MEDIASTORM, 39, 180
MEDIATOR, 39, 180
MEDIEVAL, 39, 180
MEGAMOUSE, 39
MEGASCOPE, 39
MEGASTAR, 39
Menwith Hill, 83, 161, 188, 190, 211, 224, 272, 276, 289
MERSHIP (CARILLON), 39
MESSALINE, 274
MESSIAH, 39, 269
Messitte, Peter, 73, 102, 104, 105, 106, 121, 122, 123, 148, 149, 156, 158, 159, 163, 185, 195, 196, 231, 232, 233, 234
METTLESOME, 269
MHCHAOS, 126
MICOM, 39
MICROBIC, 274
MIGHTYMAIL, 39
Mikulski, Barbara, 14, 29, 216
MILLANG, 39
MILLENIUM, 245
MILLPOOL, 274
Minihan, Ken, 31, 80
MOBLOOSE, 34
MONITOR, 39
MONOCLE, 13, 25, 39
MOONDANCE, 39
MOONFOX, 39
MOONPENNY, 274, 276, 287
MOOR, 274
MOORHAWK, 39
MORETOWN, 39
MOSES, 126
Mossad, 32, 33, 122, 217, 225, 285
MOSTWANTED, 39
MOTIF ART, 248
Motorola, 47, 48, 166
MOVIETONE III, 39

MOWLAND, 288
MUDDYSWELT, 34
MUSICHALL, 39
MUSTANG, 39
MYTHOLOGY, 39
NABOBS, 39
Nacchio, Joseph, 209, 210
Narus, 230
National Cryptologic Strategy for the 21st Century (NCS21), 80
National Geospatial-Intelligence Agency (NGA), 16, 94, 279
National Reconnaissance Office (NRO), 16, 94, 132, 281
NATIONHOOD, 39
NAUTILUS, 39
NAVIGATOR, 269
NDAKLEDIT, 39
NEEDLEICE, 13, 25
NEEDYWHAT, 34
Negroponte, John, 12, 13, 20, 21, 30, 91, 103, 109, 180
NEMESIS, 39
NERVETRUNK, 39
NETGRAPH, 39
NEWHORIZONS, 269
NEWSBREAK,, 39
NEWSDEALER, 274
NEWSHOUND, 39
NEXUS, 39
NIGHTFALL 16, 39
NIGHTFALL 32, 39
NIGHTFIRE, 274
NIGHTSURF, 269
NIGHTWATCH, 39
NOBLE EAGLE, 125
NOBLEQUEST, 39
NOBLESPIRIT, 39
NOBLEVISION, 39
NORMALRUN, 269
Northrop Grumman, 23, 26, 30, 31, 76, 101, 103, 105, 167, 196, 222
NSA
    National Security Agency, 5, 6, 10, 11, 12, 13, 14, 15, 16, 17, 18, 19, 20, 21, 22, 23, 24, 25, 26, 27, 28, 29, 30, 31, 32, 33, 34, 35, 42, 43, 44, 45, 46, 47, 48, 49, 50, 51, 52, 53, 54, 55, 56, 57, 58, 60, 62, 63, 65, 66, 67, 68, 70, 71, 72, 73, 74, 75, 76, 77, 78, 79, 80, 81, 82, 83, 84, 85, 86, 87, 88, 89, 90, 91, 92, 93, 94, 96, 97, 98, 99, 100, 101, 103, 104, 105, 106, 107, 108, 109, 110, 111, 112, 113, 114, 115, 121, 122, 123, 124, 125, 136, 137, 138, 139, 140, 141, 142, 143, 144, 145, 146, 147, 148, 149, 150, 151, 152, 153, 154, 155, 156, 157, 158, 161, 162, 163, 164, 165, 167, 168, 169, 170, 171, 172, 173, 174, 175, 176, 179, 180, 181, 182, 183, 184, 185, 186, 187, 188, 189, 190, 191, 192, 193, 194, 195, 196, 208, 209, 210, 211, 212, 213, 215, 216, 217, 218, 220, 221, 222, 223, 224, 225, 226, 227, 228, 229, 230, 231, 232, 233, 234, 236, 237, 238, 239, 240, 241, 242, 243, 245, 246, 250, 253, 256, 259, 260, 261, 264, 268, 269, 270, 271, 272, 276, 277, 278, 279, 280, 281, 285, 286, 287, 288, 289
NSOC SHIFTER, 39
NUCLEON, 39, 269, 290
NUMERIC, 39
Nurunga, 281
NuTCracker, 252
OAKSMITH, 39
OAKSTAR, 6
OBLIGATOR, 39
OCEANARIUM, 39, 181
OCEANFRONT, 39
OCTAGON, 39
OCTAVE, 39, 269, 288
OCTSKYWARD, 269
Odom, Gen. William, 50, 52, 53, 60
OFFSHOOT, 39
OILSTOCK, 35, 274
OLYMPIAD, 39
OMELET, 274
OMELET II, 274
ONEROOF, 39
ONEROOF-WORD 2000 TRANSCRIPTION, 39
OPALSCORE, 39
OPENSEARCH, 39
OPERA, 39
ORATORY, 238
ORCHID, 39
ORIANA, 39
OUTCURVE, 274

OUTERBANKS, 39
OUTFLASH, 39
OUTREACH, 39
OUTWARD, 274
PACESETTER, 39
PADDLEBOAT, 13
PADDOCK, 39
PAILETTE, 274
PAINTEDEAGLE, 316
PAINTPOT, 274
PALANKA, 274
PALINDROME, 39
PANOPTICON, 269
PAPAYA, 13
PAPERHANGER II, 39
PARADIGM, 274
PARTHENON, 39
PARTHENON II, 39
PASSBACK, 39
PASTURE, 39
PATCHING, 39
PATENTHAMMER,, 13
PATHFINDER, 39, 248, 269
PATHMASTER, 269
PATHSETTER, 35
PATRIARCH, 39
PAWLEYS, 316
PAYMASTER, 39
PAYTON, 39
PEARLWARE, 39
PEDDLER, 39
PELKEY II, 274
PENDLETON, 316
PERDIDO, 291
PERFECTO, 39
PERSEUS, 39
PERSEVERE, 39
PHOENIX, 272
PICARESQUE, 316
PICKET, 39
PIEDMONT, 316
PIEREX, 32, 39, 82
PILEHAMMER, 39
PILGRIM, 238, 239
Pine Gap, 226, 227, 281, 289
PINK FLAMINGO, 168
PINNACLE, 39
PINNAGE, 292

PINSETTER, 35
PINSTRIPE, 39
PINWALE, 39, 75, 169, 181, 228, 288, 290
PITCHFORD, 316
PITONS, 39
PIXIEDUST, 39
PIZARRO, 39
PK Electronics, 56
PLATINIZE LAN, 274
PLATINUM PLUS, 39
PLATINUMRING, 39
PLATOONWOLF, 13, 25
PLUMMER, 39
PLUS, 39, 248
PLUTO, 39
POLARFRONT, 39
POLYSTYRENE, 39
POOLFISH, 274
POPPYBASE, 39
POPTOP, 39
PORCELAIN, 40
PORTCULLIS, 40
POSTCARD, 40
POWDERKEG, 40
POWELL, 291
Powell, Colin, 90, 96, 124, 154
POWERPLANT, 13, 40
PRAIRIE DOG, 40
PRANKSTER, 40
PREDATOR, 40
PRELUDE, 40
PRESENTER, 269
PRINTAURA, 6
PRISM, 6, 237, 240, 278, 281
PRIZEWINNER, 40
PROPELLER, 40
PROSCAN, 40
PROSPERITY, 40
PROTON, 269
PROTOVIEW, 40
PUFFERFISH, 40
PUSHER, 274
PYTHON II, 40
Q Group, 173, 187, 194, 211, 215, 216, 221, 222
QUADARITE, 274
QUADRUNNER, 13, 25
QUARTERBACK, 40
QUASAR, 40

QUEST, 40
QUICKER, 40
QUICKSILVER, 40
Qwest, 209, 210
RADIANT SPRUCE II, 13, 25
RAGBOLT, 40
RAGDOLL, 274
RAGTIME, 40
RAINGAUGE, 40
RAINMAN, 40
RAKERTOOTH, 40
RAMJET, 40
RAP, 40
RAPPEL, 40
RAUCOVER, 40
RAVENWING, 269
REACTANT, 40
READOUT/IANA, 13
RECEPTION, 274
RECEPTOR, 40
RECOGNITION, 40
RED ARMY, 40
RED BACK, 40
RED BELLY, 40
RED DAWN, 40
RED DEMON, 40
RED ROOSTER, 40
RED ROVER, 40
REDALERT, 40
REDCAP, 40
REDCENT, 40
REDCOATS, 40
REDFACE, 126
REDMENACE, 40
REDSEA, 40
REDSTORM, 40
REDZONE, 40
REGULATOR, 275
RELAYER, 40
REMEDY, 292
RENEGADE, 40
RENOIR, 40, 269
Requirements Process, Overhead Tasking Distribution, 34
RESCUER, 275
REVERSE EAGLE REACH, 13
Richardson, Bill, 42, 90, 91, 96, 124, 211
RIGEL LIBRARY, 40

RIKER, 40
RIMA, 40
RIMTITLE, 34
RISKDIME, 34
ROADBED, 13, 40, 269
ROADTURN, 40
ROCKDOVE, 40
ROMAN ALLIANCE, 13, 25
ROOFTOP, 40
ROOTBEER, 40
Rosenstein, Rod, 121, 123, 158, 159, 163, 185, 193, 195, 196, 233
ROSEVINE, 40
ROTUNDPIPER, 222, 245, 246
ROWBOAT, 275
ROWLOAD, 34
ROYALNET, 291
RSOC Development Program, 13
RUNWAY, 275, 276
RUTLEY, 40, 275
SADDLEMAKER, 275
SAEDAC, 275
SAGACITY, 40
SAILBIRD, 275
SALAMANDER, 163, 167
SANDBANK, 275
SANDKEY, 34
SANDSAILOR, 40
SASPLOT, 40
SATINWOOD, 40
SATURN,, 40
SAUCEPAN, 239
SAUGUS, 239
SAYA, 40, 275
SCANNER, 40
SCAPEL, 288
Schmidt, John, 14, 65, 67
SCISSORS, 40
SCORPIONFORE, 269
SCRATCHPAD, 275
SCREENWORK, 40
SEABEACH II, 40
SEADIVER, 13, 25
SEALION, 40
SEAPLUM, 40
SEARCHLIGHT, 40
SEAWATER, 34
Secure Telephone Unit (STU-III), 153

SEEKER, 269
SELLERS, 40
SEMITONE, 40
SENIOR GLASS, 40
SENIOR SPUR/ETP, 13
SENSATION, 275
Sensitive Compartmented Information Facility (SCIF), 153
SENTINEL, 40
SETTEE, 260
SHADOWBOXER, 13, 25, 40
SHADOWCHASER, 40
SHANTY, 40
SHARK, 40
SHARKBITE, 13, 25, 40
SHARKFINN, 269
SHARKKNIFE, 40
SHARPSHOOTER, 13, 40, 275
SHAWNEE II, 275
SHILLET, 40
SHILOH, 13, 25, 40
SHIPMASTER, 40
SHOAL BAY, 288
SHORTSWING, 40
SHUFFLEBOARD, 275
SIDEKICK, 13
SIDEMIRROR,, 40
Siemens Defense Electronics Group, 47, 58
SIGDASYS, 35
SIGHTREADY, 40
SIGINT
    Signals intelligence, 10, 11, 13, 14, 17, 19, 20, 23, 24, 25, 27, 29, 33, 34, 35, 43, 45, 47, 49, 50, 52, 53, 63, 66, 69, 82, 87, 99, 104, 109, 110, 112, 118, 119, 121, 123, 125, 133, 138, 139, 140, 141, 142, 143, 144, 145, 146, 147, 153, 154, 156, 160, 161, 164, 165, 167, 168, 169, 170, 175, 179, 183, 188, 191, 195, 211, 213, 215, 222, 223, 224, 225, 226, 227, 232, 235, 236, 241, 242, 243, 244, 245, 250, 260, 277, 278, 279, 280, 281
Signals Intelligence Automation Research Center (SARC), 230
SIGNATURE, 40
Silberman, Laurence, 28, 92
SILKRUG, 40
SILKWORTH, 275, 276
SILVERFISH, 40
SILVERHOOK, 40
SILVERLINER, 40
SILVERSTREAK, 275
SILVERVINE, 40
SILVERWEED, 275
SILVERZEPHYR, 271, 290
SINGLEPOINT, 40
SINGLESHOT, 40
SINKBOX, 275
SITA, 40
SKEPTIC, 40
SKIDROWE, 269
SKILLFUL, 40
SKOPE, 269
SKYBOARD, 40
SKYCAST, 40
SKYGAZER, 40
SKYLINE, 40
SKYLOFT, 40
SKYSWEEPER, 275
SKYWRITER, 40
SLAGSTONE, 275
SLAMDANCE, 40
SLATEWRITER, 40
SLEEVEBOARD, 275
SLIDESHOW, 40
SLYGOOSE, 275
SMOKEPIT, 40
SNAKEBOOT, 40
SNAKECHARMER, 40
SNAKEDANCE II, 40
SNAKERANCH II, 40
SNAPE, 269
SNORKEL, 40
Snowden, Edward, 5, 6, 236, 237, 238, 239, 256, 262, 270, 271, 272, 278, 279, 281, 286, 287, 289
SNOWMAN, 40
SOAPOPERA, 41
SOAPSHELL, 41
SOFTBOUND, 41
SOFTRING, 41
SORCERY, 41
SOUNDER, 288
SPANISH MOSS, 41
SPARKPROOF, 275
SPARKVOYAGE, 41

SPEARHEAD, 41
Special Collection Service (SCS), 14, 121, 237
Specific Emitter Identification (SEI), 13
SPECOL, 41
SPECTAR, 41
SPELLBEAK, 34
SPHINX, 239
SPIROGRAPH, 41
SPLINTER, 41
SPLITGLASS, 269
SPLITTER, 41
SPORADIC, 41
SPOT, 35
SPOTBEAM, 41, 269
SPRINGRAY, 41
SPRINGTIME, 275
SPRINKLER, 275, 276
SPUDLITE, 41
STAIRWAY, 41
STAR SAPPHIRE, 41
STARCICLE, 13, 41
STARGLORY, 41
STARLOG, 41
STARQUAKE, 13, 25, 41
STARSTONE, 275
STARSWORD, 13, 41
STATIONMASTER, 41
STEAKHOUSE, 41
STEELKNIGHT, 290
STEEPLETOP, 275
STELLAH, 41
STELLAR, 177, 178, 179, 181, 193, 194, 209, 210, 211, 228, 230, 278, 281, 288
STELLAR WIND, 181, 193, 194, 209, 210, 211, 228, 278, 281
STINGRAY, 269
STONEGATE, 41
STOREROOM, 275
STORMCHASER, 41
STORMPEAK, 41
STOUTHEARTED, 14, 25
STOWAWAY, 41
STRAIGHTSHOT, 14
STREETCAR, 292
STROKE, 275
STRONGHOLD, 41
Studeman, Adm. William, 152, 153, 241
Stuxnet, 216, 217, 218, 219

SUBSHELL, 41
Sudan, 51, 56, 57, 62, 79, 151, 289
SUNBEAVER, 14, 25
SUNDANCE, 275
SUNDIAL, 41
SUPERCODING, 14, 41, 179, 180
SURREY, 41, 269
SWEEPINGCHANGE, 41
SWEET TEA, 175
SWEETDREAM, 41
SWEETTALK, 41
SWIFT, 111, 149, 291
SWITCHPOINT, 41
Switzerland, 44, 45, 49, 53, 57, 59, 61, 237, 260, 267, 271, 285
Syafii, Abdullah, 11
TABLELAMP, 41
TABLETOP, 275
TAILORED ACCESS OPERATIONS (TAO), 291
TALION, 41
TANGOR, 41
TAPERLAY, 269
TARN, 275
TAROTCARD, 41, 269
TARP, 41
TARSIS, 41, 275
TART, 41
TAXIDRIVER, 41
TEAS, 41
TECBIRD, 41
Technology Development Corporation (TDC), 230
TEL, 41
TELE, 41
TELESTO, 41
TELLTALE, 41
TELLURITE, 41
TEMAR, 41
TEMPTRESS, 269
TENORMAN, 275
TENORMAN II, 275
TERMINAL VELOCITY, 41
TEXTA, 35
THINKCHEW, 41
THINTHREAD, 41, 240, 278
THISTLE, 275
THOSEHOT, 34
THUNDERWEB, 41

Tice, Russell, 6, 86, 112, 113, 114, 115, 157, 278
TIDYTIPS III, 41
TIEBREAKER, 41
TIGER, 41
TIMBERLINE, 287
TIMELINE, 41
TIMEPIECE, 41
TIMETRAVELER, 41
TINKERTOY, 41
TINMAN, 34
TINSEL, 41
TIPPIE, 41
TK, 75
TOGA, 275
TOP SECRET STRAP, 272
TOPSHELF, 41
TOPSPIN II, 41
TOPVIEW, 41
Total Information Awareness (TIA), 176
TRACECHAIN, 41
TRACEROUTES, 269
TRACFIN, 269
TRACKSHOE, 275
TRACKWALKER, 275
TRAFFICTHIEF, 6
TRAILBLAZER, 24, 25, 26, 29, 30, 31, 33, 41, 175, 221, 222, 240, 278
TRAILMAPPER, 269
TRANSCRIBER, 275
TRANSIENT THURIBLE, 289
TRBUSTER, 41
TREASURE, 41
TREASURE TROVE, 41
TREASUREMAP, 269
TRED, 41
TRICKLER, 269
TRIFECTA, 41
TRINFO, 41
TRINIAN, 41
TROJAN, 275
TROLLEYMASTER, 41
TROUTMAN, 275
TRUNK MOBILE, 41
TRYSTER, 41
TSUNAMI, 41
TUNINGFORK, 269
TURBINE, 291
TURBULENCE, 175

TURMOIL, 269
TUSKATTIRE, 269
Tuvalu, 188, 190, 191
TWILIGHT, 41
TWISTEDPATH, 269
TWOBIT, 41
ULTRAPURE, 275
Unit 8200, 183, 230
USA-PATRIOT Act, 77
VAGRANT, 311
VARIATION, 276
Vatican, 56, 267
VEILED DATABASE, 41
VEILED FORTHCOMING, 41
VELODROME, 276
VENTURER II, 41
Verint, 116, 230
Verizon, 23, 30, 111, 166
VICTORY DAEMON, 41
VIEWEXCHANGE, 41
VINTAGE HARVEST, 41
VIOLATION, 41
VISIONARY, 41
VISIONQUEST, 41
VITREOUS, 292
Vodafone, 190
VOICECAST, 41, 276
VOICESAIL, 41
VOIP SEED, 41
VRK, 75
WABASH, 291
WAITRESS, 276
WAKE, 276
WALKOUT, 276
WARGODDESS, 41
WARSTOCK, 41
WATCHOUT, 41, 276
WATERWALL, 276
WAXFLOWER, 41
WAYLAND, 41
WEALTHYCLUSTER, 41, 240, 269
WEBSPINNER, 41
WEBSPINNER -- ACCESS TO DBS, 42
WESTRICK, 42
WHARFMAN II, 42
WHIRLPOOL, 42
WHITE SEA, 42
WHITE SHARK, 42

WHITE SWORD, 42
WHITESAIL, 42
WHITEWASH, 42
Whitlam, Whitlam, 281, 285, 286
WICKETKEEPER, 276
WILDFIRE, 42
Williams, Gareth, 70, 101, 191, 211, 213, 214
WINDSHIELD, 42
WINTEL, 33, 70
WINTERFEED, 42
WIREDART, 42
WIRESHARK, 269
WIREWEED, 42
WITCHHUNT, 269
WITHROW, 276
WIZARDRY, 42
WOLFPACK, 42
WORLDWIDE, 42
WRAPUP, 42
XKEYSCORE, 269, 271
X-KEYSCORE, 288
X-KEYSCORE, 290
X-KEYSCORE, 290
XVTUBA, 42
Yamantau Mountain, 17, 18
YELLOWCROWN, 276
YELLOWHAMMER, 276
YELLOWSTONE, 42, 269
YETLING, 42
YMCA, 288
ZENTOOLS, 42
ZIGZAG, 42
ZIRCON, 42, 249
ZORILLO, 276

Printed in Great Britain
by Amazon.co.uk, Ltd.,
Marston Gate.